Integrating AI, Circularity, and Ethical Innovation in Fashion

Luzia Arantes
https://orcid.org/0000-0003-1179-9113

Águeda School of Technology and Management, University of Aveiro, Portugal & Polytechnic Institute of Cávado and Ave, Portugal

IGI Global
Scientific Publishing
Publishing Tomorrow's Research Today

Vice President of Editorial Melissa Wagner
Director of Acquisitions Mikaela Felty
Director of Book Development Jocelynn Hessler
Production Manager Mike Brehm
Cover Design Jose Rosado

Published in the United States of America by
IGI Global Scientific Publishing
701 East Chocolate Avenue
Hershey, PA, 17033, USA
Tel: 717-533-8845 | Fax: 717-533-7115
Website: https://www.igi-global.com E-mail: cust@igi-global.com

Library of Congress Cataloging-in-Publication Data

(CIP Data Pending)
ISBN13: 9798260003039
Isbn13Softcover: 9798260003046
EISBN13: 9798260003053
British Cataloguing in Publication Data
A Cataloguing in Publication record for this book is available from the British Library.

Table of Contents

Detailed Table of Contents

in recycling technologies, and consumer education to accelerate circular fashion adoption. By embracing reduce, reuse, and recycle principles, India's fashion sector can transition towards a more sustainable and resilient future.

The way fashion brands connect with their customers is being redefined by the confluence of artificial intelligence (AI), augmented reality (AR), and virtual reality (VR). These technologies are producing immersive, customized, and interactive experiences that go beyond conventional shopping. The study used a qualitative exploratory methodology to examine these innovations, utilizing public data from tech partnership announcements, app reviews, retail innovation reports, and brand case studies in addition to secondary research. According to the findings, these companies are using AI and immersive technology to improve the shopping experience while also promoting more sustainable retail models, lowering return rates, and enhancing personalization. According to these results, mass-market fashion firms hoping to compete in a customer world that prioritizes digital devices are finding that the strategic application of AI-powered AR and VR is becoming a crucial tool.

The widespread use of fast fashion has led to a complicated web of social, economic, and environmental issues, which has made an immediate ethical shift in the sector necessary. The crucial role that artificial intelligence (AI) plays as a strategic enabler in this sustainability journey has been examined in this chapter. It looks at how AI might rethink and redesign so as to reduce waste in the production processes and improve supply chains for increased transparency. The chapter also looks at AI's potential to transform consumer interaction and ethical marketing by promoting tailored messaging and establishing credibility & transparency. The chapter concludes that AI and sustainability have a symbiotic future, offering the means to create a new and more ethical narrative for the fashion industry while understanding the inherent difficulties and ethical issues.

learning, computer vision, and robotics play a crucial role in identifying, sorting, and recycling textile materials more efficiently. Furthermore, AI can facilitate the development of smarter production processes that minimize waste generation from the outset. By analyzing large datasets and improving resource management, AI enables more sustainable decision-making across the textile supply chain.

Preface

INTRODUCTION

The global fashion industry stands at a critical crossroads. Long celebrated for creativity, cultural expression, and economic vitality, it is now equally scrutinized for its environmental footprint, labor inequities, and accelerating consumption cycles. The convergence of artificial intelligence (AI), circular economy principles, and ethical innovation presents not merely an opportunity for reform — but a structural imperative. *Integrating AI, Circularity, and Ethical Innovation in Fashion* emerges from this urgent context, positioning technology not as an isolated solution, but as part of a broader, systemic transformation.

Sustainability in fashion can no longer be approached through fragmented initiatives. Technological advances without ethical governance risk reinforcing inequalities. Circular business models without behavioral change struggle to scale. Ethical commitments without data-driven accountability remain aspirational. This volume is grounded in the conviction that meaningful transformation requires integration — across disciplines, sectors, and value chains. By weaving together AI-driven innovation, circular design strategies, behavioral insights, digital branding, and waste management systems, this book presents a holistic roadmap for change.

The contributions gathered here reflect diverse geographies and perspectives — from Europe to South Asia and Southeast Asia — demonstrating that the transition toward sustainable fashion is both global and locally contextualized. The chapters collectively argue that innovation must be simultaneously technological and human-centered, data-informed and ethically grounded, economically viable and socially inclusive. Rather than framing sustainability as a constraint, the authors reimagine it as a driver of competitiveness, creativity, and resilience.

CHAPTER OVERVIEW

Chapter 1: The Four Gaps of Sustainable Fashion: Why Integrated Interventions Matter

This opening chapter introduces the Conceptual Gap Model, identifying four persistent barriers to sustainable transformation: psychological, technological, ethical, and inclusion gaps. The authors demonstrate how isolated interventions, whether behavioral nudges, AI optimization, or blockchain transparency, often produce unintended consequences when not coordinated. By advocating for simultaneous, systemic interventions, the chapter reframes sustainable fashion as an ecosystem challenge requiring synchronized governance, authenticity, and equity.

Chapter 2: Sustainability of Circular Fashion in India

Focusing on India's $100 billion fashion industry, this chapter examines circular fashion through the lens of Sustainable Development Goal 12. Drawing from consumer surveys, business interviews, and eco-entrepreneur insights, it highlights both momentum and resistance. While awareness and interest are rising, practical barriers, including hygiene concerns, inventory management, and technological limitations, remain significant. The chapter underscores the importance of policy support, infrastructure investment, and consumer education to scale circular adoption.

Chapter 3: AI-Driven Immersive Technologies in Fashion Brand Communication

Here, the authors explore how AI, augmented reality (AR), and virtual reality (VR) are reshaping consumer engagement. Immersive experiences reduce return rates, personalize interactions, and support more sustainable retail models. Through qualitative analysis of case studies and retail innovations, the chapter demonstrates how digital immersion is becoming central to competitive strategy while contributing to environmental efficiency.

Chapter 4: Rebranding Sustainability: AI as a Catalyst in Ethical Fashion Marketing

This chapter examines AI as a strategic enabler in ethical marketing transformation. It explores how AI enhances supply chain transparency, waste reduction, and consumer trust through tailored communication and data-backed authenticity. Importantly, the authors do not overlook the ethical dilemmas embedded in AI deployment, emphasizing responsible governance as foundational to credible sustainability narratives.

Chapter 5: The Power of Online Branding: A Closer Look at Canary's Fashion Industry

Through an empirical study of 129 fashion designers in the Canary Islands, this chapter adapts the Brand Equity model to a digital context. By measuring awareness, relevance, differentiation, and esteem through web-based metrics, the study reveals how digital maturity and social media presence directly influence brand strength. The findings offer practical diagnostic tools for fashion marketers navigating increasingly digital marketplaces.

Chapter 6: AI in Fashion Design

This chapter explores AI's expanding role in generative design, recommender systems, trend forecasting, and education. Technologies such as generative adversarial networks (GANs) enable rapid prototyping and creative exploration, while advanced recommendation systems shift from similarity-based to compatibility-based personalization. The authors critically reflect on how AI reshapes definitions of creativity and raises new ethical and educational questions for future designers.

Chapter 7: Circular Fashion Business Model Development Using Digital Innovation in Tanggulangin Leather Bag SME

Using a case study from Indonesia, this chapter demonstrates how Business Intelligence (BI) dashboards and AI analytics can support circular transformation in small and medium-sized enterprises (SMEs). By leveraging e-commerce data and predictive insights, the proposed Circular Fashion Business Model (CFBM) integrates sustainability with competitiveness. The chapter highlights the necessity of socio-economic collaboration alongside technological adoption.

Chapter 8: Application of AI in Sustainable Textile Waste Management

Addressing one of fashion's most pressing environmental challenges, this chapter examines AI-driven solutions for textile waste reduction and recycling. Machine learning, computer vision, and robotics enhance material identification and sorting efficiency, while predictive analytics improve resource management across supply chains. The chapter positions AI as a critical tool in closing material loops and minimizing waste at scale.

CONCLUSION

This volume collectively demonstrates that the future of fashion depends not on isolated technological breakthroughs, but on integrated, ethically guided innovation. Artificial intelligence alone cannot deliver sustainability; circularity without digital intelligence cannot scale; ethical commitments without measurable transparency cannot build trust. The chapters converge on a central insight: transformation demands coordination across behavioral, technological, economic, and governance dimensions.

Importantly, the research presented here challenges the narrative that sustainability is primarily a matter of individual consumer responsibility. While behavioral change remains important, systemic transformation requires redesigning business models, regulatory frameworks, and technological infrastructures. AI emerges throughout this volume not as a substitute for ethical judgment, but as an amplifier, capable of accelerating either positive or harmful outcomes depending on how it is governed.

As editors, we hope this book contributes to scholarly discourse, informs industry practice, and inspires cross-sector collaboration. The integration of AI, circularity, and ethical innovation is not a distant ambition; it is an immediate necessity. By bringing together interdisciplinary scholarship and real-world case studies, this volume seeks to support a fashion industry that is not only innovative and competitive, but also responsible, inclusive, and regenerative.

This volume directly supports SDG 12 (Responsible Consumption and Production), SDG 9 (Industry, Innovation and Infrastructure), and SDG 13 (Climate Action), while also engaging with SDG 8 (Decent Work and Economic Growth) through its emphasis on inclusive circular business models and responsible digital transformation.

This volume aligns particularly with SDG 12 (Responsible Consumption and Production) and SDG 9 (Industry, Innovation and Infrastructure), situating AI-driven circular innovation within a global framework for responsible industrial transformation and sustainable value creation.

Chapter 1
The Four Gaps of Sustainable Fashion:
Why Integrated Interventions Matter

Koteshwar Ramesh Rakesh
http://orcid.org/0000-0002-5464-275X
Synpase International, India

Lakhminder Singh
Amity Institute of Psychology and Allied Sciences, India

Yana Agarwal
Amity Institute of Psychology and Allied Sciences, India

ABSTRACT

Sustainable fashion requires bridging four gaps: Psychological (values-behavior), Technological (lab-field effectiveness), Ethical (design-implementation), and Inclusion (equitable access). This chapter integrates behavioral insights, AI nudging, gamification, and ethical governance. Behavioral interventions increase sustainable choices 25-45% but experience habituation; AI gains (28%) are offset by rebound effects; blockchain concentrates benefits among large firms. The Conceptual Gap Model explains why isolated interventions fail: addressing one gap may widen others without simultaneous action. Transformation demands coordinated psychological, technological, ethical, and systemic approaches. Some gaps require structural business model innovation beyond technology. This perspective reframes sustainable fashion from individual behavior change toward ecosystem coordination, requiring simultaneous attention to authenticity, equity, governance, and transformation.

DOI: 10.4018/979-8-2600-0303-9.ch001

1. INTRODUCTION

1.1 Global Importance and Urgency of the Fashion Sustainability Challenge

The global fashion and apparel industry ranks as the world's second-largest polluter, responsible for approximately 10% of global greenhouse gas emissions and generating 92 million tonnes of textile waste annually, a burden projected to increase by 15% by 2030 (Ellen MacArthur Foundation, 2017; UNEP, 2025). This environmental toll extends well beyond waste metrics. The cotton industry alone consumes 16% of global insecticides while occupying only 2.5% of cultivated land; dyeing and treatment of textiles constitute the second-largest water polluter globally; and approximately 85% of all textiles produced annually end up in landfills within a year of production (World Bank, 2020; UNEP, 2025). Beyond environmental devastation, the fashion industry perpetuates profound social injustices, with an estimated 75 million garment workers facing exploitative wages and unsafe working conditions, disproportionately concentrated in low-income regions (Allais et al., 2021).

Despite this environmental and social urgency, consumer behaviour reveals a critical paradox that defines the central challenge this chapter addresses: although 90% of consumers express environmental concern and claim to value sustainability, fewer than 20% consistently make sustainable purchasing choices (The Business of Fashion and McKinsey & Company, 2021). This persistent attitude-behaviour gap, the discrepancy between stated values and actual purchasing behaviour, represents not individual moral failure but rather the outcome of systemic barriers. These barriers include price premiums (20–50% higher for sustainable alternatives), limited retail availability, widespread consumer scepticism toward greenwashing claims, and deeply entrenched purchasing habits that conventional awareness campaigns fail to overcome (Park & Lin, 2020).

This chapter argues that addressing this gap requires moving decisively beyond conventional interventions toward integrated, multi-level solutions that leverage behavioural psychology, technological innovation, and ethical design. The core proposition is that sustainable choices must be made easier, more appealing, and more rewarding than unsustainable alternatives through coordinated interventions operating simultaneously across psychological, technological, systemic, and ethical dimensions.

1.2 The Conceptual Gap Model: Four-Dimensional Framework for Understanding the Challenge

Central to this chapter is the introduction of a Conceptual Gap Model (see Figure 1) that maps the multidimensional nature of the attitude-behaviour gap, distinguishing four interconnected but analytically distinct gaps that must be addressed through integrated interventions:

Figure 1. Conceptual Gap Model - Four-Dimensional Framework for Sustainable Fashion Adoption (Authors' own work, 2025)

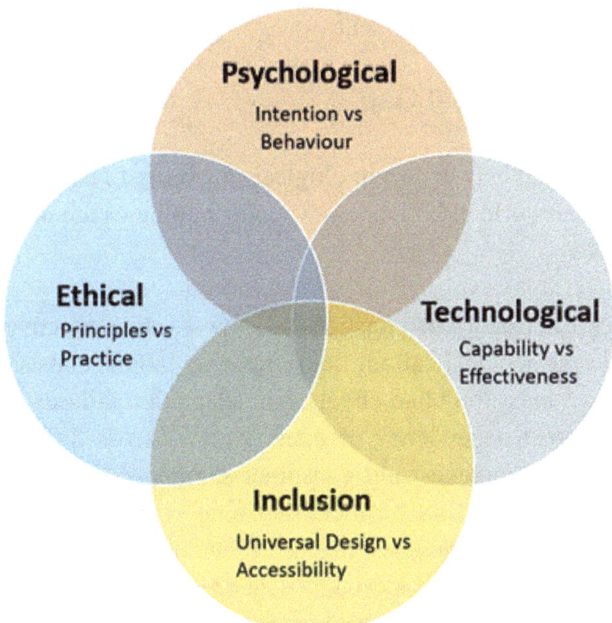

Gap 1: The Psychological Gap

Definition: The gap between environmental intention and actual behaviour; between attitudes favouring sustainability and actual purchasing choices.

- *Expression:* 90% of consumers express environmental concern; fewer than 20% make sustainable purchases
- *Drivers:* Dual-process cognitive biases, temporal discounting (preferences for immediate over long-term benefits), social conformity pressures, habitual

purchasing patterns established through years of repetition, and the visceral appeal of fast fashion design

- *Psychological mechanisms:* Habit momentum, System 1 automatic processing that bypasses System 2 reflective reasoning, where environmental values operate, immediate emotional responses overriding deliberative environmental logic

This gap exists because fashion purchasing decisions during actual point-of-purchase moments often occur under time pressure, cognitive load, and limited attention conditions where automatic System 1 processing dominates. Even highly motivated consumers find that habitual fast-fashion choices override deliberative sustainability reasoning in the moment.

Gap 2: The Technological Gap

Definition: The gap between technological capability to deliver sustainable interventions and real-world effectiveness when technologies are deployed in actual consumer contexts.

- *Expression:* Laboratory demonstrations show 25-45% effectiveness of digital nudges and AI personalization; field implementations consistently show reduced effectiveness, rebound effects, and adaptation failures
- *Drivers:* Context dependency of interventions across different device modalities, cultural contexts, and consumer segments; rebound effects where efficiency gains are offset by increased total consumption; adaptation and habituation to repeated nudges; misalignment between technological optimization and actual consumer decision-making processes
- *Technological mechanisms:* Point-of-purchase environment failures where sophisticated recommendation algorithms cannot overcome the visceral appeal of fast fashion; algorithmic targeting that works at scale but fails for personalization at the individual level; technology-driven solutions that optimize within existing systems rather than transforming systems

This gap exists because technologies developed and tested in controlled academic or corporate environments encounter unexpected challenges when deployed at scale: consumer data quality issues, platform integration failures, users' adaptation to and habituation of nudges, and the reality that algorithmic optimization cannot overcome structural barriers like price premiums and limited availability.

Gap 3: The Ethical Gap

Definition: The gap between ethical design principles (fairness, transparency, user autonomy, genuine impact) and actual implementation that risks creating manipulation, bias, greenwashing, and erosion of user trust.

- *Expression:* Fairness principles vs. algorithmic bias in implementation; transparency ideals vs. greenwashing risks; consumer autonomy aspirations vs. manipulation temptations; sustainability claims vs. actual environmental impact
- *Drivers:* Governance gaps where accountability structures are absent; misaligned incentive systems that reward engagement metrics rather than genuine environmental outcomes; insufficient external oversight of corporate sustainability claims; inadequate mechanisms for verifying environmental impact at scale
- *Ethical mechanisms:* Default nudges that increase sustainable choices but reduce perceived user autonomy; personalization systems that require granular data collection with privacy risks; greenwashing, where companies exaggerate environmental credentials without substantive operational change; rebound effects where technological solutions create an appearance of impact without genuine environmental progress

This gap exists because organizations implementing behavioural technologies face inherent tensions between maximizing adoption/engagement and preserving user autonomy; between personalization effectiveness and privacy; between apparent environmental impact and actual impact. Corporate incentive structures frequently reward growth and engagement metrics over genuine sustainability outcomes, creating structural pressures toward ethical shortcuts.

Gap 4: The Inclusion Gap

Definition: The gap between universal design intentions and actual accessibility reality, where technology-enabled sustainability solutions concentrate benefits among affluent, digitally-connected populations while excluding the communities most vulnerable to fashion industry harms.

- *Expression:* Digital platform access requires internet connectivity, digital literacy, and payment infrastructure that exclude billions of potential users; sustainable fashion technologies concentrate in wealthy nations and affluent urban centres; SMEs and informal enterprises (99% of fashion businesses) lack resources to implement advanced technologies; low-income consumers face absolute barriers to purchasing sustainable options regardless of motivation.

- *Drivers:* Technology costs (blockchain implementation $10,000-50,000 annually; AI infrastructure requirements); digital infrastructure gaps in low-income regions; skill requirements (data science expertise) inaccessible to most enterprises; market dynamics where algorithmic systems prioritize high-volume, high-margin actors over smaller sustainability-focused businesses.
- *Inclusion mechanisms:* Infrastructure inequality where sustainability solutions are accessible only to large corporations; cost barriers that exclude budget-conscious consumers who are least able to pay 20-50% premiums; geographic concentration of sustainable fashion retail; knowledge gaps that disadvantage SMEs facing certification costs ($2,000-8,000) and complex compliance requirements.

This gap exists because sustainability solutions emerging from research in developed-world academic and corporate contexts reflect the capabilities and constraints of large, well-resourced organizations. When these solutions are generalized across entire industries without explicit adaptation, they inadvertently deepen inequality by making advanced technologies accessible only to large corporations while excluding the SMEs and informal enterprises that employ millions of workers.

Table 1. The Four-Gap Model (overview)

Gap	Definition	Current Problem
Psychological Gap	Attitude vs. behavioural environmental intention vs. actual choices	Dual-process biases, habit momentum, and visceral appeal of fast fashion
Technological Gap	Capability vs. real-world effectiveness; lab success vs. field failure	Rebound effects, context dependency, habituation to nudges
Ethical Gap	Design principles vs. actual practice; autonomy ideals vs. manipulation risks	Governance gaps, greenwashing, privacy risks
Inclusion Gap	Universal design vs. accessibility reality; benefits concentrated vs. excluded	Technology costs, digital divide, SME barriers

1.3 Why an Integrated Framework Addressing All Four Gaps Is Necessary

Examination of attempted fashion sustainability interventions reveals why isolated approaches, addressing only one gap, consistently fail to achieve meaningful impact. Behavioural interventions alone (nudges, gamification, educational campaigns, social norm messaging) can shift choices at the margin among motivated populations but cannot overcome structural barriers of price, availability, and infrastructure access.

Without simultaneously addressing psychological, technological, systemic, and equity barriers, behavioural interventions risk becoming performative; generating the appearance of behaviour change while leaving fundamental barriers intact.

Technological solutions alone (AI personalization, blockchain verification, digital platforms, demand forecasting systems) can optimize within existing systems but cannot transform the systems themselves. When applied within unchanged business models, technology frequently amplifies existing inequalities by concentrating capabilities and benefits among large, technologically sophisticated organizations while leaving SMEs and informal enterprises disadvantaged. Moreover, technological solutions deployed without explicit attention to ethical design create risks of manipulation, privacy violation, and greenwashing.

Policy interventions alone (regulation, certification requirements, sustainability mandates, carbon pricing) can establish minimum standards but risk generating compliance theatre where organizations meet formal requirements while avoiding substantive operational change.

Equity-focused interventions alone (subsidies for low-income consumers, SME support programs) can expand access but may fail if psychological habits and technological barriers remain unaddressed.

Ethical governance alone (fairness frameworks, transparency requirements) can reduce risks, but cannot create motivation for participation.

Integrated approaches, by contrast, coordinate behavioural, technological, systemic, and ethical interventions to address barriers at multiple levels simultaneously. This chapter proposes that such integration must function as an ecosystem where:

- AI personalization systems nudge choices toward sustainable options, but only if simultaneously addressing price barriers through policy incentives or business model innovation
- Blockchain verification builds trust in sustainability claims, but only if implemented with governance structures ensuring transparency about the verification process itself
- Gamification sustains engagement, but only if designed with explicit attention to equity and access across socioeconomic segments
- Behavioural insights guide design, but only if psychological interventions preserve user autonomy and align with intrinsic motivation
- Systemic design restructures the ecosystem to make sustainable choices the default easier option, rather than attempting to overcome structural barriers through individual motivation

1.4 Chapter Structure and How This Chapter Addresses the Four Gaps

The subsequent sections develop an integrated framework specifying how behavioural insights, technology, ethical governance, and systemic design function together to progressively narrow the four gaps while maintaining commitment to equity, authenticity, and long-term environmental impact.

Section 2: Understanding Consumer Behaviour primarily addresses the Psychological Gap. It identifies the cognitive and affective drivers underlying the attitude-behaviour gap, examining how psychological foundations, dual-process decision-making, personal norms, emotional responses, and habitual purchasing create the initial discrepancy between environmental values and sustainable choices. This section establishes why simple awareness campaigns cannot overcome psychological barriers and what psychological mechanisms effective interventions must activate.

Section 3: AI-Driven Nudging in Sustainable Fashion addresses both the Psychological Gap (through demonstrating how algorithmic choice architecture can activate System 2 reflective processing at critical decision moments) and the Technological Gap (through documenting what works in field implementations, where intervention effectiveness proves limited compared to laboratory demonstrations, and under what contextual conditions technologies actually succeed). This section synthesizes experimental evidence revealing both promise and limitations of digital nudging.

Section 4: Gamification and Emotional Engagement addresses the Psychological Gap through emotional activation and intrinsic motivation mechanisms, while also addressing the Technological Gap by documenting how gamification designs that fail to align with psychological needs actually backfire, demonstrating the necessity of psychological sophistication in technological design.

Section 5: Ethical Framework and Responsible AI Development directly addresses the Ethical Gap by proposing governance structures, design principles, and accountability mechanisms ensuring that behavioural technologies maintain user autonomy, prevent manipulation and greenwashing, and create authentic rather than performative environmental impact. Crucially, this section also addresses the Inclusion Gap by specifying how ethical frameworks must prevent technologies from concentrating benefits among affluent populations.

Section 6: Case Studies demonstrates real-world implementations attempting to address these gaps, illustrating partial successes and persistent challenges. By examining case examples through the lens of the four gaps, this section shows where current implementations succeed and where gaps persist.

Section 7: Conclusions and Research Agenda synthesizes findings across sections, reflects on what remains unknown about gap closure, and proposes research priorities for future work. It explicitly acknowledges which gaps remain inadequately addressed and what systemic transformations would be required for genuine gap closure at scale.

1.5 Core Argument and Chapter Contribution

This chapter does not claim to fully bridge the four gaps; doing so would require a fundamental transformation of fashion industry structures, global economic incentive systems, and consumption patterns that extend beyond this chapter's scope. Rather, this chapter demonstrates how integrating behavioural insights, artificial intelligence, gamification, and blockchain technology can systematically narrow the four gaps when designed with explicit attention to psychological authenticity, technological realism, ethical integrity, and equitable access.

The novel theoretical contribution lies in the Conceptual Gap Model itself, which distinguishes analytically between four interconnected but distinct gaps, each requiring different intervention logic. Previous literature has focused primarily on the attitude-behaviour gap (our Psychological Gap) or examined technological solutions in isolation. By mapping four interconnected gaps and demonstrating how interventions addressing one gap may inadvertently widen others (for example, efficiency gains that increase consumption, or technologies that exclude low-income populations), this framework provides guidance for designing more holistic interventions.

Substantively, this chapter synthesizes behavioural economics, technology design, systems thinking, and ethical frameworks to propose practical interventions that can be implemented immediately by fashion retailers, technology companies, policymakers, and consumers, while also proposing a research agenda for validating long-term impact and addressing gaps that require structural transformation.

2. ADDRESSING THE PSYCHOLOGICAL GAP

This section addresses the Psychological Gap, the persistent discrepancy between environmental intention and actual purchasing behaviour that defines sustainable fashion's central challenge. Understanding the psychological mechanisms underlying this gap is essential because behavioural interventions can only succeed if they activate the reflective, values-aligned decision-making where pro-environmental motivation actually resides. Simple awareness campaigns consistently fail because they operate at the wrong psychological level, failing to engage the visceral and habitual dimensions of fashion consumption that override stated environmental values at the point of purchase.

2.1 The Psychological Gap: Why Attitudes Don't Translate to Behaviour

Consumer acceptance remains the critical bottleneck for sustainable fashion adoption. Research documents a significant attitude-behaviour gap: while 77% of consumers express familiarity with sustainable fashion concepts and 83% believe circular textiles can reduce environmental impact, actual purchasing behaviour remains inconsistent with these attitudes (Das & Paul, 2024). This gap is particularly pronounced among younger demographics, despite high environmental awareness; young consumers show minimal adoption of sustainable purchasing practices (Niinimäki, 2010).

The persistence of this paradox reflects deeper psychological and structural barriers that cannot be overcome through awareness alone. Price remains the most formidable barrier: sustainable fashion alternatives cost 20-50% more than conventional options, which makes conscientious consumers unable to afford products aligned with their values (Park & Lin, 2020). Geographic and infrastructure barriers compound this challenge; limited retail availability and digital access exclude significant portions of the consumer base (Busalim et al., 2022).

Beyond structural barriers, psychological mechanisms actively suppress sustainable choices. Temporal discounting leads consumers to prioritize immediate gratification over future environmental benefits. Habit momentum, the powerful tendency to repeat previous purchasing patterns, often overrides deliberative reasoning about environmental impact. Identity factors complicate the picture further; fashion serves psychological functions beyond its protective purpose, including identity expression, social status signalling, and group membership affiliation, functions that can contradict environmental considerations (Lundblad & Davies, 2016).

For sustainable fashion interventions to succeed, they must address psychological barriers at multiple levels of processing and acknowledge the legitimate competing psychological needs that fashion fulfills beyond environmental protection.

2.2 Psychological Foundations: Personal Norms and Value-Belief-Norm Theory

Value-Belief-Norm (VBN) Theory provides the theoretical foundation for understanding how personal norms activate sustainable behaviour. According to VBN theory, pro-environmental behaviour is initiated when personal values activate beliefs about environmental consequences, which subsequently facilitate awareness of personal responsibility and generate moral norms that guide conduct (Stern, 2000). Personal norms, internalized sense of responsibility function as powerful motivators for sustainable fashion choices because they operate through intrinsic moral obligation rather than external pressure.

Research demonstrates that personal norms are stronger predictors of sustainable fashion behaviour than social norms, operating through internalized moral conviction rather than perceived social pressure (Shahzad et al., 2023). This distinction carries significant implications for intervention design: effective digital systems should foster a sense of personal responsibility and environmental awareness rather than attempting to influence consumers through social pressure or price comparisons alone.

The evolution of personal norms in clothing consumption is intricate, as fashion performs psychological roles extending beyond its functional protective purpose. Clothing functions as identity language, communicating social status, group membership, and personal values. Consumers naturally experience tension between these competing psychological functions. For behavioural interventions to succeed, they must not undermine these legitimate psychological needs but rather align sustainable choices with consumers' core identity and values, aspirations, helping them see sustainable fashion as an expression of who they are, not what they should buy.

2.3 Dual-Process Decision-Making in Fashion Consumption

Fashion purchasing decisions engage both automatic (System 1) and deliberative (System 2) cognitive processes. This dual-process framework reveals why sustainable fashion interventions must operate across multiple psychological levels simultaneously:

i. *Visceral Processing (System 1 - Automatic):* Immediate emotional responses to product aesthetics, texture, brand imagery, and sensory appeal. Fast fashion excels at triggering positive visceral responses through trend driven designs, attractive retail environments, and social media marketing that creates emotional rewards for purchase. Sustainable fashion often faces disadvantages in this domain because sustainable design and marketing typically emphasize durability and environmental impact, worthy but abstract concepts that lack the visceral immediacy of fast fashion's trend-driven appeal (Norman, 2004).
ii. *Behavioural Processing (System 1 - Habitual):* Functional evaluation of convenience, price, availability, and habitual patterns. This is where sustainable fashion encounters structural barriers: higher prices, limited retail availability, and concerns about quality persistence due to limited consumer familiarity with sustainable materials create functional disadvantages. Repeated fast-fashion purchasing has established automatic behavioural scripts ("browse mall, see appealing item at low price, purchase immediately") that operate without deliberative engagement (Park & Lin, 2020).

iii. *Reflective Processing (System 2 - Deliberative):* Meaning-making around personal identity, long-term values, consequences, and social implications. This level offers the greatest opportunity for sustainable fashion interventions because it aligns with consumers' deeper environmental values and identity aspirations. Reflective processing, however, is cognitively demanding and occurs only when consumers have sufficient time, cognitive capacity, and motivation to think carefully, conditions rarely present during point-of-purchase retail moments (Onwezen et al., 2013).

The psychological challenge is that fashion purchases often occur under conditions favouring visceral and habitual processing: time pressure, competing cognitive demands, emotional states, and retail environments designed to promote immediate purchase rather than deliberate reflection. Effective sustainable fashion interventions must engage consumers emotionally (engaging visceral processing toward sustainable options) while making sustainable choices functionally competitive (simplifying and reducing barriers at the behavioural level) and aligning with deeper identity and values (supporting reflective processing). Systems operating at only one or two levels remain insufficient.

2.4 Barriers to Sustainable Fashion Adoption

Empirical research identifies six barriers contributing to the attitude-behaviour gap in sustainable fashion consumption. It is presented below in table format:

Table 1. Barriers to Sustainable Fashion Adoption

Barrier Name	Description & Statistics	Consumer Segment Most Affected	Examples	Impact on Adoption	Recommended Interventions
Price Premiums	20-50% cost premium over conventional fashion	Price-sensitive consumers; younger demographics	Sustainable tees $40-60 vs. fast fashion $10-15	Absolute barrier - prevents access regardless of motivation	Business model innovation, subsidies, and cost reduction through scale
Geographic/ Retail Availability	Limited retail infrastructure; concentrated in affluent areas	Rural populations; low-income urban areas	80% of fast-fashion consumers never access resale platforms	Search friction; information asymmetries	Online platforms; SME support; digital infrastructure investment
Greenwashing Concerns	Unclear sustainability claims; difficulty verifying impact	Educated, environmentally-aware consumers	H&M #CloseTheLoop: 73% awareness but only 1.8% participation	Consumer skepticism and trust erosion	Third-party verification; transparent methodologies; independent audits

continued on following page

Table 1. Continued

Barrier Name	Description & Statistics	Consumer Segment Most Affected	Examples	Impact on Adoption	Recommended Interventions
Fashionability Perception	Sustainability is perceived as aesthetically monotonous	Young consumers; trend-followers	Sustainable = boring, dowdy, hippie-ish stereotype	Identity/self-expression barriers	Design innovation; contemporary aesthetics; marketing repositioning
Quality/ Performance Skepticism	Unfamiliarity with sustainable materials; durability uncertainty	Quality-conscious consumers; older demographics	Questions about the longevity of eco-friendly textiles	Risk aversion: preference for known alternatives	Consumer education; trials; transparent durability data; repair services
Convenience & Habit	Effortful search; entrenched purchasing habits	Time-constrained consumers; habitual shoppers	Browse the mall, see an appealing item, and purchase it immediately	Behavioural inertia overrides reflective values	Default recommendations; simplified navigation; habit interruption

2.5 Intrinsic Motivation, Circular Consumption, and Emotional Engagement

The circular fashion economy, centered on resale, rental, repair, and garment longevity, offers psychological pathways alternative to new purchase-based sustainability, with distinct motivational profiles. Research on circular consumption motivations reveals multiple psychological drivers distinct from linear sustainability messaging:

i. *Economic Value:* Cost savings and quality-at-reduced-prices represent primary motivations for second-hand consumption, particularly among price-constrained consumers. Importantly, economic motivation is not inherently opposed to environmental benefit; consumers motivated by economic value achieve environmental outcomes as a by-product. This suggests that framing circular consumption, emphasizing value-for-money and quality, may reach consumers not primarily motivated by environmental identity (Lang & Zhang, 2019).
ii. *Environmental Responsibility:* Explicitly environmental motivations for example, reducing, reusing, recycling to minimize waste, drive adoption among environmentally-identified consumers. Research shows this motivation becomes particularly powerful when paired with visible impact metrics demonstrating the specific environmental benefits of individual choices (Laitala & Klepp, 2018).
iii. *Uniqueness and Discovery:* Access to original, retro, and discontinued items provides psychological satisfaction through uniqueness and identity expression distinct from fast fashion conformity. This motivation proves particularly powerful among younger consumers seeking individual expression and aesthetic differentiation (Lang & Zhang, 2019).

iv. *Social and Experiential Value:* The enjoyment of social shopping, particularly peer interaction and collaborative discovery, correlates strongly with adoption of circular fashion. Social shopping value, defined as psychological satisfaction derived from shopping with friends and family, significantly predicts both second-hand acquisition intention and perceived enjoyment of circular shopping experiences. This finding suggests that approaches emphasizing the social and experiential nature of circular fashion may outperform those focused solely on environmental or economic benefits (Lang & Zhang, 2019; Laitala & Klepp, 2018).
v. *Adoption Barriers in Circular Consumption:* Hygiene and cleanliness concerns about second-hand items persist despite evidence of rigorous cleaning standards. Quality uncertainty, difficulty estimating wear, damage, and remaining lifespan, creates decision friction. Social stigma persists in some contexts where second-hand purchases signal inability to afford new items, though this stigma has substantially diminished among younger cohorts who perceive circular consumption as environmentally conscious. Search costs, time and effort required to locate desired items in the correct size and condition, remain significant (Laitala & Klepp, 2018).

Self-Determination Theory and Intrinsic Motivation

Effective circular fashion platforms must satisfy three psychological needs identified by Self-Determination Theory (SDT) to maintain long-term engagement:

i. *Autonomy:* Users should feel genuine control and choice over circular consumption participation rather than coercion. Platforms should present resale, repair, and rental options as choices aligned with personal values and preferences, not requirements or moral obligations.
ii. *Competence:* Users require opportunities for mastery and skill development, learning how to assess second-hand quality, style thrifted pieces effectively, and extend garment lifespan through care and repair. Platforms providing educational content and guidance satisfy this need.
iii. *Relatedness:* Users require a connection to communities sharing similar values and interests. Platforms facilitating peer interaction, shared discovery experiences, and community recognition foster belonging and relatedness essential for sustained engagement (Ryan & Deci, 2000; Shahzad et al., 2023).

By addressing these psychological needs, circular fashion platforms can activate intrinsic motivation, engagement for its own satisfaction rather than external rewards, which research demonstrates produces more sustainable long-term behaviour change than externally-motivated compliance (Ryan & Deci, 2000).

2.6 Consumer Education and Information Processing

Despite widespread environmental awareness, many consumers lack specific knowledge about textile production impacts, garment care practices extending product lifespan, and circular economy mechanics. Educational interventions show promise but must account for cognitive biases and temporal discounting that prioritize immediate gratification over future environmental benefits (White & Simpson, 2013).

Effective consumer education in sustainable fashion requires:

i. ***Concrete Impact Visualization:*** Translating abstract environmental concepts (carbon footprint, water usage, chemical pollution) into tangible, personally-relevant metrics. For example, displaying "This garment saves 50 litres of water compared to virgin cotton production" connects environmental abstraction to a concrete quantity. Research demonstrates that concrete metrics increase both comprehension and motivation compared to general statements like "sustainable for our planet" (Park & Lin, 2020).
ii. ***Action-Specific Guidance:*** Moving beyond general sustainability awareness to specific behavioural recommendations. Rather than stating "fast fashion causes environmental damage," platforms might offer: "Extend this garment's life by 25%—30% by using cold water washing, line drying, and proper storage." Specificity increases adoption because it reduces uncertainty and the cognitive effort required for implementation.
iii. ***Temporal Bridging:*** Connecting immediate purchase decisions to long-term personal and environmental consequences. Messaging such as "This garment will likely fit and feel as good in three years" bridges temporal discounting by making future benefits salient and consequential.
iv. ***Social Validation:*** Providing evidence that sustainable choices are becoming mainstream and socially valued. Messages indicating "87% of users in your city selected this pre-owned item" leverage social conformity to reinforce that sustainable choices align with emerging norms.
v. ***Aesthetic Stereotype Reversal:*** Research indicates sustainable apparel must overcome negative aesthetic stereotypes to gain market acceptance. Sustainable fashion is frequently coded as "boring," "dowdy," or "hippie-ish" in consumer perception. Strategic marketing positioning sustainable fashion at the heart of contemporary fashion aspiration, aligning with style, chicness, and individual expression, rather than evoking antiquated or marginal imagery, proves essential (Niinimäki, 2010).

2.7 Material Innovation and Consumer Perception

Emerging sustainable materials, including bio textiles, regenerative fibres, lab-grown fabrics, and mycelium-based textiles, represent technological innovations that could reduce the environmental footprints of production. However, consumer adoption requires addressing psychological barriers distinct from traditional sustainability concerns. Consumers must overcome unfamiliarity with new materials, skepticism about performance compared to established alternatives, and concerns about whether innovative materials represent genuine sustainability or marketing innovation.

The following have been identified as potential psychological barriers to material innovation adoption:

i. ***Unfamiliarity and Quality Skepticism:*** Consumers lack experiential knowledge of new materials' functional properties. Without prior experience evaluating mycelium leather or lab-grown fabrics, consumers rely on limited signals to assess durability and performance. This information gap creates justified skepticism and risk aversion, particularly when premium pricing accompanies unfamiliar materials (Park & Lin, 2020).

ii. ***Performance Uncertainty:*** Legitimate questions persist about whether innovative materials perform comparably to conventional alternatives across important dimensions: durability, care requirements, environmental impact across the full lifecycle, and genuine versus marketed sustainability claims. When companies provide insufficient evidence addressing these concerns, consumer skepticism increases.

iii. ***Marketing Claims Validity:*** Innovative materials frequently face greenwashing concerns. Consumers encounter multiple products claiming sustainability through "revolutionary new materials," creating skepticism about whether novelty indicates genuine environmental benefit or sophisticated marketing. The Conceptual Gap Model's Ethical Gap directly addresses this concern—material innovation claims must include third-party verification and transparent impact documentation (Casino et al., 2019).

iv. ***Role of AI in Material Innovation Adoption:*** Artificial intelligence can address psychological barriers through personalization and education. AI-driven personalization could match consumers with materials aligning with their specific preferences and concerns: high-durability users receive information emphasizing innovative material longevity; consumers prioritizing certifications receive third-party verification documentation; style-conscious consumers see aesthetic styling with innovative materials paired with contemporary fashion aesthetics.

v. Lastly, educational interventions powered by AI might include interactive product comparisons showing lifecycle environmental impacts alongside functional properties, addressing quality skepticism with transparent performance data, and positioning innovative materials as aligned with contemporary fashion innovation; integrating material sustainability with aesthetic appeal rather than positioning as environmentally-conscious sacrifice (Park & Lin, 2020).

2.8 Cultural and Regional Variations in Sustainable Fashion Adoption

Sustainable fashion adoption is not uniformly distributed across global markets. Significant variations in consumer attitudes, infrastructure capacity, digital access, economic constraints, and cultural values shape adoption patterns across regions and income segments. Designing effective interventions requires understanding these contextual factors rather than applying Western, affluent-market solutions universally.

Research comparing sustainable fashion adoption across developed and emerging economies reveals substantial variations. In mature markets (North America, Western Europe), consumers express higher environmental awareness and demonstrate greater willingness-to-pay premiums for sustainability messaging, though actual adoption rates remain low (Candeloro, 2020). In emerging markets (India, Brazil, Nigeria), environmental awareness exists but competes with immediate economic constraints; sustainable options priced 50% above conventional alternatives remain inaccessible for the vast majority of consumers, regardless of environmental values (Das & Paul, 2024).

Digital platform adoption varies significantly. Research in Bangladesh and India found that 85% of consumers had never heard of reward-based sustainable fashion platforms, not due to disinterest but because digital infrastructure, platform awareness, and payment mechanisms remain concentrated in high-income segments and affluent urban areas (Das & Paul, 2024). This represents the Conceptual Gap Model's Inclusion Gap in practice: technology enabling sustainable consumption remains accessible primarily to affluent, digitally-connected populations.

Cultural dimensions shape both environmental attitudes and consumption behaviour. In collectivist cultures emphasizing social harmony and group welfare, normative appeals highlighting community environmental benefits show greater effectiveness than in individualist cultures emphasizing personal choice and autonomy (Goldstein et al., 2008; Udall et al., 2021). Conversely, individualist cultures respond more strongly to messaging emphasizing unique identity expression and personal values alignment.

Different cultural contexts value different sustainable pathways. In cultures emphasizing durability, frugality, and longevity (some East Asian contexts), circular consumption of high-quality garments aligns with existing cultural values. In cultures with strong social gifting traditions (parts of South Asia, Africa), extending garments through community sharing and gift exchange may represent more culturally-aligned pathways than anonymized resale platforms designed for individualist contexts (Laitala & Klepp, 2018).

Interventions leveraging digital nudging, AI personalization, and gamification assume digital infrastructure, internet connectivity, and payment system access that remain unequally distributed globally. Low-income regions and rural areas often lack reliable internet access and digital payment infrastructure that digital interventions require. Moreover, populations with lower digital literacy face steeper learning curves when adopting new technologies, regardless of motivation.

This creates a critical concern; AI and technology-enabled sustainability interventions risk concentrating benefits among affluent, digitally-connected populations while excluding the global majority most vulnerable to fashion industry harms. The Conceptual Gap Model's Inclusion Gap directly addresses this concern: interventions must explicitly ensure equitable access or risk deepening inequality.

Scaling sustainable fashion interventions globally requires explicit adaptation beyond literal translation. Approaches effective in Western affluent markets may prove counterproductive in emerging markets where economic constraints, different digital infrastructure, and cultural contexts create entirely different decision-making environments.

Effective global adaptation includes: (1) developing region-specific solutions rather than imposing standardized platforms; (2) addressing affordability barriers through pricing models, subsidies, or business model innovation rather than assuming consumers will pay Western premiums; (3) respecting cultural values regarding consumption, community, and identity rather than imposing Western sustainable fashion aesthetics; (4) building digital solutions accessible via low-bandwidth networks and basic mobile devices rather than requiring high-speed internet; (5) incorporating local languages, cultural references, and values into interface design and messaging; (6) partnering with local enterprises and informal-sector players rather than assuming large corporate platforms represent the only viable implementation approach.

3. AI-DRIVEN NUDGING IN SUSTAINABLE FASHION

3.1 Addressing the Psychological and Technological Gaps

This section addresses both the Psychological Gap (through demonstrating how algorithmic choice architecture can activate System 2 reflective processing at critical decision moments) and the Technological Gap (through documenting what works in field implementations, where intervention effectiveness proves limited compared to laboratory demonstrations, and under what contextual conditions technologies actually succeed). Section 3 reveals the central challenge: nudging shows substantial promise in controlled experiments, yet field deployments reveal rebound effects, habituation, and adaptation failures that substantially reduce real-world effectiveness. Understanding these gap-narrowing and gap-widening dynamics is essential for designing robust interventions that deliver sustained behaviour change rather than temporary choice shifts.

3.2 Defining Digital and Algorithmic Nudging

Digital nudging applies choice-architecture principles from behavioural economics to online interfaces, guiding consumers toward sustainable options without eliminating freedom of choice (Weinmann et al., 2016).

Table 2. Five core mechanisms adapted for sustainable fashion are given in the table below:

Nudge Type	Psychological Mechanism	Lab Efficacy	Field Efficacy	Habituation/ Backfire Risk	Autonomy Impact	Key Finding
Simplification	Hide non-sustainable options; highlight eco-choices	45%	12-18%	High - 8% decrease post-intervention (reactance)	Medium risk - reduces choice visibility	Initial lift erodes; habituation within weeks
Default Filter	Pre-select sustainable options as a starting point	100% (relative to unfiltered)	24% uplift	Medium - perceived constraint on choice	Medium - suggests default preference	Effective but requires active engagement to disable
Social Norm	Display peer behaviour; '70% of users chose recycled'	12-34%	12-20%	Low - aligns with natural conformity	Low - leverages existing social motivation	More effective in collectivist vs. individualist cultures
Reframing	Present cost differential: 'Only 10% more expensive'	23% willingness-to-pay increase	15-18% conversion lift	Medium - perceived manipulation if transparent math shows premium	Low-Medium - uses anchoring bias	Effective only when baseline frame already established
Personalized Eco-Scoring	AI calculates the composite environmental score per item	28% intention increase	22-28% (affluent only); negligible for budget-conscious	Low-Medium - data privacy concerns	Low-Medium - perceived algorithmic determination	Heterogeneous effects; fails for low-income segments

3.3 Experimental Evidence: Promise and Limitations

Recent field and laboratory experiments reveal that digital nudging's efficacy in sustainable fashion is highly context-dependent, illustrating the Technological Gap between laboratory promise and field reality.

Laboratory Effectiveness

Schürmann et al. (2023) compared simplification nudges (collapsing non-sustainable items behind an "Eco" filter) and social norm nudges (displaying "70% of users chose green items") among 461 online shoppers. Simplification increased sustainable selections by 45%, whereas social norm nudging showed no significant effect within the nudged set and only 12% uplift in non-nudged alternatives. Critically, participants exposed to simplification nudges were 8% less likely to make sustainable choices in subsequent sessions, suggesting reactance effects and habituation when cognitive friction is sharply reduced.

Field Study Findings

Coleman & Williams, (2015) conducted a randomized trial with 288 consumers on an operational e-retail site. Verbal nudges (text-based sustainability messages) produced 24% increase in eco-garment choice compared to control, significantly outperforming visual nudges (icon badges) which yielded 9% lift. However, high-involvement shoppers (those with strong fashion and environmental interest) responded most to verbal appeals, whereas low-involvement shoppers showed negligible differences, a finding demonstrating that nudge effectiveness depends critically on consumer heterogeneity.

Backfire and Stacking Effects

Mirbabaie et al. (2022) tested default, social norm, and simplification nudges alone and stacked together in a simulated e-commerce setting (n = 320). While single nudges each produced modest gains, the stacked condition led to 15% *decrease* in sustainable choices relative to control, attributed to decision fatigue and perceived manipulation. This backfire effect directly illustrates the Technological Gap: nudging techniques that work in isolation may paradoxically widen psychological gaps when combined without careful design.

Role of Intrinsic Motivation

Busalim et al. (2022) systematic review highlighted that intrinsic motivation and environmental self-identity remain the strongest predictors of green purchase behavior, with self-identified "green" consumers 2.5× more likely to select sustainable items regardless of nudge type. This finding reveals a critical limitation: nudging is substantially more effective among already-motivated consumers and may fail entirely for those lacking environmental self-identity. Nudges cannot *create* intrinsic motivation; they can only amplify existing pro-environmental orientation.

These results collectively demonstrate the Technological Gap, the substantial distance between laboratory effectiveness and real-world sustained impact. Nudges generate temporary choice shifts rather than lasting behaviour transformation, and when applied without attention to individual differences, psychological heterogeneity, and genuine motivation alignment, they risk backfiring.

3.4 AI Personalization and Eco-Scoring

AI-driven personalization extends basic nudging by leveraging consumer data to deliver hyper-relevant sustainability interventions. A six-week field deployment by Munten et al. (2024) implemented an AI engine calculating composite eco-scores (carbon, water, labour impacts) for each garment. This intervention yielded 28% increase in sustainable purchases; however, overall shopping frequency rose 12%, indicating rebound effects that partially offset environmental gains. The finding illuminates the Technological Gap: successful behavioural nudging creates new consumption patterns that may undermine environmental goals if business models continue rewarding consumption growth.

Technology Acceptance: Park and Lin (2020) demonstrated that clear eco-metric presentation on product pages boosted intentions to purchase recycled and upcycled clothing. Mirbabaie et al. (2022) found that personalized eco-recommendations with interactive visual storytelling increased perceived enjoyment, leading to 15% additional green choice uptake. These results highlight that successful personalization requires balancing instrumental utility (accurate eco-information, intuitive navigation) with hedonic factors (compelling narratives, aesthetic customization) while maintaining transparent data practices to alleviate greenwashing concerns.

3.5 Consolidated Industry Applications

Current implementations demonstrate diverse approaches to AI-driven sustainability nudging. Rather than examining isolated companies, this section consolidates approaches by technology type to reveal what works across different contexts.

Resale Marketplace Integration: ThredUp and Vinted

ThredUp and Vinted represent the resale-platform category employing AI to quantify and surface sustainability metrics. ThredUp's Eco-Impact Calculator, powered by an AI recommendation engine, quantifies estimated carbon and water savings based on users' resale histories. A January-February 2025 survey of 3,034 U.S. adults found that 78% reported increased visibility of sustainability metrics in search results after eco-score integration, with resale transactions on high-impact items increasing 22% year-over-year (ThreadUp Inc., 2025). Natural-language and image-based search features (e.g., "dusty rose linen dress" or photo uploads) drove 17% uplift in click-through rates to second-hand listings.

Vinted publishes annual Climate Impact Reports estimating average savings of approximately 2 kg CO_2e per item through peer-to-peer resale, cumulatively amounting to hundreds of kilotons avoided annually (Vinted, 2023). Post-purchase messaging ("Thank you for extending this item's life!") reinforces environmental identity, with surveys indicating environmental motivations rank among top repeat-use drivers.

Both platforms demonstrate that transparent impact visualization paired with streamlined matching algorithms can effectively narrow the Psychological Gap by connecting individual choices to concrete environmental outcomes while the Technological Gap persists: the platforms cannot overcome price barriers or address the 80% of fast-fashion consumers who lack access to resale platforms (Busalim et al., 2022).

Ethical Rating Systems: Good On You and Fashion Transparency Index

Good On You applies third-party-verified ratings to over 3,000 brands across five levels from "We Avoid" to "Great" (Good On You, 2023). Algorithmic badges appearing in search results and brand pages simplify complex supply-chain data into intuitive signals. User surveys found visible ratings increased click-through rates on highly-rated brands by over one-third, indicating enhanced consumer trust. However, increased engagement did not proportionally increase conversions, suggesting that trust signals address the Ethical Gap but cannot overcome price and availability barriers.

Fashion Transparency Index (published annually by Fashion Revolution) rates major fashion brands on disclosure of social and environmental policies, practices, and impacts (Fashion Revolution, 2025). The Index creates accountability pressure and enables consumers to systematically compare brands. By making brand disclosure visible, the Index creates reputational incentives for improvement. Over time, average transparency scores have increased from 21% (2017) to 25% (2023), suggesting that public accountability mechanisms drive gradual organizational behaviour change. However, increased engagement and trust signals did not proportionally increase conversions in either platform, suggesting that trust alone cannot overcome price and availability barriers (Good On You, 2023; Fashion Revolution, 2025).

3.6 Contextual Factors and Device-Specific Implementation

AI-driven nudging effectiveness depends critically on contextual variables often overlooked in laboratory research. Device modality shapes nudge design: mobile interfaces with limited screen real estate benefit from concise "micro-nudges" delivered via notifications. Schürmann et al. (2023) found that mobile prompts highlighting per-item carbon savings increased sustainable selections 18% compared to no notifications, whereas desktop implementations allow richer interactive elements but risk cognitive overload if overused.

Temporal framing amplifies effectiveness: priming sustainability goals at session start increases efficacy, while end-of-session alerts leverage decision inertia (Weinmann et al., 2016). Energy sector research suggests timing itself can boost efficacy 25%.

Cultural norms moderate nudge impact. Descriptive norm messages ("70% of users selected recycled denim") prove more effective in collectivist cultures; injunctive norms ("Gain the community's approval") resonate more in individualist societies (Goldstein et al., 2008). Emotional framing incorporating positive reinforcement ("You've saved 2 kg CO_2e this session!") engages without guilt fatigue (Mirbabaie et al., 2022). Algorithm transparency explaining nudge rationale in accessible language, safeguards autonomy and reduces manipulation concerns (Thaler & Sunstein, 2009).

3.7 Computational Sustainability and Responsible MLOps

Scaling AI nudging requires attention to environmental costs and data governance. Training large AI models generates substantial carbon emissions: Strubell et al. (2019) report that one NLP model generates 626,000 pounds of CO_2, approximately five times average car lifetime emissions. This reveals a critical paradox: technologies intended to reduce environmental impact create new environmental burdens.

Green AI approaches include: (1) once-for-all network architectures reducing computational requirements; (2) federated learning enabling on-device model training with bounded privacy safeguards and decentralized computation; (3) renewable-energy-powered cloud infrastructure; (4) scheduling computational tasks during low-carbon generation periods, reducing emissions by ~50%; (5) dynamic resource scaling adjusting capacity to real-time demand (Shi et al., 2020).

Data Privacy and Responsible Practices: Effective personalization hinges on granular behavioral data, raising concerns under GDPR and CCPA regulations. Embedding privacy-by-design principles like data anonymization, differential privacy, explicit consent mechanisms, maintains user trust without compromising model efficacy (Voigt & von dem Bussche, 2017). Many retailers operate legacy monolithic platforms; transitioning to microservices and headless commerce architectures facilitates incremental AI integration, enabling agile A/B testing and continuous optimization (Newman, 2015).

3.8 Addressing the Technological Gap: Why Field Effectiveness Lags Laboratory Promise

The Technological Gap persists because laboratory experiments occur in controlled environments divergent from real-world retail contexts. Consumers in real commerce face competing demands, emotional states, time pressure, and retail environments designed to promote fast, automatic purchase rather than deliberate reflection. Environmental psychology theory suggests three mechanisms explaining gap persistence:

i. ***Adaptation and Habituation:*** Repeated exposure to nudges triggers habituation, loss of effectiveness over time as consumers adapt to the signal. Schürmann et al. (2023) found 8% reduced sustainable choice in post-nudge sessions, suggesting that initial behavioural shifts erode as consumers accommodate to the intervention.
ii. ***Contextual Misalignment:*** Laboratory experiments often test nudges in isolation; real retail environments contain multiple competing nudges, defaults, and choice architecture elements. Stacking effects documented by Mirbabaie et al. (2022) reveal that well-designed individual nudges backfire when combined without explicit coordination.
iii. ***Consumer Heterogeneity:*** Nudging effectiveness varies dramatically across consumer segments. Busalim et al. (2022) find self-identified green consumers show 2.5× higher sustainable selection regardless of nudge type, whereas consumers lacking environmental identity show minimal response. Nudges cannot bridge this heterogeneity gap.
iv. ***Rebound Effects:*** Increased efficiency of sustainable options sometimes paradoxically increases overall consumption volume, offsetting environmental gains. Munten et al. (2024) document 12% increase in overall shopping frequency following eco-score implementation, suggesting that making sustainable choices easier simultaneously increases consumption.

Addressing the Technological Gap requires moving beyond individual nudges toward systemic design: coordinating choice architecture with price restructuring, availability enhancement, emotional engagement, and community support to address multiple barriers simultaneously.

3.9 Synthesis: Toward Effective, Ethical AI Nudging

Integrative approaches to AI-driven nudging include context sensitivity, technological sustainability, adaptive design, and ethical transparency. Nudges should be customized to user profiles considering values, cultural norms, and device context; richer visualizations suit desktop while simplified micro-nudges suit mobile (Schürmann et al., 2023; Coleman & Williams, 2015). Explainable AI methods increase transparency, clarifying why specific prompts appear and triggering consumer autonomy and trust (Doshi-Velez & Kim, 2017). Green AI infrastructure (like efficient architectures, edge computing, renewable-powered data centers) achieves both low carbon emission and high-performance training and serving (Strubell et al., 2019; Shi et al., 2020).

Adaptive co-evolutionary systems continuously update nudges in response to changing user behaviour, avoiding habituation and maintaining effectiveness (Scherer et al., 2023). Ethical governance consolidates privacy-by-design principles, ensures equitable access across socioeconomic segments, and implements third-party verification to protect user rights and prevent greenwashing (Voigt & von dem Bussche, 2017; Casino et al., 2019).

Ongoing multi-faceted evaluation consisting of quantitative conversion metrics, CO_2 savings calculations, trust assessments, and comprehensive environmental impact analysis guides iterative improvement (Mirbabaie et al., 2022). By synthesizing behavioural economics, data science, and ethical design, next generation AI-powered nudges move beyond superficial persuasion toward value-aligned engagement that empowers consumers to participate in building circular, low-carbon fashion economies.

4. GAMIFICATION AND EMOTIONAL ENGAGEMENT

This section addresses the Psychological Gap through emotional and social engagement mechanisms that activate intrinsic motivation and create sustained behaviour change. While Section 3 demonstrated how AI nudging can activate reflective processing at critical decision moments, this section reveals how gamification, combining game mechanics with emotional triggers and community dynamics, can sustain motivation over time by engaging the affective and social dimensions of decision-making that conscious nudging cannot reach. Gamification's power lies not in manipulating choice architecture but in transforming sustainable behaviours from obligations into sources of pride, achievement, and belonging.

4.1 Gamification Mechanics for Circular Fashion Behaviours

Contemporary sustainable fashion platforms employ game-based elements like points, badges, leaderboards, and challenges to translate abstract environmental goals into concrete, actionable tasks with immediate feedback. These mechanics harness intrinsic motivations and create reinforcement loops supporting pro-environmental behaviours.

Points systems award credits for circular actions: purchasing pre-owned items, extending garment lifespans through care, hosting clothing swaps, or participating in repair workshops. Immediate point accumulation provides feedback satisfying the psychological need for competence; users understand their actions create measurable progress (Shahzad et al., 2023). However, research reveals critical implementation nuances. Shahzad et al. (2023) documented a significant negative relationship between poorly-designed gamification and green consumption behaviour among Chinese university students, particularly when gamification emphasized superficial engagement over authentic environmental impact. Points systems must be calibrated to reflect genuine environmental benefit rather than simply rewarding platform engagement metrics.

Badges and achievements recognize accomplishments symbolizing status and mastery: "Wardrobe Lifespan Champion" for garments worn >100 times, "Circular Innovator" for completing upcycling tutorials, "Community Host" for organizing clothing swaps. These digital symbols satisfy the psychological need for mastery and serve as social signals encouraging peer emulation. Hamari et al. (2014) demonstrated that well-designed achievement systems correlate with enhanced cognitive and affective brand loyalty. However, superficial badge proliferation can generate "gamification fatigue", users cease paying attention when achievements feel arbitrary or disconnected from authentic accomplishment.

Leaderboards and social challenges foster healthy competition and collective achievement. Monthly city-wide competitions ranking users by total carbon prevented, total textiles diverted from landfills, or community swaps hosted harness social comparison while framing competition as progress toward shared environmental goals rather than zero-sum ranking. Das and Paul (2024) documented that eco-gamification pilots in Bangladesh achieved 92% consumer willingness to modify purchasing behaviour when incentivized, with 90% expressing interest in joining reward-based platforms, suggesting substantial appeal of competitive social engagement.

Narrative quests and story-driven challenges embed learning within engaging narratives: a "Repair Journey" quest sequence might include workshops on hand-mending techniques, machine-washing best practices, and fibre care, with each completed workshop contributing to quest progression and unlocking rewards. This narrative framing connects learning to identity and values, making skill development inherently rewarding rather than externally motivated (Shahzad et al., 2023).

Mirbabaie et al. (2022) documented "nudge stacking" backfire effects where combining multiple game elements (simultaneous leaderboards, points, badges, notifications) created decision fatigue and manipulative perception, resulting in a 15% *decrease* in sustainable selection. Effective gamification requires restraint, introducing mechanics strategically at critical decision moments rather than overwhelming users with simultaneous engagement attempts.

4.2 Emotional Drivers: Pride, Guilt, and Future Orientation

Emotions significantly influence sustainable fashion decision-making, functioning as both motivators and barriers. Three emotional dimensions prove particularly influential:

Anticipated pride represents positive, achievement-related emotion, strengthening self-identity and perceived efficacy. Tangney et al. (2007) demonstrate that pride functions as a moral emotion, reinforcing ethical behaviour by rewarding alignment with personal and social values. Gamified platforms leveraging pride through achievement recognition and public acknowledgment of contributions foster sustained participation. Messaging such as "You've prevented 50 kg textile waste: community leader!" connects individual actions to identity and social standing, making continued participation intrinsically rewarding (Onwezen et al., 2013).

Anticipated guilt represents a negative, self-critical emotion arising when individuals anticipate regret for unsustainable actions. Guilt activates personal norms and responsibility awareness, motivating initial behaviour change. However, excessive guilt becomes counterproductive. Research demonstrates that prolonged guilt exposure generates emotional fatigue and motivational depletion, ultimately reducing sustainable behaviour adoption (Onwezen et al., 2013). Effective emotional engagement balances guilt-based prompts ("Your shopping habits generate 500 kg CO_2 annually") with pride-based reinforcement, avoiding guilt saturation that triggers resistance.

Future-oriented framing connects present actions to long-term environmental and personal consequences, bridging temporal discounting that typically prioritizes immediate over delayed rewards. Dasandi et al. (2022) demonstrate that positive, globally-framed climate messaging increases public engagement. Platforms combining concrete present-tense feedback ("You've saved water today") with future-oriented messaging ("At this rate, you'll prevent 5 tons CO_2 this year") balance psychological needs for both immediate reinforcement and meaningful long-term impact (Onwezen et al., 2013).

4.3 Community Building and Social Engagement

Community dynamics amplify gamification's impact by leveraging social identity, peer support, and collective efficacy. Platforms embedding community-centric features transform individual behaviours into coordinated collective movements.

Collaborative challenges structure group activities like city-wide upcycling competitions, neighbourhood clothing swaps, peer repair circles, etc., creating shared objectives and mutual support. Strong social identity increases pro-environmental behaviours by fostering collective responsibility and agency (Udall et al., 2021). Users identify not merely as individuals making sustainable choices but as members of environmental communities, amplifying motivation through social belonging.

Social leaderboards and recognition publicly display peer contributions across geographic or demographic scales, reinforcing descriptive norms ("Your neighborhood prevented 100 tons of textile waste this month") and injunctive norms ("Neighborhood leaders prioritize garment longevity"). Goldstein et al. (2008) demonstrated that such social proof messaging increased conservation behaviours by 34%. Recognition systems converting individual achievement into visible community contribution strengthen social cohesion and collective environmental efficacy (Udall et al., 2021).

Peer-to-peer feedback and content-sharing platforms encouraging user-generated content like styling sustainable outfits, demonstrating repair techniques, photographing circular wardrobe rotations, etc., promote social learning and democratize expertise. Good On You's integration of community ratings and brand reviews creates knowledge exchange cycles, bolstering communal trust and informed decision-making (Good On You, 2023).

Guilds and affinity groups segment users into identity-based micro-communities: vintage fashion enthusiasts, DIY upcyclers, minimalist wardrobists. Targeted challenges and recognition within affinity groups foster belonging more powerfully than broad platform-wide competitions. Das and Paul (2024) document that social belonging within gamified platforms significantly enhances intrinsic motivation and reduces user attrition by approximately 25% compared to individual-focused competitions.

4.4 Self-Determination Theory and Sustaining Intrinsic Motivation

Self-Determination Theory (SDT) identifies three psychological needs essential for sustained engagement and intrinsic motivation (Ryan & Deci, 2000). Autonomy requires that users feel genuine control and choice over participation rather than coercion. Gamified platforms should present sustainable options as autonomous choices aligned with personal values, not moral obligations. Users need straightforward controls to disable notifications, opt out of leaderboards, or adjust challenge difficulty. When users feel manipulated despite gamification's good intentions, reactance emerges; deliberate resistance undermining intervention effectiveness (Shahzad et al., 2023). Effective design preserves perceived autonomy through transparent explanations, reversible choices, and user control over engagement intensity.

Competence requires opportunities for mastery and skill development. Platforms should provide learning pathways progressing from accessible introductory challenges (complete a social media poll about wardrobes) through increasingly sophisticated tasks (lead a community repair workshop). Tiered difficulty maintaining appropriate challenge prevents both boredom (excessive simplicity) and frustration (excessive difficulty). Users require skill-building resources enabling authentic competence development rather than pseudo-mastery from trivial achievements (Hamari et al., 2014).

Relatedness requires connection to communities sharing similar values and interests. Platforms facilitating peer interaction, collaborative challenges, and community recognition foster belonging essential for sustained engagement. Conversely, competitive leaderboards that shame lower-ranking users erode relatedness, damaging motivation (Das & Paul, 2024).

Research demonstrates that gamification aligned with SDT principles produces intrinsic motivation, engagement satisfying for its own value rather than external rewards, resulting in more sustainable long-term behaviour change than externally-motivated compliance (Ryan & Deci, 2000). Critically, external reward systems (points, badges, monetary incentives) can paradoxically *crowd out* intrinsic motivation when they undermine perceived autonomy or appear manipulative (Shahzad et al., 2023).

4.5 Blockchain-Enabled Gamification for Transparency and Trust

Blockchain technology provides immutable ledgers underpinning gamification systems, ensuring trust in sustainability claims and reward distribution. Three applications prove particularly relevant. Decentralized Reward Systems employ blockchain-based tokens for circular behaviours, enabling cross-platform redemption and broader ecosystem participation. Smart contracts automate reward issuance for verified environmental actions, ensuring fair distribution while reducing administrative overhead (Bag et al., 2024). Rather than users accumulating points only on individual platforms, tokenized rewards become portable value tradeable across sustainable fashion networks.

Immutable Impact Tracking records user activities like garment swaps, quantified carbon savings, repair completions, etc., on distributed ledgers, creating permanent environmental-footprint registries. Field trials demonstrate that transparent, on-chain recording of verifiable actions boosts participant trust by 38% and engagement by 22% compared to centralized database tracking (Wüst & Gervais, 2018).

Automated Smart Contracts enforce reward conditions, releasing tokens upon verified task completion while embedding penalty clauses deterring misuse. Smart-contract-based environmental incentives improve compliance verification and instantaneous reward delivery compared to traditional voucher systems, resulting in 20-30% higher participation rates (Bag et al., 2024).

4.6 Design Principles and Best Practices

Synthesizing research and practice reveals six guiding principles for effective gamified emotional engagement:

i. ***Value-Aligned Mechanics:*** Game elements must explicitly connect to sustainability outcomes. Awarding points proportional to kilograms of textile waste diverted reinforces that actions drive environmental progress, not just platform engagement. Superficial gamification disconnected from authentic impact generates cynicism, undermining motivation (Shahzad et al., 2023).
ii. ***Emotionally Balanced Messaging:*** Blend guilt-based initial prompts activating behavior change with pride-based reinforcement and future-oriented narratives sustaining motivation. Overreliance on single emotional framings (excessive guilt or relentless positivity) triggers emotional fatigue (Onwezen et al., 2013).
iii. ***Community-Centric Design:*** Incorporate collaborative challenges, social recognition, and content-sharing hubs leveraging peer influence and collective efficacy. Competitive elements must emphasize collective environmental progress rather than zero-sum status ranking (Udall et al., 2021).
iv. ***Transparent Operations:*** Employ blockchain or third-party verification, ensuring impact credibility and reward legitimacy, preventing greenwashing and enhancing user confidence (Bag et al., 2024).

v. ***Adaptive Evolution:*** Continuously monitor engagement to refresh challenges, adjust difficulty, and adapt emotional framings, preventing habituation and maintaining novelty (Gyulai & Revesz, 2023).
vi. ***Ethical Safeguards:*** Embed clear opt-out controls, transparent explanations for nudges, and robust privacy protections respecting autonomy and data rights; essential for fostering trust and avoiding manipulation (Voigt & von dem Bussche, 2017).

4.7 Implications and Research Directions

This integrated framework presents a scalable blueprint enabling sustainable fashion platforms to harness gamification ethically and effectively. Future research priorities include:

- Longitudinal field trials (6-12 months) assessing gamification durability, decay, rebound effects, and cost-effectiveness across diverse populations
- Cross-cultural validation examining how game mechanics, emotional framings, and social dynamics translate across cultural contexts and income segments
- Emerging technology integration exploring hybrid AR/VR experiences offering immersive sustainability education at point-of-purchase
- Multi-objective optimization algorithms balancing environmental impact, user engagement, and business performance
- Participatory co-design involving end users in framework development ensuring alignment with values, motivations, and real-life constraints

5. ETHICAL FRAMEWORK AND RESPONSIBLE AI DEVELOPMENT

This section directly addresses both the Ethical Gap (the discrepancy between ethical design principles and actual implementation that risks creating manipulation, bias, and greenwashing) and the Inclusion Gap (ensuring equitable access and preventing technologies from concentrating benefits among affluent populations). Sections 3 and 4 demonstrated how digital nudging and gamification can narrow the Psychological Gap by activating reflective processing and sustaining intrinsic motivation. However, without explicit attention to ethical design and equitable implementation, these technologies risk creating new problems: algorithmic bias that reinforces existing inequalities, greenwashing that erodes consumer trust, privacy violations that undermine autonomy, and infrastructure barriers that exclude marginalized communities. Section 5 proposes governance structures, design principles, and accountability mechanisms ensuring that behavioural technologies maintain integrity while distributing benefits equitably across all consumers.

5.1 The Ethical Paradox: Power and Peril of Behavioural Technology

Behavioural technologies create a fundamental ethical tension. When designed thoughtfully, they can help millions of consumers align purchasing choices with environmental values. Digital nudges activate reflective processing at critical decision moments; gamification transforms abstract environmental goals into emotionally rewarding engagement; personalization delivers relevant information reducing decision friction. These mechanisms work precisely *because* they engage psychological mechanisms beneath conscious awareness.

Yet this same power to influence without requiring conscious deliberation creates ethical risks. Nudges invisible to conscious scrutiny can manipulate choices while users believe they've exercised autonomous judgment. Gamification designed to maximize engagement metrics may encourage consumption patterns that undermine environmental goals. Personalization powered by granular behavioural data can implement targeting so sophisticated that users are unaware of how their choices are shaped. The more effective behavioural interventions become at influencing choice, the greater the ethical responsibility to implement them transparently and equitably (Thaler & Sunstein, 2009).

The Greenwashing Risk: Companies face inherent incentives toward greenwashing, exaggerating or misrepresenting environmental impact to gain market advantage. When platforms display eco-scores without rigorous verification, certifications without independent audit, or impact claims without transparent methodologies, consumers reasonably become skeptical. Accumulated greenwashing experiences breed cynicism that generalizes across all sustainability messaging, undermining genuine efforts. Candeloro (2020) documents how H&M's "#CloseTheLoop" campaign achieved 73% consumer awareness yet only 1.8% actual participation, suggesting that visibility without substantive environmental progress creates legitimacy gaps eroding consumer trust.

The Equity Risk: Behavioral technologies designed in Western affluent contexts reflect the capabilities and constraints of well-resourced organizations. When generalized globally without explicit adaptation, these technologies inadvertently deepen inequality by concentrating benefits among large corporations with technical sophistication while excluding SMEs, informal enterprises, and populations lacking digital infrastructure. Algorithms trained on unrepresentative datasets may systematically deliver inferior recommendations to marginalized populations, creating discriminatory outcomes beneath conscious visibility (Voigt & von dem Bussche, 2017).

The Autonomy Risk: Between influence and manipulation lies a psychological boundary that ethical design must respect. Influence preserves perceived autonomy; users feel they chose the outcome. Manipulation erodes autonomy; users feel their choice was determined by external forces. This distinction matters ethically and practically: when users perceive manipulation, reactance emerges (deliberate resistance and choice of opposite option), undermining intervention effectiveness while damaging platform trust (Mirbabaie et al., 2022).

5.2 Core Ethical Principles: Fairness, Transparency, and Accountability

Addressing ethical gaps requires systematic principles operationalized throughout platform design and organizational governance.

Principle 1: Fairness: Equitable Access and Protection Against Bias

Fairness requires that sustainable choice benefits reach all consumer populations regardless of income, digital literacy, geographic location, or demographic characteristics. It also requires protection against algorithmic bias that systematically disadvantages particular groups.

Implementation of the principle might require:

i. *Universal Design:* Sustainable fashion interventions should be accessible via low-bandwidth networks, mobile-first interfaces, and multiple languages rather than assuming high-speed internet and English fluency. Platforms should function on basic smartphones and feature simplified navigation accessible to users with limited digital literacy (Busalim et al., 2022).
ii. *Affordability Considerations:* Nudging consumers toward sustainable options becomes unethical if those options remain economically inaccessible. Interventions should address price barriers directly, through policy incentives, business model innovation redistributing cost-savings to consumers, or differential pricing making sustainable options accessible to budget-conscious segments; rather than expecting psychological activation to overcome economic constraints.
iii. *Bias Detection and Mitigation:* Regular fairness audits should assess whether recommendation algorithms, personalized messaging, and credit/financing decisions systematically treat demographic groups differently. Tools like IBM's AI Fairness 360 can detect disparate impact where algorithms produce unequal

outcomes across protected classes (Bellamy et al., 2018). When bias is detected, remediation should occur promptly.

iv. *Vulnerable Population Consideration:* Specific attention should protect consumers experiencing homelessness, linguistic isolation, low digital literacy, or limited financial resources. Platforms should incorporate feedback mechanisms enabling these populations to report problematic experiences and seek remediation (Voigt & von dem Bussche, 2017).

Principle 2: Transparency: Clear Explanation and Information Accessibility

Transparency requires openness about how systems operate, like how eco-scores are calculated, what data influences recommendations, why particular nudges appear to specific users, etc., enabling informed participation rather than hidden influence.

Implementation of the principle might require:

i. *Algorithm Explainability:* Any recommendation or nudge should be accompanied by an understandable explanation of reasoning. Rather than opaque rankings, systems should communicate: "This item scores 7/10 environmentally because it uses organic cotton (reduces water use), has a 10-year expected lifespan (extends wear), is produced with verified labor practices, but uses synthetic dyes (chemical pollution concerns)." Explainability tools like LIME or SHAP can generate understandable feature importance explanations (Doshi-Velez & Kim, 2017; Gilpin et al., 2018).

ii. *Data Transparency:* Platforms should clearly communicate what personal data is collected, how long it is retained, how it is used in algorithmic systems, and who has access to it. Consent mechanisms should be genuinely informed—not buried in lengthy terms of service—enabling users to understand what they're agreeing to (Voigt & von dem Bussche, 2017; GDPR Article 13).

iii. *Methodology Documentation:* Impact measurement methodologies should be publicly available, enabling independent verification. Companies should specify assumptions embedded in calculations (such as lifecycle assessment methodologies, temporal boundaries, system boundaries) that substantially affect results (Strubell et al., 2019). Publishing methodologies invite external scrutiny that improves rigor while building credibility.

iv. *Third-Party Verification:* Independent audits provide credibility that self-reported claims lack. Blockchain-based verification systems can create immutable records of audited claims, preventing retroactive modification (Bag et al., 2024).

Principle 3: Accountability: Organizational Responsibility and User Recourse

Accountability requires that organizations take responsibility for systemic failures, implement correction mechanisms when errors occur, and provide users with recourse when they believe recommendations or decisions are unfair.

Implementation of the principle might require:

i. *Governance Structures:* Establish ethics review boards similar to research IRBs, empowered to evaluate platform changes before deployment. Include external members representing diverse stakeholder perspectives (consumer advocates, environmental scientists, equity specialists) rather than only company employees. Ethics boards should have authority to delay problematic deployments, not merely advisory capacity (IEEE, 2019).
ii. *Audit Trails:* Maintain detailed documentation of algorithmic decisions, which version of the model generated which recommendation for which user, enabling post-hoc investigation of failures. This paper trail supports accountability when users lodge complaints (Himmelreich & Köhler, 2022).
iii. *Appeal Mechanisms:* Users should be able to contest algorithmic recommendations: "I believe this eco-score is inaccurate because..." or "This nudge feels manipulative because..." Formal appeal processes should exist where trained staff investigate complaints and implement corrections when warranted.
iv. *Impact Assessment:* Conduct regular impact assessments evaluating whether platform operations achieve intended environmental benefits or inadvertently produce harms (rebound effects, leakage to non-sustainable alternatives, increased consumption). Update systems when evidence reveals unintended consequences (Casino et al., 2019).
v. *Executive Accountability:* Designate organizational leaders responsible for ethical outcomes, potentially a Chief Ethics Officer with board-level authority to halt problematic practices. Without executive accountability, ethics becomes a marginalized function easily overridden by profit pressure.

5.3 Distinguishing Influence from Manipulation

The psychological boundary between influence and manipulation proves ethically crucial. Influence preserves autonomy; users feel they chose the outcome. Manipulation erodes autonomy; users feel determined by external forces.

Table 3. The following table shows the difference:

Influence characteristics	Manipulation characteristics
User retains transparent information about options	Information asymmetry prevents informed judgment
Choice remains genuinely available (alternatives visibly present)	Choice alternatives hidden or made unnecessarily difficult
Decision-making feels internally motivated ("I want to choose this")	Decision-making feels externally imposed ("They made me choose this")
Afterwards, users feel good about the decision made	Post-decision regret or resentment emerges

Regardless of whether it is influence or manipulation following specific safeguards should be taken into account:

- *Informed Consent:* Users must know they're being influenced. Nudges should be clearly labelled: "We're highlighting sustainable options because our research shows they reduce environmental impact." Transparent labelling paradoxically often increases nudge effectiveness by preserving autonomy perception (Thaler & Sunstein, 2009).
- *Reversibility:* Users should have straightforward controls to undo nudges: "Undo this recommendation," "Stop showing me this type of nudge," "Use a different recommendation approach." Easy opt-out demonstrates respect for autonomy and prevents reactance.
- *User Control:* Rather than platforms deciding what consumers need, users should customize how they engage: "Show me recommendations emphasizing carbon reduction," "Emphasize cost-effectiveness instead," "Hide all gamification elements." Customization acknowledges that different consumers weigh sustainability dimensions differently.
- *Emotional Honesty:* Emotional appeals (pride, guilt, belonging) are legitimate influence mechanisms but become manipulative when deceptive. Gamified rewards should genuinely reflect accomplishment, not artificially inflate achievement. Guilt appeals should connect to realistic rather than exaggerated environmental consequences.

5.4 Green AI and Responsible MLOps Practices

Scaling behavioural technologies requires attention to AI infrastructure, environmental costs and data governance. Without responsible practices, the technologies intended to reduce environmental footprint create new environmental burdens.

Computational Sustainability

Training large machine learning models generates substantial carbon emissions: Strubell et al. (2019) report that one NLP model produces 626,000 pounds of CO_2, approximately five times the average lifetime car emissions. Scaling this across thousands of personalized recommendation models creates a significant environmental cost that ethical practice must minimize.

Green AI approaches include:

- *Once-for-All Networks:* Instead of training multiple distinct models, once-for-all architectures train a single flexible model supporting multiple objectives simultaneously. This reduces redundant computation while maintaining performance (Shi et al., 2020).
- *Federated Learning:* Training models on user devices rather than centralized servers distributes computational burden and enables on-device privacy preservation. Federated learning reduces data transmission and central computation, lowering energy requirements (Kairouz et al., 2021).
- *Renewable Energy:* Where cloud infrastructure is necessary, select providers powered by renewable energy. Scheduling compute-intensive tasks during low-carbon generation periods (high wind/solar hours) can reduce emissions by approximately 50% compared to baseline timing (Shi et al., 2020).
- *Dynamic Resource Scaling:* Infrastructure provisioning should adjust capacity to real-time demand rather than over-provisioning. Algorithms predicting request volume enable appropriate capacity allocation, avoiding energy waste from underutilized infrastructure (Newman, 2015).

Privacy-by-Design and Data Governance

Personalization effectiveness depends on behavioural data, raising concerns under GDPR, CCPA, and emerging privacy regulations. Privacy-by-design embeds protection from the architecture outset rather than retrofitting compliance (Voigt & von dem Bussche, 2017).

Implementation approaches inlcude:

- *Data Minimization:* Collect only data necessary for specific functions. Rather than comprehensive behavioural tracking, collect only attributes directly relevant to recommendation generation (Voigt & von dem Bussche, 2017).
- *Differential Privacy:* Add controlled noise to individual-level data before analysis, preventing identification of specific users while preserving aggre-

gate statistical patterns enabling model training (Voigt & von dem Bussche, 2017).

- *Data Anonymization:* Remove personally identifiable information and implement data retention policies (e.g., delete individual transaction records after 90 days, retain only aggregated summaries) (General Data Protection Regulation, 2018).
- *Consent Management:* Implement genuine consent mechanisms, not buried in lengthy terms of service, with easy opt-in/opt-out. Users should control data usage at a granular level ("Use my purchase history for recommendations: Yes/No"; "Share anonymized data with research: Yes/No") (Voigt & von dem Bussche, 2017).

Architecture and Technology Stack

Many fashion retailers operate monolithic, tightly-coupled systems where integrating new AI components requires risky, system-wide modifications. Microservices and headless commerce architectures facilitate incremental integration (Newman, 2015; Pautasso & Zimmermann, 2016). This architectural transition provides multiple benefits: modularity enables AI recommendation modules, gamification engines, and blockchain verification to operate independently, supporting selective deployment and A/B testing without system-wide changes (Newman, 2015); agility allows new machine learning models to be deployed and tested without system downtime; experimentation becomes straightforward when systems are decoupled, enabling efficient A/B testing of different algorithms; and failure containment ensures that if one component malfunctions, others continue operating rather than cascading failures across the system (Pautasso & Zimmermann, 2016; Soldani et al., 2018).

5.5 Multi-Stakeholder Governance and Industry Alignment

Individual platform ethics must be embedded within broader industry governance frameworks supporting coordination across organizations.

Institutional Frameworks

- *IEEE Ethically Aligned Design:* Establishes principles for autonomous systems including transparency, accountability, and human oversight (IEEE Global Initiative on Ethics of Autonomous and Intelligent Systems, 2019)
- *OECD AI Principles:* Call for fairness, accountability, transparency, and inclusive stakeholder engagement in AI governance (OECD, 2019)

- *UNFCCC Fashion Industry Charter:* Emphasizes transparency in environmental impact reporting and alignment with Paris climate goals (UNFCCC, 2021)

These frameworks provide foundational principles that individual organizations should operationalize into internal governance structures.

Industry Standards Development

Rather than each company independently implementing ethics, industry-wide standards create a level playing field and prevent race-to-the-bottom competitive dynamics (Bellamy et al., 2018). Initiatives like the Circular Fashion Task Force develop shared methodologies for impact measurement, establishing common definitions and preventing competitive pressure toward less rigorous standards. Industry consortia coordinating best practices across companies enable collective advancement beyond what individual organizations could achieve alone.

Public-Private Partnerships

Effective governance combines regulatory mandates (what companies must do), industry standards (what companies should do), and market incentives (rewarding leading practices). This three-layer approach proves most effective because government policy alone lacks specificity for rapidly-evolving technologies; industry standards alone lack enforcement mechanisms; and market competition alone creates race-to-the-bottom dynamics where companies cut ethical corners for competitive advantage (OECD, 2019; IEEE Global Initiative on Ethics of Autonomous and Intelligent Systems, 2019). Integration of these three layers, with clear communication between government regulators, industry consortia, and market actors, creates accountability structures stronger than any single mechanism alone.

5.6 Implementation Roadmap and Maturity Progression

Organizations at different capability levels require differentiated guidance for advancing ethical AI practices. A phased maturity model, informed by frameworks like the Capability Maturity Model Integration (CMMI) applied to responsible AI (Himmelreich & Köhler, 2022), structures progression toward comprehensive ethical governance.

Level 1 (Foundational): Establish basic accountability structures and initial ethical implementation

- Designate ethics responsibility with clear reporting lines
- Conduct initial algorithmic audits identifying obvious biases using existing tools (e.g., Fairness 360)
- Develop transparency documentation for key systems
- Implement basic privacy-by-design (data minimization, retention policies)

Level 2 (Systematic): Embed ethics throughout operations and governance structures

- Formalize ethics review board with external members representing diverse stakeholder perspectives
- Deploy bias detection tools (Fairness 360, SHAP) into development workflow (Bellamy et al., 2018; Doshi-Velez & Kim, 2017)
- Implement comprehensive third-party audits using established ethical AI audit frameworks
- Transition architecture to support modularity and experimentation (Newman, 2015)

Level 3 (Leading): Innovate ethical practice beyond compliance and create industry leadership

- Achieve carbon-neutral AI infrastructure through renewable energy and efficient architectures (Shi et al., 2020)
- Implement federated learning or on-device models enabling privacy-preserving personalization (Kairouz et al., 2021)
- Develop new ethical frameworks addressing emerging technologies (blockchain, AR/VR)
- Pioneer industry standards and publish ethical practices enabling competitive learning across sector

5.7 Addressing the Inclusion Gap Through Ethical Practice

The Inclusion Gap represents a fundamental ethical challenge that responsible practice must actively prevent. Research on technology equity and digital divide shows that technological solutions without explicit equity-focused design deepen existing social inequalities (Busalim et al., 2022; Das & Paul, 2024).

Specific mechanisms for inclusion

- *Accessibility Priority:* Design for accessibility first, then enhance for power users, not vice versa. If platforms require JavaScript, fast internet, or complex interactions, they exclude billions of potential users. Accessibility-first design ensures broad reach before optimization for sophisticated users (Voigt & von dem Bussche, 2017).
- *Affordability Solutions:* Technology alone doesn't solve affordability. Address price premiums through business model innovation: cost-plus pricing models enabling SMEs to participate, subsidy programs for low-income consumers, or financing mechanisms making sustainable options accessible across income levels (Das & Paul, 2024; Park & Lin, 2020).
- *Representation in Data and Design:* Training data should represent populations globally served; if historical data reflects past inequities, models will amplify those inequities. Design teams should include members from diverse geographic regions, economic backgrounds, and cultural contexts to identify blind spots early (Himmelreich & Köhler, 2022).
- *Community-Based Implementation:* Rather than imposing top-down technology solutions, partner with communities to develop locally-appropriate approaches. This may mean prioritizing offline mechanisms (community swap events, repair workshops) alongside digital platforms, ensuring that communities without reliable digital infrastructure can participate (Das & Paul, 2024; Busalim et al., 2022).

6. CASE STUDIES AND REAL-WORLD IMPLEMENTATIONS

This section demonstrates real-world implementations attempting to address the four gaps identified in the Conceptual Gap Model. Through three consolidated case examples, Section 6 illustrates how organizations are combining behavioural insights, AI technology, gamification, and ethical governance to narrow gaps at scale. Critically, examining these implementations through the gap model lens reveals where current efforts succeed in narrowing specific gaps and where gaps persist, showing both progress and limitations that point toward the research agenda in Section 7.

6.1 Case Study Framework: Analyzing Interventions Across the Four Gaps

To assess real-world implementations systematically, each case study is evaluated across the four gaps:

- Psychological Gap addressed: Does the intervention activate reflective processing and intrinsic motivation?
- Technological Gap addressed: Does effectiveness in field deployment match laboratory promise?
- Ethical Gap addressed: Are fairness, transparency, and accountability operationalized?
- Inclusion Gap addressed: Are benefits distributed equitably across consumer populations?

6.2 Case Cluster 1: Resale Marketplace Integration (ThredUp & Vinted)

Intervention Type: AI-powered demand matching, impact quantification, and peer-to-peer transaction facilitation

Mechanism: Resale platforms use AI recommendation engines to match sellers with buyers efficiently, reducing search friction. Eco-impact calculators quantify carbon and water savings per transaction, making abstract environmental benefits concrete.

Psychological Gap Addressed: ThredUp's Eco-Impact Calculator makes environmental outcomes tangible. A January-February 2025 survey of 3,034 U.S. adults found that 78% reported increased visibility of sustainability metrics in search results after eco-score integration, with resale transactions increasing 22% year-over-year on high-impact items (ThreadUp Inc., 2025). Natural-language search features ("dusty rose linen dress") and image uploads drove 17% higher click-through rates to second-hand listings, reducing decision friction by meeting users where their natural language operates.

Vinted's annual Climate Impact Reports quantify approximately 2 kg CO_2e savings per item. Post-purchase messaging ("Thank you for extending this item's life!") reinforces environmental identity, with surveys indicating environmental motivations rank among top repeat-use drivers (Vinted, 2023). This identity reinforcement activates reflective processing: users see themselves as environmental stewards rather than merely making convenient transactions.

Technological Gap Partially Addressed: Both platforms achieve real-world effectiveness matching laboratory promise: recommendation algorithms reduce search friction, concrete metrics increase engagement. However, the Technological Gap persists: 80% of fast-fashion consumers never access resale platforms (Busalim et al., 2022), suggesting that algorithmic optimization within existing platforms cannot overcome infrastructure access barriers. Rebound effects also emerge; users may increase overall shopping volume while replacing purchases with resale, offsetting environmental gains.

Ethical Gap: Transparency is strong: both platforms publish methodology documentation, enabling independent verification of impact claims. ThredUp and Vinted practice relatively transparent data governance, though greenwashing risks persist if methodological assumptions prove overly generous. Third-party verification enhances credibility.

Inclusion Gap (Major Limitation): Access remains concentrated among affluent, digitally-connected populations. Resale platform usage correlates with income, education, and digital literacy (Laitala & Klepp, 2018). Low-income consumers most vulnerable to fashion system harms, lack internet access or smartphone technology required for participation. Rural populations lack reliable connectivity. This represents a critical Inclusion Gap limitation.

6.3 Case Cluster 2: Ethical Rating Systems (Good On You & Fashion Transparency Index)

Intervention Type: Third-party transparency, supply chain verification, algorithmic rating systems

Mechanism: Comprehensive brand assessment across social, environmental, and animal welfare dimensions, with algorithmic badges appearing on retail platforms and brand pages.

Psychological Gap Addressed: Good On You's five-level rating system ("We Avoid" to "Great") simplifies complex supply-chain data into intuitive signals, reducing decision complexity (cognitive friction). Third-party verification addresses consumer skepticism about greenwashing. User surveys found visible ratings increased click-through rates on highly-rated brands by over one-third, indicating enhanced trust and engagement (Good On You, 2023). This increases psychological motivation to explore sustainable alternatives.

Fashion Transparency Index (published annually by Fashion Revolution) rates major fashion brands based on disclosure of social and environmental policies, practices, and impacts. The Index creates accountability pressure and enables consumers to compare brands systematically across transparency metrics (Fashion Revolution, 2025). By making brand disclosure visible, the Index creates reputational incentives for improvement.

Technological Gap: Field effectiveness aligns reasonably well with laboratory promise: transparency systems increase engagement and conversion. However, the Technological Gap appears in the mismatch between trust signals and conversion to actual purchase. Good On You's ratings increase interest but don't proportionally increase sales, suggesting that trust alone cannot overcome price premiums and availability barriers. The Fashion Transparency Index shows measurable improvement in brand disclosure over time (average transparency scores increased from 21% in

2017 to 25% in 2023), demonstrating that public accountability mechanisms can drive gradual behavior change at organizational level (Fashion Revolution, 2025). However, disclosure does not automatically equal substantive operational change.

Ethical Gap (Strongest): These platforms prioritize transparency and third-party verification. Independent audits, methodology publication, and iterative improvement processes embed accountability. Good On You employs researchers who assess brands against evidence-based criteria; Fashion Revolution publishes detailed methodology enabling external scrutiny. This represents exemplary ethical practice within existing systems, though risks of greenwashing remain if underlying supply chains don't substantively change.

Inclusion Gap (Moderate Limitation): Both systems primarily reach digitally-connected, educated consumers in developed markets. While theoretically accessible to anyone with internet access, the platforms require English fluency and digital literacy that exclude significant global populations. Fashion Transparency Index focuses on large brands (covering 250 major brands globally), inherently excluding the vast majority of small enterprises. This concentration on major brands creates blind spots around SMEs and informal enterprises that employ millions of workers globally (Fashion Revolution, 2025).

6.4 Case Cluster 3: Blockchain-Enabled Transparency (Aura Consortium & Digital Passports)

Intervention Type: Immutable supply chain tracking, digital product identity, smart contracts for reward distribution

Mechanism: Blockchain ledgers create permanent records of the product journey from production through ownership cycles to end-of-life processing. Smart contracts automate reward distribution for circular behaviours.

Psychological Gap Addressed: Transparency verification creates cognitive confidence that sustainability claims are genuine. Users feel empowered knowing they can independently verify supply chain claims. Blockchain's immutability, i.e., records cannot be retroactively modified, provides psychological assurance. The Aura Blockchain Consortium's implementation demonstrates luxury-sector success: 87% of surveyed users report increased trust in traceability compared to traditional documentation (Aura Blockchain Consortium, 2025).

Tokenized incentives create gamified engagement: users accumulate blockchain-based rewards for circular actions, providing immediate feedback and a feeling of accomplishment.

Technological Gap: Field effectiveness aligns with the promise for luxury brands with resources for blockchain implementation. However, the Technological Gap widens significantly for mass-market adoption: blockchain infrastructure costs

(USD 10,000-50,000 annually) remain prohibitive for SMEs. Energy consumption of proof-of-work blockchains creates computational sustainability concerns. Implementation complexity and limited interoperability between blockchain networks reduce real-world deployment (Bag et al., 2024).

Ethical Gap: Blockchain provides immutability, supporting transparency and accountability. However, ethical risks persist: greenwashing can embed false claims into immutable records that cannot be corrected. Governance structures must accompany technology; blockchain alone does not ensure ethical data entry. Data privacy concerns emerge if personal transaction histories are recorded on transparent ledgers.

Inclusion Gap (Critical Limitation): This intervention most sharply illustrates the Inclusion Gap. Blockchain solutions concentrate among large corporations and luxury brands. SMEs, informal enterprises, and low-income consumers lack access to implementation and participation. The technology gap becomes an inclusion gap: what benefits affluent enterprises leaves others behind, deepening inequality.

6.5 Comparative Analysis: What Works Across Cases

Convergent Success Factors

1. *Transparency and Third-Party Verification:* All three case clusters succeed most when independent verification accompanies claims. Platforms with auditable methodologies and published documentation build consumer trust.
2. *Concrete Metrics:* Making abstract environmental concepts tangible (showing "2 kg CO_2 per item" rather than "environmental benefit") increases psychological engagement across cases.
3. *Integration with Existing Infrastructure:* Resale platforms, rating systems, and QR-enabled labels succeed because they integrate into existing shopping behaviours rather than requiring behavioural transformation.
4. *Emotional Engagement:* Cases connecting consumer actions to identity (stewardship, innovation, community membership) show higher sustained engagement than cases emphasizing information alone.

Persistent Limitations Across Cases

1. *Technology Gap:* Laboratory-validated interventions show reduced real-world effectiveness. Habituation, rebound effects, and context dependencies limit impact.
2. *Inclusion Gap:* All interventions concentrate benefits among affluent, digitally-connected populations. Low-income consumers, rural populations, and informal enterprises remain excluded or disadvantaged.

3. *Price Barriers Unaddressed:* None of the cases has overcome the fundamental 20-50% price premium on sustainable fashion. Technology optimizes within existing pricing structures without transforming affordability.
4. *Scale Limitations:* Successful pilots rarely scale cost-effectively to serve mass populations. Infrastructure costs, technical complexity, and adoption barriers limit geographic and demographic reach.
5. *Greenwashing Risks:* Despite transparency efforts, greenwashing concerns persist. When companies embed misleading claims, consumers lose trust across all platforms.

6.6 Critical Gaps Remaining: Where Interventions Fall Short

Examining these cases through the Conceptual Gap Model reveals where gaps persist despite implementation efforts:

i. ***Psychological Gap:*** Partially narrowed through gamification and identity reinforcement, but underlying dual-process decision-making, where visceral and habitual processing override reflective environmental values at the point of purchase, remains largely unaddressed. Nudges and transparency address the reflective level but cannot fundamentally change the immediate emotional and functional barriers that fast fashion overcomes.
ii. ***Technological Gap:*** Field effectiveness consistently lags laboratory promise. Habituation emerges within weeks, rebound effects offset efficiency gains, and consumer heterogeneity means single interventions reach only motivated segments. This gap widens as interventions scale.
iii. ***Ethical Gap:*** Cases implementing governance structures and third-party verification address this gap well. However, greenwashing risks remain: companies can manipulate methodologies while maintaining superficial transparency. Accountability structures must be embedded in organizational incentives, not merely compliance requirements.
iv. ***Inclusion Gap:*** All three case clusters illustrate this gap sharply. Interventions designed in developed-world, affluent contexts create infrastructure that replicates existing inequalities. Low-income consumers, rural populations, informal enterprises, and non-digitally-native populations are systematically disadvantaged or excluded.

6.7 Synthesis: Implications for Integrated Implementation

These case studies collectively demonstrate that isolated interventions, even well-designed ones addressing specific gaps, fail to deliver system-wide transformation.

Resale platforms address technology and psychology, but cannot overcome price barriers. Rating systems increase transparency, but don't close the ethical gap created when greenwashing persists. Blockchain provides immutability but concentrates benefits among wealthy enterprises.

Genuine progress requires orchestrated, multi-level interventions:

- *Psychological + Technological:* AI personalization paired with behavioural nudging shows promise but requires accompanying price/availability restructuring
- *Psychological + Ethical:* Transparent impact metrics paired with governance structures build trust, enabling sustained engagement
- *Technological + Inclusion:* Infrastructure investment in affordable technology and offline mechanisms enables broad participation
- *Systemic Transformation:* Business model innovation, realigning incentives from consumption growth to durability and repair

The research agenda in Section 7 proposes how to advance beyond current limitations by addressing gaps simultaneously.

7. CONCLUSIONS AND RESEARCH AGENDA

This concluding section synthesizes the integrated framework developed across Sections 2-6 through the lens of the Conceptual Gap Model. By examining what current interventions accomplish, where gaps persist despite best efforts, and what remains unknown about achieving system-wide sustainable fashion adoption, this section proposes a targeted research agenda that acknowledges both progress and limitations. The central insight is clear: no single intervention suffices; genuine progress requires orchestrated, simultaneous action across all four gaps while acknowledging that some gaps require structural transformation extending beyond technological and behavioural solutions.

7.1 What We've Learned: Evidence-Based Progress Across the Four Gaps

The table below delineates the insights acquired regarding the four gaps based on the comprehensive evidence from the literature and other sources:

Table 4. Evidence-based Progress across the Four Gaps

Gap Name	Evidence of Progress	Persistent Challenges	Key Implication
Psychological Gap	Behavioural interventions show 25-45% sustainable selection increases when combining psychological insights, AI nudging, gamification, emotional framing that balances pride/guilt/future-orientation, and community recognition that reinforces social identity	Habituation within weeks; initial shifts erode; visceral/habitual processing overrides reflective values at point-of-purchase; interventions cannot reach consumers lacking environmental self-identity; structural barriers prevent behaviour translation	Psychological gap cannot be closed through behavioural interventions alone; it requires simultaneous technological accessibility, affordability, and addressing systemic barriers.
Technological Gap	AI demand forecasting achieves 30% waste reduction; eco-scoring increases purchases by 28%; blockchain enables accountability; real-world systems demonstrate measurable environmental benefits	Rebound effects offset gains; context dependency across retail environments; computational costs substantial (626,000 lbs CO2 per model); technology costs concentrate benefits among large corporations only	Technology enables but does not determine outcomes; without simultaneous psychological motivation, equitable access, and ethical governance, technology remains insufficient and may deepen inequality
Ethical Gap	Platforms implementing bias detection and audit trails; ethics review boards with external members; independent verification validates claims; privacy-by-design protects user rights	Greenwashing risks persist (transparent methodology can be gamed); incentive misalignment (profit motives prioritize engagement over genuine outcomes); implementation gaps (most companies lack mature ethical AI); autonomy-effectiveness tension	Ethical governance is necessary but insufficient; it requires embedding in organizational incentives and industry-wide standards, not merely compliance procedures
Inclusion Gap	Some interventions show awareness of equity; SME pilots demonstrate accessibility potential; community-based implementations are emerging	80% of consumers are excluded from platforms; benefits concentrate among affluent/digitally-connected; technology costs exclude SMEs/informal enterprises; infrastructure barriers exclude rural/low-income; algorithms discriminate against marginalized groups	Technology-driven solutions risk DEEPENING inequality; inclusion must be designed-in from the outset, not retrofitted

7.2 Acknowledging What Remains Unknown

The following table illustrates how despite substantial research, some critical questions persist:

Table 5. Critical Questions Across Various Research Areas

Research Area	Key Unanswered Questions	Why This Matters
Psychological Persistence and Behaviour Change Sustainability	How long do behaviour changes persist after interventions cease? Do annual rebound effects overcome initial gains? What consumer characteristics predict sustained vs. temporary response?	If changes last <6 months, interventions provide temporary shifts without lasting impact; if rebound effects substantial, net environmental benefit may be minimal or negative
Technological Effectiveness and Environmental Impact	Do efficiency gains exceed computational carbon cost of AI model training? What's the break-even point for net environmental benefit? How much do consumption increases offset per-unit efficiency gains?	If computational costs exceed environmental savings, sustainability tech creates new environmental burdens; break-even analysis guides technology selection
Ethical Implementation in Practice	What governance structures prevent misleading claims vs. creating appearance of transparency? How do systems discriminate across demographic groups? Can platforms maintain autonomy while achieving meaningful behaviour change?	Determines whether ethical frameworks work in practice or merely create compliance theatre; reveals autonomy-effectiveness trade-offs constraining design
Equity and Access	What cost-effective technology models enable small enterprises to participate? Can offline alternatives achieve comparable impact to digital platforms? How must interventions adapt for emerging markets and low-access populations?	Without equitable participation solutions, technology deepens inequality; offline and low-cost alternatives necessary for genuine inclusion
Cross-Cultural Technology Transfer	Do Western-developed nudges work equally in emerging markets? How do effectiveness and cultural acceptability vary across regions? What design adaptations enable global applicability?	If Western technologies fail in non-Western contexts, solutions remain geographically limited; forced deployment creates new equity problems
Algorithmic Bias and Discrimination	How do recommendation systems discriminate across demographic groups? What disparate impacts persist despite bias detection efforts? Can fairness tools prevent or merely measure discrimination?	If algorithms systematically disadvantage marginalized populations, platforms deepen social inequalities; auditing must prevent, not merely document, harms

7.3 Research Agenda

Building on identified gaps, we propose six interconnected research priorities. The following table illustrates the same:

Table 6. Research Agenda Priorities

Name	Research Objective	Key Questions (main 1-2)	Recommended Methodology	Timeline	Expected Outcomes
Longitudinal Field Trials	Move beyond short-term labs to assess intervention durability and net environmental impact	Do behaviour changes persist beyond 3-6 months? What is true net environmental impact?	12-18 month RCTs with treatment/control/cessation arms; environmental accounting; heterogeneous effects	18-24 months	Evidence on durability, true impact, rebound effects, segment-specific persistence
Cross-Cultural and Equity Research	Expand beyond Western samples; ensure generalizability; prevent inequality deepening	Do Western nudges work in emerging markets? What designs increase low-income/rural access?	Multi-country RCTs (6+ regions); qualitative research with marginalized populations; participatory design	24+ months	Culturally-grounded understanding, equity-centered designs, cross-cultural generalizability evidence
Technology Integration	Explore emerging technologies (blockchain, AR/VR, IoT) for addressing gaps sustainably	Can blockchain verify without excessive computational costs? Do immersive experiences drive deeper engagement?	Pilot deployments with A/B testing; environmental impact assessments; scalability analysis	18-24 months	Technology selection guidance, environmental cost-benefit analysis, and hybrid model effectiveness
Responsible AI Development	Operationalize ethical principles into practice through responsible MLOps	What practices prevent algorithmic discrimination? What organizational structures embed ethics?	Systematic MLOps documentation; algorithmic audits; organizational studies; governance experiments	Ongoing	Practical MLOps guidelines, fairness measurement approaches, governance model comparison
Consumer-Centric Design	Shift to participatory approaches ensuring alignment with consumer values	What designs feel supportive vs. manipulative? How can marginalized populations shape design?	Participatory workshops; ethnographic research; user-centered evaluation; co-design processes	12-18 months	Autonomy perception framework, marginalized population preferences, design principles
Policy and Systems-Level	Examine systemic barriers and policy solutions for sustainable fashion competitiveness	What policy frameworks make sustainable economically competitive? What prevents greenwashing?	Policy analysis; stakeholder engagement; economic modelling; international comparative analysis	24+ months	Evidence-based policy recommendations, regulatory frameworks, systems-level intervention models

7.4 Why Orchestrated Approaches Succeed Where Isolated Interventions Fail

Throughout this chapter, we've documented that isolated interventions, however well-designed, address only one of the four gaps while leaving others unattended or inadvertently widening them. Psychological interventions alone cannot overcome affordability barriers or infrastructure constraints. Technological solutions alone concentrate benefits among affluent corporations while excluding vulnerable populations. Ethical governance alone cannot generate initial motivation or overcome structural barriers. Inclusion-focused policies alone cannot address the psychological and technological barriers preventing adoption. The following figure shows a transformation to our originally proposed gap model and highlights an integrative framework rather than isolated dimensions.

Integration works because:

- Behavioural nudging activates reflective processing where environmental values reside → BUT must pair with affordability and infrastructure to make reflection actionable
- AI personalization delivers relevant information → BUT must protect autonomy through transparency and fairness oversight to prevent perceived manipulation
- Gamification sustains emotional engagement → BUT must embed in ethical governance structures to prevent greenwashing that undermines trust
- Blockchain enables accountability → BUT must include affordable, accessible implementation pathways to reach beyond affluent markets

Figure 2. Conceptual Intervention Framework - How Psychological, Technological, Ethical, and Inclusion Dimensions Work Together (Authors' own work, 2025)

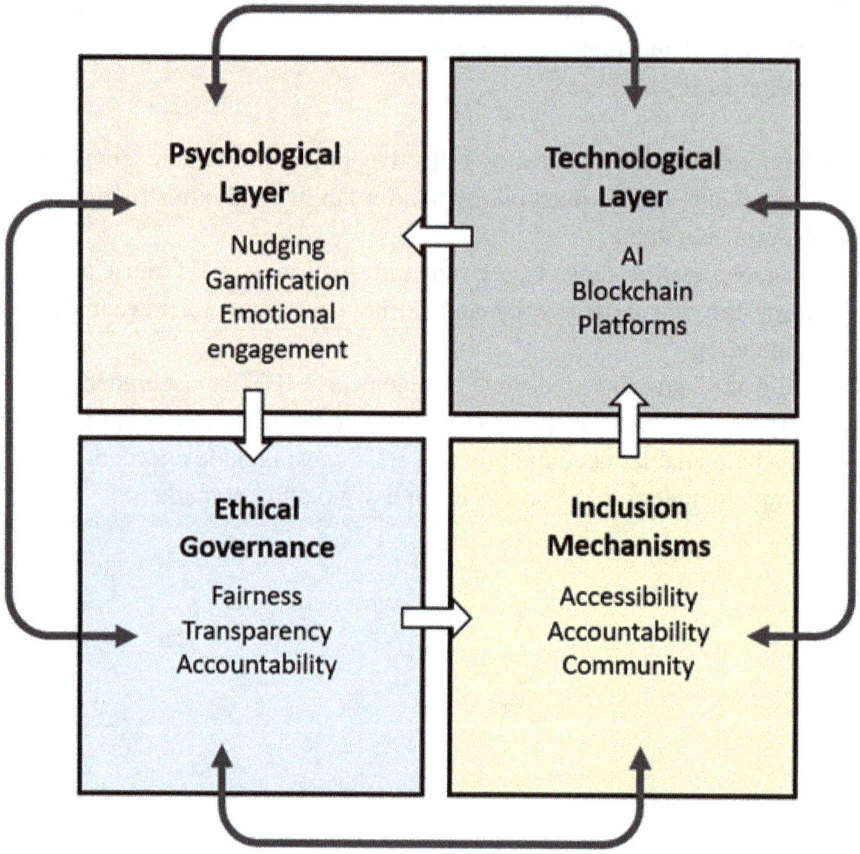

The missing piece in current approaches: Systemic business model transformation. Technology, behaviour change, and ethics can optimize within existing systems; genuine fashion sustainability requires reimagining business models aligned with circular economy principles rather than consumption growth incentives.

7.5 Directions for Industry and Policy

As we approach the final section, following directions and policy reforms are proposed for various stakeholders:

For Fashion Companies and Technology Platforms

- Invest in longitudinal research measuring real environmental impact beyond narrow engagement metrics
- Embed responsible MLOps practices and ethics governance into organizational structure and incentives
- Prioritize equity and accessibility in technology development; design for inclusion first
- Explore cooperative and stakeholder governance models balancing sustainability with business sustainability
- Collaborate with policymakers on industry-wide standards preventing race-to-the-bottom greenwashing

For Researchers and Academics

- Pursue multi-disciplinary research bridging behavioural science, computer science, environmental science, and policy analysis
- Invest in longitudinal, cross-cultural, and equity-focused field research
- Examine systemic and structural barriers alongside individual behaviour changc
- Critically assess technology's environmental costs, not merely its potential
- Engage in participatory research with marginalized communities ensuring solutions serve their needs

For Policymakers and Civil Society

- Establish regulatory frameworks requiring transparent cnvironmental impact reporting using standardized methodologies
- Implement producer responsibility and circular economy incentives making sustainable choices economically viable
- Invest in digital infrastructure and digital literacy enabling equitable access to sustainable fashion platforms
- Support SME and informal enterprise pathways to sustainability technology adoption
- Oversee and audit claims of environmental impact preventing greenwashing

7.6 Final Reflection

Throughout this chapter, we've explored how behavioural insights, artificial intelligence, gamification, and blockchain can help millions of consumers align choices with environmental values. The evidence demonstrates genuine, measurable promise: digital nudges increase sustainable selection, AI forecasting reduces waste, gamification sustains engagement, blockchain enables accountability.

Yet this chapter's most important contribution may be documenting what technology alone cannot accomplish:

- Technology cannot create affordability where supply chain costs mandate price premiums.
- Technology cannot overcome habit and visceral emotional response through reflective nudges alone.
- Technology cannot ensure equity when infrastructure and expertise concentrate among privileged populations.
- Technology cannot guarantee genuine environmental impact when incentives reward appearance over substance.

The path forward requires simultaneously advancing:

1. ***Behavioural science:*** Deeper understanding of how to sustain motivation, preserve autonomy, and activate intrinsic values
2. ***Technological innovation:*** More efficient, equitable, and ethically-sound technology that genuinely reduces environmental burden rather than shifting it
3. ***Ethical governance:*** Robust structures embedding fairness, transparency, and accountability into organizational decision-making and incentives
4. ***Systemic transformation:*** Business model innovation, policy frameworks, and investment in global equity that make sustainable choices economically feasible for all populations
5. ***Research commitment:*** Long-term funding for longitudinal, cross-cultural, participatory research measuring genuine impact rather than marketing metrics

The sustainable fashion economy we need exists at the intersection of psychology and infrastructure, technology and equity, innovation and governance. This chapter offers a roadmap for moving from isolated interventions toward that integrated vision, while acknowledging that the journey from research to real-world impact at scale remains incomplete, requiring sustained commitment from researchers, practitioners, policymakers, and consumers united around the possibility of fashion that serves both people and planet.

REFERENCES

Allais, F. B., Cappa, C., De Cock, M., Guarcello, L., & Lyon, S. (2021). *Child labour: Global estimates 2020, trends and the road forward*. ILO; UNICEF. Retrieved from https://www.ilo.org/wcmsp5/groups/public/---ed_norm/---ipec/documents/publication/wcms_797515.pdf

Aura Blockchain Consortium. (2025). *Leveraging Blockchain for Supply Chain Transparency in the Luxury Sector*. Retrieved from https://auraconsortium.com/insight/blockchain-for-supply-chain-transparency-luxury-sector

Bag, S., Rahman, M. S., Routray, S., Shrivastav, S. K., & Agrawal, S. (2024). Exploring the potential of blockchain-enabled smart contracts for achieving net-zero emissions: An empirical study. *Business Strategy and the Environment, 33*(5), 3965–3985. DOI: 10.1002/bse.3691

Bellamy, R. K. E., Dey, K., Hind, M., Hoffman, S. C., Hoey, J., Kanan, C., & Raji, I. D. (2018). AI fairness 360: An extensible toolkit for detecting, understanding, and mitigating unwanted algorithmic bias. *IBM Journal of Research and Development, 63*(4/5), 4–1. DOI: 10.1147/JRD.2019.2942287

Busalim, A. H., Fox, G., & Lynn, T. (2022). Consumer behavior in sustainable fashion: A systematic literature review and future research agenda. *International Journal of Consumer Studies, 46*(5), 1790–1815. DOI: 10.1111/ijcs.12794

Candeloro, D. (2020). Towards sustainable fashion: The role of artificial intelligence—H&M, Stella McCartney, Farfetch, Moosejaw: A multiple case study. *ZoneModa Journal, 10*(2), 91–105. DOI: 10.6092/issn.2611-0563/11837

Casino, F., Dasaklis, T. K., & Patsakis, C. (2019). A systematic literature review of blockchain-based applications: Current status, classification and open issues. *Telematics and Informatics, 36*, 55–81. DOI: 10.1016/j.tele.2018.11.006

Coleman, N. M. V., & Williams, P. (2015). Looking for My Self: Identity-Driven Attention Allocation. *Journal of Consumer Psychology, 25*(3), 504–511. DOI: 10.1016/j.jcps.2015.01.001

Das, D., & Paul, S. (2024). Promoting consumer engagement in sustainable fashion and circular textile through eco-gamification in Bangladesh. *Proceedings of the International Conference on Industrial Engineering and Operations Management, 37*, 241–252. DOI: 10.46254/BA07.20240037

Dasandi, N., Graham, H., Hudson, D., Jankin, S., vanHeerde-Hudson, J., & Watts, N. (2022). Positive, global, and health or environment framing bolsters public support for climate policies. *Communications Earth & Environment, 3*(1), 239. DOI: 10.1038/s43247-022-00571-x

Doshi-Velez, F., & Kim, B. (2017). Towards a rigorous science of interpretable machine learning. *arXiv preprint arXiv:1702.08608.* /arXiv.1702.08608DOI: 10.48550

Ellen MacArthur Foundation. (2017). *A new textiles economy: Redesigning fashion's future*. Retrieved from https://www.ellenmacarthurfoundation.org/publications/a-new-textiles-economy-redesigning-fashions-future

Fashion Revolution. (2025). *What fuels fashion?* Retrieved from https://www.fashionrevolution.org/about/transparency/

Gilpin, L. H., Bau, D., Yuan, B. Z., Bajwa, A., Specter, M., & Kagal, L. (2018, October). Explaining explanations: An overview of interpretability of machine learning. In *2018 IEEE 5th International Conference on data science and advanced analytics (DSAA)* (pp. 80–89). IEEE. DOI: 10.48550/arXiv.1806.00069

Goldstein, N. J., Cialdini, R. B., & Griskevicius, V. (2008). A room with a viewpoint: Using social norms to motivate environmental conservation in hotels. *The Journal of Consumer Research, 35*(3), 472–482. DOI: 10.1086/586910

Good On You. (2023). *How We Rate Fashion and Beauty Brands*. Retrieved from https://goodonyou.eco/how-we-rate

Gyulai, Z., & Revesz, B. (2023). Nudging in the digital world: An up-to-date systematic literature review. *Proceedings of the European Marketing Academy Conference*, Paper 117268. https://proceedings.emac-online.org/pdfs/R2023-117268.pdf

Hamari, J., Koivisto, J., & Sarsa, H. (2014). Does gamification work?—A literature review of empirical studies on gamification. *2014 47th Hawaii International Conference on System Sciences* (pp. 3025–3034). IEEE. DOI: 10.1109/HICSS.2014.377

Himmelreich, J., & Köhler, S. (2022). Responsible AI through conceptual engineering. *Philosophy & Technology, 35*(3), 60. DOI: 10.1007/s13347-022-00542-2

IEEE Global Initiative on Ethics of Autonomous and Intelligent Systems. (2019). *Ethically Aligned Design: A Vision for Prioritizing Human Well-being with Autonomous and Intelligent Systems (2nd ed.)*. IEEE. Retrieved from https://globalpolicy.ieee.org/wp-content/uploads/2019/06/IEEE19002.pdf

Kairouz, P., McMahan, H. B., Avent, B., Bellet, A., Bennis, M., Bhagoji, A. N., . . . Zhao, S. (2021). Advances and open problems in federated learning. *Foundations and Trends® in Machine Learning, 14*(1–2), 1–210. /arXiv.1912.04977DOI: 10.48550

Laitala, K., & Klepp, I. G. (2018). Motivations for and against second-hand clothing acquisition. *Clothing Cultures, 5*(2), 247–262. DOI: 10.1386/cc.5.2.247_1

Mirbabaie, M., Marx, J., & Germies, J. (2022). Digital nudge stacking and backfiring: Understanding sustainable e-commerce purchase decisions. *Pacific Asia Journal of the Association for Information Systems, 14*(12), 65–87. DOI: 10.17705/1pais.15303

Munten, P., Swaen, V., & Vanhamme, J. (2024). Exploring rebound effects in Access-Based services (ABS). *Journal of Business Research, 182*, 114758. DOI: 10.1016/j.jbusres.2024.114758

Newman, S. (2015). *Building microservices: Designing fine-grained systems.* O'Reilly Media, Inc.

Norman, D. A. (2004). *Emotional design: Why we love (or hate) everyday things.* Basic Books. DOI: 10.1145/985600.966013

OECD. (2019). *Artificial intelligence in society.* OECD Publishing., DOI: 10.1787/eedfee77-

Onwezen, M. C., Bartels, J., & Antonides, G. (2013). The self-regulatory function of anticipated pride and guilt in a sustainable and healthy consumption context. *European Journal of Social Psychology, 43*(7), 671–684. DOI: 10.1002/ejsp.1991

Park, H. J., & Lin, L. M. (2020). Exploring attitude–behavior gap in sustainable consumption: Comparison of recycled and upcycled fashion products. *Journal of Business Research, 117*, 623–628. DOI: 10.1016/j.jbusres.2018.08.025

Ryan, R. M., & Deci, E. L. (2000). Self-determination theory and the facilitation of intrinsic motivation, social development, and well-being. *The American Psychologist, 55*(1), 68–78. DOI: 10.1037/0003-066X.55.1.68 PMID: 11392867

Schürmann, C. L., Helinski, C., Koch, J., Westmattelmann, D., & Schewe, G. (2023). Digital Nudging to Promote Sustainable Consumer Behavior? An Experimental Analysis in Online Fashion Retail. https://aisel.aisnet.org/ecis2023_rp/335

Shahzad, M. F., Xu, S., Rehman, O. U., & Javed, I. (2023). Impact of gamification on green consumption behavior integrating technological awareness, motivation, enjoyment and virtual CSR. *Scientific Reports, 13*(1), 21751. DOI: 10.1038/s41598-023-48835-6 PMID: 38066018

Shi, W., Cao, J., Zhang, Q., Li, Y., & Xu, L. (2020). Edge computing: Vision and challenges. *IEEE Internet of Things Journal*, *3*(5), 637–646. DOI: 10.1109/JIOT.2016.2579198

Stern, P. C. (2000). New environmental theories: Toward a coherent theory of environmentally significant behavior. *The Journal of Social Issues*, *56*(3), 407–424. DOI: 10.1111/0022-4537.00175

Strubell, E., Ganesh, A., & McCallum, A. (2019). Energy and policy considerations for deep learning in NLP. *Proceedings of the 57th Annual Meeting of the Association for Computational Linguistics*, 3645–3650. DOI: 10.18653/v1/P19-1355

Tangney, J. P., Stuewig, J., & Mashek, D. J. (2007). Moral emotions and moral behavior. *Annual Review of Psychology*, *58*(1), 345–372. DOI: 10.1146/annurev.psych.56.091103.070145 PMID: 16953797

Thaler, R. H., & Sunstein, C. R. (2009). *Nudge: Improving decisions about health, wealth, and happiness*. Penguin.

The Business of Fashion and McKinsey & Company. (2021). *The state of fashion 2021*. McKinsey & Company. Retrieved from https://www.mckinsey.com/~/media/mckinsey/industries/retail/our%20insights/state%20of%20fashion/2021/the-state-of-fashion-2021-vf.pdf

ThreadUp Inc. (2025). *Resale Report 2024*. Retrieved from https://cf-assets-tup.thredup.com/resale_report/2024/ThredUp_2024_Resale%20Report.pdf

Udall, A. M., De Groot, J. I., De Jong, S. B., & Shankar, A. (2021). How I see me—A meta-analysis investigating the association between identities and pro-environmental behaviour. *Frontiers in Psychology*, *12*, 582421. DOI: 10.3389/fpsyg.2021.582421 PMID: 33796041

UNFCCC. (2021). *Fashion Industry Charter for Climate Action*. United Nations Framework Convention on Climate Change. Retrieved from https://unfccc.int/climate-action/sectoral-engagement-for-climate-action/fashion-charter

United Nations Environment Programme. (2025). *Fashion and textiles: Environmental impact and solutions*. UNEP Reports. Retrieved from https://www.unep.org/resources/report/fashion-and-textiles-environmental-impact-and-solutions

Vinted. (2023). *Climate Impact Report 2023*. Retrieved from https://www.vinted.com/climate-impact-report

Voigt, P., & von dem Bussche, A. (2017). *The EU general data protection regulation (GDPR): A practical guide*. Springer International Publishing., DOI: 10.1007/978-3-319-57959-7

Weinmann, M., Schneider, C., & vom Brocke, J. (2016). Digital nudging. *Business & Information Systems Engineering*, *58*(6), 433–436. DOI: 10.1007/s12599-016-0453-1

World Bank. (2019). *How Much Do Our Wardrobes Cost to the Environment*. World Bank Report. Retrieved from https://www.worldbank.org/en/news/feature/2019/09/23/costo-moda-medio-ambiente

Wüst, K., & Gervais, A. (2018). Do you need a blockchain? In *Proceedings of the Crypto Valley Conference on Blockchain Technology (CVCBT '18)* (pp. 45–54). IEEE. DOI: 10.1109/CVCBT.2018.00011

Chapter 2
Sustainability of Circular Fashion in India

N. Ramakrishnan
http://orcid.org/0000-0002-2306-2218
Christ University, India

E. V. Sreedevi Nambiar
http://orcid.org/0009-0001-4986-1456
Christ University, India

Saibal Kumar Saha
http://orcid.org/0000-0002-7842-698X
St. Xavier's University, Kolkata, India

ABSTRACT

The Indian fashion industry, valued at USD 100 billion, faces pressing sustainability challenges, including resource depletion, labor issues, and excessive textile waste. This study explores the potential of circular fashion in advancing Sustainable Development Goal 12 (SDG 12) by promoting responsible consumption and production. Through consumer surveys, business insights, and interviews with eco-entrepreneurs, the research examines awareness, adoption barriers, and opportunities in circular fashion. Findings reveal growing consumer interest in sustainable apparel, yet concerns about product quality, hygiene, and brand credibility persist. Businesses acknowledge the potential of circular models but struggle with skill shortages, inventory management, and sanitation costs. The study highlights the need for policy interventions, investment in recycling technologies, and consumer education to accelerate circular fashion adoption. By embracing reduce, reuse, and recycle principles, India's fashion sector can transition towards a more sustainable and resilient future.

DOI: 10.4018/979-8-2600-0303-9.ch002

INTRODUCTION

The Sustainable Development Goal 12 (SDG 12) proposed by the United Nations pertains to sustainable consumption and production. It has a focus on ensuring sustainable patterns with reference to consumption and production. This is vital for the sustenance of the present and future generations. If the patterns of production and consumption are not sustainable, it could lead to climate change issues, pollution, and loss of biodiversity, thus posing a threat to the well-being of humans (Hales and Birdthistle, 2023). The majority of SDG 12 research conducted in India to date has been on topics like waste management, energy efficiency, and sustainable tourism. While these are crucial areas for reaching SDG 12, further research is needed to determine how circular fashion might help India's consumption and production habits become more sustainable. With a market size of USD 100 billion and an annual growth rate of 10-12%, the Indian fashion business is one that is expanding. The sector does, however, also confront a number of sustainability issues, including the usage of resource-intensive materials, low worker wages and working conditions, and significant amounts of textile waste.

By encouraging the use of sustainable materials, minimising waste output through recycling and upcycling, and encouraging sustainable consumption practices among customers, circular fashion concepts can address these concerns (Dissanayake & Weerasinghe, 2022). Several Indian fashion companies have already begun to follow the concepts of circular fashion, which include employing sustainable materials in their goods and recovering textile waste to make new ones.

However, further research needs to be done on how widely these initiatives have been adopted and how they have affected India's fashion industry in terms of fulfilling SDG 12. Some critical factors that act as barriers for sustainable fashion include disposal of clothing, insufficiency in adapting to modern technology, issues pertaining to fashion design, and challenges affecting efficiency of the apparel and textile sector (Vishwakarma et al. 2024).

RESEARCH PROBLEM

Since India is one of the biggest consumers of resources owing to its large population the attainment of SDG 12 is critical for the sustainable development of the country. There is only limited research available on circular fashion concepts and the implementation of SDG 12 in the fashion industry in India.

RESEARCH QUESTIONS

The following are the key research questions:

1. How do customers, employees, and entrepreneurs perceive circular fashion in India?
2. What approaches could facilitate the adoption of circular fashion in India with alignment to sustainability goals?

RESEARCH OBJECTIVES

This study seeks to fill the research vacuum related to the potential for circular fashion to achieve SDG 12 in the country's fashion industry by examining the development of SDG 12 in India. The objectives of this study are outlined below:

1. To understand the preferences of customers about circular fashion.
2. To assess the perspective of circular fashion by employees and entrepreneurs with reference to related opportunities and challenges.
3. To provide insights on the approaches for adoption of circular fashion in India with alignment to the SDG 12.
4. To provide an adoption framework for sustainability in the circular fashion industry.

LITERATURE REVIEW

All participants in the supply chain, from production to distribution, must be engaged in the bioeconomy and circular economy (CE). It takes the active involvement of corporations, consumers, governments, academics, scientists, and retailers to achieve responsible consumption. In order to promote recycling, waste reduction, and changes in consumption patterns at the national level, the use of tools to quantify the environmental, economic, and social implications of the supply chain can be helpful (Iacovidou et al. 2021). New models that are in line with these results can be developed with the help of the circular economy. The goal of the CE is to use resources efficiently so that the industrial sector can profit from a variety of factors (Dwivedi et al. 2022), and approaches based on multicriteria analysis are helpful for measuring these factors (Zorpas and Saranti 2016).

Circular Economy

"Circular economy" is an economic system that has a focus on reducing consumption and waste of resources. A circular system facilitates the creation of a closed-loop system that reduces resource-related inputs, pollution, waste, and carbon emissions (Ali et al., 2024). These circular systems involve reusability, repair, recycling, resources sharing, refurbishment, and re-manufacturing (Rashid et al., 2020). The deployment of goods, machinery, and infrastructure for an extended timeframe enhances the value of critical resources, which in turn, facilitates economic growth. It is based on the concept of waste elimination through design, restoration of natural systems and utilization of existing resources. A circular economy has a focus on keeping resources in use to the best extent possible and extract maximum value before regeneration or recovery. While transitioning to a circular economy, businesses and communities may reduce their impact on environment, enhance security and resilience of resources, and enable new economic opportunities by means of innovation and efficient usage of resources (Kandpal et al., 2024). This, however, would require adjustment in structure, co-operation across sectors, investing funds for research, infrastructure, and regulatory frameworks. Apart from waste reduction, circular economy has a broader benefit on the societal front such as building economies that are more inclusive and resilient, enhanced levels of public health and wellbeing, and advancements in achieving UN Sustainable Development Goals (Schröder, 2020). Circular economy involves a large-scale transformation from linearity in production to circular creation of value wherein resources, components, and products are maintained at the maximum value for the longest time-frame (Zils et al. 2023).

Circular Supply Chain And Sustainability

Closed-loop supply chains (CLSC) focus on the following four aspects: the selection of recycling channels, Pricing decisions, Governments rewards and punishments and Coordination mechanisms. The biggest challenge faced by CLSC is related to the visibility of products (Robaina et al. 2020). Where the products are coming from and how it is remanufactured and gets back to customers have to be made transparent to operationalize CLSC. Interdependability is high among supply chain components and suitable driving solutions have to be designed for clients to effectively implement a circular economy. A sustainable closed loop supply chain has a focus on the environmental and social impacts generated as a result of raw material procurement / processing until the supply of products in the market and the post-consumer phase (Lozieno-Oviedo et al. 2024).

A circular supply chain is a closed-loop system with the goal of lowering waste and improving sustainability and efficiency. Throughout a product's entire life cycle, it entails designing and managing the flow of goods, services, and information in a way that maximises resource use and minimises waste and pollution. A circular supply chain keeps materials and components moving for as long as feasible while designing goods for reuse, refurbishment, or recycling (De Angelis, et al., 2018). This calls for cooperation and coordination among various supply chain phases, from the extraction and processing of raw materials to manufacture, distribution, usage, and end-of-life disposal. The coordination of circular practices across the entire product value chain is an important aspect in a circular supply chain (Kreye, 2025). The circular economy's key element is the circular supply chain. By extending the life of products and materials, a circular economy seeks to reduce waste and maximise resource utilisation (Morseletto, 2020). The entire economy, including how things and services are created, produced, consumed, and disposed, needs to make a systemic transition towards circular practices.

As it helps to close the loop between production and consumption by ensuring that resources are used and reused effectively, a circular supply chain is a crucial component of this shift. Businesses may construct a closed-loop system that maximises the value of resources while minimising waste and pollution by creating products for circularity, optimising the usage of resources, and putting reverse logistics practises into place (Ramasamy and Subramanian 2021). Businesses can lessen their negative effects on the environment, increase resource efficiency, and open new avenues for innovation and economic development by adopting circular supply chain practises. This in turn promotes the overarching objective of establishing a more sustainable and circular economy that is advantageous to both people and the environment.

Circular Supply Chain Management could be a promising solution for achieving sustainability in the present industrial scenario (Kaur et al. 2024). Responsible consumption and production could be attained by implementing a circular economy across the supply chain. The symbol of SDG 12 could be interpreted as an infinity symbol with an arrow mark showing the flow of resources cyclically continuously. So circular economy which encourages the flow of raw materials in a cyclical way both forward and backward across the closed-loop supply chain is one of the ways to attain responsible consumption and production and vice-versa (Symeonides et al. 2019).

If the unsustainable pattern rate as today is continued, then there is a scientific estimation that by the next 25 years, there would be serious survival issues according to the United Nations research institute for social development. Every year, the world produces 2.01 billion tons of municipal solid garbage (Srivastava & Kumar,

2020), with at least 33% of that — to put it conservatively — not being managed in an environmentally sound manner. The average amount of garbage generated per person each day is 0.74 kilos, however, it varies greatly, ranging from 0.11 to 4.54 kilograms (Marques & Marques, 2020). Despite having only 16 percent of the world's population, high-income countries produce around 34% of the world's garbage or 683 million tons (Yılmaz, 2020).

Circular Fashion And Circular Product Design

Circular fashion is the circular supply chain in the fashion industry. By extending the lifespan of materials and goods, the circular fashion movement strives to reduce waste, pollution, and resource use (Rathinamoorthy, 2019). It is a component of the larger circular economy framework, which aims to develop a closed-loop system with effective resource usage and reuse. As it involves planning and controlling the flow of materials and products in a way that maximises resource use and minimises waste and pollution throughout a product's entire lifecycle, circular fashion is closely related to circular supply chains. By implementing circular practises including product design for circularity, sustainable material sourcing, circular business models, and closed-loop cycles, circular fashion strives to keep materials and goods in use for as long as possible Dissanayake & Weerasinghe, 2022). Circular fashion involves a regenerative approach by embedding circular practices in the existing fashion system for utilizing waste and transforming it into new and useful products (D'ltria & Aus, 2023).

By making sure that materials and products are produced and maintained in a way that encourages their reuse and recycling, a circular supply chain can aid in the implementation of these circular fashion practises. In order to execute reverse logistics to recover and regenerate materials, employ sustainable and low-impact materials, optimise resource utilisation throughout the supply chain, and promote circular practises, for instance, a supply chain should be circular. Businesses can develop a closed-loop system that maximises the value of resources while minimising waste and pollution by merging circular fashion and circular supply chain practises. This could contribute to the development of a fair and sustainable fashion sector that benefits both people and the environment.

A significant sector in the European manufacturing economy, textiles and clothing (T&C) employs 1.7 million people and generates a revenue of 166 billion euros. The T&C industry contributes significantly to people's daily lives and is a significant sector of the global economy due to the volume of production and consumption (Peters and Simaens 2020). In an average, customers own more clothes than they actually need, making clothing a product that is underutilised. Because of this, clothing may only be used a few times before being discarded, causing a value loss.

This production and consumption model is often linear (Mishra et al. 2021), which leaves unrealized economic potential. Along the entire supply chain, it uses up a lot of resources, harms the environment, and may have serious negative societal effects.

A rising consumer trend is combating this general condition of inefficiency (Kumar et al. 2021), especially if customers identify a circular premium. Young people (commonly referred to as Generation Z) are typically analytical, meticulous, and rigorous in their clothing choices, exhibiting a deliberate aim to purchase apparel that has sustainable traits (Pencarelli et al. 2019). They may also develop brand loyalty based on a company's history of manufacturing and dedication to social responsibility and environmental sustainability; as a result, they demand more openness from merchants (Gazzola et al. 2020). Despite being discussed in academic and professional contexts, this consumer tendency is still little examined in the scientific literature. This shift in behavior, which is particularly pronounced in Generation Z, gives customers more leverage over clothes manufacturers and the ability to significantly alter production processes through their purchases (Pencarelli et al. 2019). Since these are the only models that can have a good impact on the environment and society, these consumers are interested in green and circular production and consumption models (D'Adamo and Lupi 2021). In this way, raising consumer awareness of the reuse and recycling potential of garments is essential for reducing unsustainable behaviour (Chaturvedi et al. 2020a).

Since it does not require new manufacture, "second-hand" fashion refers to previously worn apparel that is already a component of the circular economy (Kasavan et al. 2021). Despite the social stigma attached to buying second-hand clothing, it can aid in reducing the harmful social and environmental effects of the fashion industry. Additionally, shoppers can save money by purchasing used clothing (Kiehn & Vojkovic, 2018), especially when it comes to premium and well-known brands. Consumers can commit more money to specific wardrobe pieces, which improve their overall appearance and sense of style, by spending less overall on apparel. Finding rare and distinctive things is another advantage for shoppers in the second-hand apparel market.

Many consumers prefer not to wear apparel that is widely popular, despite high-volume standardised manufacturing runs imitating every new fashion trend. The second-hand market extends the typically brief life cycle of clothing, allowing customers to combine patterns, styles, and colours from previous collections to develop their own distinctive look. However, the second-hand market does not offer the same blatant benefits to the fashion sector. The usefulness of second-hand clothing as a remedy for the negative social and environmental effects of the fashion industry is still up in the air. It is also uncertain whether changing business practises and production techniques would be required to accomplish this. To balance the divergent expectations of customers and the fashion industry towards the second-hand clothes sector, is important.

The circular fashion economy in India is influenced by cultural practices, policies that continue to evolve, and a fragmented supply chain. From a cultural perspective, the 'raddi' system was an informal recycling activity done through 'raddi-wallahs' who collected and resold discarded items. However, a fragmented supply chain with the existence of multiple SMEs (Small and Medium Enterprises) and an informal sector that lacked the technology and capital required for recycling.

However, in a semi-urban context, clothing is viewed as an indicator of social mobility, and buying new clothes as a rise in the middle / upper class status There is a stigma associated with buying used clothes (second-hand clothes) and is viered as a sign of financial decline instead of being a choice in the personal and environmental dimensions. There are also deep-rooted beliefs that clothes may continue to have the 'bad karma' or 'negativity' of the original owner. A lack of information about the past history of the clothing and its users also impact reselling and reuse..

Policy frameworks introduced by the Indian Government

Various policy frameworks such as the National Textile Policy 2024, Niti Aayog's Circular Economy Action Plan and the Mission Lifestyle for Environment are formal mechanisms established by the Indian Government. The focus was on Extended Producer Responsibility (EPR) and promoting materials such as organic cotton which are eco-friendly.

The National Textile Policy 2024 has 'Sustainability and Environmental Responsibility' as a key element. Further, incentives for adopting green manufacturing and circular economy practices are also provided to enhance global competitiveness of exporting firms in India.

NITI Aayog's Circular Economy Action Plan was established with one of the focus areas being the Textiles and Apparel Sector. The development of a 'Comprehensive Mission Document for Circular Economy' is a key aspect of the report for the year 2024-25. An interactive dashboard to serve as a 'resource efficiency progress tracker' was also proposed.

Mission LiFE (Lifestyle for Environment) is an initiative by the Indian Government with a focus on 'longevity-oriented consumer behavior aligned with traditional reuse'.

CII National Circular Economy Framework (Edition 3) established in 2025) has a roadmap for a 'Sustainable & Resilient India' and highlighting waste minimization and recycling in the textile sector through success stories.

Integration Of Circular Fashion Into Sustainability Frameworks

A systemic shift is required to integrate circular fashion into sustainability frameworks. The shift from a Linear framework to a Circular framework involves utilization of the following:

a) Life-Cycle Assessment (LCA) as a tool for diagnostics
b) Carbon Footprinting as a metric to measure progress

While the End-of-life (EOL) stage is a key aspect in a Linear Life-cycle Assessment, the Circular Life-cycle assessment has a focus on 'Resource Recovery',

Recycled cotton has about 46% lower emissions in comparison with virgin cotton due to the avoidance of the cultivation phase. Re-selling helps to reduce emissions by 14-26% for every acquisition since production of a new item is avoided. Organic fibres utilize 91% less water and reduced Green House Gas (GHG) emissions. The textile industry accounts for approximately 10% of global carbon emissions. About 1.2 billion tons of Carbon-dioxide equivalent are emitted every year. There could be a 50% increase in Carbon-dioxide equivalent emissions by 2030, if there is no focus on circularity. Dyeing of textiles and microplastics contribute to toxic discharge resulting in water pollution.

Eco-design and Design for Sustainability (DfS) are two significant sustainability concepts that use product design to solve environmental concerns. To address environmental problems, ecodesign employs a four-level model: product improvement, product redesign, function innovation, and system innovation (Burke et al., 2023). Circular product design replaces the cradle-to-grave strategy used in previous strategies with the cradle-to-cradle method, emphasizing product design to continually improve and eventually attain indefinite resource circulation (Has, 2024). 'End-of-life thinking in product design,' 'business model innovation, "sustainable organizational values,' and 'circular supply chain management are four themes related to sustainable operations (Burke et al., 2023). Circular product design necessitates product system thinking. Such design can affect consumers' perceptions and purchase patterns, allowing industry and society to move away from wasteful resource depletion and toward the circular economy.

METHODOLOGY

To accomplish the objectives of this research, data was collected in three phases. In the first phase a questionnaire was designed to get insights from the customers about their preference and issues associated with circular fashion. For this, responses were collected from 114 different individuals who were between the age group of 18 to 30 years. For the second part of the study, insights were drawn from the business perspective and data was collected about the opportunities and issues which businesses perceived about circular fashion from 94 individuals working in the apparel sector. In the third phase eco-entrepreneurs were interviewed and their verbatim about circular fashion has been recorded. This sample size has been considered to provide a directional focus and to arrive at 'pain-points' that could be subsequently tested in detail with a larger study. Further, the focus is more towards Urban / Semi-urban areas since the theme revolves around fashion apparel. Figure 1 depicted below shows a diagrammatic representation of the research framework.

Figure 1. Research Framework

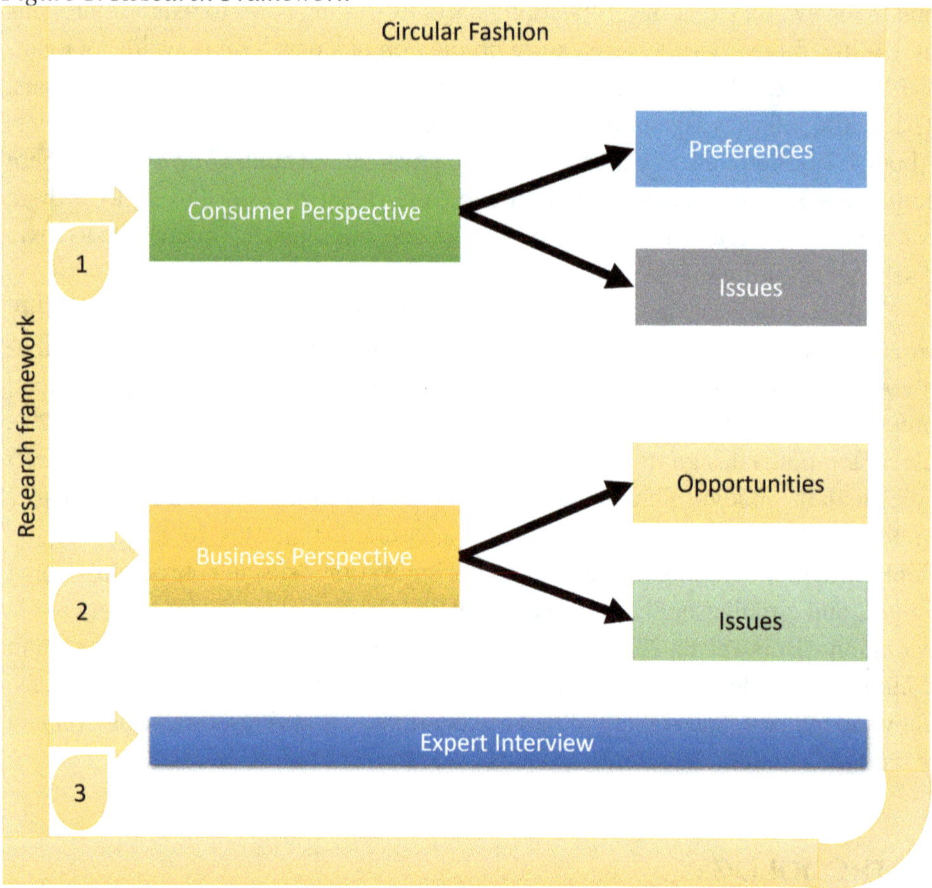

Factors associated with consumer preferences and issues

Eleven factors have been identified to be associated with consumer preferences and issues. Description of the identified consumer factors are shown in table 1.

Table 1. Description of identified consumer factors

Factors	Description	Type
Economical	As some bargain hunters are committed to finding genuine archival things in addition to their desire to purchase used goods, bargain hunters may present a business potential. (i.e. limited editions).	Preference
Green Lifestyle	Consumers may embrace a sustainable lifestyle that positions them as active participants in this decarbonization process.	Preference
Responsible Consumption	The idea of "critical consumption" can be used to describe the used-goods market since it enables customers to develop unconventional buying habits that support a more ethical and sustainable way of life for the benefit of future generations.	Preference
Climate Change	The observable effects of climate change must be addressed, and international actors are asked to get involved. Businesses could suggest environmental conservation methods to achieve global goals.	Preference
Waste Reduction	Consumers who are responsible will get a chance to reduce waste.	Preference
Cleanliness	Due to a notion of unsanitary second-hand goods, some consumer groups may find them to be unacceptable.	Issue
Low Quality	Due to their usage history, used goods could be seen as being of poorer quality than new goods. (And despite undergoing inspection prior to resale).	Issue
Lack of knowledge	Responsible consumption may be hindered by customer ignorance about actual sustainability performance, especially the implications of reuse.	Issue
Social discrimination for using recycled product	Use of used goods might be seen as a sign of low social standing, which could lead to prejudice.	Issue
Apparels won't make a big difference to the circular economy	Even though apparels contribute a large amount of the economy, consumers are not aware of it. It is one of the sectors in the high waste generation list. Since consumers are not aware of it, they think just a normal apparel recycling might to be of a value.	Issue
Brand Conscious (known brands might not give recycled products)	Some businesses have been able to achieve a preferred position in the market thanks to brand awareness. Consumers pay close attention to these details, therefore the brand may suffer if unsuitable products from these brands (or products that are viewed as having less value) are sold on the secondary market.	Issue

Factors from business perspective

Ten factors have been identified from the business perspective. Description of the identified factors are shown in table 2.

Table 2. Description of identified factors from business perspective

Factors	Description	Type
Product Variety	The market for used clothing offers a diverse range of goods, including clothing, accessories, shoes, purses, jewellery, and watches. Marginalization opportunities are increased by this.	Opportunities
Affordability	Consumers have more opportunities to engage this market area thanks to accessibility. It refers to the availability of products in an easy and quick manner thanks to the variety of digital platforms, in addition to fair and inexpensive pricing.	Opportunities
Eco design	A new life cycle may be added to used clothing. Even though the components of the "goods" are consistent, they go through reconditioning.	Opportunities
Market Penetration	The second-hand market might cater to a brand-new type of consumer cluster with distinct buying habits. Therefore, having more consumer data may be advantageous for firms.	Opportunities
Product life	It is possible to change the product life cycle to "cradle to cradle." By doing this, it would be possible to prevent waste and replace the problem of programmed obsolescence with a business model that makes the most of a product's whole (lengthened) life cycle.	Opportunities
Selling cost	Fundamental business costs, such as those incurred for creating new communication channels, changing one's voice, and creating a new cash flow plan, are those related to marketing initiatives in the new market.	Issues
Quality assurance	Costs for product quality assurance and probable remanufacturing could be included.	Issues
Inventory build up	By expanding the breadth and depth of product categories, there may be an excess of unsold stock, which could lead to immobile goods and disposal issues.	Issues
Lack of skillset	The usefulness of an economic closed loop system may be determined by a shortage of workers who can explain to customers the value of used goods.	Issues
Garment sanitation	Prior to being re-released onto the market after quality control, recovered products may incur a cost for the sanitation procedure.	Issues

Results and Discussion

Customer's perspective

93% of the respondents reported that they are concerned about the life of a product that they purchase. 53% of the respondents reported that they are aware about circular fashion while 47% said that they are not aware about it. 94% of the respondents showed interest to give their used apparels to specific centres for recycling while 6% did not.

Customer's preferences in purchase of recycled apparels

Part A of the figure 2 shows the comfort level of customers in purchase of recycled apparels. 13% of the respondents are not comfortable in purchasing recycled apparels, 36% are neutral while 52% are comfortable in purchasing recycled apparels. Customers were asked about the importance they would give to five different factors during their purchase of apparel. These factors were "Economical", "Green Lifestyle", "Responsible Consumption", "Climate Change" and "Waste Reduction". Part B of the figure 2 shows the importance given by customers to the "Economical" factor. 9% of the customers do not consider it important. 24% are neutral while 68% of the customers considered "Economical" factor as important. Part C of the figure 2 shows the importance given by customers to the "Green Lifestyle" factor. 14% of the customers do not consider it important. 22% are neutral while 64% of the customers considered "Green Lifestyle" factor as important. Part D of the figure 2 shows the importance given by customers to the "Responsible Consumption" factor. 14% of the customers do not consider it important. 19% are neutral while 67% of the customers considered "Responsible Consumption" factor as important. Part E of the figure 2 shows the importance given by customers to the "Climate Change" factor. 10% of the customers do not consider it important. 18% are neutral while 72% of the customers considered "Climate Change" factor as important. Part F of the figure 2 shows the importance given by customers to the "Waste Reduction" factor. 10% of the customers do not consider it important. 11% are neutral while 80% of the customers considered "Waste Reduction" factor as important.

Figure 2. Customer's preferences in purchase of recycled apparels

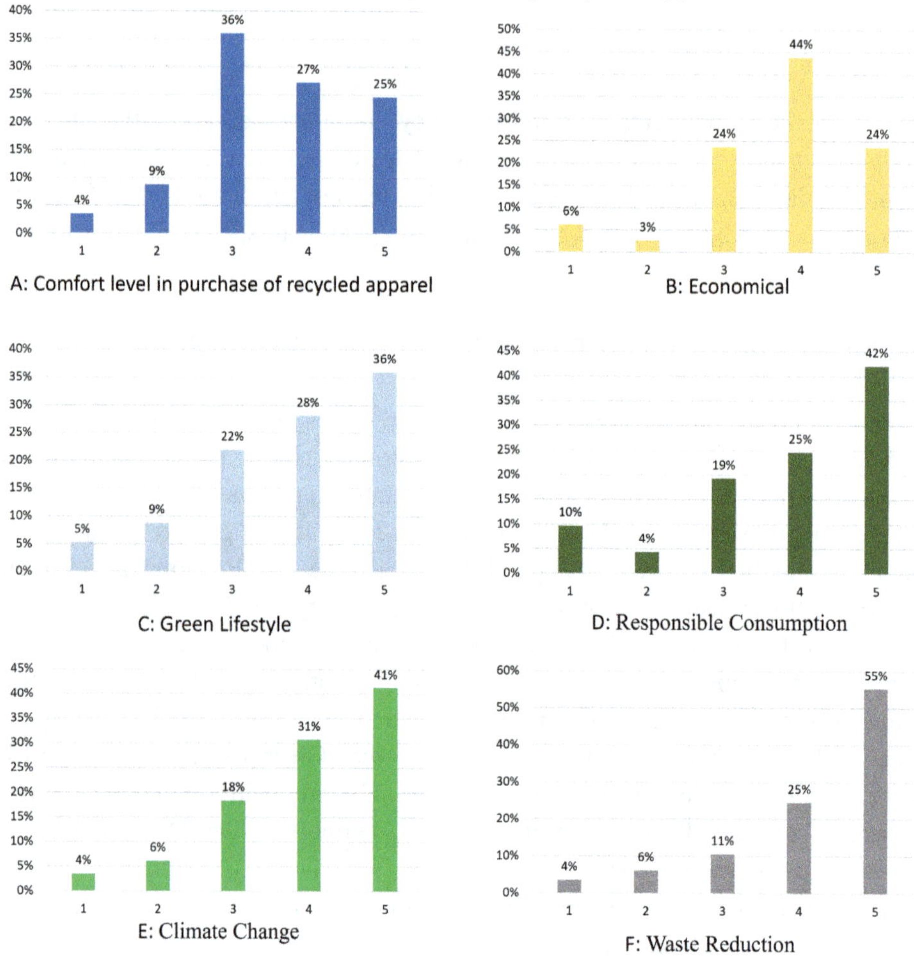

Issues customers consider while purchasing a recycled apparel

Table 3. Rating of issues customers consider while purchasing a recycled apparel

Issues customers consider while purchasing a recycled apparel	Lowest	Rating				Highest
	1	2	3	4	5	6
Cleanliness	14%	6%	19%	24%	6%	31%
Low Quality	10%	7%	26%	18%	21%	18%
Lack of knowledge	7%	15%	26%	24%	13%	15%
Social discrimination for using recycled product	16%	13%	21%	22%	18%	11%
Apparels won't make a big difference to the circular economy	32%	10%	10%	13%	18%	18%
Brand Conscious (known brands might not give recycled products)	26%	9%	16%	14%	12%	23%

Table 3 shows the rating of issues that customers consider while purchasing a recycled apparel. Six parameters were identified and responses of customers were taken on a scale of 1-6 where 1 was the lowest rating while 6 was the highest rating. "Cleanliness" emerged as the most significant concern, as 31% of respondents rated it as a major issue (6) and 24% respondents give it a rating of 4, indicating that hygiene plays a crucial role in customers' decision-making. Concerns about "low quality" are moderately distributed, with peaks at ratings 3 (26%) and 4 (18%). "Lack of knowledge" about recycled apparel is another noticeable factor, as 26% respondents give it a rating of 3 and 24% as 4. It shows that there is a knowledge gap among consumers. "Social discrimination" for using recycled products appeared to be a concern of lesser issue as the highest percentage (22%) was given to rating 4. Regarding the belief that "recycled apparel won't impact the circular economy", the majority of respondents (32%) rated this concern as 1. "Brand consciousness" which is skepticism about well-known brands offering genuine recycled products, also shows varied responses. 23% of the respondents rated this concern as 6, indicating strong skepticism, while 26% rated it as 1, suggesting that many consumers do not see this as an issue.

Business perspective

96% of the respondents reported that they are concerned about the life of a product that they sell. 72% of the respondents reported that they are aware about circular fashion while 28% said that they are not aware about it.

Opportunities identified for recycled apparels

The perspective of business towards opportunities for enhancing recycled apparels were identified in terms of enhanced product variety, affordability, eco design, market penetration, and product life as shown in figure 3. 62% of the respondents reported that product variety is an important parameter for opportunity of enhancing recycled apparels. 66% felt affordability was important. Eco design was given a rating above 3 by 66% of the respondents and market penetration was given a rating above 3 by 73%. 77% of the respondents felt product life was an important parameter for enhancing recycled apparels.

Figure 3. Opportunities identified for recycled apparels - business perspective

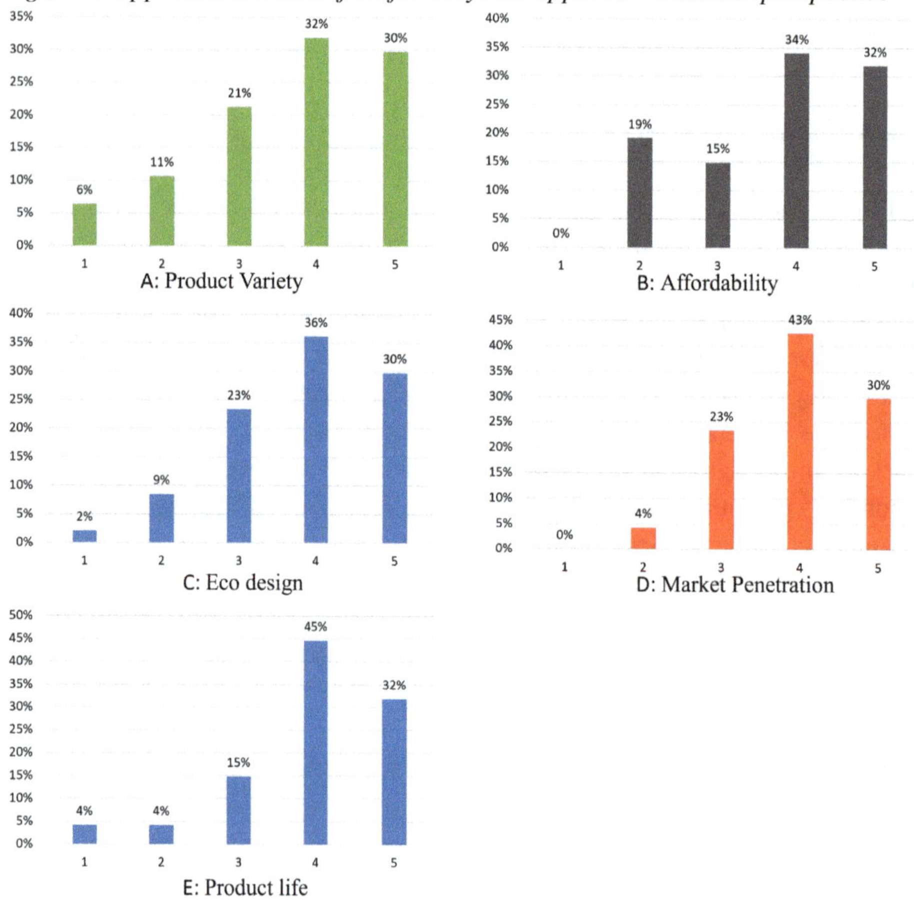

Issues associated with recycled apparels – business perspective

Table 4. Rating of issues associated with recycled apparels – business perspective

Issues associated with recycled apparels	Lowest	Rating			Highest
	1	2	3	4	5
Selling cost	9%	9%	38%	36%	9%
Quality assurance	0%	28%	34%	21%	17%
Inventory build up	2%	11%	43%	28%	17%
Lack of skillset	0%	13%	36%	38%	13%
Garment sanitation	2%	21%	26%	38%	13%

Table 4 shows the rating of issues associated with recycled apparels from the perspective of business personnels. "Lack of skillset" and "garment sanitation" are the most significant concerns, with 38% of respondents rating skill shortages at level 4 and 13% at level 5. Also, for garment sanitation 38% respondents rated at level 4 and 13% at level 5. This suggests that expertise in handling recycled materials and maintaining hygiene standards are major barriers. "Inventory buildup" and 'selling cost" are also notable challenges. For inventory buildup 28% respondents rated level 4 and 17% level 5. For selling cost 36% respondents rated at level 4 and 9% at level 5. This indicates that managing stock levels and pricing strategies require careful attention. "Quality assurance" has a more balanced distribution of ratings, with 28% rating it at level 2, 34% at level 3, and 21% at level 4, and 17% at level 5. It shows that perceptions of quality control vary among the respondents.

Insights from - Eco-entrepreneurs and employees engaged in sustainability work at their workplaces

In the third part of the study, interview was conducted with three eco-entrepreneurs in Bangalore, India who were founders of different apparel industries in India.

Eco-entrepreneur 1:

Question: How are current economic systems be an obstacle to sustainable life-style (Responsible consumption and production)?

Response: "*In our contemporary economic systems, a company's growth is judged in terms of how much revenue it can generate. As a result, business owners desired increased product sales. As a result, by using appealing marketing tactics to persuade individuals, they end up pushing unnecessary consumption beyond what we truly need to consume. Our economic model, which includes how businesses and individuals are compensated, is fundamentally broken. The dynamics and problems of the circular economy are numerous. To avoid any rebound effects, a paradigm shift in business structure is required. Only then will there be a successful shift from a linear to a circular economy."*

Question: How are the government policies to be framed to incentivize your business operations which are aimed at solving sustainability issues?

Response: *"Policies should be framed considering all the three pillars of sustainability which is economic, social, and environmental aspects. When companies operate on a complete circularity mode by following 3R's genuinely then they must be rewarded based on the value addition they do to society and the environment and should not ignore them and look at only the revenue aspect."*

Question: How to build a business model which could decouple economic growth and environmental degradation - as a Service model business?

Response: *"Our whole model is destructive where we mine metals or extract the chemical, do processing and then discard and the same cycle repeats. When we look at nature nothing is wasted – everything goes through cycles. Nature always creates everything in an elegant style which is more like an additive approach rather than a destructive way. Example – Learnings from snail shell Our circular product design should be in such a way that it can be assembled and dissembled, streams separated and recycled to fit into the circular economy model. Biodegradable and Non- Biodegradable materials have to be separated and processed in their streams."*

Eco-entrepreneur 2:

Question: What is circular fashion, and how does it differ from traditional linear fashion?

Response: *"The goal of circular fashion is to create a closed-loop system that keeps resources in use for as long as feasible while minimising waste. Contrary to conventional linear fashion, which uses the "take-make-dispose" paradigm, circular fashion aims to eliminate waste and pollution, prolong the useful lives of items and materials, and renew natural systems."*

Question: What do you think are the benefits of adopting circular fashion in the Indian apparel industry?

Response: *"Adopting circular fashion in the Indian garment sector has a number of advantages. First, it can aid in reducing waste and pollution, which can have favourable effects on the environment. Second, it can aid in lowering production costs and improving resource efficiency. Finally, it can contribute to the development of new company prospects and a rise in global market competition."*

Question: What obstacles do you perceive in the Indian clothing industry's adoption of circular fashion?

Response: *"Adopting circular fashion in the Indian garment sector is fraught with difficulties. First, it's possible that players in the sector don't fully comprehend and are unaware of the ideas of circular fashion. Second, putting into practise circular fashion principles like designing for recycling and disassembly may present technical difficulties. The adoption of circular fashion practises may also be hampered by regulations and policies."*

Question: How do you think India can adopt circular fashion in line with SDG 12?

Response: *"India will need to create a multi-stakeholder strategy that includes business, the government, civil society, and consumers in order to implement circular fashion in line with SDG 12. This could entail investing in the research and development of novel circular materials and technologies, creating policies and regulations that encourage circular fashion practices, and promoting awareness of and educating consumers and industry stakeholders on the fundamentals of circular fashion. Collaboration between Indian and foreign players may also hasten the implementation of circular fashion principles in the nation."*

Eco-entrepreneur 3:

Question: What is circular fashion, and how does it differ from traditional linear fashion?

Response: *"The term "circular fashion" refers to a comprehensive approach to fashion that considers every stage of a product's lifecycle, from the sourcing of raw materials to disposal. It contrasts from conventional linear fashion, which has an adverse effect on the environment and uses a "take-make-dispose" model. Contrarily, circular fashion prioritises the durability, recyclability, and reuse of products in order to lessen waste and pollution."*

Question: What do you think are the benefits of adopting circular fashion in the Indian apparel industry?

Response: *"There are numerous advantages to the Indian apparel sector implementing circular fashion. By lowering waste and pollution, it can aid in lessening the industry's negative environmental effects. By fostering resource efficiency, generating new business prospects, and enhancing global market competitiveness, it can also have a positive impact on the economy. By encouraging moral and ethical business practises and enhancing labour conditions, it can also increase social sustainability."*

Question: What obstacles do you perceive in the Indian clothing industry's adoption of circular fashion?

Response: *"The lack of knowledge and comprehension of circular fashion principles among industry stakeholders is one of the main obstacles to its adoption in the Indian garment sector. Implementing circular fashion principles, such as designing for recycling and disassembly, may also provide technical difficulties. Finally, the adoption of circular fashion in the industry may be hampered by regulatory and policy impediments to implementation."*

Question: How do you think India can adopt circular fashion in line with SDG 12?

Response: *"By adopting a collaborative strategy that includes business, the government, civil society, and consumers, India can implement circular fashion in line with SDG 12. This could entail investing in the research and development of novel circular materials and technologies, creating legislation and regulations that encourage circular fashion practices, and fostering consumer and industry knowledge of circular fashion. Companies may also set an example by incorporating circular fashion practises into their own supply chains and operations, as well as by highlighting circular fashion in their goods and marketing campaigns."*

Table 5 shows the key aspects of the circular fashion industry that could be explained based on various dimensions.

Table 5. Key aspects of the circular fashion industry

Dimension	Key aspect
Core concept	• Reduce-Reuse-Recycle
Business Model Dimension	• Enhanced level of services pertaining to recycling, repair, resale etc.
Design Dimension	• Design with a focus on durability, recycling potential, and environment-friendliness
Production Dimension	• Efficient utilization of resources to enhance sustainability • Usage of materials that are sustainable / have been recycled
Supply Chain Dimension	• Transparency and Traceability of the supply chain
Product Dimension	• Extended life / duration due to the possibility of repair and recycling
Consumer Behaviour Dimension	• Thoughtful consumption, Long-term use
Environment Dimension	• Reduction in waste generation, pollution, and carbon footprint due to 'closed-loop system' and recovery of materials

Application of 6R Framework in the Circular Fashion Industry

The 6R framework from a sustainability perspective is provided below (figure 4):

Figure 4. Sustainability and 6R framework.

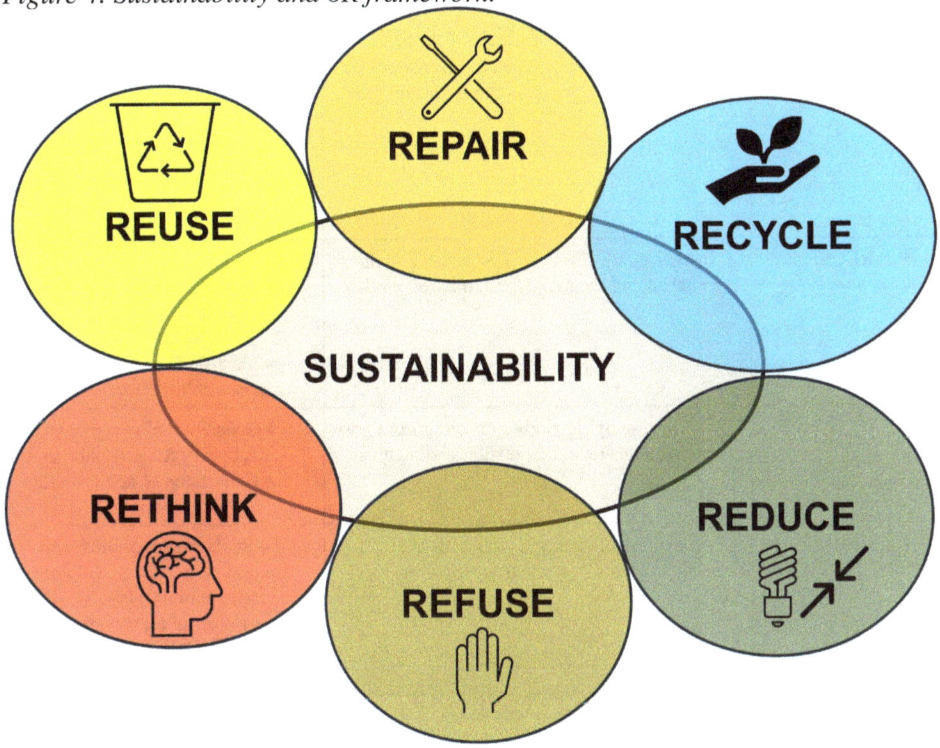

The 6R framework as shown in figure 4 could be applied in the Fashion Industry to enable a shift towards "Circular fashion" for a better future with improved sustainability. Table 6 shows the emphasis and adoption approaches for the 6Rs.

Table 6. Emphasis and adoption approaches for 6Rs.

	Emphasis	Adoption approach
R1: **REDUCE**	Reduction in consumption of raw materials / new resources (i.e., avoiding overconsumption)	• Reduction in procurement quantity • Quality-oriented focus rather than Quantity focus • Optimization in packaging (i.e. minimize non-essential packaging)
R2: **REUSE**	Increasing the lifespan of garments / clothing (i.e., enhancing the usage for garments / clothes)	• Donation / Exchange of clothes • Purchase of second-hand clothing • Identification of alternative usage possibilities for old items
R3: **RECYCLE**	Conversion of old clothes / textile pieces into new materials (avoiding textiles ending up as waste)	• Generation of new clothes / items by recycling the fabrics • Conversion of textile waste into new fibres
R4: **REPAIR**	Mending of damaged clothes rather than discarding them (i.e. extending functionality)	• Replacement of broken or damaged parts / items in clothes (e.g. buttons, zippers) • Repair of tears / holes in clothing
R5: **REFUSE**	Avoidance of purchasing or utilizing clothes that are not needed	• Identification of essential clothes and purchasing only those items • Refraining from purchasing garments / clothing materials that cannot be recycled or reused
R6: **RETHINK**	Modification of perspectives pertaining to textile and fashion industry (i.e., transform from the present to the future, by modifying the existing system)	• Innovation in textile design • Re-thinking and Re-evaluation of business models and supply chains • New methods adopted by customers for purchase of clothes / clothing materials

Apart from the above, there needs to be a focus environmental replenishment. This would involve utilization of materials that could be returned to the earth in a safe manner. This could be achieved through the usage of naturally available fibres / biodegradable materials, and also by means of deploying systems and processes (in textile production) which facilitate environmental regeneration.

Globally, the fashion industry has become a focal point for sustainability transformations. People are now more concerned about the environmental impacts and resource inefficiencies of the fashion industry. The European Union has led with progressive circularity policies such as the EU Circular Economy Action Plan. It has mandated eco-design, extended producer responsibility (EPR), and textile waste minimization (Zils et al., 2023). Brands like H&M and Patagonia have pioneered the introduction of take-back schemes and garment recycling initiatives. This shows the potential of extended producer involvement for closing the resource loops (De Angelis et al., 2018). Sweden and Denmark have demonstrated the value of integrating *eco-tax incentives* and consumer awareness campaigns to boost second-hand markets and slow fashion movements (Peters & Simaens, 2020). In China there is large-scale industrial symbiosis and technological solutions for textile waste. Factories have deployed IoT sensors and AI-enabled tracking to optimize production waste flows (Ali et al., 2024). The UK's *WRAP Sustainable Clothing Action Plan* is another best practice which uses multi-stakeholder agreements to set measurable waste reduction targets (Mishra et al., 2021). Emerging economies like Bangladesh and Vietnam have also started integrating cleaner production methods and closed-loop supply chain models to balance cost and sustainability (Kaur et al., 2024).

The transition towards circular fashion in India aligns strongly with the *Triple Bottom Line* (Elkington, 1997) and *Stakeholder Theory* (Freeman, 1984). Both these theirs emphasize balancing economic, social, and environmental priorities through collaborative stakeholder engagement. By applying these frameworks, the process by which circular supply chains could be integrated with sustainability, can be understood. Addressing the operational barriers is also required in this. Integration of *Closed-Loop Supply Chain* (CLSC) principles is critical for the Indian textile sector. It can help to tackle resource inefficiency and textile waste (Lozano-Oviedo et al., 2024). A case from European brands shows that traceability and reverse logistics can strengthen stakeholder trust and resource recirculation (Zils et al., 2023). In India, leading sustainable brands like Doodlage and B Label shows the potential of upcycling and recycling. By embedding *Design for Sustainability* (DfS) framework these brands integrated eco-design into product life cycles (Burke et al., 2023).

Diffusion of Innovation Theory (Rogers, 2003) can be used for scaling circular fashion adoption. According to the theory awareness and perceived benefits help to influence consumer uptake of sustainable clothing (Chaturvedi et al., 2020b). Kumar et al. (2021) in their research, found that Generation Z's environmentally responsible purchase intentions in India are pivotal for market shifts toward reused or upcycled fashion. Lack of consumer awareness, issues related to perceived hygiene, and gaps in the policy level are some of the barriers identified (Vishwakarma et al., 2024).

A multi-stakeholder approach is vital: firms need to collaborate with the Government. Together they can create regulatory incentives, build consumer awareness campaigns, and invest in reverse logistics. By integrating AI and IoT into textile, CLSCs can enhance resource tracking, waste minimization, and consumer engagement (Ali et al., 2024).

Implementation Scenario

Many large corporate entities are focusing on implementing circularity in the apparel sector. For example, Aditya Birla Fashion and Retail introduced the initial 'Circularity Guidelines' in India in 2024 and have a focus on rejuvenation of cotton waste. Similarly, smaller players / SMEs are also partnering with manufacturing / processing units to implement circularity. This ensures that the entir supply chain (including MSMEs) focus on the 6R Framework and establishing a benchmark for exports.

Enabling Sustainability in the Fashion Industry through AI

Sustainability is a standardized concept that generally comprises three aspects, namely the environmental, economic, and social dimensions. AI has the potential to address critical challenges across the various dimensions. Research has been done in areas related to Sustainable Development Goals with the use of Artificial Intelligence and Machine Learning to create an effective mechanism that would facilitate a circular economy (Kar et.al., 2022). AI technologies such as Machine Learning and Data Analytics can be deployed in the attainment of Sustainable Development goals. AI algorithms could be applied in areas such as optimization of energy consumption, enhancement of transportation efficiency, identification of inefficiencies in the supply chain, etc. This in turn, could be helpful in various sectors by enabling decision-making in a more informed and sustainable manner. There is also a need to mitigate the negative impacts of AI while enhancing its potential for sustainable transformation (Pimenow et.al., 2025).

Contemporary advancements in technology provide various tools to address issues pertaining to Sustainability Goals. Artificial Intelligence is one of the key technologies to enhance sustainability in the fashion industry. It could be a significant enabler in the fashion industry for transitioning towards sustainability. AI could play a role from a sustainability perspective in multiple aspects of the fashion industry such as creativity in design, management of supply chains, sales and promotional activities, control of waste, and analysis of data. Despite the limitations of AI such as the need for large data volumes, cost of implementation, etc., it could be deployed while focusing on responsible management of resources, easier access to services, and enhanced customer satisfaction from the current and future perspectives. It could be deployed for the complete lifecycle related to circular fashion, from the initial designing phase until end-of-life management.

The fashion industry has shortcomings from a sustainability dimension. A substantial exploitation of labour exists in the fashion industry which is visible in terms of workers being subjected to grueling shifts in excess of eight hours a day.

In addition, distribution logistics related to clothing and accessories have increased emission of greenhouse gases. The growth of fast fashion has also increased the pace of production and disposal of clothing, which results in enhanced generation of waste and unsustainable consumption of resources (Wren, 2022). The fashion industry involves a heavy consumption of resources in the production of clothing and accessories. There are challenges related to water pollution such as presence of heavy metals and micro-plastics in the sources of water (Akter et.al. 2022), which lead to health issues due to water consumption by the nearby residents (Hossain et.al. 2018).

The fashion industry is constantly trying to identify tools and solutions that would facilitate attainment of sustainability goals. One of the avenues is through the deployment of AI to help in sustainability improvement (Bruzzone et.al. 2022). Artificial Intelligence could enable the fashion industry to optimize many processes related to apparel production AI algorithms could be utilized by fashion apparel companies for improved management of resources facilitating reduction of cost, enhanced efficiency and effectiveness, and higher speed of production (Thomassey & Zeng, 2018).

A systematic review conducted by Ramos, Rivas-Echeverria, Perez, and Casas (2023) with an intent to explore sustainability improvement in the fashion industry through usage of AI focused on artificial intelligence-based approaches to enhance sustainability, and also on the associated advantages and limitations. Based on systematic literature review of shortlisted items from 616 articles available online, the researchers published their results as indicated below:

Functionality: 40.54% of the total articles related to AI for sustainability in the fashion industry focused on supply chain optimization, 27.03% of the articles were related to sustainable clothing and sales, 18.91% had a focus on reducing waste, and 13.52% had a focus on data analysis.

Technology: Various technologies such as Neural networks, Machine Learning Algorithms, Internet of Things (IoT), and Blockchain were deployed.

Focus: 41% of the reviewed articles focused on aspects related to satisfying the current and futuristic needs of customers, 35% of the articles were in areas pertaining to the management of waste, and 24% of the articles were related to improvement of accessibility and services.

Sustainability Using AI and Other Technologies In The Fashion Industry

Retailers in the fashion industry could optimize resource efficiency and enhance product utilization by integrating Machine Learning based Intelligence with IoT equipment. Technologies such as Computer Vision could help in online retail by enhancing precision in body measurements, which in turn reduces the rate of product returns and environmental impact (Sliyakat S, 2024).

The integration of AI/ML and IoT could facilitate circularity in the apparel sector by inventory balancing and reducing overproduction through real-time data insights. Analysis of images from two / three dimensional perspective facilitates customization / personalization in appropriate fitting of garments, thus enhancing their functional life and in achieving the sustainability-related goals (Sliyakat S, 2025).

Framework for Sustainability Using AI and Other Technologies In The Fashion Industry

A framework for Sustainability through the usage of Artificial Intelligence and other technologies in the fashion industry is provided below. This comprises the Focus areas, Functional areas, and Technologies from a sustainability perspective.

Figure 5. Framework For Sustainability Using AI and Other Technologies in the Fashion Industry

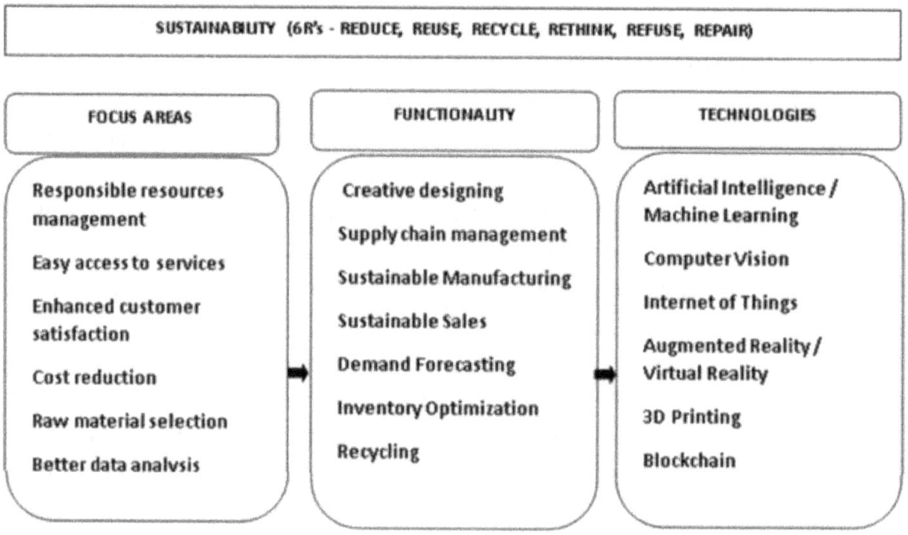

Focus Areas

The focus areas as specified in the framework indicate a commitment towards sustainability, process improvement, and consumer experience.

Responsible Resources Management

The fashion industry could contribute towards minimizing the impact on environment through responsible utilization and management of resources. This includes procuring raw materials that are sustainable such as organic cotton, recycled materials, reducing the consumption of water and energy resources by fine-tuning production processes, and also focusing on aspects such as design for durability and development of good recycling techniques.

Easy access to Services

Accessibility to services across various channels without much difficulty plays a significant role in the fashion industry. The design of clothing and its production should be able to meet the requirements of people who are specially-abled. This could be achieved while considering sizing, sensory aspects, etc.

Enhanced Customer Satisfaction

The fashion industry would need to cater to consumer needs by providing personalization and a seamless experience. This could be achieved by addressing the aesthetic needs of consumers, product recommendation in a personalized manner, etc.

Cost reduction

The focus on reducing cost an important requirement in the fashion industry. This could be attained through implementation of lean manufacturing techniques, inventory optimization, reduction in supply chain returns etc. The alignment with sustainable practices while focusing on cost reduction could include waste minimization, supply chain logistics optimization, and adoption of energy-efficient technologies.

Raw Material Selection

The selection of appropriate raw materials in the fashion apparel production process could impact the quality, visual appeal, and carbon footprint. Sustainable options in the selection of raw materials could include procurement of recycled materials, or materials that have a low carbon footprint during the production process.

Better Data Analysis

The analysis of data pertaining to customer preferences, consumer behavior, trend analysis of sales, supply chain, etc. could help in improved demand forecasting, inventory optimization, effective response to market dynamics and consumer preferences.

CONCLUSION

India has a population of 1.45 billion, and this results in a high degree of generation of waste. The adoption of manual processes for waste processing consumes more time and effort and also leads to waste management issues. Even the technology utilized for waste management in India is expensive or if imported, it is not customizable to the Indian context. In the fashion industry, circular supply chains and business models have drawn a lot of interest since they differ from the traditional "take-make-dispose" linear process. By using less resources to produce apparel and prolonging the life of products through recycling, the circular model aims to improve sustainability and reduce waste. However, now, only about 20% of clothing gets recycled or reused due to the fashion industry's dominating operational logics of bulk manufacturing, linear fourth in terms of high environmental cost, model and rapid fashion consumption. The growing second-hand market trend offers the fashion sector a chance to transition to a circular economy.

To address the severe environmental impact of the T&C business, immediate action is required. While some companies have modified their production processes and customers are choosing more sustainable products, these actions might not be sufficient to mitigate the environmental impact. Within the industry, the market for used garments is expanding, and circular economy principles might be used in this market. The possibility of unforeseen repercussions exists, though. In order to solve this problem, a framework was created to evaluate the opportunities and difficulties presented by the market for used apparel for both enterprises and consumers.

Making use of renewable sources of energy like sunlight, wind energy and hydrogen fuel to produce innovative products which could be used for economic activities intended towards sustainable development goals. Waste management is another area where there are a lot of opportunities for sustainable business operations. To develop responsible business ideas, we have to analyze the effects of the ideas on all the social, economic and environmental pillars of sustainability before implementing them to avoid any kind of rebound effects. Businesses should be pushed to reorganise their processes to include green and circular practises, which respect both human welfare and the effective use of resources. Indian businesses should educate their staff and clients about this idea and motivate them to work hard to meet the sustainability goal. The flexibility to select the sustainability area that best suits their beliefs and objectives must be available to both consumers and businesses. The circular economy's main objective is resource efficiency, but this shouldn't come at the expense of social welfare and economic justice.

The current study, which used a macro-level strategy, has several drawbacks when it comes to understanding consumer preferences. To better understand consumer preferences, future research should concentrate on particular textile and clothing industry segments, such as clothes and accessories, fast fashion, brand fashion, leisure fashion, and sports fashion. Research should also be done on how businesses are reorganising their supply chains and operations. The second-hand market is just one of the many suggested techniques for promoting the sustainability of the fashion business, in addition to increasing manufacturing efficiency and utilising sustainable textile resources, such as fiber-based clothing and clothing recycling. There is a good scope for Artificial Intelligence and other technologies to be deployed in the fashion industry to enhance efficiency and sustainability.

REFERENCES

Akter, M. M. K., Haq, U. N., Islam, M. M., & Uddin, M. A. (2022). Textile-apparel manufacturing and material waste management in the circular economy: A conceptual model to achieve sustainable development goal (SDG) 12 for Bangladesh. *Cleaner Environmental Systems*, *4*, 100070. DOI: 10.1016/j.cesys.2022.100070

Ali, Z. A., Zain, M., Pathan, M. S., & Mooney, P. (2024). Contributions of artificial intelligence for circular economy transition leading toward sustainability: An explorative study in agriculture and food industries of Pakistan. *Environment, Development and Sustainability*, *26*(8), 19131–19175. DOI: 10.1007/s10668-023-03458-9

Burke, H., Zhang, A., & Wang, J. X. (2023). Integrating product design and supply chain management for a circular economy. *Production Planning and Control*, *34*(11), 1097–1113. DOI: 10.1080/09537287.2021.1983063

Chaturvedi, P., Kulshreshtha, K., & Tripathi, V. (2020a). Investigating the determinants of behavioral intentions of generation Z for recycled clothing: An evidence from a developing economy. *Young Consumers*, *21*(4), 403–417. DOI: 10.1108/YC-03-2020-1110

Chaturvedi, P., Kulshreshtha, K., & Tripathi, V. (2020b). Investigating determinants of behavioral intentions for recycled clothing. *Young Consumers*, *21*(4), 403–417. DOI: 10.1108/YC-03-2020-1110

De Angelis, R., Howard, M., & Miemczyk, J. (2018). Supply chain management and the circular economy: Towards the circular supply chain. *Production Planning and Control*, *29*(6), 425–437. DOI: 10.1080/09537287.2018.1449244

Dissanayake, D. G. K., & Weerasinghe, D. (2022). Towards circular economy in fashion: Review of strategies, barriers and enablers. *Circular Economy and Sustainability*, *2*(1), 25–45. DOI: 10.1007/s43615-021-00090-5

Dwivedi, A., Moktadir, M. A., Chiappetta Jabbour, C. J., & de Carvalho, D. E. (2022). Integrating the circular economy and industry 4.0 for sustainable development: Implications for responsible footwear production in a big data-driven world. *Technological Forecasting and Social Change*, *175*, 121335. DOI: 10.1016/j.techfore.2021.121335

Elkington, J. (1997). *Cannibals with Forks: The Triple Bottom Line of 21st Century Business*. Capstone.

Freeman, R. E. (1984). *Strategic Management: A Stakeholder Approach*. Pitman.

Gazzola, P., Pavione, E., Pezzetti, R., & Grechi, D. (2020). Trends in the fashion industry. The perception of sustainability and circular economy: A gender/generation quantitative approach. *Sustainability (Basel), 12*(14), 5808. DOI: 10.3390/su12072809

Hales, R., & Birdthistle, N. (2023). The sustainable development goals–SDG# 12 responsible consumption and production. In *Attaining the 2030 sustainable development goal of responsible consumption and production* (pp. 1–10). Emerald Publishing Limited. DOI: 10.1108/978-1-80455-840-920231001

Has, M. (2024). *Sustainable Products: Life Cycle Assessment, Risk Management, Supply Chains, Ecodesign.* Walter de Gruyter GmbH & Co KG.

Hossain, L., Sarker, S. K., & Khan, M. S. (2018). Evaluation of present and future wastewater impacts of textile dyeing industries in Bangladesh. *Environmental Development, 26*, 23–33. DOI: 10.1016/j.envdev.2018.03.005

Iacovidou, E., Hahladakis, J. N., & Purnell, P. (2021). A systems thinking approach to understanding the challenges of achieving the circular economy. *Environmental Science and Pollution Research International, 28*(19), 24785–24806. DOI: 10.1007/s11356-020-11725-9 PMID: 33289042

Kandpal, V., Jaswal, A., Santibanez Gonzalez, E. D., & Agarwal, N. (2024). Circular economy principles: shifting towards sustainable prosperity. In *Sustainable energy transition: Circular economy and sustainable financing for environmental, social and governance (ESG) practices* (pp. 125–165). Springer Nature Switzerland. DOI: 10.1007/978-3-031-52943-6_4

Kar, A. K., Choudhary, S. K., & Singh, V. K. (2022). How can artificial intelligence impact sustainability: A systematic literature review. *Journal of Cleaner Production, 376*, 134120. https://doi.org/doi:10.1016/j.jclepro.2022.134120

Kasavan, S., Yusoff, S., Guan, N. C., Zaman, N. S. K., & Fakri, M. F. R. (2021). Global trends of textile waste research from 2005 to 2020 using bibliometric analysis. *Environmental Science and Pollution Research International, 28*(33), 44780–44794. DOI: 10.1007/s11356-021-15303-5 PMID: 34235692

Kaur, M., Palazzo, M., & Foroudi, P. (2024). Circular supply chain management in post-pandemic context. A qualitative study to explore how knowledge, environmental initiatives and economic viability affect sustainability. *Qualitative Market Research, 27*(4), 572–607. DOI: 10.1108/QMR-10-2023-0140

Kiehn, K., & Weller Vojkovic, A. (2018). Millennials motivations for shopping second-hand clothing as part of a sustainable consumption practice.

Kreye, M. (2025). Circularity in supply chains versus circular supply chains: Identifying the need for transformation in manufacturing. *Supply Chain Management, 30*(3), 339–352. DOI: 10.1108/SCM-05-2024-0295

Kumar, A., Prakash, G., & Kumar, G. (2021). Does environmentally responsible purchase intention matter for consumers? A predictive sustainable model developed through an empirical study. *Journal of Retailing and Consumer Services, 58*, 102270. DOI: 10.1016/j.jretconser.2020.102270

Lozano-Oviedo, J., Cortés, C. E., & Rey, P. A. (2024). Sustainable closed-loop supply chains and their optimization models: A review of the literature. *Clean Technologies and Environmental Policy, 26*(4), 999–1023. DOI: 10.1007/s10098-023-02730-w

Marques, L., & Marques, L. (2020). Waste and Industrial Intoxication. *Capitalism and Environmental Collapse*, 97-129.

Mishra, S., Jain, S., & Malhotra, G. (2021). The anatomy of circular economy transition in the fashion industry. *Social Responsibility Journal, 17*(4), 524–542. DOI: 10.1108/SRJ-06-2019-0216

Morseletto, P. (2020). Targets for a circular economy. *Resources, Conservation and Recycling, 153*, 104553. DOI: 10.1016/j.resconrec.2019.104553

Pencarelli, T., Ali Taha, V., Škerháková, V., Valentiny, T., & Fedorko, R. (2019). Luxury products and sustainability issues from the perspective of young Italian consumers. *Sustainability (Basel), 12*(1), 245. DOI: 10.3390/su12010245

Peters, J., & Simaens, A. (2020). Integrating sustainability into corporate strategy: A case study of the textile and clothing industry. *Sustainability (Basel), 12*(15), 6125. DOI: 10.3390/su12156125

Pimenow, S., Pimenowa, O., Prus, P., & Niklas, A. (2025). The Impact of Artificial Intelligence on the Sustainability of Regional Ecosystems: Current Challenges and Future Prospects. *Sustainability (Basel), 17*(11), 4795. https://www.mdpi.com/2071-1050/17/11/4795. DOI: 10.3390/su17114795

Ramasamy, R., & Subramanian, R. B. (2021). Synthetic textile and microfiber pollution: A review on mitigation strategies. *Environmental Science and Pollution Research International, 28*(31), 41596–41611. DOI: 10.1007/s11356-021-14763-z PMID: 34100210

Ramos, L., Rivas-Echeverría, F., Pérez, A. G., & Casas, E. (2023). Artificial intelligence and sustainability in the fashion industry: A review from 2010 to 2022. *SN Applied Sciences, 5*(12), 387. DOI: 10.1007/s42452-023-05587-2

Rashid, A., Roci, M., & Asif, F. M. (2020). 26. Circular manufacturing systems. *Handbook of the circular economy*, 343.

Rathinamoorthy, R. (2019). Circular fashion. *Circular economy in textiles and apparel: Processing, manufacturing, and design*, 13-48.

Robaina, M., Murillo, K., Rocha, E., & Villar, J. (2020). Circular economy in plastic waste-Efficiency analysis of European countries. *The Science of the Total Environment*, *730*, 139038. DOI: 10.1016/j.scitotenv.2020.139038 PMID: 32438212

Rogers, E. M. (2003). *Diffusion of Innovations* (5th ed.). Free Press.

Schröder, P. (2020). *Promoting a just transition to an inclusive circular economy*. Royal Institute of International Affairs.

Sliyakat, K. (2025). Machine learning-powered IoT (MLIoT) for retail apparel industry. In Tarnanidis, T., Papachristou, E., Karypidis, M., & Manda, V. (Eds.), *Sustainable practices in the fashion and retail industry* (pp. 345–372). IGI Global Scientific Publishing.

Sliyakat, S. (2024). IoT driven by machine learning (MLIoT) for the retail apparel sector. In Tarnanidis, T., Papachristou, E., Karypidis, M., & Ismyrlis, V. (Eds.), *Driving green marketing in fashion and retail* (pp. 63–81). IGI Global., DOI: 10.4018/979-8-3693-3049-4.ch004

Srivastava, M., & Kumar, M. (2020). Impact of Solid Municipal Waste. *Resilience, Response, and Risk in Water Systems: Shifting Management and Natural Forcings Paradigms*, 303.

Symeonides, D., Loizia, P., & Zorpas, A. A. (2019). Tire waste management system in Cyprus in the framework of circular economy strategy. *Environmental Science and Pollution Research International*, *26*(35), 35445–35460. DOI: 10.1007/s11356-019-05131-z PMID: 31127515

Thomassey, S., & Zeng, X. (2018). *Artificial intelligence for fashion industry in the big data era*. Springer Ser Fashion Bus., DOI: 10.1007/978-981-13-0080-6

Vishwakarma, A., Mehrotra, D., Agrahari, R., Kharub, M., Gupta, S., & Jagtap, S. (2024). Breaking barriers: Paving the path to sustainable fashion – insights for a greener apparel and textile sector. *Journal of Advances in Management Research*, *21*(3), 376–397. DOI: 10.1108/JAMR-05-2023-0112

Wren, B. (2022). Sustainable supply chain management in the fast fashion industry: A comparative study of current efforts and best practices to address the climate crisis. *Clean Logistics Supply Chain*, *4*, 100032. DOI: 10.1016/j.clscn.2022.100032

Yılmaz, F. (2020). Is there a waste Kuznets curve for OECD? Some evidence from panel analysis. *Environmental Science and Pollution Research International*, *27*(32), 40331–40345. DOI: 10.1007/s11356-020-09109-0 PMID: 32666443

Zils, M., Howard, M., & Hopkinson, P. (2023). Circular economy implementation in operations & supply chain management: Building a pathway to business transformation. *Production Planning and Control*, *36*(4), 501–520. DOI: 10.1080/09537287.2023.2280907

Zorpas, A. A., & Saranti, A. (2016). Multi-criteria analysis of sustainable environmental clean technologies for the treatment of winery's wastewater. *International Journal of Global Environmental Issues*, *15*(1/2), 151–168. DOI: 10.1504/IJGENVI.2016.074359

Chapter 3
AI-Driven Immersive Technologies in Fashion Brand Communication

Nikita Singh
http://orcid.org/0000-0001-5493-4640
Lovely Professional University, India

Sarishti Dutt
http://orcid.org/0009-0008-2064-4416
Lovely Professional University, India

Jyoti Rani
http://orcid.org/0000-0002-5577-7808
Parul University, India

ABSTRACT

The way fashion brands connect with their customers is being redefined by the confluence of artificial intelligence (AI), augmented reality (AR), and virtual reality (VR). These technologies are producing immersive, customized, and interactive experiences that go beyond conventional shopping. The study used a qualitative exploratory methodology to examine these innovations, utilizing public data from tech partnership announcements, app reviews, retail innovation reports, and brand case studies in addition to secondary research. According to the findings, these companies are using AI and immersive technology to improve the shopping experience while also promoting more sustainable retail models, lowering return rates, and enhancing personalization. According to these results, mass-market fashion firms hoping to compete in a customer world that prioritizes digital devices are finding that the strategic application of AI-powered AR and VR is becoming a crucial tool.

DOI: 10.4018/979-8-2600-0303-9.ch003

INTRODUCTION

The fashion business is changing dramatically as it adopts the convergence of virtual reality (VR), augmented reality (AR), and artificial intelligence (AI), which are radically changing the way fashion brands interact with their clientele (Bucea-Manea-Ţoniş et al., 2021). These developments are giving customers a new degree of involvement and personalisation by producing immersive, personalised, and interactive experiences that go well beyond the conventional shopping paradigm (Kim et al., 2023). At first, high-end fashion brands were the first to embrace these innovative technologies, leveraging them to improve customer engagement, inventiveness, and accuracy. But the trend has quickly spread to mass-market fashion businesses, who are using AI-enhanced AR and VR more and more to appeal to consumers who are tech-savvy and convenience-driven. From limited premium applications to widespread accessibility, this change represents a larger democratisation of smart technology in retail. The first luxury brands to use AI, AR, and VR into their retail strategies were Burberry, Dior, Gucci, and Louis Vuitton (Jung et al., 2021). While AR and VR made it possible for virtual try-ons and immersive digital showrooms, which let buyers experience things in new ways without having to be physically there, they also used AI to enhance creative processes and increase design precision. Customers could explore things in three dimensions straight from search results thanks to Burberry's partnership with Google, for example, which increased customer engagement and confidence when making purchases. Dior's use of augmented reality (AR) to create virtual accessory try-ons showed how these technologies could help close the gap between digital and physical shopping by offering realistic previews that boost customer happiness and decrease uncertainty. By empowering consumers to make better decisions, these advances not only enhanced the shopping experience but also assisted in lowering return rates (Singh & Kulkarni, 2023).

Mainstream companies like Uniqlo, H&M, and ASOS have followed the luxury sector's example and used AI-powered AR and VR to satisfy changing consumer demands. With the help of its mobile app, Uniqlo's AI stylist provides tailored outfit suggestions based on user preferences, current trends, and weather conditions. This results in a highly customised purchasing experience that appeals to contemporary customers looking for relevance and ease (Aslam & Davis, 2024). In order to improve customer connection, H&M has combined digital and physical retail spaces by experimenting with augmented reality window shopping experiences and integrating AI-driven product recommendations into its app and in-store kiosks. In order to solve typical issues like fit uncertainty in online shopping, ASOS's creative "See My Fit" feature uses augmented reality (AR) to enable virtual try-ons and AI algorithms to suggest sizes and styles based on consumer profiles (Barone & Stagno, 2023). Walmart's acquisition of Zeekit, an AI and AR-powered virtual fitting room platform, is another example of how big-box stores are boosting accessibility and customer confidence by allowing customers to see clothing on a variety of body shapes, encouraging inclusivity, and lowering reluctance to make online purchases (Khatib et al., 2023).

Mass-market fashion companies' extensive use of AI-enhanced AR and VR technology is a reaction to changing consumer expectations and behaviours. Customers of today are more and more digital natives who value ease of use, customisation, and immersive experiences that fit in well with their digital lives. Fashion firms are being forced to constantly adapt as a result of the increased engagement criteria set by the growth of social media shopping, mobile commerce, and virtual influencers. In addition to satisfying these needs, AI-powered AR and VR help create more environmentally friendly retail models by reducing return rates, which lessen waste (Pakharuddin & Kamarudin, 2023). These technologies assist optimise manufacturing and inventory management by allowing buyers to virtually try on clothing and obtain personalised recommendations, which is in line with the growing consumer preference for sustainable and ethical design. These innovations were investigated using a qualitative and exploratory research methodology that included secondary research and public data from retail innovation reports, app reviews, technological partnership announcements, and brand case studies. This all-encompassing strategy made it possible to conduct a thorough analysis of the ways in which AI, AR, and VR are being applied across various brands and retail settings. Key themes like efficiency gains, inclusion, the results of consumer interactions, and the smart use of technology were the focus of the study. According to research, these businesses are incorporating AI and immersive technology as essential elements of their retail strategies to improve personalisation, develop captivating brand experiences, and advance sustainable practices rather than just using them as gimmicks (Viswanathan, 2024).

Efficiency improvements were demonstrated by the way AI algorithms expedite inventory forecasting and product recommendations, lowering operating expenses and raising customer happiness by promptly providing pertinent options. With AR try-ons and virtual fitting rooms supporting a range of body sizes and preferences, inclusivity emerged as a crucial advantage, resolving a long-standing issue in the fashion retail industry. The concrete economic value of these technologies was demonstrated by the results of consumer interactions, which showed stronger engagement, higher conversion rates, and lower return rates. Additionally, it was discovered that mass-market fashion companies seeking to compete in a customer-centric, digital-first world where customers expect seamless integration of technology in their purchasing journeys must strategically deploy AI-powered AR and VR (Upreti et al., 2024). AI, AR, and VR are predicted to play an increasingly larger part in the fashion business as it develops, interacting with new trends like digital fashion, the metaverse, and AI-driven haptic feedback. With these developments, customers will be able to interact with virtual clothing in ways that closely resemble real-world touch and movement, making for ever more realistic and immersive shopping experiences. By combining these technologies, firms will be able to stand out in a competitive market and develop stronger emotional bonds with their clientele. This is expected to encourage new kinds of creativity and personalisation (Akram et al., 2022).

Fashion retail is undergoing a revolution thanks to the confluence of AI, AR, and VR, which is moving intelligent and immersive customer experiences from expensive exclusivity to widespread acceptance. The necessity to satisfy the needs of tech-savvy customers who want individualised, practical, and interesting shopping experiences is what is driving this change (Patel, 2024). Examples of how mass-market fashion companies are strategically utilising these technologies to boost customer pleasure, encourage sustainability, and increase operational efficiency include Uniqlo, H&M, ASOS, and Walmart. The results emphasise that the smooth integration of AI-powered immersive technologies, which are quickly becoming essential tools for firms looking to prosper in a fast-evolving digital world, is the key to the future of fashion retail. The relationship between fashion firms and their clientele will continue to change as these technologies advance and become more widely available, opening up new avenues for creativity, inclusivity, and long-term success (Har et al., 2022).

UNDERSTANDING THE ROLE OF AI, AR, AND VR IN FASHION RETAIL

By converting traditional shopping into immersive, customised, and interactive experiences that engage customers at previously unheard-of levels, the fashion retail industry is undergoing a fundamental transformation thanks to the integration of artificial intelligence (AI), augmented reality (AR), and virtual reality (VR). To fully appreciate these technologies' combined influence on the fashion customer journey, one must comprehend their many functions and interactions (Chaudhary et al., 2024). Fundamentally, artificial intelligence describes computer systems that are able to carry out operations like learning, reasoning, and decision-making that normally demand for human intellect. AI drives algorithms in the fashion retail industry that examine large datasets to forecast trends, customise suggestions, maximise stock, and improve customer support via chatbots and virtual stylists. Customers can see things in their physical surroundings using smartphones, tablets, or AR glasses thanks to augmented reality, which superimposes digital features onto the real world. With the use of this technology, consumers may virtually try on clothing and accessories to see how they would appear on them or in their environment (Pierdicca et al.,

2017). Customers can tour virtual stores, watch fashion presentations, or try on clothing in a 3D virtual fitting room thanks to virtual reality, which immerses users in completely digital surroundings, frequently through headgear. A new paradigm in fashion retail is being pushed by the convergence of AR and VR, which offer the sensory and experience aspects of digital connection, and AI, which concentrates on data-driven intelligence and decision-making (Dear, 2019).

By facilitating real-time personalisation and predictive fitting two essentials for providing smooth and fulfilling customer experiences AI greatly expands the potential of AR and VR. For instance, in AR and VR platforms, AI algorithms leverage user data such as past purchases, browsing habits, body measurements, and even social media activity to dynamically customise product recommendations. This implies that when a consumer digitally trys on a jacket via an augmented reality app, AI can recommend related products based on current fashion trends and the user's personal interests, resulting in a tailored and user-friendly purchasing experience (Xie et al., 2022). AI-powered predictive fitting tackles fit uncertainty, one of the most enduring issues in online apparel industry. AI algorithms can forecast the ideal size and fit for each customer by analysing data from many sources, such as 3D body scans, customer reviews, and return trends. AI algorithms can forecast the ideal size and fit for each customer by analysing data from many sources, such as 3D body scans, customer reviews, and return trends. By reducing the amount of waste produced by returned goods, this collaboration between AI and immersive technologies not only improves customer pleasure but also advances more environmentally friendly retail practices (Nnenna Ijeoma Okeke et al., 2024). From discovery and contemplation to purchase and post-buy involvement, AI, AR, and VR play a significant part in the customer experience, radically changing how customers engage with fashion brands. AI-driven chatbots and recommendation engines assist consumers in navigating extensive product catalogues during the discovery stage by displaying options that suit their requirements and preferences. By allowing users to instantaneously see things on their bodies or in their actual surroundings, augmented reality applications help consumers bridge the gap between online shopping and in-person trials. By providing immersive virtual stores where consumers can peruse collections, go to live fashion events, or interact with brand narratives in ways that go beyond geographical constraints, virtual reality (VR) goes beyond this (Joy Onma Enyejo et al., 2024). AI-driven personalisation at the point of sale guarantees that pricing, promotions, and product recommendations are customised to optimise relevance and conversion. Although AR and VR can facilitate virtual style sessions or digital wardrobe management, AI continues to improve the consumer experience after the purchase through personalised follow-ups, styling recommendations, and loyalty programs. Through this thorough integration, the customer journey is changed from a transactional, linear process to a dynamic, interactive one that encourages stronger emotional bonds and brand loyalty (Mustafa Ayobami Raji et al., 2024).

The transition from strictly transactional purchasing to immersive, experience-driven engagement is one of the biggest changes made possible by AI, AR, and VR in fashion retail. Conventional retail has historically emphasised the simple exchange of commodities, with buyers choosing items based on still photos or in-person inspections and completing transactions with little to no contact after the sale. However, this model has been reimagined as a result of the development of digital technology and shifting consumer expectations (Pereira et al., 2022). Customers of today look for significant experiences that amuse, uplift, and personally connect in addition to goods. This is made possible by AR and VR technologies, which provide environments in which consumers may engage with items in realistic ways, such as digitally putting on clothing, reading brand narratives, or taking part in virtual fashion shows. By making every encounter feel pertinent and customised, AI personalises these experiences, increasing user pleasure and engagement. Because users frequently post AR try-ons or VR experiences on social media, this immersive method also encourages social sharing and community development, which naturally expands brand reach (Kovács & Keresztes, 2024). Furthermore, the move towards immersive experiences is consistent with broader patterns in consumer behaviour, especially among younger generations that place a higher importance on digital integration, convenience, and personalisation. By restricting access to physical stores and forcing retailers to quickly innovate in digital engagement, the COVID-19 pandemic hastened this change. By restricting access to physical stores and forcing retailers to quickly innovate in digital engagement, the COVID-19 pandemic hastened this change. For example, AI stylists offer individualised advice that replicates the knowledge of in-store colleagues, and virtual fitting rooms ease the hassle of online purchasing by addressing fit and style issues up front. Additionally, these technologies allow firms to gather useful information about consumer preferences and behaviours, which can be utilised to improve supply chain efficiency, optimise product development, and fine-tune marketing campaigns (Adulyasak et al., 2024). By decreasing waste and encouraging more thoughtful consumption, the use of AI, AR, and VR in fashion retail not only improves customer experience and operational efficiency but also advances sustainability objectives. These technologies assist reduce return rates, which are a major source of environmental impact because of transportation emissions and discarded inventory, by increasing fit accuracy and personalisation. Digital showrooms and virtual try-ons allow firms to embrace more flexible and demand-driven production methods by eliminating the need for physical samples and surplus inventory. Additionally, immersive experiences inspire customers to interact with things more carefully, developing a greater respect for quality and craftsmanship over the disposable mentality of quick fashion. This change reflects the industry's increasing dedication to moral behaviour and environmental stewardship (Karadayi-Usta, 2024).

Fashion retail is being revolutionised by AI, AR, and VR, each of which has unique but complimentary roles to play. AR superimposes digital information on the real world to improve product visualisation and interaction; VR immerses customers in completely digital environments that increase the potential for brand engagement; and AI offers the intelligence and predictive power that propels personalisation and operational optimisation. When combined, these technologies turn the consumer journey from a transactional procedure into an engaging, personalised, and emotionally impactful experience (Uchechukwu Christopher Anozie et al., 2024). Fashion firms are being forced to embrace AI-powered AR and VR as strategic imperatives as a result of this development, which reflects broader shifts in customer expectations towards convenience, inclusion, and sustainability. These technologies will further transform how customers find, interact with, and buy fashion as they develop and become more integrated, establishing new benchmarks for creativity and involvement in the retail sector (Gauri et al., 2021).

CASE STUDIES OF COMMERCIAL FASHION BRANDS

AI Size Prediction and "See My Fit" AR Feature With its "See My Fit" tool, ASOS was the first to utilise augmented reality and artificial intelligence to boost online shoppers' confidence and lower return rates. "See My Fit," created in collaboration with the Israeli augmented reality startup Zeekit, lets buyers see apparel on 16 distinct virtual models in sizes 4–18, representing a range of body shapes (Kholoud FADEL, 2024). With consideration for size, shape, and fit, the AR technology digitally projects the outfit onto the chosen model in a realistic way, creating pictures that nearly mimic actual photos. This technology solves a major issue in online clothing shopping fit uncertainty by enabling users to visualise how an item may seem on a body shape similar to their own, enabling them to make better informed purchasing decisions. In addition, ASOS uses AI-powered size prediction tools, such the "Fit Assistant," which gathers user information like height, weight, age, and fit preferences in order to suggest the best size (Gill, 2015). It has been demonstrated that by boosting customer confidence and happiness, the combination of AR visualisation and AI sizing may improve online engagement and drastically lower return rates. A major advancement in the application of immersive technology for mass-market fashion retail was made when ASOS became the first European retailer to test this technology (Su, 2025).

AI Kiosks and AR Displays in Store Connecting Digital and Real-World Experiences In order to establish a smooth transition between digital interaction and real stores, H&M has embraced AI and AR. In order to improve the physical shopping experience with immersive technology, the company introduced in-store augmented reality displays that let shoppers virtually try on clothing and see digital fashion collections. In-store AI-powered kiosks also offer tailored product recommendations based on demographics, regional trends, and past browsing and purchase activity. AI examines regional sales trends and returns to optimise stock assortments for each location, guaranteeing that stores sell goods that suit local consumer tastes. This data-driven personalisation also extends to inventory management (Konina, 2023). In order to democratise access to fashion beyond the confines of physical stores, H&M is also investigating digital showrooms and fashion collections that are available worldwide. These programs demonstrate how H&M strategically uses AI and AR to close the gap between online convenience and brick-and-mortar stores, resulting in a hybrid shopping experience that boosts customer pleasure and engagement while promoting sustainability by cutting waste and overstock (Alanadoly et al., 2024).

Integration of AI Stylists for Trend, Climate, and User Preference-Based Customisation With a focus on supply chain optimisation, trend forecasting, and customised style, Uniqlo heavily utilises AI in its retail operations. To provide useful, everyday outfit suggestions that speak to customers' actual needs, the brand's AI stylist combines information on weather patterns, new fashion trends, and user preferences. AI-powered trend forecasting predicts popular styles and materials by analysing sales data, fashion events, and social media, allowing Uniqlo to effectively design and supply collections that satisfy current demand (Usui, 2024). AI-powered heat mapping in stores monitors how customers walk and interact with displays, enabling Uniqlo to improve product placements and store layouts for better shopping experiences. Supply chain automation minimises overstock and reduces stockouts by using predictive models to estimate demand and automate restocking. Additionally, Uniqlo's AI technologies enable dynamic pricing and personalised marketing, which customise offers for each unique customer. Uniqlo is positioned as a leader in integrating AI into everyday clothes retail because to this thorough integration, which also increases operational efficiency and provides a highly customised and convenient shopping experience (Nguyen et al., 2022).

Fitting rooms that are virtual AI and AR for Accessibility and Diverse Body Representation Walmart's dedication to improving online clothing purchasing using AI and AR-powered virtual fitting rooms is demonstrated by its acquisition of Zeekit, the same Israeli AR firm that partners with ASOS. Zeekit's platform promotes accessibility and diversity by allowing users to digitally try on clothes using digital avatars that represent a variety of body types, sizes, and races (Ivanov et al., 2023). Walmart consumers can now see how clothes fit and move on bodies similar to their own thanks to this technology, which boosts confidence while making purchases online and lowers return rates. Walmart overcomes common e-commerce obstacles like fit uncertainty and lack of tactile experience by combining AI-driven sizing suggestions with augmented reality visualisation. By reducing return waste and raising consumer happiness, this clever use of immersive technology advances Walmart's overarching objective of making fashion retail more simple, accessible, and sustainable ("Virtual Fashion," 2024). Together, these case studies show how top fashion shops are leveraging AI, AR, and VR to revolutionise the shopping experience. With data-driven sizing and personalised virtual try-ons, ASOS's "See My Fit" and AI size prediction address online fit issues. AI kiosks and augmented reality displays help H&M bridge the gap between digital and physical retail, improving inventory efficiency and personalisation. By using AI for trend forecasting, in-store behaviour research, and customised style, Uniqlo improves customer satisfaction and streamlines business processes. Walmart's virtual fitting rooms, powered by Zeekit, highlight accessibility and inclusion by representing a range of body types with AI and AR to increase customer trust. When taken as a whole, these developments demonstrate how important immersive and intelligent technologies are to increasing consumer engagement, decreasing returns, and developing sustainable fashion retail models (Mollel & Chen, 2025).

CONSUMER ACCEPTANCE AND ENGAGEMENT

The fashion industry's adoption of virtual reality (VR), augmented reality (AR), and artificial intelligence (AI) has changed how customers engage with companies, goods, and services. Even while these technologies have revolutionary potential—from virtual try-ons to personalized shopping experiences—their uptake is dependent on a number of intricate psychological, demographic, and practical considerations. Market statistics and recent research show a complex picture: consumers are cautiously optimistic about AI-designed clothing, with functionality taking precedence over expressiveness or beauty (Lee & Kim, 2024). Although worries about data privacy and technological complexity still exist, AR use has increased, especially among younger groups, because it may connect physical and digital retail experiences. There are clear generational differences as Gen Z adopts immersive technologies more quickly than previous generations due to familiarity and a need for interaction. However, obstacles including digital weariness, limits in interface design, and mistrust of data processing procedures still prevent broad adoption (Chan & Lee, 2023).

Customers assess AI-generated clothes pragmatically, giving more weight to usefulness than aesthetic value. The most positively regarded feature of AI-designed apparel, according to a 2024 survey of 505 American consumers, was practicality (such as comfort and durability), which scored 12% higher than aesthetics and 18%

higher than expressiveness. Since 72% of luxury buyers now demand AR try-on features as standard, augmented reality has evolved from a marketing gimmick to a vital retail tool. This change is motivated by observable advantages: Virtual fitting rooms increase conversion rates by 94% while decreasing return rates by 25–38% (Dubey et al., 2020). As demonstrated by Saks Fifth Avenue's virtual try-on program, which increased revenue per client by 19%, users report feeling more confident about their purchase selections while utilizing AR. With adoption concentrated on high-engagement scenarios like virtual fashion shows, virtual reality's role is still more specialized. 2.3 million people attended Balenciaga's 2023 virtual reality runway, which let viewers explore designs in a gamified setting. This is a 410% increase over their past in-person events (Choi & Lee, 2024).

Technology that makes buying easier is becoming more and more popular among time-constrained consumers. AR-integrated stores enable instantaneous product visualization in real-world scenarios, resulting in 94% greater conversion rates. For instance, by removing measuring guessing, Simply Wardrobes' augmented reality app, which projects virtual wardrobes into users' homes, raised revenue by 77% in just one month. Personalization tools driven by AI also lessen choice fatigue: Repeat purchase rates are increased by 35% using algorithms that examine surfing and previous purchase history. Notwithstanding these benefits, 68% of customers are hesitant to divulge biometric information (such as facial scans for virtual try-ons) for fear of abuse. Mistrust has increased as a result of high-profile breaches, such as the 2024 Charlotte Tilbury lawsuit over the improper keeping of facial geometry. Only 22% of AR apps provide a clear explanation of how user data is stored or monetized, indicating that transparency gaps still exist. Older consumers are disproportionately impacted by this opacity; compared to their Gen Z counterparts, customers aged 55 and beyond are 43% less likely to use AR technologies (Mahajan & Taggar, 2025).

Users' comfort level with digital interfaces has a strong correlation with adoption rates. 60% of Baby Boomers need tutorials or in-store help, whereas 81% of Gen Z can use AR apps with ease. This gap is made worse by complex UI design; apps with cluttered menus have 50% greater abandonment rates among inexperienced users. In order to combat this, companies such as Zara have integrated augmented reality navigation into their physical stores and used QR codes to initiate guided experiences. Gen Z customers, who were raised in an era of constant connectedness, are remarkably receptive to immersive technology (Perry et al., 2019).

KEY CHALLENGES IN IMPLEMENTATION

Despite its revolutionary potential, the incorporation of artificial intelligence (AI), augmented reality (AR), and virtual reality (VR) into fashion retail and creative processes is fraught with difficulties. Brands have to negotiate a challenging terrain of social, economic, and technological obstacles, from infrastructure constraints to moral conundrums. According to a 2025 industry analysis, 48% of fashion companies have difficulty ensuring algorithmic fairness in AI-driven suggestions, and 63% of them regard implementation costs as their biggest challenge. Rapid technological advancement has made these difficulties worse, necessitating constant adaptation to stay competitive. In order to chart the route toward sustainable implementation, this paper analyzes the key obstacles preventing broad acceptance and draws on technical studies, user feedback, and empirical data (Karimova et al., 2025).

There are significant hardware constraints on current AR/VR systems, especially when it comes to obtaining accurate body representation. Only 22% of users had compatible devices, despite the fact that high-end VR headsets like Meta Quest Pro offer 16K resolution for accurate virtual try-ons. A 2024 survey revealed that 68% of consumers thought digital clothing draping was "unnatural" on mobile AR platforms, indicating that most relied on smartphone-based AR, which has trouble simulating fabrics accurately. These problems are made worse by device fragmentation: With ARKit, Android devices process ARCore data 37% more slowly than their iOS equivalents, resulting in uneven user experiences. An additional level of complexity arises from integration with current retail systems. API endpoints for real-time AR/VR data synchronization are frequently absent from legacy inventory management systems. To link 3D product models with stock-keeping units (SKUs) for Zara's 2025 AR catalog deployment, a 14-month backend redesign was necessary, resulting in a $2.7 million middleware development expense. Such technical debt is expensive for smaller firms; according to 73% of regional labels, the main obstacle to AR adoption is the expense of app integration (Quattelbaum et al., 2022).

Despite declining development costs, the cost of basic AR/VR capabilities is still high. While AI-powered virtual try-ons demand $120,000 to $500,000 in machine learning infrastructure, a marker-based augmented reality software currently costs between $15,000 and $50,000. These numbers do not include recurring costs, such as the $18,000 in cloud rendering fees required to operate a 100-product VR showroom and the $7–$12 per user hour added for AI model retraining. These expenses take up 9–15% of marketing budgets for firms with yearly sales under $5 million, which is an unsustainable ratio considering current ROI timescales. 71% of consumers refuse to provide their body measurements for virtual fitting services, demonstrating the continued mistrust that consumers have for data handling procedures. Scrutiny has increased because to high-profile breaches, such the 2024 release of 1.2 million facial scans from a high-end AR app. Operational complexity is increased by adhering to changing legislation such as the EU's AI Act; for example, real-time emotion detection algorithms now need explicit opt-ins, which lowers adoption rates by 19% in pilot tests (Dhatrak et al., 2024).

FUTURE DIRECTIONS AND INNOVATIONS

With the quick development of AI, AR, VR, and immersive digital platforms, the fashion industry is poised for a technological revolution. The future of fashion will be characterized by emotional intelligence, customization, and the smooth transition between the real and virtual worlds as customer expectations change and digital-native generations assume a central role. Here are some of the most exciting trends and developments influencing fashion branding and retail in the coming years (Silvestri, 2020).

The fashion industry is changing as a result of generative AI. From basic text instructions or mood boards, sophisticated models such as DALL-E, Midjourney, and bespoke fashion AIs can produce unique patterns, silhouettes, and complete collections. AI is used as a co-creator by designers, who quickly prototype hundreds of iterations and make real-time adjustments based on user feedback. AI-powered systems examine each customer's body type, preferred styles, and even social media activity to recommend or create custom ensembles. Brands may now provide "made-to-order" collections thanks to AI, which cuts waste and supports sustainability objectives. Adidas introduced an AI-powered sneaker design platform in 2025 that allows users to collaborate on creating limited-edition sneakers. This tool has increased customer engagement by 32% and reduced unsold inventory by 40% (Alto, 2023).

By identifying and reacting to users' emotions in real time, emotion-aware AI has the potential to completely transform the shopping experience. Based on identified emotions, these systems can recommend colors, styles, or collections using computer vision, voice analysis, and biometric sensors (e.g., uplifting styles when a user appears down). Adapt the structure, speed, or tone of digital interactions to the emotional state of the customer. Create stronger bonds with your clients by helping them feel appreciated and understood. An emotion-aware virtual stylist was tested by a top luxury retailer, increasing session durations by 22% and increasing Gen Z shoppers' conversion rates (Qishu, 2024).

With AI and AR technology smoothly merging into platforms like TikTok, Instagram, and Snapchat, social commerce is also changing. The boundaries between content, community, and commerce are becoming more hazy thanks to shoppable AR filters, influencer-driven digital collections, and live shopping events. This is increasing engagement and conversion rates, especially among Gen Z and millennials. Meanwhile, a new area for fashion branding is developing: the metaverse. Companies are creating completely immersive virtual flagships where consumers can browse collections, go to virtual events, and buy digital and real products for their avatars and themselves. The combination of digital-only wearables and NFTs is increasing brand exclusivity and generating new revenue streams. Crucially, these developments are increasing access to underdeveloped markets and customers who prefer mobile devices (Scholz & Smith, 2016). While AI-driven localization guarantees that recommendations are inclusive of a variety of body types and culturally relevant, lightweight AR and AI applications designed for low-bandwidth areas are enabling sophisticated fashion experiences on older smartphones. Consequently, fashion is growing more innovative, democratic, and globally interconnected. In conclusion, hyper-personalization, emotional intelligence, and immersive digital interaction will characterize the next era of fashion, allowing firms to establish more meaningful connections with a wider range of consumers than in the past (Joy et al., 2022).

CONCLUSION

In summary, the fashion sector is entering a revolutionary period as a result of the quick uptake of AI, AR, and VR technologies, which is radically changing how companies interact with customers and provide value. Mass-market stores are now able to provide individualized, immersive, and interactive experiences that appeal to today's tech-savvy consumers thanks to what started out as exclusive tools for luxury businesses. By improving inventory management and lowering return rates, these technologies are increasing operational savings in addition to improving customer engagement and satisfaction through features like virtual try-ons, AI-driven recommendations, and inclusive digital fitting rooms.

Importantly, because virtual experiences can fit a variety of body sizes and preferences while reducing waste, the combination of AI, AR, and VR is assisting brands in addressing long-standing issues linked to sustainability and inclusion. The strategic use of these smart technologies is becoming crucial for brands looking to stay competitive and relevant as consumer expectations continue to change in a world that is mobile-first and socially connected. With the promise of even more realistic, imaginative, and emotionally compelling shopping experiences, the fashion industry is set to further embrace innovations like digital fashion, the metaverse, and AI-powered haptic feedback. The future of fashion retail will ultimately be redefined by the smooth integration of these technologies, which will promote stronger client relationships, increased inclusion, and sustainable growth in an increasingly digital environment.

In conclusion, the customer journey is being transformed from a transactional process to an immersive, interactive, and highly personalized experience thanks to the combination of artificial intelligence, augmented reality, and virtual reality. While AR and VR help consumers see products in their own environments or explore virtual stores and fitting rooms, AI's capacity to analyze large data sets allows brands to provide predictive fitting, personalized recommendations, and dynamic customer support. This convergence supports more sustainable retail operations by cutting waste and optimizing inventory, while also improving consumer pleasure and engagement and addressing long-standing issues like fit uncertainty and return rates. Whether through AI-driven size prediction, AR-powered virtual try-ons, or customized in-store and online experiences, case studies from top brands like ASOS, H&M, Uniqlo, and Walmart show how these technologies are being strategically deployed to boost accessibility, inclusivity, and operational efficiency. Fashion shops that want to stay competitive and relevant must seamlessly integrate AI, AR, and VR as consumer expectations continue to shift toward ease, personalization, and digital connectivity.

The fashion business is undergoing a fundamental transformation as a result of the integration of artificial intelligence, augmented reality, and virtual reality. This is changing the way that customers and brands interact throughout the whole customer journey. The widespread adoption of these technologies is influenced by a complex combination of generational preferences, trust issues, and technological barriers, even though they present previously unheard-of possibilities for personalization, convenience, and immersive engagement—such as virtual try-ons, AI-driven recommendations, and interactive digital showrooms. While older generations continue to be more hesitant, frequently put off by privacy concerns and complicated interfaces, younger consumers—particularly Gen Z—are setting the pace for adoption of these advances, appreciating the smooth blending of digital and physical experiences. Brands are reaping quantifiable benefits from the strategic application of AI, AR, and VR, such as increased brand distinction, lower return rates, better customer retention, and increased operational efficiency. By increasing accessibility to fashion and decreasing waste through improved fit prediction and on-demand production, these technologies are also advancing more general objectives of sustainability and inclusivity. Significant obstacles still exist, nevertheless, namely in the areas of implementation costs, data privacy, algorithmic fairness, and the requirement for constant technological advancements. Future developments like emotion-aware purchasing, generative AI for design, social commerce integration, and the emergence of the metaverse hold the potential to significantly transform fashion retail. These developments will increase access to underserved markets and mobile-first consumers in addition to strengthening client engagement. The ability of businesses to use these sophisticated, immersive technologies to produce more sustainable, inclusive, and meaningful experiences for a wide range of global consumers will ultimately determine the direction of fashion.

REFERENCES

Adulyasak, Y., Cohen, M. C., Khern-Am-Nuai, W., & Krause, M. (2024). Retail Analytics in the New Normal: The Influence of Artificial Intelligence and the Covid-19 Pandemic. *IEEE Engineering Management Review*, *52*(1), 268–280. DOI: 10.1109/EMR.2023.3337415

Akram, S. V., Malik, P. K., Singh, R., Gehlot, A., Juyal, A., Ghafoor, K. Z., & Shrestha, S. (2022). Implementation of Digitalized Technologies for Fashion Industry 4.0: Opportunities and Challenges. *Scientific Programming*, *2022*, 1–17. DOI: 10.1155/2022/7523246

Alanadoly, A. B., Sidhu, S. K., & Richards-Carpenter, N. (2024). AI Landscape in Fashion: Insights on Transforming Design, Supply Chains, Marketing, and Consumer Experiences. In Raj, P., Rocha, A., Dutta, P. K., Fiorini, M., & Prakash, C. (Eds.), *Illustrating Digital Innovations Towards Intelligent Fashion* (Vol. 18, pp. 417–439). Springer Nature Switzerland., DOI: 10.1007/978-3-031-71052-0_16

Alto, V. (2023). *Modern generative AI with ChatGPT and OpenAI models: Leverage the capabilities of OpenAI's LLM for productivity and innovation with GPT3 and GPT4*. Packt Publishing.

Anozie, U. C., Onyenahazi, O. B., Ekeocha, P. C., Adekola, A. D., Ukadike, C. A., & Oloko, O. A. (2024). Advancements in artificial intelligence for omnichannel marketing and customer service: Enhancing predictive analytics, automation, and operational efficiency. *International Journal of Science and Research Archive*, *12*(2), 1621–1629. DOI: 10.30574/ijsra.2024.12.2.1436

Aslam, U., & Davis, L. (2024). Analyzing consumer expectations and experiences of Augmented Reality (AR) apps in the fashion retail sector. *Journal of Retailing and Consumer Services*, *76*, 103577. DOI: 10.1016/j.jretconser.2023.103577

Barone, A. M., & Stagno, E. (2023). AI-powered Self-service Technologies. In A. M. Barone & E. Stagno, *Artificial Intelligence along the Customer Journey* (pp. 23–35). Springer Nature Switzerland. DOI: 10.1007/978-3-031-48792-7_2

Bucea-Manea-Ţoniş, R., Gurgu, E., Martins, O. M. D., & Simion, V. E. (2021). An Overview of How VR/AR Applications Assist Specialists in Developing Better Consumer Behavior and Can Revolutionize Our Life. In Dutta, T., & Mandal, M. K. (Eds.), *Consumer Happiness: Multiple Perspectives* (pp. 231–253). Springer Singapore., DOI: 10.1007/978-981-33-6374-8_12

Chan, C. K. Y., & Lee, K. K. W. (2023). The AI generation gap: Are Gen Z students more interested in adopting generative AI such as ChatGPT in teaching and learning than their Gen X and millennial generation teachers? *Smart Learning Environments*, *10*(1), 60. DOI: 10.1186/s40561-023-00269-3

Chaudhary, P., Raut, N., Patil, H., & Kate, N. (2024). Up-Skilling in Fashion Retail. In Malik, R., Sharma, A., & Chaudhary, P. (Eds.), *Transforming Education with Virtual Reality* (1st ed., pp. 323–336). Wiley., DOI: 10.1002/9781394200498.ch19

Choi, D., & Lee, H. (2024, January 20). AI-Designed Clothing and Perceived Values: What can Move Consumers' Minds with the AI-Designed Clothing? *Bridging the Divide*. Bridging the Divide. DOI: 10.31274/itaa.17098

Dear, K. (2019). Artificial Intelligence and Decision-Making. *RUSI Journal*, *164*(5–6), 18–25. DOI: 10.1080/03071847.2019.1693801

Dhatrak, M., Jadhav, S., Harkal, A., Kankrale, A., & Gupta, S. (2024). AI-Powered Virtual Try-On System: Enhancing Fit Prediction and User Comfort Through Deep Learning. *2024 5th International Conference on Communication, Computing & Industry 6.0 (C2I6)*, 1–6. DOI: 10.1109/C2I663243.2024.10895137

Dubey, A., Bhardwaj, N., Abhinav, K., Kuriakose, S. M., Jain, S., & Arora, V. (2020). *AI Assisted Apparel Design* (Version 2). arXiv. DOI: 10.48550/ARXIV.2007.04950

Enyejo, J. O., Obani, O. Q., Afolabi, O., Igba, E., & Ibokette, A. I. (2024). Effect of Augmented Reality (AR) and Virtual Reality (VR) experiences on customer engagement and purchase behavior in retail stores. *Magna Scientia Advanced Research and Reviews*, *11*(2), 132–150. DOI: 10.30574/msarr.2024.11.2.0116

Fashion, Virtual: Production and Display. (2024). The Frontiers of Society. *Science and Technology*, *6*(7). Advance online publication. DOI: 10.25236/FSST.2024.060720

Gauri, D. K., Jindal, R. P., Ratchford, B., Fox, E., Bhatnagar, A., Pandey, A., Navallo, J. R., Fogarty, J., Carr, S., & Howerton, E. (2021). Evolution of retail formats: Past, present, and future. *Journal of Retailing*, *97*(1), 42–61. DOI: 10.1016/j.jretai.2020.11.002

Gill, S. (2015). A review of research and innovation in garment sizing, prototyping and fitting. *Textile Progress*, *47*(1), 1–85. DOI: 10.1080/00405167.2015.1023512

Har, L. L., Rashid, U. K., Chuan, L. T., Sen, S. C., & Xia, L. Y. (2022). Revolution of Retail Industry: From Perspective of Retail 1.0 to 4.0. *Procedia Computer Science*, *200*, 1615–1625. DOI: 10.1016/j.procs.2022.01.362

Ivanov, A., Mou, Y., & Tawira, L. (2023). Avatar personalisation vs. Privacy in a virtual try-on app for apparel shopping. *International Journal of Fashion Design, Technology and Education, 16*(1), 100–109. DOI: 10.1080/17543266.2022.2125589

Joy, A., Zhu, Y., Peña, C., & Brouard, M. (2022). Digital future of luxury brands: Metaverse, digital fashion, and non-fungible tokens. *Strategic Change, 31*(3), 337–343. DOI: 10.1002/jsc.2502

Jung, J., Yu, J., Seo, Y., & Ko, E. (2021). Consumer experiences of virtual reality: Insights from VR luxury brand fashion shows. *Journal of Business Research, 130*, 517–524. DOI: 10.1016/j.jbusres.2019.10.038

Karadayi-Usta, S. (2024). Role of artificial intelligence and augmented reality in fashion industry from consumer perspective: Sustainability through waste and return mitigation. *Engineering Applications of Artificial Intelligence, 133*, 108114. DOI: 10.1016/j.engappai.2024.108114

Karimova, G., LeMay, S. A., Müller, A., & Klumpp, M. (2025). From the Shallows to the Shelves and Back: A Review, Synthesis, and Research Agenda for Socially Sustainable, AI -Driven Digital Fashion Supply Chains. *Business Ethics, the Environment & Responsibility*, beer.12839. DOI: 10.1111/beer.12839

Khatib, D. M. E., Al Falasi, F., Anani, H. A., & Shurrab, W. (2023). The Effect of Virtual Reality and Augmented Reality on Managing Projects. *2023 International Conference on Business Analytics for Technology and Security (ICBATS)*, 1–10. DOI: 10.1109/ICBATS57792.2023.10111112

Kholoud, F. A. D. E. L. (2024). *Understanding How Algorithms Shape Consumer Choices: A Retail Consumer Framework*. DOI: 10.5281/ZENODO.11544950

Kim, J.-H., Kim, M., Park, M., & Yoo, J. (2023). Immersive interactive technologies and virtual shopping experiences: Differences in consumer perceptions between augmented reality (AR) and virtual reality (VR). *Telematics and Informatics, 77*, 101936. DOI: 10.1016/j.tele.2022.101936

Konina, N. Yu. (2023). Artificial Intelligence in the Fashion Industry—Reality and Prospects. In Popkova, E. G., & Sergi, B. S. (Eds.), *Anti-Crisis Approach to the Provision of the Environmental Sustainability of Economy* (pp. 273–280). Springer Nature Singapore., DOI: 10.1007/978-981-99-2198-0_29

Kovács, I., & Keresztes, É. R. (2024). Digital Innovations in E-Commerce: Augmented Reality Applications in Online Fashion Retail—A Qualitative Study among Gen Z Consumers. *Informatics (MDPI), 11*(3), 56. DOI: 10.3390/informatics11030056

Lee, G., & Kim, H.-Y. (2024). Human vs. AI: The battle for authenticity in fashion design and consumer response. *Journal of Retailing and Consumer Services, 77*, 103690. DOI: 10.1016/j.jretconser.2023.103690

Mahajan, A. I., & Taggar, R. (2025). Augmented Reality Adoption: Exploring Security Concerns and Consumer Resourcefulness in the Era of Society 5.0. *International Social Science Journal, 75*(255), 241–259. DOI: 10.1111/issj.12548

Mollel, J., & Chen, Y. (2025). Does AR virtual try-on boost online apparel purchase intentions? An integration of TAM, IDT, FIT perception and body esteem. *Young Consumers, 26*(3), 385–402. DOI: 10.1108/YC-08-2024-2196

Nguyen, K., Le, M., Martin, B., Cil, I., & Fookes, C. (2022). When AI meets store layout design: A review. *Artificial Intelligence Review, 55*(7), 5707–5729. DOI: 10.1007/s10462-022-10142-3

Okeke, N. I., Alabi, O. A., Igwe, A. N., Ofodile, O. C., & Ewim, C. P.-M. (2024). AI in customer feedback integration: A data-driven framework for enhancing business strategy. *World Journal of Advanced Research and Reviews, 24*(1), 2036–2052. DOI: 10.30574/wjarr.2024.24.1.3207

Pakharuddin, N. D., & Kamarudin, S. (2023). Retail Sector Emerging Technologies: AI and Augmented Reality Present and Future Perspective. *2023 2nd International Engineering Conference on Electrical, Energy, and Artificial Intelligence (EICEEAI)*, 1–7. DOI: 10.1109/EICEEAI60672.2023.10590317

Patel, K. (2024). Revolutionizing Customer Experience: Integrating Blockchain with AR and VR in Retail. In B. Verma, A. Mittal, M. Raman, & B. Sindhav (Eds.), *Augmenting Retail Reality, Part B: Blockchain, AR, VR, and AI* (pp. 1–22). Emerald Publishing Limited. DOI: 10.1108/978-1-83608-708-320241003

Pereira, A. M., Moura, J. A. B., Costa, E. D. B., Vieira, T., Landim, A. R. D. B., Bazaki, E., & Wanick, V. (2022). Customer models for artificial intelligence-based decision support in fashion online retail supply chains. *Decision Support Systems, 158*, 113795. DOI: 10.1016/j.dss.2022.113795

Perry, P., Kent, A., & Bonetti, F. (2019). The Use of Mobile Technologies in Physical Stores: The Case of Fashion Retailing. In Piotrowicz, W., & Cuthbertson, R. (Eds.), *Exploring Omnichannel Retailing* (pp. 169–195). Springer International Publishing., DOI: 10.1007/978-3-319-98273-1_8

Pierdicca, R., Frontoni, E., Pollini, R., Trani, M., & Verdini, L. (2017). The Use of Augmented Reality Glasses for the Application in Industry 4.0. In De Paolis, L. T., Bourdot, P., & Mongelli, A. (Eds.), *Augmented Reality, Virtual Reality, and Computer Graphics* (Vol. 10324, pp. 389–401). Springer International Publishing., DOI: 10.1007/978-3-319-60922-5_30

Qishu, L. (2024). Implementation method of intelligent emotion-aware clothing systembased on nanofibre technology. *Industria Textila (Bucuresti), 75*(01), 3–14. DOI: 10.35530/IT.075.01.202379

Quattelbaum, B., Breckenfelder, C., Voigt, J., & Maas, L. (2022). Possibilities and limits of virtual and augmented reality in the purchase decision process for clothing. *Communications in Development and Assembling of Textile Products, 3*(1), 42–50. https://doi.org/DOI: 10.25367/cdatp.2022.3.p42-50

Raji, M. A., Olodo, H. B., Oke, T. T., Addy, W. A., Ofodile, O. C., & Oyewole, A. T. (2024). E-commerce and consumer behavior: A review of AI-powered personalization and market trends. GSC advanced research and reviews, 18(3), 066-077.

Scholz, J., & Smith, A. N. (2016). Augmented reality: Designing immersive experiences that maximize consumer engagement. *Business Horizons, 59*(2), 149–161. DOI: 10.1016/j.bushor.2015.10.003

Silvestri, B. (2020). The Future of Fashion: How the Quest for Digitization and the Use of Artificial Intelligence and Extended Reality Will Reshape the Fashion Industry After COVID-19. *ZoneModa Journal, V. 10 N. 2*, 61-73 Paginazione. DOI: 10.6092/ISSN.2611 0563/11803

Singh, H., & Kulkarni, P. (2023). *A review on application of modern AR/VR technologies in brand*. 050010. DOI: 10.1063/5.0175843

Su, B. (2025). *Ai-Driven Innovations for Sustainable E-Commerce Returns Management. SSRN*. DOI: 10.2139/ssrn.5126388

Upreti, K., Gangwar, D., Vats, P., Bhardwaj, R., Khatri, V., & Gautam, V. (2024). Artificial Neural Networks for Enhancing E-commerce: A Study on Improving Personalization, Recommendation, and Customer Experience. In Shaw, R. N., Siano, P., Makhilef, S., Ghosh, A., & Shimi, S. L. (Eds.), *Innovations in Electrical and Electronic Engineering* (Vol. 1115, pp. 141–153). Springer Nature Singapore., DOI: 10.1007/978-981-99-8661-3_11

Usui, T. (2024). Uniqlo: A Pathway to Becoming a Multinational Through Global Business Model Development. In Makino, S., Uchida, Y., & Kasahara, T. (Eds.), *Transformation of Japanese Multinational Enterprises and Business* (pp. 161–186). Springer Nature Singapore., DOI: 10.1007/978-981-99-8616-3_5

Viswanathan, J. (2024). Artificial Intelligence: Transforming the Future of Retail. [IJSR]. *International Journal of Science and Research (Raipur, India), 13*(9), 174–178. DOI: 10.21275/SR24901234506

Xie, Z., Yu, Y., Zhang, J., & Chen, M. (2022). The searching artificial intelligence: Consumers show less aversion to algorithm-recommended search product. *Psychology and Marketing, 39*(10), 1902–1919. DOI: 10.1002/mar.21706

Chapter 4 Rebranding Sustainability: A.I. as a Catalyst in Ethical Fashion Marketing

Pritesh Pradeep Somani
http://orcid.org/0000-0002-0039-0358
Balaji Institute of International Business, Sri Balaji University, Pune, India

Ushmita Gupta
http://orcid.org/0000-0002-6442-1248
Balaji Institute of International Business, Sri Balaji University, Pune, India

ABSTRACT

The widespread use of fast fashion has led to a complicated web of social, economic, and environmental issues, which has made an immediate ethical shift in the sector necessary. The crucial role that artificial intelligence (AI) plays as a strategic enabler in this sustainability journey has been examined in this chapter. It looks at how AI might rethink and redesign so as to reduce waste in the production processes and improve supply chains for increased transparency. The chapter also looks at AI's potential to transform consumer interaction and ethical marketing by promoting tailored messaging and establishing credibility & transparency. The chapter concludes that AI and sustainability have a symbiotic future, offering the means to create a new and more ethical narrative for the fashion industry while understanding the inherent difficulties and ethical issues.

DOI: 10.4018/979-8-2600-0303-9.ch004

INTRODUCTION: THE UNRAVELLING THREAD OF FAST FASHION

Fast fashion is a business model where clothing is created, produced, and sold quickly and cheaply to closely follow new trends in fashion. It is distinguished by the quick translation of runway or celebrity-inspired trends into mass-produced clothing for broad consumer markets. This approach places a strong emphasis on frequent inventory turnover, short product life cycles, and affordability. With an estimated market value of USD 1.7 trillion and the creation of jobs for over 300 million people globally, the fast fashion business is an important economic sector on a global scale. Zara, Shein, UNIQLO, Forever 21, and H&M are the major players in the fast fashion industry. On the contrary, some of these brands have faced allegations of greenwashing, wherein sustainability claims were found to be misleading or overstated, raising concerns about the credibility of environmental responsibility narratives within the industry.

Despite its glitz and inventiveness, the modern fashion business has long been associated with the unappealing themes of mass production, excessive consumption, and environmental damage. Since the turn of the twenty-first century, fast fashion has been a source of growth, and the production of clothing has increased exponentially. According to the forecasts, people are opting for less expensive clothing that is typically thrown away quickly, disregarding sustainable textiles and clothing quality (Hanan Samir Berry, 2020).

The ethical and ecological impact of the textile industry is a major concern, given the enormous amounts of water used in its manufacturing, the widespread problem of microplastic pollution, and the social inequalities that occur within global supply chains. 79 trillion Liters of water are used annually, and more than 92 million tons of garbage are generated because of the fashion business. Based on these environmental effects, we describe the necessity of a fundamental shift in the fashion industry's business strategy. The industry is facing several key changes: like a slowdown in manufacturing, the adoption of sustainable practices across the supply chain, and a change in how consumers shop. People are buying less new clothing and are making their garments last longer.(Niinimäki, 2020).

Fashion firms are under more pressure than ever to shift to sustainability as consumers grow more conscious and demanding and as authorities tighten their control. This change, which is known as ethical fashion branding, is more than just a fad; rather, it represents a fundamental reassessment of brand identity. Mitigating the climate catastrophe requires a shift toward responsible purchasing patterns in a variety of areas, including fashion. The importance stems from the predicted 63% rise in apparel consumption worldwide between 2015 and 2030.

In the span of 40 years from 1975 to 2018 has seen a 120% increase in textile production, which was in line with a rise in per capita fashion consumption from 5.9 to 13 kg. This increase has led to increased land use and resource consumption for this business, which has increased water pollution and greenhouse gas (GHG) emissions. Nowadays, people are buying more clothes, and in order to boost sales, these things are being sold for less money; this is known as fast fashion. (Olivar Aponte, 2024).

Although the goal of sustainability is admirable, there are frequently difficulties in putting it into practice. It is challenging for companies to effectively monitor and reduce their environmental and social impact due to the industry's convoluted and opaque supply chains and ineffective legacy procedures. For instance, it has become commonplace for UK clothing retailers to create CSR policies in response to the growing demand for ethical apparel. These policies influence their supplier agreements and garment sourcing practices. Retailers are increasingly offering ethical clothing lines manufactured by Fair Trade producers or using organic cotton. (Goworek, 2011).

AI has made considerable advances into fast fashion sector, delivering novel technology solutions, more effective operational procedures, and access to vital consumer and industry data. In the ever-changing world of today, businesses who use AI effectively have a competitive edge. Initially, executives in the creative and expressive fashion industry were uninterested in AI automation. But as we move into the hyper-digital era, AI technologies could completely transform the fashion industry and generate significantly more growth and income than those that stick to more conventional methods.

AI has a very big impact on the fashion industry, affecting every phase from production and design to marketing, sales, and shipping.

Moreover, Artificial intelligence (AI) technologies, such as Internet of Things (IoT), blockchain, machine learning and predictive analytics are no longer merely sci-fi ideas. They are becoming into essential tools that may assist brands in reorganizing all aspect of their business, from marketing and customer engagement to design and production. This chapter will explore how AI is a strategic driver for ethical transformation rather than just an efficiency tool, significantly altering consumer perceptions of sustainability and brand positioning. These tools are touted as game-changing technologies that reduce waste, increase transparency, and lessen overproduction. Solutions like strategic partnerships and R&D expenditures are explored alongside problems like exorbitant prices, rapid fashion tastes, and a lack of recycling techniques. (Deeksha Gupta Ganguly, 2025)

ETHICAL IMPERATIVES IN THE FASHION INDUSTRY

The shortcomings of the traditional fast-fashion paradigm are directly addressed by the idea of ethical fashion. (Sustainability in Fashion and Textiles, 2013). The goal of ethical fashion is to create apparel in a way that safeguards the environment and people. To safeguard people, ethical fashion prioritizes making sure that employees receive fair treatment, are employed in secure settings, and have their rights upheld. To preserve the environment, ethical fashion makes sure that resources are sourced ethically, that production doesn't damage the environment but rather enhances it, and that fashion delight extends beyond consumption to encompass other circular possibilities. It includes a wide range of actions meant to reduce damage to the environment and to humans. (bluedesign, n.d.).

A major change is occurring in the contemporary fashion business, which is well-known for its substantial effects on the environment and society. Fashion firms are being urged by a growing movement to embrace ethical methods that address the detrimental impacts of the industry. These ideas are revolutionizing the design, manufacture, and consumption of apparel, fostering a more ethical and sustainable sector. Fast fashion has grown astronomically as a result of conspicuous consumption and has an impact on social justice, ecological sustainability, and economic sustainability. One possible solution to all these problems is the efficient marketing of sustainable fashion. Three fundamental pillars—economic viability, social justice, and environmental responsibility—have made this shift more than just a fad. (Ray & Nayak, 2023)

1. **Environmental Responsibility:** Fast Fashion industry is the second largest polluters in the world, it contributes significantly to textile waste, chemical pollution, and water usage. These problems are made worse by the "take-make-dispose" business model used by fast fashion. Fast fashion comes at an astonishing environmental and social cost. Brands that embrace environmental responsibility must lessen their ecological impact. This entails employing environmentally friendly resources such as recycled fibres and organic cotton, utilizing circular economy models to cut waste, and embracing production methods that save energy and water. Brands may reduce their carbon footprint and attract the increasing number of environmentally concerned consumers by putting the health of the world first. (Environmental Sustainability in the Fashion Industry, 2025).

Businesses should prioritize using materials like recycled polyester, hemp, and organic cotton in order to reduce waste and resource consumption; they should also use zero-waste cutting and recycling to reduce waste; they should use efficient technologies like drip irrigation and renewable energy to conserve water and energy; and they should use low-impact materials and sustainable farming practices to minimize carbon emissions.

Waste is disposed of by businesses as well as by customers who discard clothing. Preconsumer waste, sometimes referred to as production waste, is made up of fibres, yarn, and fabric waste from scrap or unused materials that are produced during the clothes manufacturing process. Deadstock is another type of pre-consumer trash that is frequently disregarded. Deadstock is made up of brand-new, unused clothing that has been returned or unsold and is classified as waste by businesses. There are reports that there are companies incinerating brand new clothing, this further generates carbon emissions. Another facet of quick fashion is post-production waste which is used and disposed by the consumers. (Bansal, 2024)

2. **Social Equity and Labour Ethics:** The fashion business has a long history of social injustice in addition to environmental harm. The global supply chain frequently takes advantage of underprivileged populations, from low pay and hazardous working conditions to problems with racial and gender inequalities. Ensuring fair labour standards and human dignity for all workers, from farmers to factory workers, is what social equity in fashion means. This entails providing safe working conditions, offering a liveable salary, and encouraging diversity and inclusion at all organizational levels.

Transparency is a goal of ethical brands so that customers can know that the people who created their clothes were treated fairly and with respect. At its most basic level, social equity in fashion refers to justice and fairness in the fashion sector. This qualification explores the significance of how fashion affects people and communities worldwide, going beyond simple aesthetics and trends. The term includes making certain that everyone involved, from consumers to garment workers, has fair access to resources, opportunities, and courteous treatment. It pushes the sector to abandon exploitative methods and adopt a paradigm that prioritizes shared prosperity and human dignity. (Lorne Michael Cousins).

This preliminary interpretation is essential to comprehending the ensuing intricacies of social justice in the form of equitable and fair distribution of social resources in this field. It ensures that all workers along the supply chain receive fair compensation, have secured working conditions, and moral treatment in the organisation (Patsy Perry, 2018).

3. **Economic Viability and Long term Value Creation:** Although many people believe that ethical fashion is too costly, it is increasingly evident that sustainable methods can eventually be profitable. The conventional fast fashion strategy is vulnerable to supply chain concerns and public reaction since it relies on

inexpensive labour and materials. On the other hand, ethical brands prioritize quality and durability over quantity to create a more robust business strategy. A stronger brand reputation and increased consumer loyalty are the results of this strategy. Additionally, cutting-edge company strategies like clothes rentals, repair services, and second-hand markets foster a circular economy and generate new revenue streams, demonstrating that purpose and prosperity can coexist.

Economically, the fashion sector has mostly been outsourced to the Far East, which has destroyed once-thriving European economies in several places. (Our vision of fashion in a circular economy, 2023). In terms of the environment, harmful textile processes and dyes have harmed natural ecosystems and increased irrigation water demands. Developing a lucrative company plan while adhering to ethical and sustainable standards (Sasha N. Sarokin, 2024).

The industry is changing for the better due to the shift toward ethical fashion, which is motivated by the ideas of social justice, environmental responsibility, and economic sustainability. This shift aims to create a new paradigm where brands prosper by putting people and the environment first, not only lessening harm. The fashion industry can transform from a significant contributor to global issues into a potent force for good by adopting sustainable practices, fair labour standards, and circular business models, demonstrating that a prosperous company and a sustainable future are not mutually contradictory.

Merely implementing these strategies is insufficient for a brand. Communicating these initiatives in an authentic manner to a sceptic and knowledgeable customer base is the real problem. This is what ethical fashion branding is all about. It involves integrating sustainability into a brand's storyline, establishing credibility, and cultivating a strong bond with customers who share these ideals. As marketing evolved, businesses were able to deliberately craft their brands. The results of Aaker's Dimension model showed five strong dimensions: sincerity, excitement, competence, sophistication, and ruggedness. These dimensions are also comparable to the Big-5 human personality scale. (Moura, 2021)

ARTIFICIAL INTELLIGENCE AS A CATALYST FOR SUSTAINABLE FASHION

In the quest for sustainability, artificial intelligence (AI) is a potent strategic enabler that provides creative answers to some of the most important environmental and social issues facing the globe. AI can boost resource management, expedite procedures, and encourage better decision-making in a range of businesses by employing its capacity to analyse vast volumes of data and discover nuanced patterns. (Brynjolfsson, 2014)

In recent years, artificial intelligence as well as machine learning have transformed some of the major industries like transportation, healthcare, banking, education, and entertainment This has led to major improvements in accuracy and efficiency in the organisations. ML models have had to get more complicated to perform better, which means there are more parameters to estimate. These developments do have a price, though, since the resources needed to train and operate these models have increased dramatically. (Verónica Bolón-Canedo, 2024)

Environmental projects can be significantly enhanced by AI's capacity to predict outcomes and optimize systems. AI systems may, for instance, analyse real-time data in the energy industry to estimate energy demand to lessen dependency on fossil fuels., improve grid distribution, and more successfully integrate renewable energy sources.

Moreover, AI-powered agricultural systems use satellite and sensor data to guide precision farming, which increases crop yields while using less water, fertilizer, and pesticide. In addition to helping with waste management by offering intelligent sorting and recycling systems, artificial intelligence (AI) can be used for environmental monitoring, such as tracking deforestation using satellite imagery or identifying pollution sources.

REIMAGINING FASHION SUPPLY CHAINS THROUGH AI

Supply chain optimization can be greatly aided by AI solutions, which offer automation, enhanced analytics, and predictive capabilities. Businesses may improve their overall ability to respond to market changes, increase productivity, reduce costs, and streamline their supply chains with the help of AI technologies in various ways. Integrating AI into current systems and procedures and encouraging an organizational culture of data-driven decision-making are frequently necessary for successful implementation. (Baukh, 2024)

One of the biggest hurdles to sustainable fashion is the lack of visibility within complex global supply chains. AI integrates a number of important technologies to play an essential role in creating a sustainable and transparent supply chain. Businesses that are ethical and environmentally responsible need to maximize operations and increase visibility, which these technologies offer. AI-powered systems can provide a new level of transparency and efficiency The creation of an open and sustainable supply chain is greatly aided by artificial intelligence. By combining three essential technologies—predictive analytics, blockchain, and the Internet of Things (IoT), it is completely changing how businesses run their operations. (Behare, Bhosale, Sharma, Shitole, & Sane, 2024)

As we know, supply chain optimization and sustainability go hand in hand. Eco-friendly practices, waste minimization, and carbon footprint reduction could assist businesses in developing a more sustainable global supply chain. Modern technology, data-driven decision-making, and collaboration are all used in supply chain optimization. Businesses that optimize experience resilience, cost savings, efficiency, and customer satisfaction. A good supply chain is essential for businesses to stay profitable and for the global economy to thrive, especially in today's increasingly complicated market.(Surjeet Dalal a, 2024). Some of the important tools are enumerated below:

- **Predictive Analytics for Demand Forecasting:** The ethical fashion movement, which places a high value on sustainability, openness, and ethical labour standards, is at the front of this development. However, ethical fashion companies frequently have major operational difficulties, especially when predicting customer demand precisely. Since ethical manufacturers seek to reduce waste and prevent overstocking, accurate demand forecasting is not only a financial problem but also a moral requirement, in contrast to fast fashion, which lives on overproduction and rapid inventory turnover.

This is where AI through predictive analysis can analyse historical sales data, social media trends, and even based on weather patterns to create highly accurate forecasts of demand. This helps brands produce only what is needed, significantly reducing overproduction and the resulting waste.

Brands like Zara, Nike, Amazon, and Stitch Fix have already changed their decision-making processes in mainstream retail and fashion thanks to predictive analytics. Even though these labels might not all be considered “ethical,” ethical fashion companies can use the same resources and techniques to guarantee data-driven sustainability—by just creating what is required, when required, and nothing more. Some of the companies are also using Google Cloud AI and AWS forecast as well to scale up their forecasting operations with built in AI based infrastructure (Oyebode Kayode, 2025).

By utilizing data and predictive analytics, artificial intelligence (AI) is transforming the analysis of fashion trends. AI supports and improves the process of fashion trend analysis in various ways, like:

AI analyses the habits of the consumer and their shopping patterns to understand what drives fashion choices. This data makes it easier for companies to tailor their products and marketing to better suit what customers want. AI facilitates market segmentation according to geography, demography, and other pertinent variables.

By ensuring that fashion products are suited to certain target audiences, this segmentation enables a more detailed grasp of regional or specialty trends.

AI helps with tracking and evaluating rivals' tactics in the fashion sector. Businesses can modify their strategies to remain competitive by knowing what works in the market.

AI also makes it possible to monitor the social media sites and websites which are pertaining to fashion in real time. Artificial intelligence (AI) systems instantly reveal which trends are becoming increasingly popular by monitoring hashtags, mentions, and engagement metrics.

In the fashion sector, predictive analytics is revolutionizing ethical brands by enabling them to make more responsible and sustainable choices. These businesses can eliminate guesswork and only produce what is required by using AI to analyse enormous volumes of data. This creates a potent synergy between technology and sustainability and not only boosts their bottom line but also reflects their basic principles of encouraging ethical behaviours and minimizing waste (Baukh, 2024).

- **Blockchain for Traceability:** Blockchain technology makes the supply chains transparent and traceable by securely tracking the assets and recording transactions on a decentralized network. By confirming the origins of materials and products, blockchain technology in the fashion industry may prevent counterfeiting activities, guarantee product authenticity, and encourage sustainable practices as well.

Blockchain technology, often integrated with AI, creates a secure, decentralized, and immutable record of every step a garment takes—starting from the source of its raw materials to its final point of sale. This combats problems like greenwashing by enabling customers to track a product's route and validate its ethical claims. (Omkar Singh, 2024). For example, one of the popular fast fashion brands, H&M has positioned itself as sustainability conscious brand with initiatives like ‘conscious collection’. These claims project the brand as eco friendly and emphasizes] the use of sustainable materials, recycled polyester, and organic cotton.

- **IoT for Real-Time Monitoring:** By linking items and devices, the Internet of Things is transforming the fashion sector and establishing an intelligent network that improves customer satisfaction and operational effectiveness. RFID tags, smart fabrics, and connected gadgets are examples of Internet of Things technologies that allow for real-time tracking of inventories, decrease loss and theft, and increase supply chain transparency. Body metrics can be tracked using smart textiles with sensors integrated, providing capabilities beyond that of conventional apparel. These developments open the door for goods that monitor health indicators, adjust to changing environmental circumstances, or communicate with other gadgets, adding new levels of customization and value to the fashion industry.

IoT sensors can also be used to monitor environmental conditions in factories, such as water and energy consumption, in real time. After being analysed by AI algorithms, this data offers practical suggestions for increasing the productivity and cutting down on the resource consumption. IoT devices gather data in real time about various client interactions, such as location, product usage, browsing history, and buying patterns. (Ushmita Gupta, 2024)

REDEFINING DESIGN AND PRODUCTION WITH AI

The biggest environmental effects are identified in the early phases of clothing design and manufacture. Fashion firms may radically change to a more ethical and sustainable paradigm by incorporating artificial intelligence (AI) into these core procedures in a planned way. This will cut waste and promote resource efficiency. In our opinion, generative AI is about acceleration and augmentation rather than merely automation. This entails providing technology to fashion experts and creatives so they may complete some jobs significantly faster and devote more time to duties that are unique to people. Additionally, it entails developing mechanisms to improve customer service (Mondalek, 2023).

- **Generative Design and Production Optimization:** A revolutionary approach to design is provided by generative AI, which produces inventive patterns and silhouettes that are by nature more sustainable. By maximizing the utilization of raw materials, this technology goes beyond aesthetics. Pattern nesting optimization is the method by which AI models may simulate an infinite number of fabric layouts to determine the most effective way to arrange and cut pattern elements. By drastically reducing fabric waste, this advanced geometric analysis helps manufacturers get closer to a zero-waste manufacturing strategy. The system guarantees that every square inch of material is used efficiently by visualizing these intricate arrangements, which directly contributes to cost savings and environmental preservation. Traditionally, fashion designers invest a lot of work in making unique prints and patterns. These days, generative AI helps with this process by creating original designs in response to predetermined guidelines or style references. For example, to develop fresh hues and patterns for their existing styles, Adidas has experimented with AI-generated shoe designs. Machine learning is used in the company's FutureCraft effort to produce design alternatives that might not be possible with just conventional human inventiveness. (Dilmegani, Cem, 2025)

Beyond surface patterns, generative AI can be used to build textile structures. By learning from pre-existing textile databases, MIT researchers have created systems that can produce new fabric weave patterns. Automated weaving machinery can subsequently be used to physically create these AI-generated structures. (Dilmegani, Cem, 2025)

- **Sustainable Sourcing and Material Innovation:** At the core of fashion are materials, leather, and textiles. They define its essential essence like the material, its structure, its texture, colour, touch, and behaviours express its appeal, is inextricably tied to the volume, feel, aspect, and overall character of a garment. Textiles are also one of the most intricate materials. An almost infinite number of options are made possible by the various properties of fibres, as well as by their preparation, yarn assembly, treatments, finishes, structural combinations, and printing methods. The ideal combination of qualities comes from the extensive knowledge and traditional craftsmanship of textile designers, traditional weavers, ancestral knitters, and the manufacturers. Every combination contributes to the unique individuality of a cloth. The development of artificial intelligence is making it a vital tool for tackling these issues like resource efficiency, clean chemistry, waste reduction, material innovation, and recycling techniques. Let us examine how these important sectors of material development are being transformed by AI.

i. Large datasets covering a material's whole lifecycle, from its genesis to its end of life, can be analysed by AI-driven machine learning algorithms. This makes it possible for brands to make supply chain decisions based on data. Important parameters, such as energy and water consumption and the carbon footprint of different textiles, can be processed and assessed by the algorithms. Innovative sustainable materials like mycelium leather, recycled polyester, and bio-based polymers being discovered and adopted more quickly thanks to these capabilities. AI helps brands choose substitutes that support their sustainability objectives and lessen their overall ecological impact by giving each material a thorough environmental profile. For example, EUCOTTON regenerative cotton suppliers in Spain are already using this technology to improve production efficiency and consume less water.

ii. AI can optimize the usage of raw materials from the extraction stage through precision blending, which involves analysing the properties of various fibres to recommend the best blends and enhance yarn quality while cutting down on waste from rejected ingredients. Raw material allocation is another axis. AI models assist firms minimize overordering and material waste by forecasting the quantity of raw fibres needed to reach production targets. For example, AI is already being used by businesses like Smartex and Oshima to detect fabric flaws, minimizing waste by halting production when problems are discovered. They use cloud-based quality control that analyse fabric rolls at a very high speed and ensures the minimum loss of material.
iii. AI is also helping the fashion sector transition to a circular economy, where textiles may be reused instead of ending up in landfills, and reducing post-production waste, which tackles the major issue of overproduction.AI makes it possible to recycle and possibly reuse the fibres more quickly and efficiently, from sorting robotization to material identification and blend separation. For example, company called Newretex, uses robots to sort textile waste according to material composition and colour identification, NIR (near-infrared) sensors and cameras are among its essential tools.
iv. Lastly, 3D visualisation of materials is one of the most effective ways to prevent overproduction while also releasing design originality. While material simulation and color control remain extremely challenging to convert into physical reality, platforms such as ColorDigital GmbH's DMix are striving to improve digital texture mapping accuracy in order to capture the smallest details and nuances of a variety of materials. For example, companies like Vizoo, (3D scanner and software for photorealistic 3D visualization), VSK Technology, (whose NAO Virtual Knitting Machine can realise 100 different fabric constructions per second and display these on screen in real time) and Hohenstein Fitting Lab which are actively using the digital simulation techniques. (Fashion meets AI: The next step in material innovation, 2024)

- **On-Demand Manufacturing:** AI plays a key role in the fashion industry's transition from large-scale, speculative production runs to an on-demand, or made-to-order, manufacturing model. This strategy does away with the requirement for expensive deadstock and extra inventory, thereby addressing the widespread issue of overproduction. AI can automate every step of the process for bespoke or customized products, from the customer's specific request to the design's automated creation and delivery to a nearby production partner. This makes the supply chain more responsive and effective by reducing waste and directly matching output to customer demand. This phase's incorporation of AI guarantees that clothing is only manufactured once a buyer has been confirmed, radically altering the production and consumption of fashion goods.

AI's contribution to the fashion industry is growing quickly as developments in automation, computer vision, and predictive analytics make the sector more sustainable and effective. Soon, AI should be able to do things like.

- AI-powered fashion assistants can improve personalization.
- Enhance sustainability through improved trash reduction and recycling strategies.
- Boost supply chain management and production efficiency. (inGrade)

AI-POWERED ETHICAL MARKETING AND CONSUMER ENGAGEMENT

A crucial and developing topic, ethical marketing using AI is concerned with applying AI in a way that respects consumer rights, fosters trust, and adheres to moral standards. AI presents major ethical issues that marketers need to solve even while it provides strong capabilities for efficiency and customisation.

Using ethical AI in marketing offers substantial commercial advantages that go beyond risk control. Businesses may gain trust and brand loyalty by handling customer data responsibly and transparently. This improves their reputation and gives them a competitive advantage. By guaranteeing adherence to data regulations and avoiding expensive penalties, this proactive strategy also helps reduce legal and financial risks. Additionally, by protecting user privacy and offering truly beneficial and pertinent material, ethical AI improves the consumer experience. Finally, businesses may expand their audience and integrate their marketing with social responsibility by tackling algorithmic prejudice and promoting diversity and fairness.

Businesses should prioritize data governance and create clear policies to ensure responsible data gathering and security in accordance with international legislation before implementing an ethical AI marketing framework. For AI systems to remain fairness and adhere to the ethical standards, regular, objective audits are essential. Additionally, it's critical to train staff members on the ethical implications of their job and to promote openness with consumers by being open and honest about the use of AI. Lastly, also preserving human oversight is essential to guaranteeing that judgments produced by AI are examined and verified, particularly for high-risk applications.

Fashion industry's innovation processes in design, production, marketing, and consumer relations are already being altered by artificial intelligence (AI). assistance. In the fashion business, the application of AI technologies—especially generative AI like ChatGPT—has produced creative results and enhanced the workflows in the companies. (Sanjida Sumaia Mimmo, 2025).

The goal of rebranding is to shift consumer perception. AI provides novel ways to tell a brand's sustainability story, building trust and fostering a community of conscious consumers. For example, customers need to trust a brand for them to think that it will live up to its promises. Customers of Apple have faith that their Apple watches and phones will live up to the company's promises (Kotler, n.d.).

The fashion business is being redefined by AI-driven platforms that enable consumers to customize apparel. Customers can choose from a wide range of customization options on these platforms by using AI algorithms. These possibilities include choosing fabrics, colours, and designs, as well as adding personal touches like embroidery or monograms. Consumers can design one-of-a-kind items that suit their own tastes and fashion sense. By assisting clients in making design decisions and offering visual samples of the finished product, AI makes sure that the customizing process is smooth and easy to use. This improves the purchasing experience and satisfies the rising fashion need for uniqueness and self-expression. Customers and fashion brands benefit from AI-powered customization since it increases consumer happiness and product uniqueness.

Fashion brands must comprehend the consumer behaviour so as to customize their products and make well-informed decisions. AI plays a key role in this by thoroughly evaluating consumer data. To learn more about consumer behaviour, artificial intelligence (AI) algorithms analyse data from a variety of sources, including browser history, online purchases, and brand interactions. AI may assist fashion firms in better understanding their target market by spotting patterns and trends. AI technologies have enabled the efficient processing and analysis of vast volumes of market research data. They can gather and examine data from a variety of sources, such as consumer sentiment, social media trends, and industry studies. Fashion companies may learn a lot from this data about customer trends, rival tactics, and changing consumer tastes.

Applications for augmented reality (AR) try-on have revolutionized the online apparel and accessory shopping. Customers can use cell phones or other devices to virtually try on fashion goods thanks to augmented reality. AR offers a realistic and engaging try-on experience by superimposing digital apparel models onto the customer's real-world photos or live videos. Consumers can make more assured selections about what to buy by seeing how a specific item of clothing fits and matches their personality. AR try-on improves the online purchasing and lowers the amount of ambiguity involved in online clothes purchases, which increases consumer satisfaction and lowers return rates. (Takyar, 2023)

Customer experience has been redefined as a result of the COVID-19 epidemic, shifting buying habits from offline to online, and the quick advancement of artificial intelligence (AI). This shift has created profitable opportunities for businesses to use chatbots to engage with customers and improve customer service. The purpose of this study was to investigate the characteristics of AI chatbots that influence the online consumer experience in the e-retailing industry. (Chee, The impact of AI chatbot adoption on customer experience in e-retailing, 2025)

Figure 1. (Source: https://techpacker.com/blog/design/how-artificial-intelligence-is-revolutionizing-the-fashion-industry/)

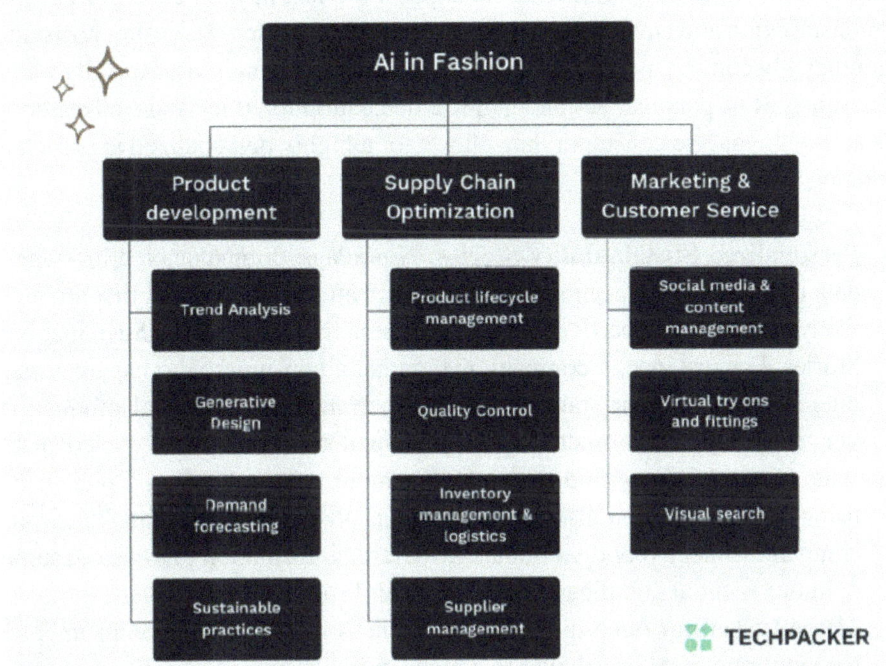

PERSONALIZATION AND RESPONSIBLE TARGETED MESSAGING

Targeted messaging and customisation have emerged as essential strategies for influencing consumer behaviour and maintaining competitiveness in the fast fashion sector. Brands build highly customized experiences by utilizing a tremendous quantity of client data, such as demographics, social media activity, browsing history, and purchase trends. This can include dynamic website layouts that highlight products depending on a user's previous interests, as well as tailored product recommendations and special offers delivered straight to a customer's phone or email. In addition to raising average order values and conversion rates, this tactic promotes customer loyalty and a smoother shopping experience. Moreover, in e-commerce for fashion, collaborative filtering can be used to improve customisation. But there are drawbacks to this degree of targeting. Concerns about data privacy and possible customer manipulation can arise from the unrelenting quest for hyper-personalization. Furthermore, ethically conscious consumers, particularly Gen Z, who are becoming more conscious of the industry's social and environmental effects, are increasingly criticizing the marketing strategies that support the fast fashion cycle for causing overconsumption and environmental waste. In order to preserve consumer trust in a sector that is becoming increasingly scrutinized, organizations must carefully weigh the advantages of personalization against a dedication to ethics and transparency. AI's ability to analyse consumer data allows for a highly personalized approach to marketing

- **Personalized Sustainability Stories:** Nowadays, companies are leveraging data to highlight environmentally friendly features of a product that are most likely to appeal to a particular customer using the Personalized Sustainability Stories. For instance, a company may target a consumer who has expressed interest in fair labour standards with a narrative about ethical production, whereas another customer may be presented content about recycled materials. Customers may find sustainability more approachable and personable using this tactic, but it also raises questions about "greenwashing," in which companies selectively disseminate favourable information to sway consumer opinions without significantly altering their broader business plan.
- **Micro-targeting:** According to TrendBible 'A micro trend is a consumer behaviour trend that is particular to a niche or industry, ready for the mass market, and actionable. Micro trends, which have a shorter lifespan than macro trends, typically trickle down from the former and give marketers, designers, and innovators a chance to capitalize on these new consumer attitudes.' (TrendBible, 2023). Using micro-targeting, marketers can precisely divide up their audience and send messages that speak to particular values and habits.

Brands may give highly customized marketing content by identifying certain consumer groups, such as those interested in vegan leather or locally produced products, by analysing large databases. This has the potential to make marketing campaigns more successful, but it also runs the danger of deceiving customers. Since brands use targeted messaging to create a perception of sustainability that doesn't align with their actual business operations, hyper-personalized, value-driven marketing that lacks a genuine commitment to sustainable practices may ultimately mislead consumers and feed the fast fashion cycle.

BUILDING TRANSPARENCY AND TRUST

Trust is the bedrock of ethical fashion branding. AI can facilitate a new level of transparency that goes beyond simple claims (Swaminathan, 2019). In the fashion industry, supply chain transparency refers to a company's capacity to completely reveal details about its manufacturing process. This contains information on where raw materials are sourced, the production facilities that are used, and the working conditions at every level. This entails providing consumers with the knowledge they need to make well-informed decisions about what to buy and to match those selections with their beliefs.

A major change from conventional, linear models to more dynamic and responsive systems is represented using AI in fashion supply chains. The potential of AI to establish circular supply chains—where resources are used more effectively and waste is reduced—is highlighted by various academic studies. In addition to tracking products, this entails assisting with material reuse, recycling, and repurposing. Reverse logistics optimization, which makes sure that commodities are put back into the supply chain for future use, can be greatly aided by AI. (Directory, 2025).

In addition, AI-powered chatbots on a brand's website can provide instant, detailed answers to customer questions about sustainability practices, materials, and labour standards, making information readily available and fostering a sense of openness (Chee, 2025).

CHALLENGES AND ETHICAL CONSIDERATIONS IN AI ADOPTION

(Gorkhe, Kudare, Behare, Kulkarni, & Waghulkar, July,2024)While the potential of AI is vast, its adoption is not without its challenges and ethical dilemmas. The fast fashion business has long been criticized for its negative effects on the environment and society because of its quick production cycles and cheap prices. A new set of ethical issues has surfaced as technology becomes increasingly integrated into its operations, especially with regard to data gathering and utilization. Although the industry's reliance on AI and advanced analytics increases productivity, it also presents serious issues with algorithmic fairness, data privacy, and the human aspect. A more comprehensive understanding of the ethical impact of rapid fashion can be obtained by looking at these problems.

- **Gathering Large databases:** Fast fashion companies gather a ton of customer data to tailor marketing, optimize supply chains, and forecast trends. A customer's past purchases, surfing habits, social media activities, and even body measurements from virtual fitting rooms are all included in this. This data collection is unique in its speed and scope. The technique itself raises concerns about customer consent and the true purpose of the data, even though this "big data" can help prevent overproduction by more precisely estimating demand. An ecosystem of hyper-personalization and targeted advertising can be made possible by the unrelenting pursuit of consumer insights, which can result in the development of comprehensive profiles that go far beyond a basic purchasing history. (Directory, 2025)
- **Data Privacy and Security:** There are serious concerns to data security and privacy when such a vast database is gathered. Because of their enormous digital footprints, fast fashion companies are often the target of hackers. Sensitive consumer data, such as payment information, personal information, and lifestyle preferences deduced from purchasing patterns, may be made public by a data breach, which could result in identity theft or financial fraud. Concerns regarding manipulation and discriminatory behaviour, such as tailored pricing, where a brand may charge different customers varying amounts depending on their perceived willingness to pay, are also raised using this data for targeted advertising. For a globalized sector that depends on a dispersed supply chain, maintaining compliance with laws like the CCPA and GDPR is a difficult and continuous task. (Alhitmi, Mardiah, Al-Sulaiti, & Abbas, 2024).
- **Algorithmic Bias:** Although algorithms are the backbone of contemporary fast fashion, their objectivity depends on the quality of the data they are trained on. Algorithmic bias is fundamentally a systematic inaccuracy in an algorithm's output caused by biases in the data used to train the algorithm or faulty assumptions in the algorithm itself. It perpetuates societal preconceptions in a variety of ways. Unintentional biases in the coding, faulty algorithm design, or distorted training data can all contribute to this bias. Algorithmic bias can seriously impede the advancement of sustainability and social responsibility in the context of ethical fashion. Products are frequently ranked according to price, profit margins, and popularity by algorithms employed in social media and fashion e-commerce. Due to their potential higher production costs and limited marketing expenditures, ethical and sustainable prod-

ucts may become under-represented. As a result, customers are less exposed to these alternatives, which sustains fast fashion's popularity and the moral and environmental issues that go along with it. Moreover, recommendation system based on data including only slender, Western models, for instance, might regularly offer clothing styles that are unflattering or not easily accessible for people who are plus-sized or of different ethnicities. In a different setting, algorithms designed just to maximize sales can suggest trendy, throwaway items over long-lasting, ethically made apparel, so deliberately impeding the expansion of the sustainable fashion industry.

The first step in reducing the detrimental effects of algorithmic bias in the fashion business is to comprehend how it functions. Businesses and consumers can take action to advance justice, accountability, and transparency in the digital fashion industry by acknowledging the possibility of prejudice in algorithms. This entails backing ethical companies that place a high priority on social and environmental responsibility, encouraging data variety, and advocating for algorithmic auditing.

- **Lack of Human Element and displacement of labour:** Businesses who want to compete in the fast fashion sector must outperform their rivals in terms of speed, efficiency, and cost. (Walden, 2024) Unethical labour decisions are the result of these forces. To find cheap labour, many fast fashion businesses outsource their production to small, developing nations. Fast fashion's growing globalisation since the 1990s made outsourcing much simpler for businesses, enabling the exploitation of workers from poorer nations with laxer social and environmental laws and lower minimum salaries. Therefore, there are worries that human labour is being undervalued in the fast fashion industry is concerning.

Moreover, as the fast fashion is moving toward automation and data-driven decision-making is leading to undervalue and displacement of labour. As AI can expedite processes from design to production, this could result in the loss of jobs for garment workers, especially in countries where physical labour is cheap. Richer countries that control fast fashion businesses rely on low-cost production in economically disadvantaged areas, creating a vicious cycle whereby these nations become economically dependent on fast fashion contracts. For example, Shein's Case: Ethical Issues in the Fast Fashion Industry.

- **Lack of standardisation:** The absence of uniform data gathering and reporting is a major problem in the fast fashion sector. With multiple levels of suppliers and manufacturers worldwide, the supply chain is infamously complex and disjointed. It is quite challenging to track the origin of a product or its effects on the environment and society because different businesses and geographical areas utilize different systems and techniques for documenting information. This lack of consistency leads to discrepancies and makes it more difficult to paint a complete and honest picture of the ethical performance of the sector. It is challenging to hold companies responsible for their actions or to enable customers to make well-informed purchase decisions in the absence of a global standard.

- **Intellectual Property and Design Theft**: Fast fashion companies are frequently chastised for their practice of stealing designs from luxury designers and independent artists. They may offer trendy things for a fraction of the price thanks to this appropriation of intellectual property, which undermines the original designers' creativity and means of subsistence.

AI'S ENVIRONMENTAL FOOTPRINT AND ENERGY CONCERNS

Although it is still in its early phases, the direction of the confluence of AI and sustainability is obvious. The two will develop a mutually beneficial relationship as AI technology advances and becomes more widely available, as well as customer demand for ethical products rises. AI will not only increase the effectiveness and scalability of sustainable methods, but it will also play a crucial role in the story of ethical fashion in general. AI's long-term effects on fashion supply chains are substantial.

AI has the power to change the sector into one that is more responsible and sustainable, where resources are used more effectively and employees are treated properly. All parties involved in this change, including suppliers, customers, legislators, and brands, must work together. Making ensuring AI is applied in a way that helps everyone in the supply chain—not just a few—is crucial.

The possibility of more supply chain automation is one of the main long-term effects. It will enable a future where AI makes it easier and more cost-effective for all brands, not just luxury ones, to adopt sustainable practices.

AI is transforming the recycling of clothing and the transition to a circular fashion paradigm. Brands can improve this process' efficiency and maximize the use of important resources by implementing AI-powered technologies. From design to end-of-life, the garment industry can shift from a wasteful, linear paradigm to a sustainable, circular one by incorporating AI into every step. In addition to helping the environment, this opens new avenues for efficiency and creativity. (Circular economy introduction, 2017)

AI'S ENVIRONMENT FOOTPRINT

Although artificial intelligence (AI) is heralded as a game-changer, there is a serious worry about how it will affect the environment. AI technology has a significant carbon footprint during its development, upkeep, and disposal, which is also known as the Green Dilemma. The energy required to train and run AI models increases dramatically with the complexity of datasets and models. Climate change is made worse by this rise in energy consumption, which has a direct impact on greenhouse gas emissions. The amount of processing power needed to train state-of-the-art AI models has doubled every 3.4 months since 2012, according to OpenAI researchers. (Kanungo, 2023)

POLICY & REGULATORY FRAMEWORKS

To lower carbon emissions and create a more sustainable future, the European Union (EU) is making great progress. The numerous EU laws and directives that have been and will be implemented in the upcoming years in the phased manner. It will have a significant influence on the fashion and textile industries due to their significant carbon footprint. Soon, fashion brands both domestically and internationally will need to understand how these regulations will impact their business. The European Union is enacting laws to improve the life cycle and recycling of textiles while lowering waste. The goal of achieving a circular economy by 2050 includes enhancing the sustainability of the fashion sector. (European, 2025)

CONCLUSION: WEAVING A NEW NARRATIVE FOR ETHICAL FASHION MARKETING

According to researchers, the fashion industry is experiencing disruptive and transformative changes in the front and back ends of the value chain as a result of the implementation of Industry 5.0 technologies. These changes are producing more innovative (faster, smarter, and efficient) business models, products, services, and processes. Nevertheless, a variety of obstacles and hindrances that impact the rate of acceptance have kept the use of digital technologies in the fashion sector in an exploratory stage for a long time (e.g., budgetary limits, insufficient competence, reluctance to adoption).

The "take-make-dispose" mentality is coming to an end. Artificial intelligence holds the key to the necessary change of the fashion business. AI provides the means to create a new course based on sustainability, openness, and moral responsibility, as this chapter has shown. Brands can radically lessen their environmental footprint and transform sustainability from a niche ideal into a key component of profitable operations by utilizing AI for supply chain efficiency, sustainable design, and authentic marketing. AI is a catalyst, not just a tool, that can improve the industry's efficiency, ethics, and long-term resilience. Understanding this technological convergence is not only advantageous for all parties involved—academics, practitioners, and professionals—but also essential for forming a more responsible fashion industry.

REFERENCES

Alhitmi, H. K., Mardiah, A., Al-Sulaiti, K. I., & Abbas, J. (2024). Data security and privacy concerns of AI-driven marketing in the context of economics and business field: An exploration into possible solutions. *Cogent Business & Management*, *11*(01), 2393743. Advance online publication. DOI: 10.1080/23311975.2024.2393743

Baukh, O. (2024, September 11). How Artificial Intelligence is Revolutionizing the Fashion Industry. Retrieved September 2025, from https://techpacker.com/blog/design/how-artificial-intelligence-is-revolutionizing-the-fashion-industry/

Behare, N., Bhosale, S. P., Sharma, S., Shitole, V. C., & Sane, A. C. (2024, July 23). Quantum ethics: Ensuring integrity and security in supply chain operations. In *Quantum Computing and Supply Chain Management: A New Era of Optimization* (pp. 284–314). IGI Global., DOI: 10.4018/979-8-3693-4107-0.ch019

bluedesign. (n.d.). Retrieved from bluedesign.com: https://www.bluesign.com/en/ethical-fashion/

Brynjolfsson, E. a. (2014). *The Second Machine Age: Work, Progress, and Prosperity in a Time of Brilliant Technologies*. W. W. Norton & Company.

Chee, J. S. (2025, January). The impact of AI chatbot adoption on customer experience in e-retailing. *Issues and Perspectives in Business and Social Sciences*, 27-36. DOI: 10.33093/ipbss.2025.5.1.3

Chee, J. S. (2025, January). The impact of AI chatbot adoption on customer experience in e-retailing. *Issues and Perspectives in Business and Social Science*, *5*(1), 27–36. DOI: 10.33093/ipbss.2025.5.1.3

Circular economy introduction. (2017). Netherlands. Retrieved Sep 5, 2025, from https://www.ellenmacarthurfoundation.org/topics/circular-economy-introduction/overview

Dalal, S., Lilhore, U. K., Simaiya, S., Radulescu, M., & Belascu, L.Surjeet Dalal a. (2024, December 1). Improving efficiency and sustainability via supply chain optimization through CNNs and BiLSTM. *Technological Forecasting and Social Change*, *209*, 123841. Advance online publication. DOI: 10.1016/j.techfore.2024.123841

Deeksha Gupta Ganguly, R. B. (2025). *Sustainable Practices in the Fashion and Retail Industry*. IGI Global., DOI: 10.4018/979-8-3693-9959-0.ch022

Dilmegani, C. (2025, August). *Generative AI in Fashion: Top 10 Use Cases & Examples.* (AI Multiple Research) Retrieved September 2025, from https://research.aimultiple.com/generative-ai-fashion/

Directory, S. (2025, January 29). *How Can AI Improve Supply Chain Transparency in Fashion?* Retrieved September 2025, from https://fashion.sustainability-directory.com/: https://fashion.sustainability-directory.com/question/how-can-ai-improve-supply-chain-transparency-in-fashion/

Environmental Sustainability in the Fashion Industry. (2025, May 23). (G. E. Network, Compiler) Geveva. Retrieved 2025, from https://www.genevaenvironmentnetwork.org/resources/updates/sustainable-fashion/

Fashion meets AI: The next step in material innovation. (2024, October 25). Premiere Vision The Art & heart of fashion. Retrieved from https://www.premierevision.com/en/articles/6dc27294-75fa-ef11-90cb-00224888722c/fashion-meets-ai-the-next-step-in-material-innovation#:~:text=AI%20adjusts%20these%20processes%20based,reducing%20energy%20and%20material%20waste

Gorkhe, M., Kudare, R., Behare, N., Kulkarni, M. V., & Waghulkar, S. (July,2024). *Quantum Computing and Supply Chain Management: A New Era of Optimization.* IGI Global. DOI: 10.4018/979-8-3693-4107-0.ch017

Goworek, H. (2011). Social and environmental sustainability in the clothing industry: A case study of a fair trade retailer. *Social Responsibility Journal*, *7*(1), 74–86. DOI: 10.1108/17471111111114558

Hanan Samir Berry, R. K.-D. (2020, November 27). Measuring Saudi Mothers' Awareness of Sustainable Children's Clothing. *Open Journal of Social Sciences*, *8*, •••. Retrieved August 2025, from https://www.scirp.org/reference/referencespapers?referenceid=2870108

inGrade. (n.d.). Retrieved from inGrade.io: https://ingrade.io/how-ai-is-revolutionizing-the-fashion-industry/

Kotler, P. (n.d.). *The Marketing Journal.* Retrieved from https://www.marketingjournal.org/: https://www.marketingjournal.org/brand-purpose-to-beneficence-philip-kotler/

Lorne Michael Cousins, P. P. (n.d.). Fashion Sustainability Directory. Retrieved from https://fashion.sustainability-directory.com/term/social-equity-in-fashion/

Mondalek, A. (2023). Generative AI: Unlocking the future of fashion. *McKinsey & Company.* Retrieved September 2025, from https://www.mckinsey.com/industries/retail/our-insights/generative-ai-unlocking-the-future-of-fashion

Moura, P. D. (2021, January 2). *Live Innovation.* Retrieved September 2025, from https://liveinnovation.org/: https://liveinnovation.org/brand-personality-understanding-aakers-5-dimension-model/

Niinimäki, K. P., Peters, G., Dahlbo, H., Perry, P., Rissanen, T., & Gwilt, A. (2020, April 1). The environmental price of fast fashion. *Nature Reviews. Earth & Environment, 1*(4), 189–200. DOI: 10.1038/s43017-020-0039-9

Olivar Aponte, N. H. (2024, August). ast fashion consumption and its environmental impact: a literature review. *Sustainability: Science. Practice and Policy, 20*(1). Advance online publication. DOI: 10.1080/15487733.2024.2381871

Omkar Singh, N. S. (2024, September). AI, IoT, and Blockchain in Fashion: Confronting Industry. *International Journal of Communication Networks and Information.* Retrieved September 2025, from https://ijcnis.org/

Our vision of a circular economy for fashion. (2023, May 9). *Ellen Macarthur Foundation Periodical.* Retrieved from https://www.ellenmacarthurfoundation.org/our-vision-of-a-circular-economy-for-fashion

Oyebode Kayode, A. L. (2025). Predictive Analytics for Demand Forecasting in Ethical Fashion:. *Research Gate.* Retrieved 2025, from researchgate.net

Patsy Perry, J. F. (2018). *Luxury fashion supply chain management* (5th ed.). Edinburgh: Kogan Page. Retrieved 2025, from research.manchester.

Ray, S., & Nayak, L. (2023, April 4). Marketing Sustainable Fashion: Trends and Future Directions. *Sustainability (Basel), 15*(7), 6202. Advance online publication. DOI: 10.3390/su15076202

Sanjida Sumaia Mimmo, A. R. (2025). Integrating Artificial Intelligence Across the Fashion. *Applied IT & Engineering.* Eman Publishers. Retrieved from https://publishing.emanresearch.org/CurrentIssuePDF/EmanPublisher_9_5948engineering-3110210.pdf

Sasha, N., & Sarokin, N. M. (2024, March 10). Pursuing profitability in slow fashion: Exploring brands' profit contributors. (Elsevier, Ed.) *Journal of Cleaner Production, 444.* DOI: 10.1016/j.jclepro.2024.141237

Sustainability in Fashion and Textiles. (2013). Taylor & Francis., DOI: 10.4324/9781351277600

Swaminathan, K. L. (2019). *Strategic Brand Management Building, Measuring and Managing Brand Equity* (5th ed.). Pearsons., Retrieved 2025, from.

Takyar, A. (2023, April 19). AI in fashion: Use cases, benefits, implementation and future trends. *LeewayHertz - AI Development Company.* Retrieved from https://www.leewayhertz.com/ai-use-cases-in-fashion/#the-rise-of-ai-in-the-fashion-industry

TrendBible. (2023). What is a Micro Trend? *Glossory.* Retrieved from https://www.trendbible.com/trendterms/micro-trend/#:~:text=A%20Micro%20Trend%20is%20a,into%20these%20emerging%20consumer%20mindsets

Ushmita Gupta, P. S. (2024). *Revolutionizing Retail IoT Applications for Enhanced Customer Experience.* Taylor & Francis. Retrieved August 2025, from https://www.taylorfrancis.com/chapters/edit/10.1201/9781003458401-5/revolutionizing-retail-ushmita-gupta-pritesh-somani-nitesh-behare-rashmi-mahajan-meenakshi-singh-vishwanathan-iyer

Verónica Bolón-Canedo, L. M.-F. (2024, September 28). A review of green artificial intelligence: Towards a more sustainable future. *Neurocomputing, 599,* 128096. Advance online publication. DOI: 10.1016/j.neucom.2024.128096

Chapter 5

The Power of Online Branding:

A Closer Look at Canary's Fashion Industry

Gonzalo Díaz Meneses
http://orcid.org/0000-0001-6260-385X
University of Las Palmas de Gran Canaria, Spain

Maica Amador-Marrero
http://orcid.org/0009-0005-8156-3618
University of Las Palmas de Gran Canaria, Spain

Neringa Vilkaitė-Vaitonė
http://orcid.org/0000-0002-4208-149X
Vilnius Gediminas Technical University, Lithuania

ABSTRACT

The present study seeks to assess the Brand Equity in the network of new fashion designers in the Canary Islands. To this end, we have adapted the Brand Equity model to an online context and proposed a set of metrics for four dimensions: estimate, relevance, awareness, and differen-tiation. The multidimensional approach to online Brand Equity was employed to measure the online Brand Equity of 129 fashion designers from the Canary Islands. The study's findings re-vealed that the number of social media profiles significantly impacts brand awareness and differentiation. Moreover, the digital maturity level influences brand relevance and overall Brand Equity . Our study highlights the practical value of web data-driven

DOI: 10.4018/979-8-2600-0303-9.ch005

metrics for measuring online Brand Equity, which can be utilised for diagnostic, evaluative, or predictive purposes. The study's outcomes have substantial implications for marketers in the fashion industry aimed at improving online Brand Equity

1. INTRODUCTION

In recent years, there has been a growing interest in digital marketing and its role in boosting digital transformation across all industries (Konopik, Jahn, Schuster, Hossbach & Pflaum, 2022). Technology and digitalisation have played a pivotal role in supporting businesses, particularly through digital marketing. Research has shown that social networks such as Meta Group, TikTok, and Twitter, now known as X, can provide valuable user information (Warbung, Wowor, Walean & Mandagi, 2023). Furthermore, web metrics have emerged as a critical avenue of interest for brands (Barman, 2013). Websites and social media platforms can help brands position themselves among consumers and gain insights into their behaviour and preferences. In this context, the structural brand dimensions of awareness, estimation, relevance, and differentiation can be measured and operationalised to manage organisations on the internet effectively (Khan, 2009; Yoo, B. & Donthu, 2001). The fashion industry has experienced rapid growth thanks to the online context (Chen, 2023). As such, fashion designers must build Brand Equity based on online metrics. By leveraging the power of digital marketing and web metrics, businesses can gain valuable insights into their target audience and position themselves for success in the digital age.

Researchers have explored various aspects of Brand Equity, highlighting dimensions such as awareness, esteem, relevance, and differentiation, which significantly influence consumer decisions and brand experiences (Briggs & Hollis, 1997; Godey, Manthiou, Pederzoli, Rokka, Aiello, Donvito & Singh, 2016; Forero & Duque, 2014; Srivastava & Shocker, 1991; Keller, 1993; Faircloth, Capella, & Alford, 2001; de Chernatony, 1997; Redhill, 1999). From a consumer-based perspective, Brand Equity is best understood as the value attributed by customers rather than product features, with Brand Stature linked to awareness and esteem, and Brand Strength associated with relevance and differentiation. While much of the literature has focused on brick-and-mortar businesses, recent research increasingly emphasises the need for updated measurement tools that capture social media and digital marketing dynamics (Davic, Vinhas & Hair, 2015; Dwivedi, Ismagilova, Hughes, Carlson, Filieri, Jacobson, Jain, Karjaluoto, Kefi, Krishen, Kumar, Rahman, Raman, Rauschnabel, Rowley, Salo, Tran & Wang, 2021).

Studies on regional brands highlight that cultural identity, local values, and tourism influence brand perception in regional markets (Pina & Dias, 2021; Karimkhan,

2023). In the fashion industry, regional authenticity is a differentiating factor. Cultural narratives and artisanal traditions reinforce the perception of uniqueness and trust in the brand (Rodrigues & Rodrigues, 2019; Dumitriu, Militaru, Deselnicu, Niculescu & Popescu, 2019). The authors conclude that regional fashion ecosystems thrive when digital strategies merge cultural authenticity with global competitiveness (Chen, Sherren, Smit, & Lee, 2023; Ameen, Cheah & Kumar, 2022). This represents an important gap in research: although the global literature addresses digital brand value, few studies contextualise these dynamics in small island economies. The Canary Islands offer a unique empirical setting to examine how digitalisation and cultural identity interact in brand value construction.

Against this backdrop, this study examines the measurement and interpretation of online Brand Equity within the network of fashion designers in the Canary Islands' emerging fashion industry. The sector was selected due to its pivotal role in diversifying the islands' economic landscape. By enhancing the value of mass tourism, fashion contributes to broader diversification efforts. For example, the internationally recognised Moda Cálida initiative not only advances the fashion sector but also indirectly supports tourism through increased visibility and global exposure. Beyond this, the study seeks to provide insights into strengthening the online presence of fashion designers through social media strategies and data-driven web technologies. Importantly, fashion branding in the Canary Islands must be understood within its socio-economic context: tourism dominates the economy and programmes such as Gran Canaria Moda Cálida and Tenerife Moda leverage fashion to diversify income, promote culture and position the islands as international destinations. These initiatives enable regional governments to project identity abroad and support local designers—often operating with limited resources—through grants, training, digital communication and participation in global trade fairs. Within this context, a central challenge remains whether local brands can sustain digital engagement and technological adoption over time, despite structural constraints.

To establish a robust connection between global frameworks and the regional context of the Canary Islands, Table 1 synthesises the principal antecedents of online Brand Equity, its digital adaptation, and its application within insular economies. This comparative lens highlights both the structural challenges and the strategic opportunities associated with transferring global Brand Equity models to a tourism-driven and resource-constrained regional setting. In doing so, the table not only bridges theoretical and contextual perspectives but also provides the conceptual foundation upon which the research questions of this study are formulated.

Table 1. Online Brand Equity: Global antecedents, digital adaptation and regional application

Global antecedents of online Brand Equity	**Digital adaptation**	**Regional application (Canary Islands)**
Brand Equity dimensions: awareness, esteem, relevance, differentiation.	Online metrics: website traffic, backlinks, visit duration, bounce rate.	Tourism-driven visibility: fashion as cultural showcase.
Consumer-based Brand Equity models: customer perspective over product features.	Social media strategies: Instagram, TikTok, influencer marketing, user-generated content (UGC).	Use of cultural narratives, authenticity, and local identity to differentiate brands
Brand Stature = Awareness & Esteem and Brand Strength = Relevance & Differentiation	Content marketing: quality, storytelling, co-creation, live streaming	Resource constraints: SMEs limited budgets for content production and campaigns
Global competitiveness in fashion: differentiation and consumer trust	Product line diversity: haute couture, prêt-à-porter, swimwear, accessories…	Tourism-linked collections (swimwear, ceremonial wear), sustainability, artisan crafts

Adopting novel methods to assess intangible values and performance is imperative (Gaitniece, 2018). Also, applying the Brand Equity model in the online marketplace is essential due to several factors:

a) Digital transformation: consumer interactions have shifted significantly to online platforms, necessitating an updated approach to Brand Equity.
b) Increased competition: the online marketplace is crowded, making strategic differentiation crucial for standing out.
c) Consumer behaviour: online consumers access information and alternatives more readily, requiring brands to leverage digital touchpoints effectively.
d) Metrics and analytics: digital tools provide detailed insights into consumer behaviour, allowing for data-driven brand strategy optimisation.
e) Personalisation and engagement: digital platforms enable personalised marketing, enhancing relevance and engagement with targeted audiences.
f) Global reach: the internet allows brands to reach a global audience, requiring consistent yet locally adaptable brand messaging.
g) Social media influence: social media shapes brand perceptions, making it vital to use these platforms to build awareness, engagement, and loyalty.

This chapter aims to examine how online Brand Equity can be measured and explained in the context of the Canary Islands' fashion industry (Spain), with a specific focus on the role of digital metrics, social media strategies and cultural factors. The objective is to adapt established Brand Equity models (traditional theories) to the online marketplace, identify their antecedents in digital environments and assess their applicability in a regional and tourism-driven economy like Canary Islands.

The research questions guiding this study are:

RQ1: How can we adapt the Brand Equity model to the online marketplace?
RQ2: What are the antecedents of Brand Stature in the online market?
RQ3: What are the antecedents of Brand Strength in the online market?
RQ4: What are the antecedents of Brand Equity in the online market?

To address those questions, we assessed online Brand Equity within the emerging network of fashion designers in the Canary Islands. We adapted the Brand Equity model to the online context of the fashion designer network and considered the most appropriate digital metrics. Additionally, we identified the factors contributing to Brand Strength and stature by examining dimensions such as awareness, esteem, relevance, and differentiation. Finally, we identified the online factors influencing Brand Equity and measured the overall structural impact of Brand Strength and stature on Brand Equity. Our analysis involved measuring online metrics essential for assessing Brand Equity: backlinks for esteem, reflecting authority and trustworthiness; visit length, pages viewed, and bounce rate for user engagement and content relevance; and social media likes for positive sentiment. Relevance was gauged through domain authority and social media engagement, while awareness was assessed by website traffic and social media reach. Differentiation was measured by content originality and social media comment interactions, highlighting user engagement and distinctiveness. Collectively, these metrics provide a comprehensive overview of Brand Equity in the digital landscape.

The present study is organised into five distinct sections in addition to the introduction. The first section, a comprehensive literature review, identifies and systematises critical online metrics and precursors of the Brand Equity phenomenon. The second section delves into the methodological framework, encompassing the fieldwork, measuring instruments, and research context. The third section presents a statistical analysis and empirical evidence derived from the research. Next, a discussion section examines the significance of the findings in the context of other studies. Finally, the article concludes with a summary of its theoretical contribution, limitations, and future research directions.

Figure 1. Chapter structure. Source: Own elaboration

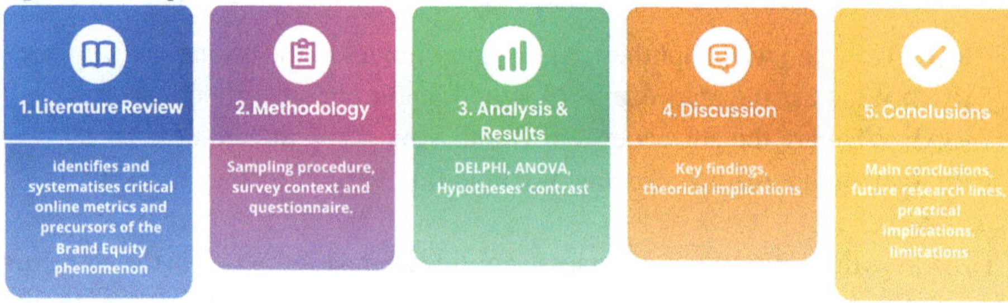

2. LITERATURE REVIEW

Having outlined the objectives and research questions, the following section reviews the existing literature on Brand Equity. The literature review is divided into four thematic blocks: (2.1) digital brand metrics, (2.2) social media strategies and (2.3) online precursors of Brand Equity. This structure provides both conceptual depth and local context, connecting global frameworks with the Canary Islands, Spain.

2.1 Digital Brand Metrics

Brand value in digital contexts encompasses awareness, valuation, relevance, and differentiation (Christodoulides, De Chernatony, Furrer, Shiu & Abimbola, 2006; Aaker, 2011). In online environments, web-based indicators serve as proxies for consumer perceptions. Key indicators such as website traffic, social media reach, external links, visit duration, and bounce rate jointly reflect consumer awareness, website authority and perceived value (Makrides, Vrontis & Christofi, 2019; Kamerer, 2020). The interdependence of these indicators is notable: low relevance often translates into higher bounce rates and weaker engagement (De Oliveira, Silveira & Luce, 2015). While earlier research relied mainly on traditional digital metrics, more recent literature calls for integrating complementary measures such as digital sentiment and search share as broader indicators of brand performance in ecosystems (France, S., Davcik, N. S., & Kazandjian, 2025). Studies further suggest that consumer-based brand equity in digital environments is strongly shaped by online engagement, electronic word of mouth (eWOM), and communication effects. This underscores the importance of digital interactivity and co-creation as integral components of online brand value (Enes, de, Demo, Porto & Zulato, 2024).

Additional studies confirm that digital indicators extend beyond traffic and bounce rate, as online advertising and engagement strongly influence brand awareness and perception (Barreda, Bilgihan, Nusair & Okumus, 2015; Drivas, Sakas, & Giannakopoulos, 2021; Ratra & Neelam, 2018). Similarly, trust and identity play mediating roles in linking digital presence to Brand Equity (Shawky, 2020; De Paula, & Chaves, 2017).

2.2 Social Media Strategies

Social media has become a crucial component of digital branding, not only enhancing visibility but also redefining consumer brand relationships through interaction, co-creation, and loyalty-building practices. Previous studies show that strong, high-quality interactions on social platforms foster durable brand-consumer ties (Godey et al., 2016; Zeeshan,& Hussain, 2017).

Recent evidence indicates that formats such as live streams, short videos (e.g., TikTok or Instagram Reels), and influencer collaborations significantly increase consumer trust, loyalty, and engagement (Shahbaznezhad, Dolan & Rashidirad, 2022; Gupta & Srivastava, 2023). Instagram and TikTok are particularly relevant for fashion branding given their visual nature and suitability for user-generated content (UGC), aligning well with fashion trends (Park & Namkung, 2022; Hase, Boczek & Scharkow, 2023).

Beyond visibility, social media contributes to brand differentiation. Storytelling, cross-platform campaigns, and authenticity-driven narratives now complement metrics such as likes, shares, and comments, expanding reach through eWOM (Cuevas-Molano, Matosas-López & Bernal-Bravo, 2021; Enes et al., 2024). Moreover, platforms are increasingly shaped by AI-driven algorithms and niche communities, where sentiment and search share emerge as critical measures of impact (France et al., 2025). Recent findings show that influencer engagement and follower dynamics shape consumer trust and loyalty, highlighting the nuanced role of status consumption and social media credibility in Brand Equity (Romão, M. T., Moro, S., Rita, P., & Ramos, 2019; Upadhyay, Paul & Baber, 2022; Husain, Ahmad & Khan, 2022; Heidari, Zarei, Daneshfar & Dokhanian, 2023; Wies, Bleier & Edeling, 2023).

For regional brands in the Canary Islands, social media represents an essential tool to overcome geographic isolation and connect with international markets. By embedding cultural narratives, authenticity, and tourism-driven positioning into their digital strategies, SMEs can strengthen competitiveness despite resource limitations (Paun, 2023).

2.3 Online Precursors of Brand Equity

Digital maturity remains a critical antecedent, with validated models confirming its role in shaping connected consumer behaviour and competitive capacity (Mettler, T., & Pinto, 2018, Rossmann, 2018; Nichifor & Brătucu, 2021; Laaber, F., Florack, A., Koch, T., & Hubert, 2023). Content strategies further integrate storytelling and eWOM as assets of branded content (Koivisto, E., & Mattila, 2023; Llorente-Barroso, Kolotouchkina & Ferreira, 2023). Digitalisation requires skills that go beyond IT, involving the integration of marketing strategy with specialised technologies such as social media, websites, and analytics (Christodoulides et al., 2006; Aaker, 2011). Early studies developed staged models of digital maturity, ranging from no online presence to advanced e-commerce capabilities (Kincl, & Štrach, 2012; Kamerer, 2020). At the lower end, brands without websites or social profiles rely on indirect consumer mentions, while higher levels include functional websites, mobile optimisation, and interactive features enabling transactions (De Oliveira et al., 2015).

Recent approaches emphasise that digital maturity is not static but dynamic, evolving toward omnichannel integration where online and offline experiences converge (Kraus, S., Durst, S., Ferreira, J. J. M., & Veiga, 2021). In this updated view, digital presence progresses from basic visibility to advanced engagement, incorporating SEO, personalised consumer journeys, and analytics.

For fashion SMEs in the Canary Islands, this progression often stalls at intermediate stages due to resource constraints. This makes public initiatives such as Gran Canaria Moda Cálida critical in helping brands achieve higher levels of digital maturity. A strong digital presence enhances visibility, credibility and trust (France et al., 2025). By differentiating through tailored online experiences and cultural authenticity (Enes et al., 2024), regional brands can strengthen both awareness and esteem within Brand Equity. Based on this, the following hypotheses are put forward:

H1: The digital level determines Brand Equity.

H1a: The digital level determines the brand's awareness.

H1b: The digital level determines the estimation of the brand.

H1c: The digital level determines the brand's relevance.

H1d: The digital level determines the brand's differentiation.

Social media is widely recognised as a cornerstone of modern marketing, enhancing visibility, engagement, and trust in consumer–brand relationships (Godey et al., 2016; Zeeshan & Hussain, 2017). Platforms such as Instagram and TikTok have proven particularly effective, as authentic content, influencer marketing, and user interactions—namely, likes, comments, and shares—strengthen awareness and loyalty (Cuevas-Molano et al., 2021; Park et al., 2022; Hase, Boczek & Scharkow, 2023). More recent studies highlight that social media strategies go beyond visibility, driving brand differentiation through co-creation, authenticity-driven storytelling, and cross-platform campaigns (Enes et al., 2024; Paun, 2023; Nobre & Ferrerira, 2021). These dynamics are increasingly shaped by AI-driven algorithms and niche online communities, where sentiment and search share become critical measures of impact (France et al., 2025). For fashion brands in the Canary Islands, social media offers a means to overcome geographic isolation and connect with international markets. Collaborations with tourism-driven micro-communities have demonstrated particular effectiveness, enabling small designers to expand their reach while incorporating local cultural narratives into global fashion conversations. On this basis, the following hypotheses are put forward:

H2: The number of social media platforms used determines Brand Equity.

H2a: The number of social media platforms used determines the brand's awareness.

H2b: The number of social media platforms used determines the estimation of the brand.

H2c: The number of social media platforms used determines the brand's relevance.

H2d: The number of social media platforms used determines the brand's differentiation.

Content marketing quality is a key factor in brand equity, as it demonstrates how effectively brands create and share various types of content to engage with consumers. Research shows that it is not the amount, but the quality and relevance of content—such as posts, videos, infographics, newsletters, or live streams—that shape how consumers perceive brand value (De Oliveira et al., 2015; France et al., 2025). Good content builds awareness, encourages loyalty, and enhances brand image by making the brand appear reliable and trustworthy (Enes et al., 2024). Interactive features, such as storytelling, user-generated content, or 360° fashion shows, enable brands to stand out and foster strong consumer–brand relationships (Koivisto et al., 2023). In the Canary Islands, incorporating local stories and craft traditions into digital content provides local fashion SMEs with an opportunity to compete globally with something unique and authentic. Based on this, the following ideas are proposed:

H3: Content format variety used determines Brand Equity.

H3a: Content format variety determines the brand's awareness.

H3b: Content format variety determines the estimation of the brand.

H3c: Content format variety determines the brand's relevance.

H3d: Content format variety determines the brand's differentiation.

Product line diversity is a key driver of Brand Equity, as the breadth and creativity of collections shape consumers' perceptions of relevance, uniqueness, and value. A wider product range—covering haute couture, prêt-à-porter, swimwear, or accessories—reinforces awareness and loyalty by meeting diverse needs (Mosarrat, 2012; Chen, 2023). Furthermore, innovative and well-segmented product lines boost consumer engagement and strengthen brand image, while also supporting differentiation in competitive markets (Kamerer, 2020; Nobre et al., 2021). For Canary Island designers, product diversification often centres on ceremonial wear, swimwear, and ready-to-wear segments, which are closely linked to the tourism-driven economy. Maintaining cultural coherence and sustainable practices within these diverse collections builds both trust and loyalty. As a result, regional brands are positioned as distinctive players in global fashion ecosystems. Based on this, the following hypotheses are put forward:

H4: Diversity of product lines determines Brand Equity.

H4a: Diversity of product lines determines the brand's awareness.

H4b: Diversity of product lines determines the estimation of the brand.

H4c: Diversity of product lines determines the brand's relevance.

H4d: Diversity of product lines determines the brand's differentiation.

Drawing on prior research, we posit that Brand Equity in digital fashion contexts is shaped by four key antecedents: digital level, content format variety, product line diversity, and number of social media platforms. Each factor is expected to influence distinct dimensions of Brand Equity—awareness, estimation, relevance, and differentiation—reflecting the multidimensional nature of consumer–brand relationships in online environments. Accordingly, the conceptual model in Figure 1 integrates these antecedents into a coherent framework for empirical testing.

Figure 2. Conceptual model. Source: Own elaboration

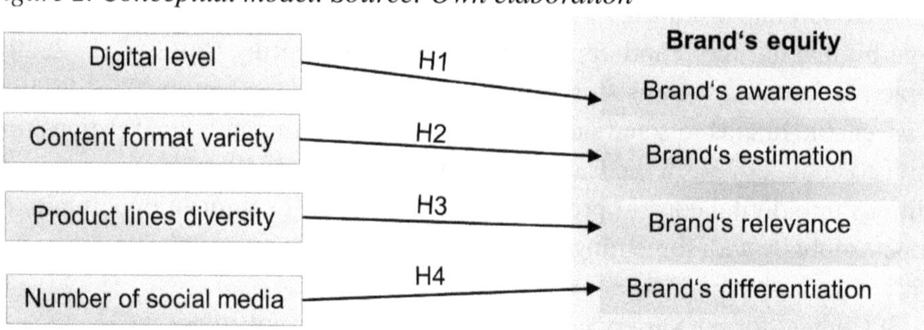

Building on this review, the next section presents the methodological approach adopted to operationalise the proposed model and to assess online Brand Equity in the Canary Islands' fashion industry.

3. METHODOLOGY

We developed a comprehensive database sampling framework to conduct a survey that aligns with our stated objectives. Our sampling framework comprises 129 fashion designers hailing from the Canary Islands. Although we initially set a theoretical sample size of 100 fashion designers, this number increased during our fieldwork. Our sample units were selected using a simple random procedure, which employed a probabilistic method to gather data from fashion designers affiliated with five different official networking platforms, namely Moda Cálida, Isla Bonita, Tenerife Moda, Moda Lanzarote, and Moda Fuerteventura, which are funded by The Canary Islands government, as well as independent new fashion creators from the same region. We assumed a 7% sampling error and established a reliability interval of 95.5%, Table 02.

To gather and collate information about the universe of new fashion designers, we recruited 100 students of a market research course for tourism from the University of Las Palmas de Gran Canaria, who were instructed to extract the necessary metrics from the sampling units' websites after being assigned one different designer to each student and survey taker. These students collected and tabulated metrics in April 2023, operating from the computer classroom of the Faculty of Business, Economics, and Tourism, under the careful supervision of authors and lecturers to ensure that all operations were well-coordinated. Following the gathering session, the authors meticulously scrutinised the database, detecting and resolving internal inconsistencies, missing values, and omitted responses.

Table 2. Technical sheet of the research. Source: Own elaboration

Methodological procedure	**Analysis of web metrics and social networks. Database**
Population	N=250
Sample error	The assumed sample error was 5.95% for a reliability interval of 95.5%. (Z=1,96)
Geographical scope	Canary Islands
Contact form	Through the designer platforms: Moda Cálida, Isla Bonita, Tenerife Moda, Moda Lanzarote and Moda Fuerteventura. Also, reports on fashion fairs and events in the Canary Islands.
Sample	129
Sample selection method	Random simple sampling by assigning one or two fashion designers to each student from ULPGC
Fieldwork date	April 2023

The database boasts eleven distinct dimensions. Upon analysis, it has come to light that the variables within the said database can be broadly classified into four distinct categories concerning the dimensions of Brand Equity . This classification has been duly illustrated in Figure 03 for reference and clarity.

Figure 3. Brand Equity and online metrics Source: Own elaboration

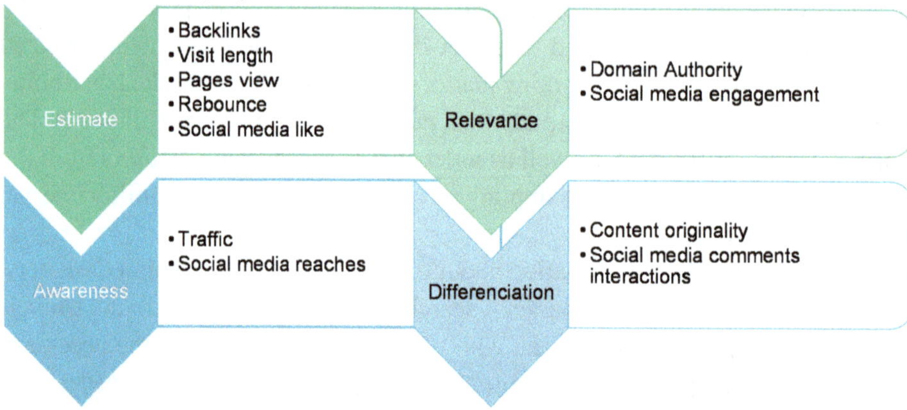

Upon collecting identification information for the new fashion designers, our team proceeded to extract the remaining metrics using specialised software, as presented in Table 03. The measurement indicators on the dimensions of Brand Equity were extracted from diverse software tools, except social media metrics, which were extracted manually.

Table 3. Description of metrics and software. Source: Own elaboration

DIMENSION	SOFTWARE	METRICS	DESCRIPTION
Estimate	Semrush	Backlinks	A link that connects one website to another
	Semrush	Visit length	Average time per visit
	Semrush	Pages view	Average number of times a page was viewed
	Semrush	Rebounce	% visitors entering a website and exiting without interaction
	Manual	Social media like	Average number of likes on Facebook, Twitter, Instagram, TikTok, LinkedIn, Pinterest
Awareness	Semrush	Traffic	Number of visitors
	Reach	Social media reaches	Scope impressions

continued on following page

Table 3. Continued

DIMENSION	SOFTWARE	METRICS	DESCRIPTION
Relevance	Moz	Domain Authority	Domain score
	Keyhole	Social media engagement	Engagement CTR on Facebook, Twitter, Instagram, TikTok, Linkedin, Pinterest
Differentiation	Siteliner	Content originality	% of original content
	Mediatoolkit	Social media comments interactions	Average number of comments interactions on Facebook, Twitter, Instagram, TikTok, Linkedin, Pinterest

Table 04 presents specific information related to the research study. The table contains dichotomous variables that indicate the existence or absence of various product lines and content formats. Additionally, the table shows a variable that provides details about fashion platforms. This variable has six values associated with each new fashion designer platform, which connects to a different island. Furthermore, the table exhibits variables for social media platforms, which gather information about the designers' community and network management. Finally, the table includes a variable that describes each new fashion designer's digital marketing maturity level. This variable has six dimensions, which provide a comprehensive overview of the digital development stage achieved by each designer. In addition, there are some variables regarding the classification details of the fashion designers, such as their names, fashion brands, contact numbers, email addresses, product line diversity and URLs.

Table 4. The specific information about the new fashion designers. Source: Own elaboration

VARIABLES	VALUES
New fashion designers' platforms	(1) Moda Cálida, (2) Isla Bonita, (3) Tenerife Fashion, (4) Lanzarote Fashion, (5) Fuerteventura Fashion and (6) independent designers.
Product lines	Accessories, ceremony, ready-to-wear men, ready-to-wear women, swimwear, women's swimwear, men's swimwear, children's fashion, and lingerie
Content marketing formats	Post, PPS, video, infographic, newsletter, case study, whitepaper, ebook, report/review, webinar, live streaming, games, contest, quizzes, press release, radio, TV, guides, celebrity endorsement, rating, events, interactive demos, checklist, databases and calculators
Social media	Facebook, Twitter, Instagram, TikTok, Linkedin, Pinterest, Whatsapp, Youtube and Vimeo.
Digital maturity levels	(0) no website, no social media, (1) no website, no networks, but has mentions in social media, (2) no website, no social media, but appears in SERP, (3) has a simple blog-style website, (4) has a simple blog-style website and profiles on social media, (5) has a mobile-friendly website, requests information with forms and allows price inquiries, (6) has a website that allows commercial transactions

New variables have been generated changing the original values, which will be used in a subsequent statistical analysis. In order to make meaningful comparisons, we had to standardise the values or carry out basic calculations like adding and subtracting. Furthermore, this also involved transforming the initial 88 variables into 20 new ones listed in Table 05.

Table 5. Transformation of original variables into new ones. Source: Own elaboration

NEW VARIABLE	FORMULA WITH OLD VARIABLES
V1 Traffic	Standardised number of visitors from the website
V2 Reaches	Standardised sum up total of reach rate (Facebook) + reach rate (Twitter) + reach rate (Instagram) + reach rate (TikTok) + reach rate (Pinterest) + reach rate (Linkedin)
V3 Brand Stature Awareness	Sum up V1 Traffic + V2 Reaches
V4 Backlinks	Standardised number of links that connect one website to another
V5 Visit length	Standardised times a page was viewed
V6 Rebounce	Standardised % visitors
V7 Likes	Standardised sum up total of like rate (Facebook) + like rate (Twitter) + like rate (Instagram) + like rate (TikTok) + like rate (Pinterest) + like rate (Linkedin)
V8 Brand Stature Estimate	Sum up V4 Backlinks + V5 Visit length + V6 Rebounce + V7 Likes
V9 Domain Authority	Standardised the Domain score
V10 Engagement	Standardised sum up total of Engagement rate (Facebook) + Engagement rate (Twitter) + Engagement rate (Instagram) + Engagement rate (TikTok) + engagement rate (Pinterest) + Engagement rate (Linkedin)
V11 Brand Strength Relevance	Sum up V9 Domain Authority + V10 Engagement
V12 Content originality	Standardised % of original content
V13 Social media comments interactions	Standardised sum up total of Interactions rate (Facebook) + Interactions rate (Twitter) + Interactions rate (Instagram) + Interactions rate (TikTok) + Interactions rate (Pinterest) + engagement rate (Linkedin)
V14 Brand Strength Differenciation	Sum up V12 Content originality + V13 Social media comments interactions
V15 Brand Equity	Sum up V3 Brand Stature Awareness + V8 Brand Stature Estimate + V11 Brand Strength Relevance + V14 Brand Strength Differenciation
V16 Number of social media	If it does not exist = 0; If social media profile exists =1 1/0 (Facebook) + 1/0 (Twitter) + 1/0(Instagram)+ 1/0(TikTok) + 1/0 (Pinterest) + 1/0 (Linkedin) + 1/0 (WhatsApp) + 1/0 (Youtube) + 1/0 (Vimeo)

continued on following page

Table 5. Continued

NEW VARIABLE	FORMULA WITH OLD VARIABLES
V17 Product lines diversity	They do not design this product line = 0; They design this product line=1 1/0 (complements) + 1/0 (footwear) + 1/0 (lingerie)+ 1/0 (sportwear) + 1/0 (swimwear women) + 1/0 (swimwear men) + 1/0 (swimwear)+ 1/0 (ceremony) + 1/0 (ready-to-wear women) + 1/0 (ready-to-wear children) + 1/0 (ready-to-wear men)
V18 Fashion Collection diversity	Sum up (complements + footwear) + (ready-to-wear women + ready-to-wear men + ready-to-wear children) + (swimwear women + swimwear men + swimwear) + Ceremony
V19 Content format variety	If it does not exist = 0; If content format exists =1 1/0 (post) + 1/0 (PPS) + 1/0 (video)+ 1/0 (infographic) + 1/0 (newsletter) + 1/0 (case study) + 1/0 (whitepaper) + 1/0 (eBook) + 1/0 (webinar) + 1/0 (livestreaming) + 1/0 (games) + 1/0 (contest) + 1/0 (quizzes) + 1/0 (press release) 1/0 (radio) + 1/0 (TV) + 1/0 (guides)+ 1/0 (celebrity endorsement) + 1/0 (rating) + 1/0 (events) + 1/0 (interactives demos) + 1/0 (checklist) + 1/0 (calculators) + 1/0 (databases)
V20 Digital level	No website, no networks= 0; No website, no networks, but has mentions in social media= 1; No website, no networks, but appears in SERP= 2; Has a simple blog-style website= 3; Has a simple blog-style website and profiles on social media= 4; Has a mobile-friendly website, requests information with forms and allows price enquiries= 5; Has a website that allows commercial transactions= 6

The Delphi was designed to assess these dimensions, with each one broken down into specific items that reflect the most significant aspects of each dimension according to the literature. For instance, (Aaker, 2011) identifies brand awareness as a crucial measure of brand strength, while esteem and relevance are discussed by (Keller, 2013) as critical components of consumer perception and preference. Differentiation has also been extensively explored by (Kapferer, 2008) as a crucial element for a brand to distinguish itself in a competitive market. It is essential to mention that we conducted a Delphi survey, in which we interviewed five digital marketers who have experience in the new fashion designers' market, Table 06. Moreover, they are actively involved in the tourism and fashion industries and are specialists in both digital and traditional marketing, Table 07. The consulted experts agreed with this four-dimensional categorisation and the inclusion of the corresponding items. None of the experts expressed disagreement with this classification, supporting its theoretical and practical validity in the context of our study. Our objective was to gather their opinions about the significance of the variables needed, Table 06, to calculate Brand Equity in the Canary Islands marketplace. Our approach involved weighing every variable within the awareness, estimate, relevance, and differentiation dimensions. This will enable us to develop a tool to evaluate the new fashion designers' marketplace.

Table 6. Technical sheet of the Delphi research. Source: Own elaboration

Methodological procedure	Delphi interview
Sample error	The assumed sample error was 5.95% for a reliability interval of 95.5%. (Z=1,96)
Geographical scope	Gran Canaria
Contact form	Through professional social network: LinkedIn
Sample	5
Sample selection method	Digital marketers who have experience in the new fashion designers' market.
Fieldwork date	August 2023

Table 7. Profile of the respondents and their opinion. Source: Own elaboration

Expert	Date	Gender	Age	Education	Profession	Professional experience
1.	17/08/2023	Female	26	Master's Degree in Marketing and International Trade	Bank cashier	2 years
2.	17/08/2023	Female	25	Master's Degree in Marketing and International Trade and PhD Candidate in Fashion Marketing	Project manager	2 years
3.	19/08/2023	Female	31	Postgraduate in Marketing for Hospitality and Tourism	Head of Production, Events and Communication	9 years
4.	19/08/2023	Female	32	Master's Degree in Marketing and International Trade	Design technique	7 years
5.	21/08/2023	Female	37	Degree in Business administration and management	Project manager	11 years

Based on this methodological framework, the following section reports the empirical results derived from the analysis of online metrics and social media indicators.

4. RESULTS

The section on the analysis of results is divided into four headings that respond to the research questions formulated in the introduction.

RQ1: How can we adapt the Brand Equity model to the online marketplace?

In this study, we have explored the possibility of measuring Brand Equity dimensions by drawing a logical equivalence between traditional brick-and-mortar indicators and digital metrics. Our review of literature suggests that brand awareness can be represented by traffic and social media reach, while brand estimate can be evaluated based on online metrics such as backlinks, visit length, pages view, rebounce, and social media likes. Brand relevance may be judged by examining DA and social media engagement, while content originality and social media comments can indicate the level of brand differentiation in digital marketing. We carefully considered these equivalences during preliminary transformations, as reflected in Table 04. Our results demonstrate that Brand Equity dimensions can indeed be adapted to the online context, owing to the logical similarities between offline and online indicators. Moreover, we have successfully formulated the total market Brand Equity value, as presented in Tables 08 and 10.

As part of our research, we employed a Delphi survey, engaging five experts to evaluate the significance of each dimension and variable in measuring online Brand Equity for emerging fashion designers in the Canary Islands, as presented in Table 09. The results of the survey, presented in Table 5, detail the experts' responses regarding the cruciality of every brand dimension. Based on the survey findings, we identified four primary dimensions for calculating Brand Equity value: awareness, estimate, differentiation, and relevance, as shown in Table 10. Our analysis indicates that web traffic and TikTok reach are the most significant variables for the awareness category, while page views and visit length are crucial for the estimate category. Furthermore, unique content stands out as a critical variable concerning differentiation. Finally, our study reveals that DA is the most vital variable for relevance.

Table 8. Delphi survey descriptive results. Source: Own elaboration

AWARENESS	Expert 1	Expert 2	Expert 3	Expert 4	Expert 5			
Item	Score	Score	Score	Score	Score	Mean	SD	Mean/SD
Visits	6	10	6	18	5	9	5.39	1.67
Facebook reach	1	2	5	5	5	3.6	1.95	1.85
Twitter reach	1	2	2	7	4	3.2	2.39	1.34
Instagram reach	9	2	5	15	6	7.4	4.93	1.50
Tik Tok reach	4	2	2	15	5	5.6	5.41	1.03

continued on following page

Table 8. Continued

AWARENESS	Expert 1	Expert 2	Expert 3	Expert 4	Expert 5			
Item	**Score**	**Score**	**Score**	**Score**	**Score**	**Mean**	**SD**	**Mean/SD**
Pinterest reach	1	2	2	1	3	1.8	0.84	2.15
Linkedin reach	1	2	5	8	2	3.6	2.88	1.25
						34.2	23.78	1.44
ESTIMATE	Expert 1	Expert 2	Expert 3	Expert 4	Expert 5			
Item	**Score**	**Score**	**Score**	**Score**	**Score**	**Mean**	**SD**	**Mean/SD**
Backlinks	4	0	6	2	4	3.2	2.28	1.40
visit length	6	10	4	1	3	4.8	3.42	1.40
Page view	5	10	6	1	4	5.2	3.27	1.59
rebounce percentage	2	5	6	3	2	3.6	1.82	1.98
Facebook likes	1	3	2	0	4	2	1.58	1.26
Twitter likes	0	3	2	1	3	1.8	1.30	1.38
Instagram likes	5	3	2	4	4	3.6	1.14	3.16
Tik Tok likes	1	3	2	3	2	2.2	0.84	2.63
Pinterest likes	0	3	2	0	2	1.4	1.34	1.04
Linkedin likes	1	1	2	1	2	1.4	0.55	2.56
						29.2	17.54	1.66
RELEVANCE	Expert 1	Expert 2	Expert 3	Expert 4	Expert 5			
Item	**Score**	**Score**	**Score**	**Score**	**Score**	**Mean**	**SD**	**Mean/SD**
Domain authority	8	4	6	2	4	4.8	2.28	2.10
Facebook CTR	1	3	4	0	3	2.2	1.64	1.34
Twitter CTR	1	3	1	0	3	1.6	1.34	1.19
Instagram CTR	6	3	4	3	3	3.8	1.30	2.91
TikTok CTR	2	3	1	2	3	2.2	0.84	2.63
Pinterest CTR	0	3	1	0	2	1.2	1.30	0.92
Linkedin CTR	1	2	4	1	2	2	1.22	1.63
						17.8	9.93	1.79
DIFFERENTIATION	Expert 1	Expert 2	Expert 3	Expert 4	Expert 5			
Item	**Score**	**Score**	**Score**	**Score**	**Score**	**Mean**	**SD**	**Mean/SD**
Unique content	25	4	6	2	5	8.4	9.40	0.89
Facebook Comments	0	2	3	0	3	1.6	1.52	1.06
Twitter Comments	0	2	3	1	2	1.6	1.14	1.40
Instagram Comments	4	2	3	1	4	2.8	1.30	2.15
TikTok Comments	3	2	1	2	3	2.2	0.84	2.63
Pinterest Comments	0	2	1	0	2	1	1.00	1.00
Linkedin Comments	1	2	1	1	1	1.2	0.45	2.68

continued on following page

Table 8. Continued

AWARENESS	Expert 1	Expert 2	Expert 3	Expert 4	Expert 5			
Item	**Score**	**Score**	**Score**	**Score**	**Score**	**Mean**	**SD**	**Mean/SD**
						18.8	15.64	1.20
	100	**100**	**100**	**100**	**100**	100	66.90	6.10

Table 9. Expert opinion. Source: Own elaboration

Expert	Opinion
1.	The current digital landscape emphasises the critical role of website visits in reaching target audiences effectively. While platforms like Facebook, Twitter, and LinkedIn are well-established, the growing significance of Instagram and TikTok cannot be overlooked. Engagement metrics such as likes and comments, alongside indicators like bounce rates and click-through rates, provide valuable insights into audience interaction and content effectiveness. Ultimately, a comprehensive approach that considers both visitor acquisition and interaction evaluation is essential for understanding and navigating the complexities of digital engagement.
2.	While all social media platforms hold significance, their valuation can differ based on the specific context. For instance, Pinterest may receive a lower score due to limited familiarity with its functionality. However, website visits take precedence over social media likes as they signify a higher potential for actual purchases. This preference also influences the cost per click, as user engagement with advertisements is more likely when there is genuine interest. In the case of Canary Islands fashion brands, the importance of each platform may be re-evaluated, taking into account their capacity to inspire and facilitate sales.
3.	All social media platforms are important, but the assessment of each may vary depending on the context. For example, Pinterest may receive a lower score due to unfamiliarity with the platform. However, website visits are prioritized over likes on social media, as they indicate a greater potential for sales. This also impacts the cost per click, as interested users are likely to engage with advertising content. In the case of Canary Islands fashion brands, the significance of each platform may change, considering their ability to inspire and drive sales.
4.	It needs to focus on content-related items like unique content and authority which contribute to SEO and better positioning. Metrics such as page views and bounce rate also help improve content quality and engagement. Social media metrics, especially reach, were given priority, though their importance varies across platforms and businesses. Likes were treated equally due to limited points. Similarly, CTR and comments were prioritized.
5.	It's essential to emphasize elements related to content, such as originality and credibility, which play a role in SEO and enhanced visibility. Analytical measures like page views and bounce rate aid in refining content quality and fostering engagement. Social media indicators, notably reach, were prioritized, although their significance varies depending on the platform and industry. Likes were uniformly valued due to a constraint in available points. Likewise, emphasis was placed on click-through rates (CTR) and comments.

Table 10. Brand Equity formulation for the new fashion industry in the Canary Islands. Source: Own elaboration

Brand stature		Brand Strength		Brand Equity
Awareness	**Estimate**	**Relevance**	**Differentiate**	
34.2	29.2	17.8	18.8	100

It is assumed that assigning a monetary value to every variable weighing its importance will lead to the calculation of the Brand Equity for the Canary Islands' new fashion designer marketplace.

RQ2: What are the antecedents of Brand Stature in the online market?

In order to test Hypotheses 1a, 2a, 3a, and 4a, we conducted two linear regression analyses, with the independent variables being the postulated antecedents of brand stature. As depicted in Table 11, the results suggest that brand awareness is solely predicted by the number of social media profiles the new fashion designer possesses. However, we found no evidence to support the notion that product line diversity, content format diversity, and maturity level significantly affect brand awareness.

Table 11. Linear regression to explain awareness within brand stature. Source: Own elaboration

Model Summary[b]

Model	R	R Square	Adjusted R Square	Std. Er.Estimate	Durbin-Watson
1	.409[a]	.167	.140	1.53003	1.988

ANOVA[a]

Model		Sum of Squares	df	Mean Square	F	Sig.
1	Regression	58.330	4	14.583	6.229	<.001[b]
	Residual	290.282	124	2.341		
	Total	348.612	128			

Coefficients[a]

Model		Unstand.Coefficients		Stand.Coefficients	t	Sig.	Collinea.Statistics	
		B	Std. Error	Beta			Tolerance	VIF
	(Constant)	-1.673	.459		-3.648	<.001		
V1	Number of social media	.436	.110	.360	3.963	<.001	.814	1.228
V2	Product lines diversity	.015	.101	.013	.153	.879	.951	1.051
V3	Content format variarity	.059	.036	.135	1.635	.105	.983	1.017
V4	Digital level	.016	.086	.017	.188	.852	.827	1.209

Collinearity Diagnostics[a]

Model	Dimension	Eigenvalue	Condition Index	Variance Proportions				
				(Constant)	V1	V2	V3	V4
1	1	4.287	1.000	.00	.01	.01	.01	.01
	2	.328	3.615	.00	.00	.25	.72	.01
	3	.225	4.368	.01	.12	.70	.18	.06
	4	.102	6.496	.15	.87	.02	.01	.21
	5	.059	8.533	.83	.00	.01	.08	.71

a. Dependent Variable: Awareness within Brand Stature

In order to test hypotheses 1b, 2b, 3b, and 4b, as presented in Table 12, a linear regression analysis was conducted to investigate the association between the dimensions of the estimate and the corresponding precursors that determine them. However, the analysis results indicate that none of the precursors exhibits a statistically significant impact, implying that neither social networks, digital maturity level, product lines diversity, nor content format variety influence the Brand Stature concerning the estimate dimension.

Table 12. Linear regression to explain estimate within brand stature. Source: Own elaboration

Model Summary[b]

Model	R	R Square	Adjusted R Square	Std. Error of the Estimate	Durbin-Watson
1	.092[a]	.008	-.024	1.84993	1.868

ANOVA[a]

Model		Sum of Squares	df	Mean Square	F	Sig.
1	Regression	3.587	4	.897	.262	.902[b]
	Residual	424.358	124	3.422		
	Total	427.945	128			

Coefficients[a]

Model		Unstand.Coefficients		Stand. Coefficients	t	Sig.	Collinea.Statistics	
		B	Std. Error	Beta			Tolerance	VIF
1	(Constant)	-.227	.555		-.410	.683		
V1	Number of social media	-.091	.133	-.068	-.686	.494	.814	1.228
V2	Product lines diversity	.045	.122	.034	.371	.711	.951	1.051
V3	Content format variarity	-.001	.044	-.002	-.023	.982	.983	1.017
V4	Digital level	.088	.104	.083	.845	.400	.827	1.209

Collinearity Diagnostics[a]

Model	Dimension	Eigenvalue	Condition Index	Variance Proportions				
				(Constant)	V1	V2	V3	V4
1	1	4.287	1.000	.00	.01	.01	.01	.01
	2	.328	3.615	.00	.00	.25	.72	.01
	3	.225	4.368	.01	.12	.70	.18	.06
	4	.102	6.496	.15	.87	.02	.01	.21
	5	.059	8.533	.83	.00	.01	.08	.71

Dependent Variable: Estimate within Brand Stature

RQ3: What are the antecedents of Brand Strength in the online market?

In order to test Hypotheses 1c, 2c, 3c, and 4c, we conducted a linear regression analysis to assess the relevance within Brand Strength, as presented in Table 13. Our findings indicate that the maturity level of a new fashion designer is significantly relevant to Brand Strength. However, no discernible influence was observed from social media, content formats, or product line diversity. These results suggest that while social media, content formats, and product line diversity may be important factors in other areas of the fashion industry, they do not seem to impact Brand Strength in this context significantly.

Table 13. Linear regression to explain relevance within Brand Strength. Source: Own elaboration

Model Summary[b]

Model	R	R Square	Adjusted R Square	Std. Error of the Estimate	Durbin-Watson
1	.274[a]	.075	.045	1.38738	1.969

ANOVA[a]

Model		Sum of Squares	df	Mean Square	F	Sig.
1	Regression	19.362	4	4.840	2.515	.045[b]
	Residual	238.680	124	1.925		
	Total	258.041	128			

Coefficients[a]

Model		Unstand.Coefficients		Stand.Coefficients	t	Sig.	Collinea.Statistics	
		B	Std. Error	Beta			Tolerance	VIF
1	(Constant)	-1.230	.416		-2.956	.004		
V1	Number of social media	.063	.100	.061	.635	.526	.814	1.228
V2	Product lines diversity	.033	.092	.032	.356	.722	.951	1.051
V3	Content format variarity	.029	.033	.076	.874	.384	.983	1.017
V4	Digital level	.180	.078	.220	2.317	.022	.827	1.209

Collinearity Diagnostics[a]

Model	Dimension	Eigenvalue	Condition Index	Variance Proportions				
				(Constant)	V1	V2	V3	V4
1	1	4.287	1.000	.00	.01	.01	.01	.01
	2	.328	3.615	.00	.00	.25	.72	.01
	3	.225	4.368	.01	.12	.70	.18	.06
	4	.102	6.496	.15	.87	.02	.01	.21
	5	.059	8.533	.83	.00	.01	.08	.71

Dependent Variable: Relevance within Brand Strength

In order to examine Hypotheses 1d, 2d, 3d, and 4d, as evidenced by the data in Table 14, we conducted a linear regression analysis to differentiate within Brand Strength. We found that a higher number of social media profiles for the new fashion designer is positively associated with greater Brand Strength due to the differentiation value. However, no statistically significant correlation was found between product line diversity, content format variety, or digital maturity level.

Table 14. Linear regression to explain differentiation within Brand Strength. Source: Own elaboration

Model Summary[b]

Model	R	R Square	Adjusted R Square	Std. Error of the Estimate	Durbin-Watson
1	.236[a]	.056	.025	1.40874	2.259

ANOVA[a]

Model		Sum of Squares	df	Mean Square	F	Sig.
1	Regression	14.498	4	3.624	1.826	.128[b]
	Residual	246.084	124	1.985		
	Total	260.582	128			

Coefficients[a]

Model		Unstand.Coefficients		Stand. Coefficients	t	Sig.	Collinea.Statistics	
		B	Std. Error	Beta			Tolerance	VIF
1	(Constant)	-.882	.422		-2.089	.039		
V1	Number of social media	.207	.101	.198	2.045	.043	.814	1.228
V2	Product lines diversity	-.019	.093	-.018	-.199	.842	.951	1.051
V3	Content format variarity	.012	.033	.032	.365	.716	.983	1.017
V4	Digital level	.055	.079	.068	.703	.483	.827	1.209

Collinearity Diagnostics[a]

Model	Dimension	Eigenvalue	Condition Index	Variance Proportions				
				(Constant)	V1	V2	V3	V4
1	1	4.287	1.000	.00	.01	.01	.01	.01
	2	.328	3.615	.00	.00	.25	.72	.01
	3	.223	4.368	.01	.12	.70	.18	.06
	4	.102	6.496	.15	.87	.02	.01	.21
	5	.059	8.533	.83	.00	.01	.08	.71

Dependent variable: differentiation within Brand Strength

Our findings indicate that the number of social media profiles is a significant factor in determining Brand Strength.

RQ4: What are the antecedents of Brand Equity in the online market?

In order to rigorously examine and quantify the determinants of Brand Equity, we conducted a linear regression analysis to test Hypotheses 1, 2, 3, and 4. The independent variables used for the analysis were consistent with those presented in Table 15. Our findings revealed that digital maturity level had a statistically significant effect on Brand Equity. However, contrary to our original expectations, we could not establish causal links between social media, product lines, content format diversities, and Brand Equity. Table 16 summarises the hypotheses testing results, showing that only four hypotheses were supported while sixteen were rejected.

Table 15. Linear regression to explain Brand Equity. Source: Own elaboration

Model Summary[b]

Model	R	R Square	Adjusted R Square	Std. Error of the Estimate	Durbin-Watson
1	.337[a]	.114	.085	3.74117	1.726

ANOVA[a]

Model		Sum of Squares	df	Mean Square	F	Sig.
1	Regression	222.684	4	55.671	3.978	.005[b]
	Residual	1735.552	124	13.996		
	Total	1958.236	128			

Coefficients[a]

		Unstand.Coefficients		Stand. Coefficients			Collinea.Statistics	
Model		B	Std. Error	Beta	t	Sig.	Tolerance	VIF
1	(Constant)	-4.012	1.122		-3.577	<.001		
V1	Number of social media	.075	.247	.026	.303	.762	.951	1.051
V2	Product lines diversity	.099	.088	.095	1.119	.265	.983	1.017
V3	Content format variety	.339	.209	.151	1.619	.108	.827	1.209
V4	Digital level	.615	.269	.214	2.287	.024	.814	1.228

Collinearity Diagnostics[a]

				Variance Proportions				
Model	Dimension	Eigenvalue	Condition Index	(Constant)	V1	V2	V3	V4
1	1	4.287	1.000	.00	.01	.01	.01	.01
	2	.328	3.615	.00	.25	.72	.01	.00
	3	.225	4.368	.01	.70	.18	.06	.12
	4	.102	6.496	.15	.02	.01	.21	.87
	5	.059	8.533	.83	.01	.08	.71	.00

Dependent Variable: Brand Equity

Table 16. Summary of hypotheses testing results. Source: Own elaboration

Hypotheses	*Results*
H1: The digital level determines Brand Equity	Accepted
H1a: The digital level determines the brand's awareness	Rejected
H1b: The digital level determines the estimation of the brand	Rejected
H1c: The digital level determines the brand's relevance	Accepted
H1d: The digital level determines the brand's differentiation	Rejected
H2: The number of social media platforms used determines Brand Equity	Rejected
H2a: The number of social media platforms used determines the brand's awareness	Accepted
H2b: The number of social media platforms used determines the estimation of the brand	Rejected
H2c: The number of social media platforms used determines the brand's relevance	Rejected
H2d: The number of social media platforms used determines the brand's differentiation	Accepted
H3: Content format variety used determines Brand Equity	Rejected
H3a: Content format variety determines the brand's awareness	Rejected
H3b: Content format variety determines the estimation of the brand	Rejected
H3c: Content format variety determines the brand's relevance	Rejected
H3d: Content format variety determines the brand's differentiation	Rejected
H4: Diversity of product lines determines Brand Equity	Rejected
H4a: Diversity of product lines determines the brand's awareness	Rejected
H4b: Diversity of product lines determines the estimation of the brand	Rejected
H4c: Diversity of product lines determines the brand's relevance	Rejected
H4d: Diversity of product lines determines the brand's differentiation	Rejected

These findings are interpreted in the discussion section, where their theoretical and practical implications are examined in relation to the broader literature and the regional context of the Canary Islands.

5. DISCUSSION

This research aimed to assess the online Brand Equity of the fashion designers' network in the Canary Islands. Our approach relied on web data analysis to measure Brand Equity, which is recognised as a crucial factor in achieving online competitiveness (Aaker, 2011; Keller, 2013). The online Brand Equity of fashion designers in the Canary Islands was evaluated using four dimensions: estimation, awareness, relevance, and differentiation. These dimensions have been extensively documented in academic literature and are widely acknowledged as necessary in assessing Brand Equity (Chernatony, 1997; Redhil, 1999). It should be noted that a

Delphi study was conducted to reinforce the significance of specific dimensions of Brand Equity. Experts' endorsement provides strong theoretical validation of their applicability in the regional context.

Strong brand awareness is crucial for fashion brands since it improves the attitude towards the brand (Kapferer, 2008). According to our research, the number of social media profiles significantly determines both brand awareness and differentiation. This finding is consistent with the current theoretical knowledge of social media's impact on online Brand Equity (Baniyani, A., Ahmadi, M. H., Motamedi, M., & Gholami, 2021; Foroudi, 2019; Dülek, B., & Saydan, 2019). Regression analysis has also shown that having more social media profiles significantly impacts brand differentiation. With over half of the world's population (4.89 billion) using social media, it is clear that social media provides vast opportunities for raising brand awareness and differentiation (Herhausen, D., Miočević, D., Morgan, R. E., & Kleijnen, 2020). Thus, a multi-platform strategy is not only beneficial but essential for fashion designers seeking to maximise reach and strengthen online competitiveness (Wies et al., 2023; Enes et al., 2024).

The implication for marketers in the fashion industry is clear: limiting activity to a few social media platforms restricts visibility and engagement. Ideally, a fashion designer should build a presence on diverse platforms—such as Facebook, Instagram, TikTok, LinkedIn, Pinterest, WhatsApp, YouTube, or Vimeo—to connect with different audience segments and reinforce brand loyalty. This multi-platform approach allows designers to effectively build their brand's online presence, improve interaction rates, and differentiate themselves from competitors.

However, our results also indicate that diversity in product lines, content formats, and digital level did not significantly impact brand awareness, estimation, or differentiation. This finding contrasts with parts of the existing literature and suggests two possible explanations: first, that regional SMEs face resource constraints limiting the impact of these strategies; and second, that cultural authenticity and niche branding may weigh more heavily than breadth of offerings or content volume in insular contexts (Koivisto et al., 2023; Chen, 2023). These results provide a better understanding of what drives Brand Equity in the Canary Islands and highlight areas requiring further exploration. We also found no significant effect on the brand estimation dimension. This underscores a gap in both our empirical evidence and the broader literature, which has yet to conclusively identify the determinants of brand estimation in digital environments. Future research should investigate this dimension in greater depth, as it remains critical to assessing Brand Equity comprehensively.

Regarding Brand Strength, our findings suggest that digital maturity plays a more decisive role than social media, content formats, or product line diversity. For fashion designers in the Canary Islands, achieving advanced digital maturity—through optimised websites, transactional functionalities, and integrated online–offline strategies—is crucial for enhancing Brand Equity. This aligns with prior studies emphasising the importance of digital capability in achieving competitiveness (Hariani, M., & Sinambela, 2020; Kraus, 2021; Dülek et al., 2019). Our research further demonstrates that the multidimensional Brand Equity model can be effectively adapted to the online marketplace. The combination of specific metrics—such as backlinks, visit length, pages viewed, bounce rate, social media likes, domain authority, and engagement—offers a robust framework for capturing all four dimensions of Brand Equity. Unlike traditional approaches, this method relies on objective, data-driven indicators obtained from web analytics, thereby reducing subjectivity and enhancing measurement reliability. Tools such as Semrush, Moz, Siteliner, and Mediatoolkit proved valuable in extracting these data.

Beyond technical metrics, several strategic factors emerge as critical to sustaining online Brand Equity in regional fashion industries: trust, authenticity, and sustainability. Consumers increasingly demand transparency and cultural narratives that reflect genuine identity, while sustainability has become a decisive driver of competitiveness (Hu, Chen, Chen & He, 2020;, Ameen et al., 2023). For SMEs in peripheral regions such as the Canary Islands, competitiveness depends not only on digital maturity but also on their ability to differentiate through cultural value, ecological practices, and innovation. Finally, the rise of artificial intelligence, influencer marketing, and omnichannel strategies introduces both opportunities and challenges (France et al., 2025; Paun, 2023). These tools expand the possibilities for personalisation, predictive analytics, and consumer engagement, yet they also raise concerns about ethics, bias, and consistency across platforms. In sum, while digital metrics provide valuable insights, the sustainable growth of online Brand Equity in the Canary Islands depends on balancing data-driven optimisation with long-term values of authenticity, cultural identity, and consumer trust.

6. CONCLUSIONS

This research contributes to the literature by attempting to adapt and apply the traditional Brand Equity model to the online context. Specifically, the study endeavours to unravel the mechanisms through which Brand Equity is shaped and reinforced in online contexts, thereby providing an alternative interpretation of the traditional brick-and-mortar model.

The present study investigated the antecedents of Brand Equity in the digital realm, focusing on the fashion industry in the Canary Islands. Through a mixed-methods approach, the findings suggest that the number of social media profiles significantly increases brand awareness while the digital maturity level enhances relevance. Notably, the study reveals that Brand Stature and strength have distinct antecedents. Contrary to expectations, there was no evidence that product line diversity or content format variety influences Brand Equity. Nevertheless, experts identified specific variables within each dimension, providing a more nuanced understanding of critical factors that drive Brand Equity in the digital landscape.

Furthermore, the Delphi study highlights that not all metrics are equally important, with web traffic and TikTok reach identified as crucial for awareness. In practical terms, these findings imply that online Brand Equity must be managed by embracing digital transformation and considering the dimensions of digital capability. Social media emerges as a critical tool to increase brand awareness and differentiation, with experts recommending creating a wide range of social media profiles to gain visibility and uniqueness. Unique content and domain authority are also identified as critical factors for differentiation and relevance, respectively.

The results of this study have significant implications for marketers and fashion designers in the Canary Islands, providing clear guidelines for the practical measurement of Brand Equity. By prioritising specific metrics and dimensions, decision-making and resource allocation can be informed by quantitative measures of Brand Equity. Furthermore, the Delphi experts developed a proposal to assign a monetary value to each variable, which can be used to quantify Brand Equity and inform strategic decisions. Ultimately, this research enhances our understanding of the antecedents of Brand Equity in the digital landscape and contributes to developing practical methodologies for measuring and improving Brand Equity. From a practical perspective, the results suggest that Canary Islands fashion designers should prioritise strengthening their digital maturity and multi-platform presence, but without overlooking content quality and cultural authenticity. Investments in professional training for SMEs in analytics and digital storytelling would enhance competitiveness. For policymakers, initiatives such as Gran Canaria Moda Cálida should be reinforced with funding lines and knowledge transfer programmes that enable small designers to integrate omnichannel strategies and sustainability practices. This alignment between industry stakeholders and regional institutions can transform fashion into a strategic lever for tourism, identity, and economic diversification in the Canary Islands.

Further research opportunities arise from the unexpected results. Additionally, it's important to note that quality, rather than quantity, is vital to improving Brand Equity through content marketing. The study found no significant relationship between the variety of content formats and Brand Equity, indicating that the quality of content may be more important than the quantity. This result highlights the need for a greater focus on content marketing quality. The lack of relationship between product line diversity and Brand Equity is also surprising and requires further investigation to identify the factors contributing to this dissociation. Understanding these factors will help improve brand perception and enhance Brand Equity management strat-

REFERENCES

Aaker, D. A. (2011). *Building strong brands*. Simon & Schuster.

Ameen, N., Cheah, J. H., & Kumar, S. (2022). It's all part of the customer journey: The impact of augmented reality, chatbots, and social media on the body image and self-esteem of Generation Z female consumers. *Psychology and Marketing*, *39*(11), 2110–2129. DOI: 10.1002/mar.21715

Baniyani, A., Ahmadi, M. H., Motamedi, M., & Gholami, M. (2021). Providing a model for brand strength in the banking industry using Yazd city banks. *Asia Pacific Management Review*, *26*(2), 78–85. DOI: 10.1016/j.apmrv.2020.08.003

Barman, H. (2013). Web analytics metrics for Internet business models. In *Impact of IT applications in accounting and finance*. Global Publishing House.

Barreda, A. A., Bilgihan, A., Nusair, K., & Okumus, F. (2015). Generating brand awareness in online social networks. *Computers in Human Behavior*, *50*, 600–609. DOI: 10.1016/j.chb.2015.03.023

Briggs, R., & Hollis, N. (1997). Advertising on the web: Is there response before click-through? *Journal of Advertising Research*, *37*(2), 33–46. DOI: 10.1080/00218499.1997.12466659

Chen, Y. (2023). How blockchain adoption affects supply chain sustainability in the fashion industry: A systematic review and case studies. *International Transactions in Operational Research*, *0*, 1–29. DOI: 10.1111/itor.13273

Chen, Y., Sherren, K., Smit, M., & Lee, K. Y. (2023). Using social media images as data in social science research. *New Media & Society*, *25*(4), 849–871. DOI: 10.1177/14614448211038761

Christodoulides, G., De Chernatony, L., Furrer, O., Shiu, E., & Abimbola, T. (2006). Conceptualising and measuring the equity of online brands. *Journal of Marketing Management*, *22*(7–8), 799–825. DOI: 10.1362/026725706778612149

Cuevas-Molano, E., Matosas-López, L., & Bernal-Bravo, C. (2021). Factors increasing consumer engagement of branded content in Instagram. *IEEE Access : Practical Innovations, Open Solutions*, *9*, 143531–143548. DOI: 10.1109/ACCESS.2021.3121186

Davic, N., Vinhas, R., & Hair, F. (2015). Towards a unified theory of brand equity: Conceptualisations, taxonomy and avenues for future research. *Journal of Product and Brand Management*, *24*(1), 3–17. DOI: 10.1108/JPBM-06-2014-0639

De Chernatony, L. (1997). Integrated brand building using brand taxonomies. *Journal of Product and Brand Management, 6*(1), 56–63.

De Oliveira, M. O., Silveira, C. S., & Luce, F. B. (2015). Brand equity estimation model. *Journal of Business Research, 68*(12), 2560–2568. DOI: 10.1016/j.jbusres.2015.06.025

De Paula, E., & Chaves, S. (2017). Identity, positioning, brand image and brand equity comparison: A vision about quality in brand management. *Independent Journal of Management & Production, 8*(4), 1246–1263. DOI: 10.14807/ijmp.v8i4.637

Drivas, I. C., Sakas, D. P., & Giannakopoulos, G. A. (2021). Display advertising and brand awareness in search engines: Predicting the engagement of branded search traffic visitors. En Business intelligence and modelling (pp. 3–15). DOI: 10.1007/978-3-030-57065-1_1

Dülek, B., & Saydan, R. (2019). The impact of social media advertisement awareness on brand awareness, brand image, brand attitude, and brand loyalty: A research on university students. *International Journal of Contemporary Economics and Administrative Sciences, 9*(2), 470–494.

Dumitriu, D., Militaru, G., Deselnicu, D. C., Niculescu, A., & Popescu, M. A. M. (2019). A perspective over modern SMEs: Managing brand equity, growth and sustainability through digital marketing tools and techniques. *Sustainability (Basel), 11*(7), 2111. DOI: 10.3390/su11072111

Dwivedi, Y. K., Ismagilova, E., Hughes, D. L., Carlson, J., Filieri, R., Jacobson, J., Jain, V., Karjaluoto, H., Kefi, H., Krishen, A. S., Kumar, V., Rahman, M. M., Raman, R., Rauschnabel, P. A., Rowley, J., Salo, J., Tran, G. A., & Wang, Y. (2021). Setting the future of digital and social media marketing research: Perspectives and research propositions. *International Journal of Information Management, 59*, 102168. DOI: 10.1016/j.ijinfomgt.2020.102168

Enes, Y. de S. O., Demo, G., Porto, R. B., & Zulato, T. S. (2024). What is next for consumer-based brand equity in digital brands? Research itineraries and new challenges. *Sustainability (Basel), 16*(13), 5412. DOI: 10.3390/su16135412

Faircloth, J., Capella, L., & Alford, B. (2001). The effect of brand attitude and brand image on brand equity. *Journal of Marketing Theory and Practice, 9*(3), 61–75. DOI: 10.1080/10696679.2001.11501897

Forero, M., & Duque, E. (2014). Evolución y caracterización de los modelos de brand equity. *Suma de Negocios, 5*(12), 158–168. DOI: 10.1016/S2215-910X(14)70038-2

Foroudi, P. (2019). Influence of brand signature, brand awareness, brand attitude, and brand reputation on the hotel industry's brand performance. *International Journal of Hospitality Management*, *76*, 271–285. DOI: 10.1016/j.ijhm.2018.05.016

France, S., Davcik, N. S., & Kazandjian, B. (2025). Digital brand equity: The concept, antecedents, measurement, and future development. *Journal of Business Research*, *181*, 115273. DOI: 10.1016/j.jbusres.2025.115273

Gaitniece, E. (2018). Digital marketing performance evaluation methods. *CBU International Conference Proceedings*, 6, 135–140. DOI: 10.12955/cbup.v6.1145

Godey, B., Manthiou, A., Pederzoli, D., Rokka, J., Aiello, G., Donvito, R., & Singh, R. (2016). Social media marketing efforts of luxury brands: Influence on brand equity and consumer behavior. *Journal of Business Research*, *69*(12), 5833–5841. DOI: 10.1016/j.jbusres.2016.04.181

Gupta, A. K., & Srivastava, V. (2023). Modelling the impact of social media marketing for apparel brands: Evidence from India. *International Journal of Internet Marketing and Advertising*, *18*(2–3), 242–262. DOI: 10.1504/IJIMA.2023.129665

Hariani, M., & Sinambela, E. A. (2020). The effect of price perception, service quality, and product diversity on Superindo customer loyalty in Surabaya. Journal of Science. *Technology in Society*, *1*(1).

Hase, V., Boczek, K., & Scharkow, M. (2023). Adapting to affordances and audiences? A cross-platform, multi-modal analysis of the platformization of news on Facebook, Instagram, TikTok, and Twitter. *Digital Journalism (Abingdon, England)*, *11*(8), 1499–1520. DOI: 10.1080/21670811.2022.2128389

Heidari, S., Zarei, M., Daneshfar, A., & Dokhanian, S. (2023). Increasing sales through social media marketing: The role of customer brand attachment, brand trust, and brand equity. *Marketing and Management of Innovations*, *14*(1), 224–234. DOI: 10.21272/mmi.2023.1-19

Herhausen, D., Miočević, D., Morgan, R. E., & Kleijnen, M. H. P. (2020). The digital marketing capabilities gap. *Industrial Marketing Management*, *90*, 276–290. DOI: 10.1016/j.indmarman.2020.07.022

Hu, M., Chen, J., Chen, Q., & He, W. (2020). It pays off to be authentic: An examination of direct versus indirect brand mentions on social media. *Journal of Business Research*, *117*, 19–28. DOI: 10.1016/j.jbusres.2020.05.032

Husain, R., Ahmad, A., & Khan, B. M. (2022). The role of status consumption and brand equity: A comparative study of the marketing of Indian luxury brands by traditional and social media. *Global Business and Organizational Excellence, 41*(4), 48–67. DOI: 10.1002/joe.22156

Kamerer, D. (2020). Reconsidering bounce rate in web analytics. *Journal of Digital & Social Media Marketing, 8*(1), 58–67. DOI: 10.69554/EJGO6858

Kapferer, J. N. (2008). *The new strategic brand management: Creating and sustaining brand equity long term* (4th ed.). Kogan Page.

Karimkhan, F. (2023). Ethics in fashion and Gucci's blackface sweater: Will the fashion industry finally learn from its mistakes? *Journal of Media Ethics, 38*(2), 123–125. Advance online publication. DOI: 10.1080/23736992.2023.2194289

Keller, K. L. (1993). Conceptualizing, measuring, and managing customer-based brand equity. *Journal of Marketing, 57*(1), 1–22. DOI: 10.1177/002224299305700101

Keller, K. L. (2013). *Strategic brand management: Building, measuring, and managing brand equity* (4th ed.). Pearson.

Khan, B. M. (2009). Operationalising Young and Rubicam's BAV™ as a consumer-based brand equity measure. *Journal for International Business and Entrepreneurship Development, 4*(4), 314–333. DOI: 10.1504/JIBED.2009.033744

Kincl, T., & Štrach, P. (2012). Measuring website quality: Asymmetric effect of user satisfaction. *Behaviour & Information Technology, 31*(7), 647–657. DOI: 10.1080/0144929X.2010.526150

Koivisto, E., & Mattila, P. (2023). Fashion in the metaverse: Consumer engagement through immersive experiences. *Journal of Business Research, 158*, 113672. DOI: 10.1016/j.jbusres.2023.113672

Konopik, J., Jahn, C., Schuster, T., Hossbach, N., & Pflaum, A. (2022). Mastering the digital transformation through organisational capabilities: A conceptual framework. *Digital Business, 2*(2), 100019. DOI: 10.1016/j.digbus.2021.100019

Kraus, S., Durst, S., Ferreira, J. J. M., Veiga, P. M., Kailer, N., & Weinmann, A. (2021). Digital transformation in business and management research: An overview of the current status quo. *International Journal of Information Management, 63*, 102466. DOI: 10.1016/j.ijinfomgt.2021.102466

Laaber, F., Florack, A., Koch, T., & Hubert, M. (2023). Digital maturity: Development and validation of the Digital Maturity Inventory (DIMI). *Computers in Human Behavior, 143*, 107709. DOI: 10.1016/j.chb.2023.107709

Llorente-Barroso, C., Kolotouchkina, O., & Ferreira, I. (2023). E-WOM as an asset of branded content strategies: A conceptual approach to the role of consumers in building brand equity. In *Handbook of research on the future of advertising and brands in the new entertainment landscape* (pp. 367–383). IGI Global.

Makrides, A., Vrontis, D., & Christofi, M. (2019). The gold rush of digital marketing: Assessing prospects of building brand awareness overseas. *Business Perspectives and Research*, *8*(1), 4–20. DOI: 10.1177/2278533719860016

Mettler, T., & Pinto, R. (2018). Evolutionary paths and influencing factors towards digital maturity: An analysis of the status quo in Swiss hospitals. *Technological Forecasting and Social Change*, *133*, 104–117. DOI: 10.1016/j.techfore.2018.03.009

Mosarrat, F. (2012). Brand elements lead to brand equity: Differentiate or die. *Information Management and Business Review*, *4*(4), 223–233. DOI: 10.22610/imbr.v4i4.983

Nichifor, E., & Brătucu, G. (2021). How the digital maturity level is shaping the connected consumer future? *Journal of Smart Economic Growth*, *6*(2), 19–39.

Nobre, H., & Ferreira, A. (2021). Digital marketing and social media: Why bother? *Business Horizons*, *64*(6), 739–749. DOI: 10.1016/j.bushor.2021.09.001

Park, C. I., & Namkung, Y. (2022). The effects of Instagram marketing activities on customer-based brand equity in the coffee industry. *Sustainability (Basel)*, *14*(3), 1657. DOI: 10.3390/su14031657

Paun, D. (2023). Digital presence and competitive advantage in fashion retailing. *Journal of Retailing and Consumer Services*, *75*, 103464. DOI: 10.1016/j.jretconser.2023.103464

Pina, R., & Dias, Á. (2021). The influence of brand experiences on consumer-based brand equity. *Journal of Brand Management*, *28*(2), 99–115. DOI: 10.1057/s41262-020-00215-5

Ratra, K., & Neelam, N. (2018). Brand awareness quotient: Digital marketing and consumer engagement. En Digital marketing and consumer engagement: Concepts, methodologies, tools, and applications (pp. 460–473). DOI: 10.4018/978-1-5225-5187-4.ch024

Redhil, D. (1999). Brand research and the global conundrum. [Former Series]. *Design Management Journal*, *10*(1), 75–80. DOI: 10.1111/j.1948-7169.1999.tb00245.x

Rodrigues, C., & Rodrigues, P. (2019). Brand love matters to millennials: The relevance of mystery, sensuality and intimacy to neo-luxury brands. *Journal of Product and Brand Management, 28*(7), 830–848. DOI: 10.1108/JPBM-04-2018-1842

Romão, M. T., Moro, S., Rita, P., & Ramos, P. (2019). Leveraging a luxury fashion brand through social media. *European Research on Management and Business Economics, 25*(1), 15–22. DOI: 10.1016/j.iedeen.2018.10.002

Rossmann, A. (2018). Digital maturity: Conceptualisation and measurement model. En *Proceedings of the Thirty-Ninth International Conference on Information Systems (ICIS)*, San Francisco, CA.

Shahbaznezhad, H., Dolan, R., & Rashidirad, M. (2022). The role of social media content format and platform in users' engagement behavior. *Journal of Interactive Marketing, 53*(1), 47–65. Advance online publication. DOI: 10.1016/j.intmar.2020.05.001

Shawky, R. (2020). The role of trust in understanding the impact of social media marketing on brand equity and brand loyalty. *Journal of Relationship Marketing, 19*(4), 287–308. Advance online publication. DOI: 10.1080/15332667.2019.1705742

Srivastava, R., & Shocker, A. D. (1991). Brand equity: A perspective on its meaning and measurement (MSI Report No. 91-124). Cambridge, MA: Marketing Science Institute.

Upadhyay, Y., Paul, J., & Baber, R. (2022). Effect of online social media marketing efforts on customer response. *Journal of Consumer Behaviour, 21*(3), 554–571. DOI: 10.1002/cb.2031

Warbung, C., Wowor, M., Walean, R., & Mandagi, D. (2023). The impact of social media marketing on beauty clinic brand equity: The case of Zap Manado. *International Journal of Professional Business Review, 8*(4), 1–26. DOI: 10.26668/businessreview/2023.v8i4.1389

Wies, S., Bleier, A., & Edeling, A. (2023). Finding Goldilocks influencers: How follower count drives social media engagement. *Journal of Marketing, 87*(3), 383–405. DOI: 10.1177/00222429221125131

Yoo, B., & Donthu, N. (2001). Developing and validating a multidimensional consumer-based brand equity scale. *Journal of Business Research, 52*(1), 1–14. DOI: 10.1016/S0148-2963(99)00098-3

Zeeshan, S., & Hussain, I. (2017). Social Media Marketing and Brand Equity: A Literature Review. *Journal of Marketing Management, 16*(1), 47–64.

Chapter 6
AI in Fashion Design

Sunil Sankathala
http://orcid.org/0009-0004-7809-7647
Ajeenkya D.Y. Patil University, India

Samruddhi Kale
Ajeenkya D.Y. Patil University, India

Gayatri Arun Gaware
Ajeenkya D.Y. Patil University, India

Susanta Das
http://orcid.org/0000-0002-9314-3988
Ajeenkya D.Y. Patil University, India

ABSTRACT

AI has changed the face of design, production, recommendations, and education in fashion. With AI generative models like GANs, sketching and adding textures can be automated, so designers can create quicker and engage in design without guided steps. AI produced recommender systems rarely need to be limited to suggestions based on "similarity," instead they progressed into recommending for "compatibility," and they have the opportunity for personalization. AI is able to generate educational opportunities and improve learning by exploring design tools and virtual modeling, despite the technological low resource and infrastructure challenges. In addition, there have been advancements in marketing research, trend forecasting, and content generation. AI systems developed with each new technology produce new standards, change the definition of creativity, offer opportunities for innovation, and allow us to create a society that continually asks: ethical, creative and sustainable questions.

DOI: 10.4018/979-8-2600-0303-9.ch006

1. INTRODUCTION

Fashion is a major industry for Generative Artificial Intelligence (GenAI) adoption, since GenAI has the potential to enhance inspiration and efficiency across various stages of the industry, electronics industry benefits of ventures $150 and $275 billion dollars of operating profit for fashion and luxury industries over the next three to five years as GenAI efficiencies are realized. The combination of artistic expression and demand for commercial production makes fashion a natural environment for exploring the capabilities of GenAI. The emergence of foundational models, such as, GPT-4 and Stable Diffusion, has transformed the use of GenAI in the industry and created a desire to consolidate everything we know about GenAI as it currently stands and will in the future for fashion brands (Shi et al., 2025). To contextualize the developments in both the academic and industry settings, the research has reviewed more than 470 academic publications and over 300 GenAI products, and classified and categorized all the developments into thirteen tasks that were grouped into four broader areas. The overall goal of the research was systematic review of the benchmarks and procedures proposed for training or fine-tuning neural networks to generate different types of fashion data (text, image, video, 3D fashion etc.). The advancement of Large Language Models (LLMs) is also intended to integrate previously separate tasks into single workflows, essentially building better verticals to make more cohesive and workable methods (Shi et al., 2025).

The fashion industry is complicated in that fashion itself is subjective, especially when it comes to the learning of what it is that makes an outfit fashionable. Fashionable outfits tend to be visually harmonious and convey a stylish look that has some relation to the current trends in fashion, so constructing outfits is challenging due to the subjective criteria loosely governing what it is to be fashionable, and the difficulty in quantifying the criteria. Fashion subjectivity complicates the process of gaining meaningful knowledge from fashion data thus hindering the ability to develop reliable models for fashion analytics and recommendations (Shirkhani et al., 2023). Creating harmonious combinations of garments requires an appreciation for nuanced details and the number of attributes that define items by their style and compatibility. Within fashion recommendation systems (FRS), two primary functions will be touched upon: compatibility and outfit completion. Compatibility refers to the act of assessing whether the specific different articles of clothing in a combination are compatible or do well together, while outfit completion will assess whichever is the most suitable item to complete a partially assembled outfit (Shirkhani et al., 2023). A conceptual model is routinely used in these instances to define each of these overlapping terms to aid our exploration of fashion compatibility/togetherness. This serves to remind us of the subjective and multifaceted characteristics of fashion compatibility as well as assist with subsequent explorations into more - 'sophisticated' fashion recommendation modelling (Shirkhani et al., 2023).

This chapter discusses the trends in the fashion research by addressing the trends through a bibliometric analysis. The databases to be used in data collection towards the analysis include PubMed and Lens.org databases. Graphs, tables, and word clouds are also used to summarize the trends in publication growth, country-based research input, and the preferred publishers, as well as create the visual maps of the keywords and research themes with the help of VOSviewer software. The combination of these approaches gives a solid idea of the research history and transformation of the activities in the sphere of AI in Fashion.

2. BASIC OF AI

Artificial Intelligence (AI), also known as Machine Intelligence, develops technologies that allow computers and machines to function intelligently. This encompasses machines that can learn, perform, and reason independently. AI research has worked to develop reasoning, planning, learning, knowledge representation, language processing, perception, and movement/manipulation of physical objects. Planning, perception, movement, and manipulation of objects are central concepts in AI; knowledge representation and reasoning are central themes for allowing machines to think with structured information to solve complex tasks (Díaz-Soloaga & Pelzer-Peinado, 2024). AI also used aspects of probability and economic models to rationalize uncertainty or incomplete data. Early algorithms struggled to dimension, compounded by mathematical descriptions "combinatorial explosion," driving home the need for intuitive approaches to problem solving in AI design. Logic programming is a foundation for AI and encompasses conditional constructs, e.g. if, if-else, for, etc (Soloaga & Peinado, 2024).

3. AI IN FASHION SECTOR

As interest in artificial intelligence technology has risen, fears about robots replacing people in fashion design, similar to what has happened in other areas, have arisen. As a consequence of this shift, research has been conducted to develop systems that would allow clothing to be designed based on customer preferences using cognitive information technology. For AI-based systems to create custom designs, for example, part of one project was to develop a platform that studied the preferences, emotions and taste of fashion trend-setters. AI's use in various industries including fashion has increased tremendously due to the convergence of sophisticated algorithms, increased processing speed, and an abundance of data (Kaya & Aytaç, 2024). Across the fashion value chain, AI is increasingly being used to respond quickly and efficiently to the design, sales, and marketing processes. Fashion, once deemed a traditional industry, is moving through the transition to digital. AI has greatly increased its applicability in almost every industry, including fashion, changing the way we design, sell, and market products. AI applications have made way for more personalized customer service and support experiences in particular. Chatbots and smart assistants have increased number of purchases and strengthened service experiences (Kaya & Aytaç, 2024). Natural language understanding and sentiment analysis are expanding and streamlining online shopping experiences. In short, the range of ability and usefulness of AI in fashion keeps growing, with further exploration of its utility to the design process and contribution to design needed in the near future (Kaya & Aytaç, 2024).

4. DATA SOURCING APPROACH

A review of IT companies using AI technologies in garment design was carried out. Articles and academic papers were searched using English and Korean keywords published on platforms such as Google, Naver and Google Scholar. Only applications of AI in fashion design that exist in practice were included. Problems from the usage of AI in fashion design were adapted from real AI projects in fashion design. An examination of AI-based design tools resulted in the selection of nine AI-based garment design tools with actual commercial offerings and use, which drew input from large technology companies and major fashion companies. Duplicates were dispelled from the final consideration (Choi et al., 2023). The analysis was similar to a comparative approach in which four fashion design experts read each article, and a five-step garment development framework was referenced to determine similarities and differences in the AI design process. The design workflows for the nine AI garment design tools were coded and categorized. If there was a discrepancy in our interpretation of the code, we searched for the actual name of the tool to apply a fair perspective (Choi et al., 2023).

5. ALGORITHMS

Artificial Intelligence (AI) is an important part of the industry, including fashion, by employing algorithms. Machine Learning, a conduit of AI, gives computers the capacity to explore massive amounts of data. Through the evaluation of this data, they identify patterns and automate the decision process. More so, it does so faster and more accurately than in the past. Machine learning is categorized as supervised, unsupervised, and reinforcement learning. In supervised learning, the machine is trained with labelled data in effort to have a better understanding of the data set (Soloaga & Peinado, 2024). In deep learning, the machine substitute learns in part by making assumptions using artificial neural networks to predict based on the data given. Another transformative approach to AI is Generative AI, which does not stop at exploring patterns, rather enables the AI to produce entirely new and original content. This originality introduces new ideas related to creativity, and does not stop at designing clothes. For example, there are platforms like Neural Fashion AI, who develop photorealistic images of garments by exploring existing designs (Soloaga & Peinado, 2024). The fashion industry has seen various use cases of Generative AI with brands like Gucci collaborating with digital artists to create an AI-generated collection utilizing manipulated digital images of its existing products. Generative models generate different dimensions of new content from a corpus of input data and doesn't require labels. This means that generative models can be used in a variety of creative applications including design, fashion, art, music, and speech synthesis. Generative AI is often referred to as a more powerful from of extended intelligence that amplifies human creativity and decision-making potential. It has the power to supplement individual professionals' strengths, allow for innovation at a faster response rate, and facilitate more extensive consumer engagement across the fashion landscape by specifying collaboration versus co-creation (Soloaga & Peinado, 2024). The incorporation of intelligent tools into fashion design continues to grow, supporting critical practice stages such as ideation, sketching, and creative development. Natural language models such as ChatGPT, alongside text-to-image generators such as DALL·E, Midjourney, and Stable Diffusion, have enabled greater accessibility to high-quality content generation and subsequently the design process itself for practitioners in the creative industries, including fashion. Generative AI tools, including Generative Adversarial Networks (GANs) and semi-automated generative modelling tools like DeepVogue, facilitate creative evolution by allowing advanced sketching and rendering exercises (Jin et al., 2024). However, despite various advancements, there remains a gap in understanding the integration of generative AI products in a commercial context; how they can appropriately be embraced in the traditional fashion design process to generate support to early-stage creativity. Attention to user behavior and needs is critical, as fashion designers often develop individual ways of collecting inspiration. There is very limited investigation into how designers cooperate with generative AI tools, during the concept and development stage, in the design process. The impact of generative AI on creativity and design process remains unclear, and critical ethical and practical considerations such as authorship, intellectual property, data privacy and algorithmic bias, must also be addressed if we expect the use of AI in fashion design to be responsible and broadly adopted. A mixed-methods approach was utilized to explore designer practice with Midjourney and DALL·E to generate fashion (Jin et al., 2024).

6. VIRTUAL TRY-ON

Is changing the face of the fashion and apparel industry by allowing customers to digitally try on clothing and accessories, without having to go into a fitting room. Through artificial intelligence, virtual try-on technology enhances the shopping experience by enabling real-time visualization of garments, while also providing an effective resolution for customer uncertainty, decreasing return rates, and increasing conversion rates. The technology also enhances personalization based on unique style preferences and body types, which results in increased customer satisfaction and greater potential for repeat purchases. For fashion brands, virtual try-on means reductions of costs and time lost to leaning on physical samples to represent their product. Virtual try-on also allows brands to promote a wider range of product through simulation, reducing manufacturing and logistical costs. Additionally, the capacity to share virtual try-on experiences on social media strengthens organic marketing, which further and lengthens impressions regarding brand awareness and consumer engagement (Singh, 2024).

7. LITERATURE REVIEW

7.1. AI Image-Generation

Recent developments in AI-based image synthesis have made a significant impact on the creative industries, especially in fashion design. With Generative Adversarial Networks (GANs) and Variational Autoencoders (VAEs) providing capabilities to generate high-quality images, students and designers have access to unprecedented tools to facilitate multiple purposes of the design process. They can be used for many purposes, such as producing digital fashion design sketches or allowing fashion designers to see 2-D images mapping onto models and providing new ways to visualize garments in ways previously unavailable through the application of technology and the internet (Zhang & Liu, 2024). GAN-based image generators have received a considerable amount of attention from the fashion industry because they use images from an existing image database to enable users to create new visuals in ways that previously would have required a substantial amount of time and effort. Recently, diffusion-based text-to-image AI has been rapidly embraced in many creative fields outside of fashion design, including art, illustration, graphic design, and architecture (Zhang & Liu, 2024). The three steps of diffusion modelling involve the first step where relevant visual parts are found based on a user provided prompt, second, random noise is added to distract from the image data and randomize the image for the third step denoising and getting the image to align with the prompt, and the system recognizes to keep the randomness so that each generated image is different and original. Working with texts to images with new generative AI for the intended output can be tricky at times and therefore open to the emergence of prompt engineering on the part of the user in order to refine the descriptions and control better the predicted generated images (Zhang & Liu, 2024).

7.2. Application and Challenges of AI in Fashion Design Learning

The use of Artificial Intelligence (AI) in fashion design education has greatly improved the learning of students by enhancing creativity, developing critical thinking skills, and expanding understanding of the design process. AI tools, especially those that create 3D designs and virtual apparel, are one of the most engaging for students that have visual and kinesthetic learning styles. Unlike outdated format and relatively rudimentary AI tools, tools such as ChatGPT and Midjourney help students to explore design variations, get immediate feedback, and brainstorm concepts very quickly, which often translates to greater efficiency and creativity (Khairulanwar & Jamaluddin, 2025). AI's confirmed capabilities such as natural language processing and image analysis give students an opportunity to explore responses based on clothing attributes, predicted user preferences, and given a virtual fashion stylist for ideas, input, and feedback. AI has been effective at providing students with virtual simulation environments in different contexts, that help them visualize and tests their ideas in real time, while minimizing material and time-costs of testing ideas, thus increasing constraints and expanding the possibilities for experimentation (Khairulanwar & Jamaluddin, 2025). On the other hand, obstacles exist to students being able to adopt AI in fashion education. The first were considered technical issues; for example, students who were having difficulties with understanding basic AI concepts, students who were lacking fundamental knowledge in AI and digital design tools, and having limited experience using foundational software tools such as Adobe Illustrator. Beyond this were issues around resources, these were complicated by barriers concerning the pedagogical gap in many fashion program curriculums was not preparing the student to manage digital changes. There is much more that needs to be done (Khairulanwar & Jamaluddin, 2025).

7.3. The use of Artificial Intelligence (AI) in fashion design education

AI in FDE as greatly improved the learning of students by enhancing creativity, developing critical thinking skills, and expanding understanding of the design process. AI tools, especially those that create 3D designs and virtual apparel, are one of the most engaging for students that have visual and kinesthetic learning styles. Unlike outdated format and relatively rudimentary AI tools, tools such as ChatGPT and Midjourney help students to explore design variations, get immediate feedback, and brainstorm concepts very quickly, which often translates to greater efficiency and creativity (Choi et al., 2023). AI's confirmed capabilities such as natural language processing and image analysis give students an opportunity to explore responses based on clothing attributes, predicted user preferences, and given a virtual fashion stylist for ideas, input, and feedback. AI has been effective at providing students with virtual simulation environments in different contexts, that help them visualize and tests their ideas in real time, while minimizing material and time-costs of testing ideas, thus increasing constraints and expanding the possibilities for experimentation. On the other hand, obstacles exist to students being able to adopt AI in fashion education (Choi et al., 2023). The first were considered technical issues; for example, students who were having difficulties with understanding basic AI concepts, students who were lacking fundamental knowledge in AI and digital design tools, and having limited experience using foundational software tools such as Adobe Illustrator. Beyond this were issues around resources, these were complicated by barriers concerning the pedagogical gap in many fashion program curriculums was not preparing the student to manage digital changes. There is much more that needs to be done (Choi et al., 2023).

7.4. Limitations of Traditional Tools and Emerging Solutions through Generative AI

AutoCAD, Photoshop, and VR based tools represent traditional fashion design tools that are too time-intensive and cumbersome and often limited in areas of user interaction and customization of a toolkits. Evolutionary Algorithm (EA) based systems allow for the encoding of features and characteristics configurable for a fashion artifact, however, without an understanding of fashion domain knowledge mostly provide impractical outputs. Techniques for the generation of a sketch have implemented Generative Adversarial Networks (GANs) and Variational Autoencoders (VAEs) but the results can be blurry, while exhibiting potential for producing photorealistic and diverse images (Yan et al., 2022). Sketch-based style transfer which maps sketches onto full-colour renderings of fashion images only partially solves the above problem due to challenges of irregular texture mapping along with addressing conflicts between sketch and texture data. Texture-based style transfer implements visual texture and structure mapping for generating realistic garments by utilizing both sketches and texture as input data and interacts bi-directionally by conditioning on each image domain for transfer. A two activity proposed model that employs a Sketch Generation Module, and B, Conditional Feature Interaction Module, along with Cross-Domain Translation, and Indicative Two Training Schemes, to control and synthesize results based on sketches & texture input data (Yan et al., 2022).

7.5. The Generative Adversarial Network

The Generative Adversarial Network (GAN) model is based on zero-sum game theory and includes two neural networks, a generator and a discriminator. A generator generates fake data based on the real distribution of the data examples, while a discriminator predicts whether samples are real or fake. GANs use nonlinear mapping functions in both networks, generally using convolutional neural networks (CNNs). GAN research has attempted to improve training stability and control, including conditional GANs (cGANs), which give external output, hierarchical generation models, and Laplacian GANs, which benefit detail and the coherence of the sample. Alternative loss functions, like the Wasserstein distance, also have helped with gradient vanishing during training and GE trained with the Wasserstein distance. The use of these additional approaches or models helps produce more consistent learning and more realistic output data. When considered that the target use of GANs is generating realistic synthetic data, there is increased individual use of GANs in creative and design settings or prospective data generation (Liu et al., 2019).

7.6. Tools

7.6.1. Chat GPT

The study used a qualitative research approach to explore the use of artificial intelligence in the fashion industry. Descriptive content analysis and document analysis were used, with ChatGPT as the primary model. The data was collected through document analysis, revealing that AI can streamline tasks and processes in fashion design, enhancing efficiency and supporting creative work. The findings led to the development of practical suggestions for further advancements in AI in the fashion industry (Kaya & Aytaç, 2024).

7.6.2. TPACK (Technological Pedagogical Content Knowledge)

TPACK framework was chosen for developing a design ideation education model merging technology, with the intention of improving student learning outcomes. The model supports the natural intersection of content, pedagogy and technology to create a positive, productive, and engaging educational experience. It is especially useful in the discipline of fashion design education because we are able to include new technologies such as generative AI. The framework has seven components that act as the foundation of our modelling of education, connecting to technological knowledge, content knowledge and pedagogical knowledge (Lee & Suh, 2024). We applied the intersection of technology content and pedagogical knowledge and learning when considering how to use generative AI in the design ideation process, formulating fashion design prompts, and supporting pedagogy. The TPACK framework demonstrates the education, and learning outcomes related to the use of generative AI in the fashion design ideation model, as a foundational model for the development and implementation of technology integrated education in design (Lee & Suh, 2024).

7.6.3. Prompt guide for design

Ideation was developed to enhance the utilization of ChatGPT and Midjourney in fashion design education. The design guide takes students through two phases firstly with design inspiration and then with design idea generation. In the first phase, students will explore and research and then identify themes from which, they will derive their design concepts. They will then build and refine prompts for the purposes of the generative AI tools, and finally compile these into a concept board. In the second phase, students will research the design elements they want to use, generate ideas, build and enhance prompts and finally compile these into a design ideation board (Lee & Suh, 2024). The layout of the prompt guide was informed by approaches to fashion design and product development tasks, prompt engineering literature, and generative AI tools. The first version of the prompt guide was pre-tested with a group of experienced fashion designers to assess its effectiveness and usability as a design ideation guide. Directions were added to each step of the prompt guide, and an additional section was added to support different forms of visual outputs. The prompt guide supports the learner in systematically navigating from inspiration to visual ideation experiences, and provides a structured approach to recall and employ generative AI tools in their fashion design process (Lee & Suh, 2024).

7.6.4. Outfit recommendation systems

Started by asking users to provide clothing items and contextual information, and then made recommendations based on users' historical usage patterns and inferred personal styles. Work in the area frequently utilized visual data from users' clothing collections as well as feedback from the user's social network to continually improve recommendations over time, similar in many ways to how Netflix improves its recommendations. In some cases, models were also designed to leverage online retailer information to recommend complementary items as well from places the user had clothing items from (Shirkhani et al., 2023). There have been two dominant research approaches in recent work on outfit recommendation systems: outfit compatibility scoring, often through uni- or multi-modal neural networks, which learn feature representations of clothing items and score how much men the clothing aligns with a user's style preferences, and sequential modelling, which treats clothing items as an ordered time step (i.e., there are some patterns exhibited in what order garments make sense together) in order to make sure there is completeness and coherence in the outfit generation process (e.g., temporal pattern) (Shirkhani et al., 2023). Bi-directional LSTM networks have even been used to learn dependencies between items and how dynamic fashion preferences relate to this process. In other recent studies, outfit recommendation has been enhanced by incorporating semantic representations of visual features. Research has used attention-based fusion approaches to incorporate product images with product textual descriptions in models to produce improved representation understanding of clothing items. There are also deep learning architectures that have created various representations, both visual and semantic, in a shared latent representation space that improved the ability to interpret how styles and functions exemplify preferences. In addition, new ranking loss functions have become more intuitive in exploring the subtlety of human beliefs about clothing and fashion (Shirkhani et al., 2023).

7.7. Visual Intelligence in Fashion Recommendation Models

In many different fields, including fashion, computer vision is an increasingly powerful method for deriving useful information from images. The main functions of computer vision include object detection, object classification, object recognition, and object segmentation; they are vital for understanding information in the context of images. Within the fashion space, computer vision facilitates entity detection, visual analysis, image generation, and personalized recommendation. Rapidly developing into a digital, social, and personalized space, the fashion industry is experiencing increasingly advanced vision-based challenges such as, modelling style, trend forecasting, interactive searching and outfit recommendation (Shirkhani et al., 2023). The development of smart fashion systems over the last few years has developed the use of computer vision from simple object detection to in-depth analysis and creative generation. More specifically, these systems can not only detect certain fashion items, but can interrogate design elements and provide personalized suggestions or recommendations. The complexities of fashion create a variety of unique challenges, and potentially one of the most unique challenges is bridging the gap between low levels of image features and high levels of semantic meaning (Shirkhani et al., 2023). Field research has categorized tasks in fashion vision as low-level pixel/mask operations, mid-level concept/recognition, and high-level forum/analysis. Convolutional Neural Networks have proven a productive approach to bolster these applications in supporting an improved performance in areas such as recognizing objects, segmentation of images and improving textures. The application of deep learning methodologies is expected to yield even better results in fashion object detection and semantic segmentation by capturing more accurate and meaningful visual information (Shirkhani et al., 2023).

7.8. Deep Learning Approaches in Fashion Landmark

Landmark detection plays a crucial role in fashion detection, as it helps identify and locate the target points for mapping garments onto the target person's body visually. Landmark detection estimates where the virtual garment should be accurately rendered. Landmark detection provides visualizations of clothing fit and appearance through recognizing dimensions and shapes of the human body, for immersive and personalized experiences in virtual fitting applications. Landmark detection involves estimating visibility of landmarks, using CNNs to extract local feature maps, and combining local feature maps into the final feature maps which estimate clothing properties and classifications (Guo et al., 2023). In the fashion sector, we have improved landmark detection so that points being tracked can be predicted (e.g.: corners of necklines, hemlines, and wrist cuffs) and allow for higher specificity of clothing retrieval and examination. Many of the underlying models on landmark detection have been improved, including a grammar model that uses neural networks with structured domain knowledge to predict location and classify clothing. Likewise, a deep end-to-end architecture has used part affinity fields (PAF) to iteratively refine probabilistic mapping of landmark location (Guo et al., 2023). Other recent achievements include using a global-local embedding module to get a better prediction of landmark heatmaps with respect to more global knowledge of what garments are. Improvements to fashion landmark detection technology improve precision and accuracy in the interpretation and analysis of clothing items in digital environments (Guo et al., 2023).

8. MARKET TREND ANALYSIS

Artificial intelligence has changed the game for market trend analysis within the fashion industry by acquiring and processing large amounts of data in real time from sources like social media, ecommerce shopping habits, and fashion blogs. More sophisticated natural language processing and image recognition algorithms can understand consumer feelings and the way consumers use sentiment to develop a particular preference. With that in mind, AI has also allowed more rapid identification of newly emerging trends, but it can also leverage inventory planning, informed product design and development decisions, and even track current and future competitors. AI can help you identify trends that can improve marketing strategy, predict upcoming market trends in the future, and allow fashion brands to use data/statistics/strategy to make informed decisions, stay competitive, and deliver the personalized experience consumers expect (Singh, 2024).

Artificial intelligence (AI) has the potential to transform the fashion industry by tackling environmental and ethical issues through innovative and data-centric solutions. AI-related technologies have improved sourcing sustainable materials, producing goods more efficiently, reducing waste, and managing supply chains, among other concerns. There are AI algorithms that have identified sustainable materials, enhanced production in factories, and discovered opportunities for recycling and upcycling. AI has also improved energy consumption, reduced emissions, and increased transparency in supply chain management. With these capabilities, fashion retailers and brands can help their customers make more informed decisions, as well as demonstrate responsible behaviour, and gain support and trust among consumers. As consumers become more aware of environmental and ethical issues, AI is positioned to assist in the evolution of a more sustainable and accountable fashion industry (Singh, 2024).The application of fashion trend forecasting in the fashion industry is intended to achieve the skill of fashion forecast that has been associated with popular fashion concepts, materials, and even colors, and all associated aspects which involve the production of a fashion trend. The application of fashion trend forecasting in the fashion industry is made possible and sustained by a premise which involves facts which have been developed and associated with past, current, and future aspects which involve all of the fashion industry. The application of AI in a similar fashion to all other applications within society has also been utilized within the fashion industry. However, this application of AI shall specifically be addressed and examined within this paper to fulfill a discussion and examination of the application of AI within the fashion industry in context to the application of fashion trend forecasting within the fashion industry. The application of AI within the application of fashion trend forecasting has hence made a great contribution to a creation of benefits which involve all individuals associated with all of the fashion industry, and has developed all aspects associated with a consideration of ethics (Wilson & Bowles, 2024).

9. BIBLIOMETRIC ANALYSIS ON AI IN FASHION

The chapter explores the field of AI in Fashion by analysing the data available in the field of research through the use of a bibliometric tool (PubMed and Lens.org). PubMed dataset is visualized using VOSviewer that allows pointing out the relationships between the key terms and major research themes and their development over time. Moreover, the Lens.org data is examined to investigate the phenomena of publication, the geographical distribution of the research, document type, primary publishers, and the coverage of the disciplines. The findings are introduced in graphs, tables and word clouds as a holistic perspective of the Cognitive Nexus research landscape.

Figure 1 is a VOSviewer network diagram that shows the knowledge structure of AI in Fashion research. The bibliographic data retrieved in the PubMed database are visualized with the help of the VOSviewer to demonstrate relationships between the most common keywords in the literature for the period of 1995 to 2010. The keywords are “human”, “female”, “animals”, “male”, “mice”, “rats” (fashion rats), “adult”, “cell line”, “adoptosis”, and “protein binding”.

The dominant nodes at the core of the network including the ones of “humans”, “animals”, “male” and “female” suggest that a lot of the fashion-related studies within the field of AI are wrapped into larger biomedical and behavioural and experimental research, particularly that one, in which the analysis of humans is centralized and the validation of the models is conducted. High activity of human being provokes preoccupation with consumer behavior, personalization and user-centric AI applications in fashion.

Clusters associated with in vitro methods, cell analysis, and protein analysis, as well as experimental models, indicate that the application of AI in fashion frequently employs computational and analytical methods in the life sciences and biomedical research, especially in the fields of image analysis, pattern recognition, and predictive modelling. This is the interdisciplinary quality of AI in the fashion industry in which the techniques initially used in medical research and images of biological data are shifted into clothes recognition, fabric recognition, and digital fittings.

The other apparent cluster focuses on empirical experimentation and testing of models with demonstrated connection between AI algorithms and validation systems. These relations highlight the best practices when working in AI, including that models should be tested on a wide variety of datasets and that they should be prepared by showing strength before implemented in real fashion work.

In general, Figure 1 shows that the subject of AI in fashion is a very interdisciplinary topic, as it combines notions of computer science, data analytics, human studies, experimental sciences. The visualization of the network indicates usages of AI methods to bridge different fields to assist fashion-related uses like intelligent design, consumer personalization, automated analysis, and decision support systems.

Figure 1. VOSViewer Network Visualization on AI in Fashion (Source: PubMed Database; generated by using VOSviewer) (Data may vary slightly)

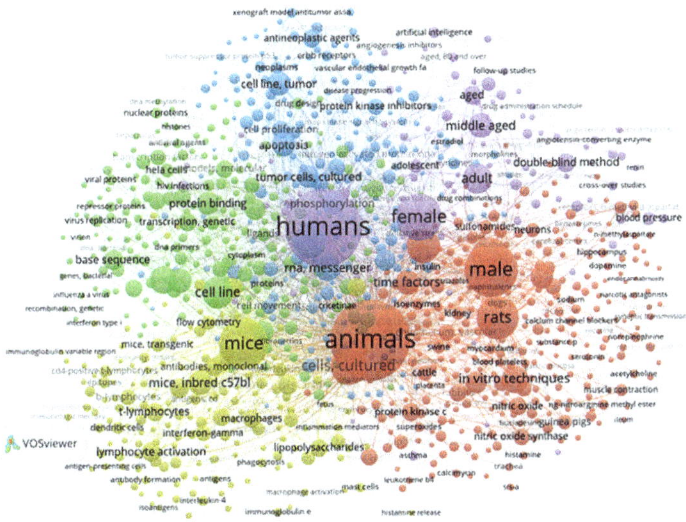

Figure 2 shows the overlay visualization of publications concerning AI in Fashion, which have been produced with the help of VOSviewer. Contrary to the network visualization, the overlay view focuses more on the dynamic nature of research topics by colouring the keywords using the average year of publication for the period of 1995 to 2010.

In the figure, the size of the node indicates the frequency of the occurrence of the keyword and colour gradients indicate trends in time where dark blue and purple shades depict previous research and the light blue and yellow depict more current research. According to this, it is possible to understand the way AI-related work in the fashion industry has developed with time. The presence of older keywords (blue-purple) like those related to experimental methods, in vitro experiments, biochemical analysis, and animal models is an indication of the initial application of AI methods based on biomedical and life-science research. Fashion-related AI applications were later informed by these pioneering studies that provided analytical models and computation methods.

The keywords containing green colours, such as humans, cell line, image-based analysis, and data modelling, are the transitional stage, in which AI research started to pay more attention to human-centric datasets and applied analytics, which is similar to use cases of fashion such as visual recognition, pattern analysis, and consumer behavior modelling.

Keywords highlighted in yellow are more recent and present the direction of research in progress. They are linked with the more developed AI applications, greater application of machine learning, smart systems, and applied decision-making models, which denote the transition to practical fashion solutions like virtual try-on applications, recommendation algorithms, sustainability analysis, and customized fashion experiences.

In general, Figure 2 illustrates a distinct time line of the transition of experimental research to applied, human-cantered AI systems. The overlay visualization serves to verify that AI in fashion is still a very dynamic area of development, which is becoming increasingly more informed by the new data-based and consumer-oriented technologies, establishing its topicality in both academic studies and the industry-driven innovation.

Figure 2. VOSViewer Overlay Visualization on AI in Fashion (Source: PubMed Database; generated by using VOSviewer) (Data may vary slightly)

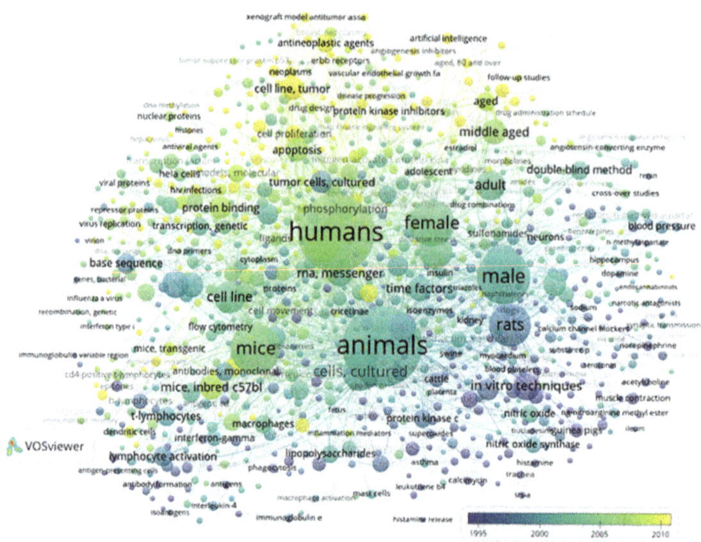

The visualization of the bibliometric network that was created in Figure 3 under the title AI in Fashion for the period of 1995 to 2010. The colour intensity in this visualization means finding the concentration and frequency of key occurrences with yellow area denoting high density of research, green denoting regular activity, and blue denoting lower density of research.

The keyword that is most focused is the keywords animals, human, male, and female. This suggests that much of the AI-related research in the fashion application is based on human- and biology-cantered research, especially the ones that use experimental analysis, behavioural modelling, and image-based interpretations. The areas of basic research are important towards AI methodology subsequently used to address fashion-related areas of concern including body measurement analysis, visual perception, and pattern recognition.

Denser scopes (green) comprise such words as cell line, mice, in vitro techniques, protein binding, and flow cytometry. These keywords are methodological and analysis-based approaches, wherein AI methods are applicable in complex data processing and feature mining-functions, which can be extended to other texts in fashion such as textile analysis, fabric classification, and quality monitoring.

Areas (blue) of low density indicate new or new-space topics research that include new computational methods, new special modelling methods, and cross-disciplinary applications. The areas represent the possible directions of future research, as AI can even more be combined with fashion tech, sustainability analytics, smart clothes, and consumer-focused intelligent systems.

The results of the density visualization as a whole remind that AI research that links into the fields of fashion is highly focused on the main analytical and people-oriented issues, and the growing peripheral ones are indicative of further diversification. The illustration proves that AI in the fashion industry is an interdisciplinary domain that is relying significantly on other fields of science and is gradually shifting towards specialized and application-focused innovations that are applicable in the fashion sector.

Figure 3. VOSviewer Density Visualization on AI in Fashion (Source: PubMed Database; generated by using VOSviewer) (Data may vary slightly)

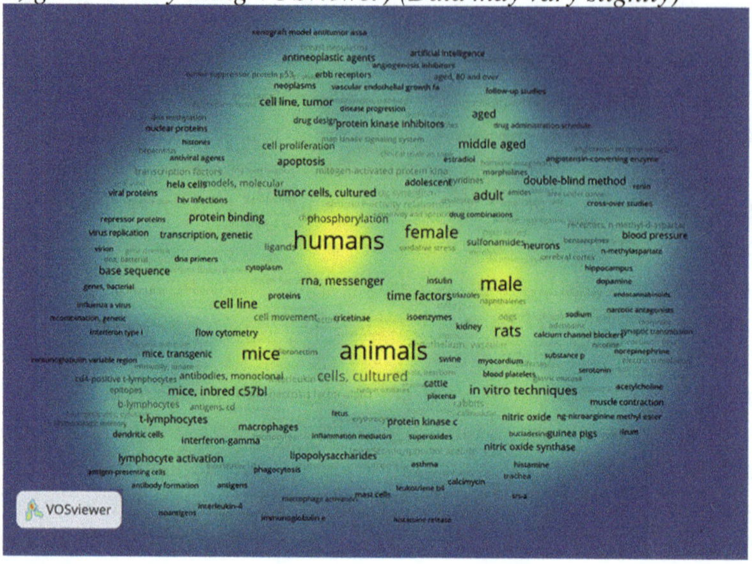

Figure 4 illustrates the trend of annual publication of studies regarding AI in Fashion during 1995- 2025, according to Enterprise basis of PubMed. The late 1990s are relatively stable in terms of the number of publications, which suggests that the initial research activity was conducted regarding AI approaches to fashion.

It is evident that there is a good rise in the number of publications between 2000 and about 2012 with 2010-2012 yielding the most publications. This growth indicates key trends in the field of machine learning, computer vision, and data analysis, which underpinned the use of these fields in fashion image recognition, design automation, and consumer behavior analysis.

The number of publications decreases after 2013, however, is evenly distributed during 2016-2020, which is rather indicative of more specialized and practical studies than rather extensive and generalized research. The reduction is stronger beginning in 2021, potentially because of the delays in databases updates, search terms, or shifting AI-in-fashion literature to more industry-focused and interdisciplinary publication sources. In general, this trend reflects a development of the research on AI in Fashion, with more advanced and mature applications existing today, as compared to the initial foundational research.

Figure 4. Yearly Wise Publication on AI in Fashion (Source: PubMed Database) (Data may vary slightly)

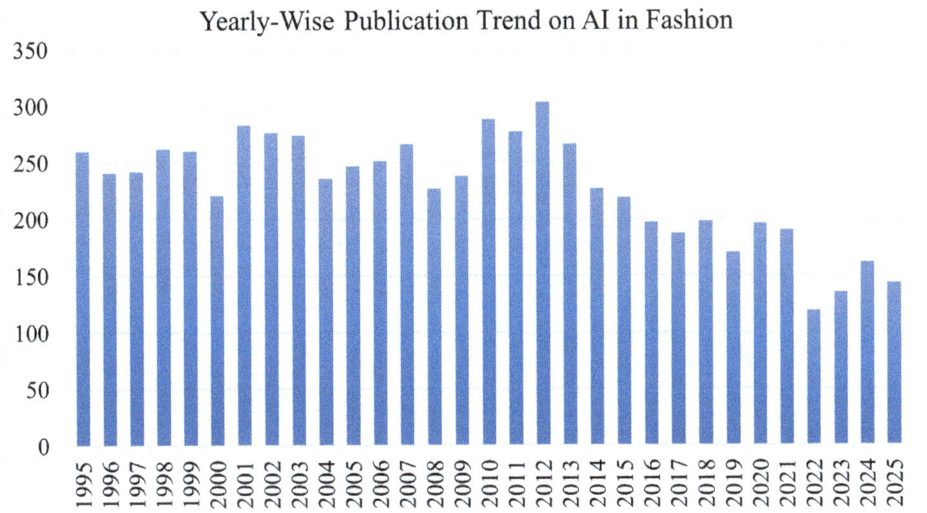

Figure 5 shows the distribution of country-by-country of research publications on AI in Fashion based on data accessed via Lens.org (2025). The findings indicate that the contribution to research is very disproportionate around the globe with the top nations taking control.

The U.S. stands out as the most active agent having 13,938 publications which is hence an indicator of a thriving ecosystem in the area of artificial intelligence research, digital retail technologies and fashion innovation. United Kingdom comes after, with 8,105 publications, which suggests that it is actively researching and developing AI-based fashion analytics, sustainability, and consumer behavior among scholars and industry participants.

The Netherlands (3,102), Switzerland (2,700), and Germany (1,971) are among the European countries with a high level of research activity, which proves the emphasis of Europe on smart textiles, data-oriented design, and ethical AI in fashion. England (1,234) does its share, making the UK become even stronger in terms of leadership. Asian leaders of Chinese (179), Japanese (256), and Indian (159) indicate a moderate level of publication activity, which demonstrates increasing yet underdeveloped research endeavours in fashion production using AI and e-commerce personalization. The numbers of contributions in Australia, Italy, France, Brazil, Egypt and Canada are relatively smaller implying niche or developing research populations. This figure shows that Fashion AI is focused on developed economies and has opportunities to further grow and cooperate in other areas.

Figure 5. Country-Wise Publication on AI in Fashion (Lens.org, 2025) (Data may vary slightly)

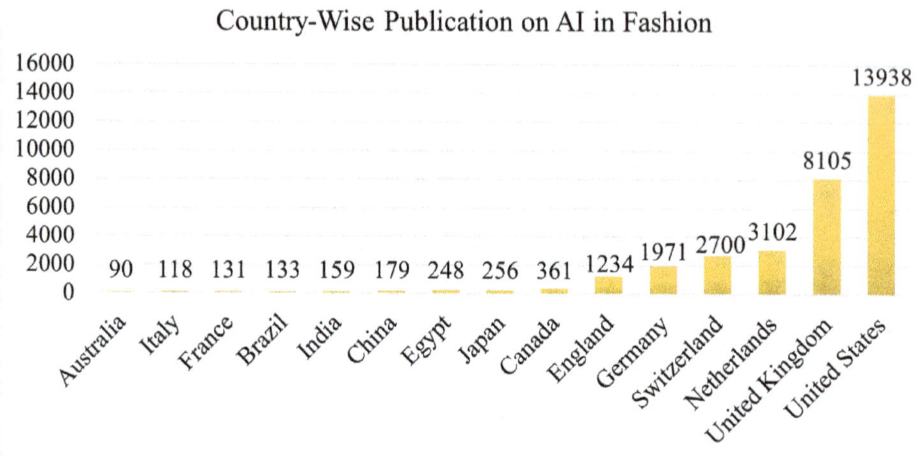

Figure 6 demonstrates the share of types of publications in the research of AI in Fashion according to the data of Lens.org (2025). The heatmap demonstrates the supremacy, variety, and maturity of academic work within the field of this study.

Journal Articles have the most outstanding category of publications with 73,412 publications which is a clear demonstration that AI in Fashion is an established and actively researched field of study. When it comes to the scientific rigor, development of theory, and empirical validation, the heavy use of peer-reviewed journal articles demonstrates the scientific rigor of the particular field. The other major types of publication are Reports (7,212) and Dissertations (6,349), implying that we have the large contribution of the institutional research institutions, industry white papers, and the postgraduate academic research. This is an indication of both applied industry-level and extensive scholarly research of AI applications in fashion, including trend predicting, smart fabrics, supply chain management, and sustainability.

Conference Proceedings Articles (5,069) and Books (4,961) also highlight the dispositional and dynamic reaction of the field as new concepts are often discussed at conferences and grouped together into the more substantial scholarly work. The count of Chapters (3,658) and Preprints (2,772) denote the continuity of experimental work and the prevalence of the new research results. The noteworthiness of smaller dataset (121), editorials (149), review (83), and clinical trials (15) is indicative of the specialization and the non-clinical focus of AI in Fashion research.

Altogether, the heat map shows that the research intensity is rather high; journal-based scholarship is at the centre of the research, but various formats of secondary publications are available to facilitate innovation, education, and applied research in the AI-fashion ecosystem.

Figure 6. Heatmap on Publication Type of AI in Fashion (Lens.org, 2025) (Data may vary slightly)

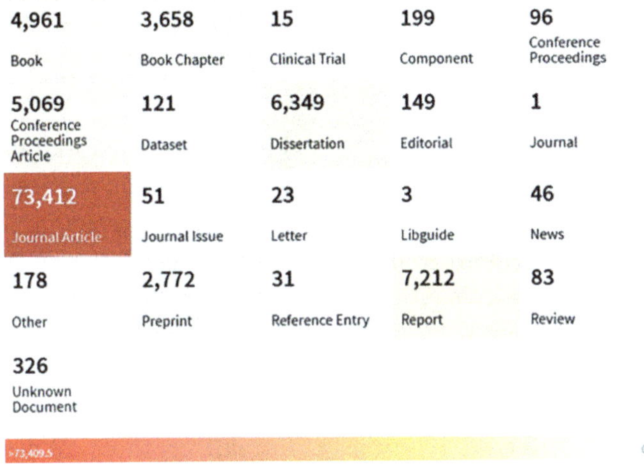

The Table 1 shows the 15 Top publishers in the area of research on AI in Fashion, according to the data on publications collected in Lens.org (2025). The table mentions the top scholarly and professional publishers of academic dissemination in this interdisciplinary area.

Table 1. Top 15 Publisher on AI in Fashion (Lens.org, 2025) (Data may vary slightly).

Serial Number	Publisher	Count
1	Elsevier BV	5460
2	Springer Science and Business Media LLC	4250
3	BMJ	3092
4	MDPI AG	1574
5	Wiley	1488
6	IEEE	1304
7	Oxford University Press (OUP)	1210
8	Institute of Electrical and Electronics Engineers (IEEE)	1084
9	Frontiers Media SA	1064
10	American Society for Microbiology	953

continued on following page

Table 1. Continued

Serial Number	Publisher	Count
11	American Mathematical Society (AMS)	923
12	Office of Scientific and Technical Information (OSTI)	702
13	ACM	681
14	JSTOR	659
15	Springer Berlin Heidelberg	637

Elsevier BV holds 5,460 publications, and it is represented well in all journals including computer science, artificial intelligence, materials science, sustainability, and applied design-core domains which apply to AI-driven fashion research. Close behind Springer Science and Business Media LLC, the developer shows 4,250 publications, meaning that it covers the field of interdisciplinary AI-specific applications in a comprehensive way, such as data analytics, smart manufacturing, and digital transformation in fashion.

BMJ (3,092 publications) and MDPI AG (1,574 publications) are proving the increased overlap between AI in fashion and health, ergonomics, wearables, and smart textiles, particularly in the field of sustainability and people-cantered design. Reliable sources like Wiley (1,488) and IEEE (1,304) highlight the technological and engineering background of AI in fashion, i.e., machine learning, computer vision, IoT-enabled clothing, and automation.

Contributors to theoretical, ethical, and open-access perspectives of research include Oxford University Press (1,210) and Frontiers Media SA (1,064), and such organizations as the American Society of Microbiology (953) and American Mathematical Society (923) show some methodological and analytical contributions to AI modelling and textile innovation.

The publishers like ACM, which is the Association of Computer Science (681), and JSTOR, which is the Journal of science (659), draw attention to the role of computing, human-computer interaction, and archival scholarship in the studies of AI in fashion. Lastly, institutional and institutionally supported research dissemination is indicated by the reports of Springer Berlin Heidelberg (637), and OSTI (702). On the whole, the table shows that AI in Fashion research is an almost interdisciplinary field with a wide variety of technology-oriented, open-access, scholarly, and institutional publishers, which testifies to the fact that the field has rapidly grown and has become scholarly across the globe.

10. CONCLUSION

Artificial intelligence is changing the fashion industry as we know it, actively providing new creative ideas and effective manufacturing processes. With technologies like generative design, predictive indicators, and virtual sampling, brands can reduce costs, improve performance, and enhance client satisfaction by improving execution. AI technologies also allow brands to forecast possibilities and trends in consumer markets faster, and in a more sustainable fashion than traditional approaches. These same technologies can inform and personalize consumer shopping experiences, helping fashion brands quickly produce fashion indices all while consuming fewer resources in a more sustainable manner. AI will not replace human creativity but will enhance human creativity, allowing fashion designers and brands to explore new creative possibilities, play with new fabrics and qualities, and identify and create more unique collections. In an increasingly digital fashion world especially, AI will be an important part of the fashion design process, including how fashion is created, distributed, and provided to the consumer. The way AI can combine creative expression and data-driven decision-making allows it to be a powerful asset to paving a sustainable and future-changing space in the fashion world.

REFERENCES

Choi, W., Jang, S., Kim, H. Y., Lee, Y., Lee, S., Lee, H., & Park, S. (2023). Developing an AI-based automated fashion design system: Reflecting the work process of fashion designers. *Fashion and Textiles, 10*(1), 39. Advance online publication. DOI: 10.1186/s40691-023-00360-w

Díaz-Soloaga, P., & Pelzer-Peinado, I. (2024). Comunicación de moda e inteligencia artificial:el caso de Neural Fashion AI. *Universitas (Accra), 41*(41), 15–52. DOI: 10.17163/uni.n41.2024.01

Guo, Z., Zhu, Z., Li, Y., Cao, S., Chen, H., & Wang, G. (2023). AI Assisted Fashion Design: A review. *IEEE Access : Practical Innovations, Open Solutions, 11*, 88403–88415. DOI: 10.1109/ACCESS.2023.3306235

Jin, Y., Yoon, J., Self, J., & Lee, K. (2024). Understanding fashion designers' behavior using generative AI for Early-Stage concept ideation and revision. *Archives of Design Research, 37*(3), 25–45. DOI: 10.15187/adr.2024.07.37.3.25

Kaya, Ö., & Aytaç, S. (2024). *Fashion sector and artificial intelligence applications*. Cankiri Karatekin Universitesi Iktisadi Ve Idari Bilimler Fakultesi Dergisi. DOI: 10.18074/ckuiibfd.1520744

Khairulanwar, A. B. M., & Jamaluddin, K. A. (2025). Artificial Intelligence in Fashion Design Education: A phenomenological Exploration of Certificate-Level Learning. *International Journal of Academic Research in Business & Social Sciences, 15*(3). Advance online publication. DOI: 10.6007/IJARBSS/v15-i3/24604

Lee, J., & Suh, S. (2024). AI Technology Integrated Education Model for empowering fashion Design ideation. *Sustainability (Basel), 16*(17), 7262. DOI: 10.3390/su16177262

Lens, (2025). Scholar search: AI in Fashion https://www.lens.org/lens/search/scholar/list?q=ai%20in%20fashion&n=10

Liu, L., Zhang, H., Ji, Y., & Wu, Q. J. (2019). Toward AI fashion design: An Attribute-GAN model for clothing match. *Neurocomputing, 341*, 156–167. DOI: 10.1016/j.neucom.2019.03.011

Pubmed, *Search: AI in Fashion* https://pubmed.ncbi.nlm.nih.gov/?term=AI+in+Fashion&sort_order=asc

Shi, W., Wong, W., & Zou, X. (2025). Generative AI in fashion: Overview. *ACM Transactions on Intelligent Systems and Technology*, 3718098. Advance online publication. DOI: 10.1145/3718098

Shirkhani, S., Mokayed, H., Saini, R., & Chai, H. Y. (2023). Study of AI-Driven Fashion Recommender Systems. *SN Computer Science*, *4*(5), 514. Advance online publication. DOI: 10.1007/s42979-023-01932-9

Singh, S. (2024). Umetna inteligenca v modni in oblačilni industriji. *Tekstilec*, *67*(3), 225–240. DOI: 10.14502/tekstilec.67.2024001

VOSViewer. (https://www.vosviewer.com/)

Wilson, R., & Bowles, O. (2024). Artificial intelligence and trend forecasting in the fashion industry: Ethical and anticipated ethical issues. *Proceedings of the International Conference on AI Research.*, *4*(1), 75–81. DOI: 10.34190/icair.4.1.3186

Yan, H., Zhang, H., Liu, L., Zhou, D., Xu, X., Zhang, Z., & Yan, S. (2022). Toward intelligent design: An AI-Based fashion designer using generative adversarial networks aided by sketch and rendering generators. *IEEE Transactions on Multimedia*, *25*, 2323–2338. DOI: 10.1109/TMM.2022.3146010

Zhang, Y., & Liu, C. (2024). Unlocking the potential of artificial intelligence in fashion design and E-Commerce applications: The case of Midjourney. *Journal of Theoretical and Applied Electronic Commerce Research*, *19*(1), 654–670. DOI: 10.3390/jtaer19010035

Chapter 7

Circular Fashion Business Model Development Using Digital Innovation in Tanggulangin Leather Bag SME:

A Big Data-Inspired BI and AI-Assisted Approach

Rahaju Saraswati
http://orcid.org/0009-0003-6244-1856
Universitas Pembangunan Nasional Veteran Jawa Timur, Indonesia

Firra Rosariawari
Universitas Pembangunan Nasional Veteran Jawa Timur, Indonesia

Erwan Adi Saputro
http://orcid.org/0000-0001-8832-7128
Universitas Pembangunan Nasional Veteran Jawa Timur, Indonesia

Susilowati Susilowati
Universitas Pembangunan Nasional Veteran Jawa Timur, Indonesia

ABSTRACT

This chapter explores how digital innovation, such Business Intelligence (BI) and Artificial Intelligence (AI), can accelerate the transition of traditional fashion SMEs toward circular and sustainable business models. Using the Tanggulangin leather

DOI: 10.4018/979-8-2600-0303-9.ch007

bag industry in East Java, Indonesia, as a case study, it demonstrates how data-driven insights derived from e-commerce analytics can inform market understanding, strategic design, and resource optimization. The BI dashboard reveals market dynamics by visualizing product distribution, pricing, and consumer behaviour, while AI techniques complement this by uncovering hidden patterns and predicting emerging trends. The insight from this strategy form the basis for developing the Circular Fashion Business Model (CFBM), which positions data as a strategic asset linking sustainability and competitiveness by embedding it through digital innovation. The chapter concludes that circular transformation requires both technological innovation and socio-economic collaboration among key stakeholders.

INTRODUCTION

The fashion world has been famous for its new ideas and ways of doing things. As the fashion world gets bigger, the bad effects it has on nature and people are also increasing. Quick production, lots of trash, and too much buying have led to practices that are not sustainable and need quick fixes (Niinimäki et al., 2020). The fashion industry has long been associated with innovation and creativity. However, as it expands, its negative environmental and social impacts have intensified. Fast production cycles, excessive consumption, and high waste generation have driven unsustainable practices that require urgent intervention (Abdelmeguid et al., 2024). In response, the Circular Business Model (CBM) promotes recycling, reuse, and repair within closed-loop systems that benefit both society and the environment. The Ellen MacArthur Foundation (2021) estimates that CBM strategies could account for 23% of the global fashion market by 2030, unlocking economic opportunities worth USD 700 billion. Despite this potential, the industry remains dominated by linear production models, and small- and medium-sized enterprises (SMEs) often lack the capabilities needed to transition toward circularity. Arranz et al. (2024) report that only 18.1% of European SMEs have fully adopted circular practices, largely due to feasibility concerns and resource constraints, indicating the need for gradual integration and strategic support.

In this context, digital technologies such as Big Data, Business Intelligence (BI), and Artificial Intelligence (AI) offer valuable tools for SMEs to bridge capability gaps. Big Data enables firms to extract insights from sources such as e-commerce platforms, social media, and supply chains, improving forecasting accuracy, personalization, and operational efficiency (Madsen et al., 2020; Quan & Hien, 2023; Silva et al., 2019). Complementing this, BI transforms raw data into actionable insights through analytics and visualization, supporting strategic decision-making in resource-constrained environments (Akbar et al., 2022; Gonçalves et al., 2023;

Maghsoudi & Nezafati, 2023; Ragazou et al., 2023). Meanwhile, AI techniques such as machine learning enable predictive and prescriptive analytics for trend forecasting, customer segmentation, and inventory management (Afifah, 2024; Kunz et al., 2023; Muhammad et al., 2022). Together, these technologies can accelerate the adoption of circular business practices and enhance SME competitiveness through data-driven decision-making.

Despite increasing scholarly attention to digitalization and circular fashion, existing studies remain fragmented. Prior research often examines Big Data, BI, and AI separately or focuses primarily on large firms with advanced digital infrastructures. Consequently, limited empirical work has explored how these technologies can be integrated into a coherent decision-support framework to operationalize circular business models in fashion SMEs, particularly in developing-country contexts. This gap highlights the need for empirical studies demonstrating how data-driven insights can be translated into actionable circular strategies at the organizational level.

The relevance of digital technologies is particularly evident for small creative industries in developing countries, where resource constraints heighten the need for efficient and competitive strategies. One such case is Sidoarjo, East Java, home to the Tanggulangin leather bag and suitcase cluster. Established in 1939 and later organized under the Koperasi Industri Tas dan Koper (INTAKO), the cluster grew to more than 300 SMEs with assets approaching IDR 13.8 billion and gained national recognition for product quality and craftsmanship (Wahyuningsih, 2016). However, this success was severely disrupted by the Lapindo mudflow disaster, which forced nearly 70% of craftsmen into bankruptcy, followed by declining demand during the COVID-19 pandemic and increased competition from low-cost imports. Today, many SMEs rely on custom orders and struggle with declining sales, inefficient resource use, and limited product innovation.

In this situation, digital innovation presents a critical opportunity. AI-driven BI tools can support SMEs in improving efficiency, reducing waste, and identifying sustainable market niches. Accordingly, this chapter proposes a circular business model for the Tanggulangin cluster supported by AI-based BI tools. By analysing e-commerce data and visualizing insights through a BI dashboard, the study demonstrates how local SMEs can enhance competitiveness while transitioning toward more sustainable and circular business practices.

BACKGROUND AND THEORETICAL FOUNDATIONS

Big Data in the Fashion and Creative Industries

Big Data refers to extremely large and complex datasets often generated at high velocity and variety that require advanced data management, storage, and processing techniques to extract meaningful insights and support scalable decision-making (Strengholt, 2020). The rapid advancement of Big Data technologies has created both opportunities and challenges for the fashion industry, where firms increasingly rely on data-driven approaches to enhance competitiveness and innovation (Gong, 2024).

In the fashion industry, Big Data is generated across multiple stages of the value chain, including supply chain operations, e-commerce transactions, social media interactions, and consumer reviews. Rather than functioning as isolated information sources, these heterogeneous datasets collectively support complex decision-making related to product development, branding strategies, demand forecasting, and market responsiveness(Xue et al., 2023). Empirical evidence further indicates that Big Data analytics is transforming the fashion retail sector by improving trend prediction accuracy, strengthening consumer engagement, enhancing operational performance, and reducing waste (Quan & Hien, 2023; Silva et al., 2019).

Collectively, these studies suggest that Big Data is not merely a technological asset but a foundational enabler of more adaptive and resource-efficient fashion operations. By enhancing demand prediction, supply chain visibility, and material traceability, Big Data reduces uncertainty across key stages of the product lifecycle and supports efforts to mitigate overproduction and material waste (Madsen et al., 2020; Quan & Hien, 2023). However, the strategic value of Big Data does not reside in data availability alone. Its contribution to circularity depends on complementary analytical and decision-support technologies, such as Business Intelligence and Artificial Intelligence that transform large, fragmented datasets into interpretable insights and forward-looking intelligence (Madsen et al., 2020; Silva et al., 2019). In this sense, Big Data provides the informational infrastructure upon which more advanced, insight-driven, and circular decision-making systems can be built.

Business Intelligence as a Strategic Enabler

While Big Data provides the volume and variety of information necessary to understand consumer behavior and supply chain dynamics, such data only gains strategic relevance when it is translated into actionable knowledge (Madsen et al., 2020; Silva et al., 2019). This translational role is fulfilled by Business Intelligence (BI), which functions as an intermediary layer between raw data and managerial decision-making. BI refers to a set of technologies and practices that transform heterogeneous historical and real-time data into structured insights through analytics, reporting, and visualization, thereby supporting strategic and operational decisions (IBM, 2021). Positioned alongside predictive tools such as Artificial Intelligence, BI plays a distinct yet complementary role by enabling organizational sense-making—helping decision-makers interpret patterns, evaluate performance, and align actions with strategic objectives, particularly in data-rich but resource-constrained environments (Gonçalves et al., 2023; Ragazou et al., 2023).

Empirical studies further demonstrate that BI enhances operational efficiency and organizational decision-making across multiple contexts. Rather than functioning merely as a reporting tool, BI systems consolidate fragmented data into intuitive dashboards that clarify essential performance metrics and support timely decision processes (Gonçalves et al., 2023; Maghsoudi & Nezafati, 2023). This integrative capability strengthens firms' understanding of customer behavior and market dynamics, allowing organizations to refine marketing strategies and tailor offerings with greater precision. The democratization of data access is another recurring theme: BI empowers users through self-service analytics and user-friendly visualizations, fostering data-driven cultures and accelerating decision cycles across different managerial levels (Ajax et al., 2025; Ragazou et al., 2023). Evidence further indicates that BI's performance impact is amplified when paired with organizational learning and innovation practices, which enhance firms' adaptability in fast-changing environments (Anjaningrum et al., 2024). Sector-specific studies also show how BI integrates operational, market, and sustainability data to support supply chain coordination, trend forecasting, and sustainable production—capabilities that are increasingly critical in the fashion and apparel industry (Ahmad et al., 2020). Practical implementations, such as dashboard-based forecasting systems in retail settings, illustrate how BI not only improves managerial interpretation of transactional data but also strengthens predictive capabilities through techniques like exponential smoothing (Akbar et al., 2022).

Taken together, these studies demonstrate a converging view of BI as a multifaceted tool that enhances visibility, learning, forecasting, and strategic responsiveness, particularly for firms that must navigate complex and dynamic markets.

Artificial Intelligence for Decision-Making

Artificial Intelligence (AI) is a broad term that refers to computational tools designed to create seemingly intelligent entities capable of solving specific tasks. Zwingmann (2022) distinguishes AI into two main types, General AI (Strong AI), an envisioned form of AI that could solve new problems using human-like cognitive abilities, and Narrow AI, a practical and currently achievable form that solves well-defined tasks for which it has been trained. Narrow AI underpins most real-world applications today and encompasses a diverse set of technique such as Machine Learning (ML), Deep Learning (DL), and Natural Language Processing (NLP) that enable organizations to move beyond descriptive analytics toward predictive and prescriptive insights. By leveraging these methods, organizations can process large volumes of historical and real-time data, anticipate future outcomes, and automate decision-making processes at scale.

Recent research demonstrates that AI is increasingly shaping decision-making in the fashion and creative industries by enhancing prediction, personalization, and sustainability-oriented design. AI-driven models enable firms to uncover complex behavioural, textual, and market patterns that would be difficult to detect through manual analysis alone. For example, natural language processing tools such as BERT have been shown to extract sustainability-related insights directly from consumer reviews, supporting product designers in aligning offerings with circularity and eco-friendly principles (Saidani et al., 2021). At the operational level, AI-powered decision-support systems help retailers optimize inventory, assortment, and logistics by modelling customer behaviour in online markets (Pereira et al., 2022), while deep learning forecasting models capture nonlinear price–demand relationships to improve pricing and inventory decisions under volatile demand conditions (Kunz et al., 2023). AI also supports strategic marketing decisions: clustering and decision tree techniques reveal how designers engage with social media and identify behavioural patterns that can guide more effective digital strategies (Muhammad et al., 2022), and hybrid approaches that combine human creativity with machine learning allow firms to tailor content, select influencers, and strengthen brand awareness more efficiently (Afifah, 2024).

Taken together, these studies demonstrate that AI extends organizational decision-making beyond descriptive and diagnostic analytics toward predictive and prescriptive capabilities (Kunz et al., 2023; Zwingmann, 2022). Across the fashion and creative industries, AI applications can be synthesized into three dominant functions: predicting demand and market dynamics (Kunz et al., 2023; Pereira et al., 2022), interpreting unstructured data such as consumer reviews and social media content (Muhammad et al., 2022; Saidani et al., 2021), and augmenting strategic decisions in design and marketing through human–machine collaboration (Afifah, 2024). When integrated with Big Data infrastructures and operationalized through BI systems, AI enables firms not only to anticipate future outcomes but also to embed these insights into routine managerial processes (Pereira et al., 2022; Zwingmann, 2022). As such, AI constitutes a critical analytical engine that strengthens sustainability-oriented decision-making, operational efficiency, and strategic adaptability in the fashion and creative sectors.

Circular Business Model

A circular economy is an economic system in which production and distribution are organized to maintain the value of resources for as long as possible (Larsson, 2018). Instead of following a linear sequence of extraction, production, consumption, and disposal, materials are kept in circulation through repeated cycles long as possible, thereby reducing waste and generating additional value within broader ecosystems (Ellen MacArthur Foundation, 2016). To translate this system-level perspective into business practice, organizations increasingly adopt Circular Business Models (CBMs), which bridge the gap between system-level circular economy principles and firm-level implementation by embedding circularity into day-to-day operations to maintain material value for as long as possible.

CBMs offer multidimensional value to organizations by first addressing environmental sustainability. Through strategies such as resource efficiency, product life extension, and closed-loop material flows, CBMs reduce waste generation and dependence on virgin resources, thereby lowering ecological impacts and supporting natural system regeneration (Bocken et al., 2016; Linder & Williander, 2017; Zucchella & Previtali, 2019). These environmental gains then translate into economic advantages, as circular practices enable cost savings through material recovery, create new revenue streams such as maintenance, refurbishment, leasing, and product-as-a-service, and enhance resilience by reducing exposure to volatile raw material markets. Ultimately, the integration of CBMs strengthens strategic positioning and competitiveness, enabling firms to differentiate through circular innovation, improve supply chain performance, foster stronger customer relationships, and reinforce brand credibility in sustainability-driven markets (Bocken et al., 2016; Geissdoerfer et al., 2020; Linder & Williander, 2017). Moreover, by framing waste as a valuable input and enabling regenerative practices, CBMs contribute to long-term societal and ecosystem well-being, further solidifying their role as a strategic pathway toward circular and resilient business ecosystems (Zucchella & Previtali, 2019). Taken together, these insights demonstrate that CBMs are not merely operational tools but a comprehensive framework that enables firms to align environmental, economic, and strategic objectives within a circular economy context.

Circular Business Model in Fashion Industry

Today's fashion industry remains largely dominated by linear production and consumption models characterized by fast production cycles, low-cost materials, and rising consumption, making it one of the most resource-intensive and polluting sectors globally. Millions of tonnes of clothing are produced each year, worn only a limited number of times, and subsequently discarded, with a truckload of textiles burned or landfilled every second (Ellen MacArthur Foundation, 2019). This linear system is not only environmentally unsustainable but also economically inefficient, as significant material value and potential revenue are lost at the end of short product lifecycles. In response, the adoption of circular business models has emerged as a strategic pathway for retaining material value, extending product lifespans, and reducing environmental impacts within the fashion industry.

Circular fashion builds on circular economy and sustainable development principles, extending beyond clothing to include footwear, home textiles, and related products. It considers the entire product lifecycle, from design and sourcing to use and end-of-life, with the objective of ensuring sustainability at each stage. The term was introduced by Anna Brismar (2017) who defined circular fashion as garments, shoes, or accessories designed, produced, and circulated responsibly to remain in use as long as possible in their most valuable form before safely returning to the biosphere. The Ellen MacArthur Foundation (2019) further conceptualizes circular fashion as a restorative and regenerative system in which textiles retain maximum value during use and are reintegrated into the economy rather than becoming waste, supported by renewable inputs, innovative business models, and effective recycling solutions.

Operationalizing this vision relies on CBMs, with four models particularly prominent in the fashion industry: rental, resale, repair, and remaking or recycling. Although these models share the goal of keeping products and materials in circulation, they differ in operational complexity and decision-making requirements. Rental models shift consumption from ownership to access and require accurate demand forecasting and lifecycle cost management. Resale models reintroduce used garments through second-hand platforms or brand-led initiatives, capturing residual value while relying on quality assessment and pricing strategies. Repair models extend product lifecycles through restoration and customization but depend on consumer participation and skilled labor availability. Remaking and recycling models transform used items through redesign, upcycling, or material recovery, demanding robust reverse logistics and material traceability.

Collectively, these models provide practical pathways for advancing the fashion industry toward a circular economy. When effectively implemented, CBMs can generate multiple revenue streams, improve resource productivity, enhance product margins, and strengthen customer loyalty. By extending product value and diversifying sourcing, CBMs can also increase firms' resilience to supply chain disruptions and raw material price volatility.

Despite their potential benefits, the implementation of circular business models in the fashion industry faces several interrelated barriers. Rathinamoorthy (2019) categorizes these barriers into cultural, technological, market, and governmental dimensions, with cultural resistance often emerging as a particularly significant obstacle. Prior studies suggest that these barriers are not isolated but mutually reinforcing (Hartley et al., 2021). For example, regulatory constraints can create technical limitations, which increase operational costs and generate market resistance; higher costs, in turn, suppress consumer demand and reinforce cultural attachment to linear consumption patterns.

Complementing this perspective, Abdelmeguid et al. (2022), classify implementation challenges into hard and soft barriers. Hard barriers include systemic, technological, and external pressures such as business model innovation requirements, regulatory frameworks, stakeholder expectations, and financial constraints, while soft barriers encompass organizational inertia and consumer behavioral resistance. Taken together, these studies suggest that the difficulty of implementing circular fashion models is not solely technological or financial, but fundamentally managerial and strategic. Overcoming these barriers requires decision-support capabilities that can reduce uncertainty, coordinate stakeholders, and support informed choices across complex circular value chains.

Digital Innovation for Circular Fashion Business Model

In response to the complexity of implementing CBMs, digital innovation emerges as a critical enabler for translating the theoretical foundations of circular business models into scalable organizational practices. By transforming fragmented operational, market, and sustainability-related data into actionable insights, digital innovation supports strategic alignment, enhances resource efficiency, and enables sustainable value creation across interconnected value-chain activities. Within this context, technologies such as big data analytics, BI, and AI serve as key enablers for advancing circular business practices in the fashion industry. When integrated, these technologies form a cohesive digital decision-making framework that supports data-driven managerial strategies and facilitates the operationalization of circular business models in the fashion industry. Empirical studies indicate that such integration enhances transparency, improves resource efficiency, accelerates product development, and expands market access, thereby helping organizations address key implementation barriers associated with circularity (Abdelmeguid et al., 2024; Casciani & D'Itria, 2024; Colombi & D'Itria, 2023).

Within this framework, Big Data functions as the foundational informational layer by capturing diverse and continuous data streams across circular value chains. BI and AI serve complementary and interdependent roles in operationalizing circular strategies.

BI system function as an analytical tool that translate fragmented operational, market, and sustainability data into structured insights that support transparency, performance monitoring, and coordination across circular activities (Gonçalves et al., 2023; Maghsoudi & Nezafati, 2023). Supporting firms in identifying inefficiencies, tracking resource utilization, and evaluating trade-offs across circular business models, thereby addressing managerial and organizational barriers such as limited visibility, fragmented decision-making, and resistance to change (Ahmad et al., 2020; Akbar et al., 2022)

Complementing BI's sense-making and monitoring capabilities, AI strengthens CBM implementation by enabling predictive and adaptive decision-making under uncertainty addressing CBM barriers related to cost uncertainty, demand volatility, and scalability. AI-driven analytics allow firms to model complex interactions across circular lifecycles by enabling more responsive and data-driven circular strategies (Kunz et al., 2023; Pereira et al., 2022; Saidani et al., 2021).

Taken together, these studies illustrate that digital innovation enables circular business models not by replacing managerial judgment, but by augmenting it through data-driven insight, predictive intelligence, and structured decision-support. By integrating Big Data as the informational foundation, BI as the interpretive and coordination layer, and AI as the predictive and adaptive engine, firms can more effectively address the managerial, technological, and market barriers that constrain CBM implementation. Consequently, digital innovation emerges as a critical enabler for scaling circular fashion business models, transforming circularity from a conceptual ambition into a viable and resilient operational strategy.

CASE STUDY: TANGGULANGIN LEATHER BAG & SUITCASE SMES

The Tanggulangin leather bag and suitcase industry, known nationally for its high-quality leather products, is in Tanggulangin District, Sidoarjo Regency, East Java, Indonesia, and has been a vital icon of the region's economy since its establishment in 1939. The industry originated in Kedensari Village and later spread to surrounding villages with Kedensari remaining the main production hub. Over time, it developed into a major destination for leather product shopping, attracting both domestic and international tourists. To strengthen collaboration among local artisans, 27 craftsmen established the Koperasi Industri Tas dan Koper (INTAKO) in 1976. The cooperative functions as a hub for production coordination, marketing, training, raw material supply, and financial management, enabling members to improve product quality and business performance collectively. Its operating capital is sourced from member contributions, allowing gradual but steady institutional growth. By the mid-2000s, INTAKO had grown to around 350 MSEs, generating annual revenues of about IDR 13.8 billion. Over the years, it gained national recognition for cooperative excellence and product quality, solidifying Tanggulangin's reputation as a leading center of Indonesian leather craftsmanship (Wahyuningsih, 2016).

However, this success was later disrupted. The Lapindo mudflow disaster in Porong, Sidoarjo, in 2006 had a devastating indirect impact on the Tanggulangin leather industry. Although the mudflow did not physically inundate the industrial cluster, it severely disrupted access routes and local trade, leading to a sharp decline in sales and cooperative revenues by about 30 percent. At the same time, public misperceptions that Tanggulangin was part of the affected area further eroded consumer confidence. As a result, nearly 70 percent of SMEs under INTAKO ceased operations, triggering a long-term downturn production downturn and threatening the survival of the cluster's cooperative-based industry (Wahyuningsih, 2016).

The COVID-19 pandemic sharply reduced consumer demand and disrupted traditional market channels for Tanggulangin's leather industry. The shift to online shopping decreased local store traffic, while low-cost synthetic imports, especially from China, further eroded local producers' competitiveness. Many SMEs responded by downscaling operations and substituting synthetic materials for genuine leather to reduce production costs, although high labor wages and reliance on imported components continue to constrain pricing strategies. Limited consumer awareness of product authenticity further reduces the perceived value of handmade leather goods. Additionally, the dominance of online marketplaces has weakened brand recognition, as many SMEs now sell unbranded products through intermediaries. Despite efforts to innovate, such as incorporating batik patterns or carved motifs into products, the sector's recovery remains constrained by cost pressures, insufficient marketing capacity, and limited support for branding and market access.

From a theoretical perspective, the Tanggulangin leather bag and suitcase SMEs represent an analytically suitable case for examining how digital innovation can enable circular business model implementation under resource-constrained conditions. The cluster is characterized by fragmented production structures, limited digital maturity, weak brand visibility, and high exposure to demand volatility conditions that mirror the implementation barriers to circularity identified in the literature. At the same time, the presence of a cooperative institution (INTAKO) provides an organizational platform for collective learning, data aggregation, and coordinated decision-making. These features make Tanggulangin an appropriate empirical setting to explore how Big Data-derived market information, operationalized through BI tools and complemented by AI-enabled analytics, can support evidence-based circular strategies in fashion MSMEs.

These challenges highlight the need for strategic renewal through digital transformation. To remain competitive and sustainable, the Tanggulangin leather industry must move beyond conventional production and marketing approaches by adopting data-driven decision-making aligned with circular economy principles. In this context, this study develops a Circular Fashion Business Model informed by BI-based insights derived from e-commerce data, illustrating how digital decision-support tools can guide Tanggulangin's transition toward more resilient and circular business practices.

METHODOLOGICAL APPROACH

Building on the contextual and theoretical justification presented in the preceding section, this study adopts a data-driven methodological approach to operationalize circular business model development in the Tanggulangin leather bag and suitcase industry. The study employs an exploratory mixed-method approach that integrates qualitative and quantitative techniques, in which artificial intelligence is used primarily for market pattern discovery through machine learning–based analysis, while business intelligence tools support data organization, visualization, and strategic interpretation for Circular Fashion Business Model development.

The methodological approach was implemented through three sequential stages. The first stage focuses on data collection and processing, encompassing both digital market preference data and contextual information on the Tanggulangin leather industry. The second stage involves the development of a BI dashboard to organize and visualize processed market data in a structured and interpretable manner. The third stage consists of the analytical interpretation of BI outputs and their systematic integration with the operational realities of Tanggulangin leather SMEs to develop a Circular Fashion Business Model.

Data Collection and Processing

This study employs two primary data sources: digital market preference data from online marketplaces and contextual data on the operational conditions of leather micro and small enterprises (MSEs) in Tanggulangin. Combining these data enables the analysis to capture both external market demand and internal industry conditions, forming the empirical foundation for Circular Fashion Business Model development.

Market preference data were collected from the Shopee platform using a Chrome-based web scraping plugin. Shopee was selected due to its high user traffic in Indonesia, as reported in national internet usage surveys (APJII, 2022, 2023). Data were retrieved from the first 20 pages of search results using the keyword "tas kulit", yielding publicly available product attributes such as product descriptions, prices, sales volumes, customer ratings, shop names, and seller locations. These variables serve as indicators of market demand, product positioning, and consumer preferences.

The collected data were subsequently processed to ensure consistency and semantic clarity. Textual data were cleaned and standardized in Python through the removal of non-informative elements, including hashtags, numerical tokens, and stopwords. Semantic representations of product descriptions were generated using the DistilUSE multilingual SentenceTransformer to capture contextual meaning beyond keyword frequency. The resulting embeddings were compiled into a keyword dataset and visualized through a word cloud to identify dominant terms and emerging fashion themes in the digital leather bag market.

To examine market structure, artificial intelligence was operationalized through a machine learning–based clustering approach. Products were segmented using a combination of quantitative and qualitative attributes, including price, sales volume, customer ratings, leather type, and bag type. A K-Means clustering algorithm was applied to a standardized feature matrix integrating numerical variables and TF-IDF–based textual features, which were reduced using Singular Value Decomposition (SVD) to improve interpretability. The optimal number of clusters was selected based on silhouette scores to ensure statistical coherence and market relevance.

In parallel, contextual data on the Tanggulangin leather industry were collected from secondary sources, including academic studies, news reports, and informal interviews with MSE actors associated with the INTAKO cooperative. These qualitative insights provide context on production structures, constraints, and innovation practices, enabling market patterns to be interpreted considering local capabilities and ensuring that the proposed business model aligns with operational realities.

BI Development and Analysis

Once the datasets were collected and standardized, BI techniques were employed to organize, visualize, and explore digital market data in a structured manner. A BI dashboard was developed to support the systematic examination of product trends, pricing patterns, and consumer preferences related to leather products. Microsoft Power BI was selected due to its flexibility in integrating multiple data sources, automated data refresh capabilities, and interactive features, which make it particularly suitable for small and medium-sized enterprises. The cleaned and structured datasets were imported into Power BI and connected through shared attributes such as product ID. This relational structure enables an interpretable and interactive exploration of market patterns and product characteristics, thereby providing an analytical foundation for subsequent Circular Business Model development.

Circular Fashion Business Model Development

The Circular Fashion Business Model (CFBM) was developed to translate descriptive insights derived from the BI dashboard into a strategic plan that generates value for Tanggulangin's leather SMEs. Grounded in the fundamental principles of the circular economy, namely resource efficiency, product durability, and material regeneration, the model seeks to align data-driven market understanding with sustainable business strategies, thereby supporting the transformation of the Tanggulangin leather industry toward circularity.

The CFBM was developed through a structured process to ensure analytical rigor and contextual relevance. The process began with a systematic analysis of the BI dashboard to derive empirically grounded insights related to market demand trends, consumer preferences, material usage patterns, pricing dynamics, and sustainability indicators relevant to the fashion sector. These insights represent the external, data-driven perspective that informs how circular value can be created and captured. In parallel, the existing operational and strategic conditions of Intako MSMEs were mapped onto each component of the Business Model Canvas to establish a comprehensive baseline of current practices, including value propositions, key resources, production processes, distribution channels, and customer relationships. Subsequently, selected BI-derived insights were strategically aligned and integrated into relevant Business Model Canvas components to ensure conceptual coherence and practical relevance guided by CBM theory. The final CFBM canvas was then constructed by synthesizing internal MSME conditions with external market and sustainability insights, resulting in a business model configuration that not only reflects current operational realities but also embeds circular strategies aimed at extending product lifecycles, reducing material waste, and enhancing long-term economic and environmental value creation.

BI DASHBOARD VISUALIZATION

The BI dashboard works as a visualization layer within the data-driven process, providing a consolidated interface through which market characteristics are explored prior to detailed insight extraction. The dashboard consists of two pages: Leather Bag Market Overview and Product Analysis & Insights.

The first page of the dashboard, Leather Bag Market Overview, illustrates the dominant types of leather bag products in the e-commerce market, the profiles of sellers and buyers, the geographic concentration of market activity, and overall market behavior in terms of sales volume, pricing, and consumer ratings. This page includes key indicator cards summarizing essential metrics, such as the number of stores and products, total units sold, average price, and average rating. In addition, several charts present product distributions across key analytical categories, including gender, leather type, material, and sales volume. A geographic map, complemented by supporting charts, visualizes the spatial distribution of stores and sales across provinces and cities, thereby highlighting the relationship between store density and sales performance. Figure 1 presents the first page of the dashboard, providing a comprehensive overview of the leather bag market landscape.

Figure 1. Leather Bag Market Overview – The First Page of the Developed Dashboard

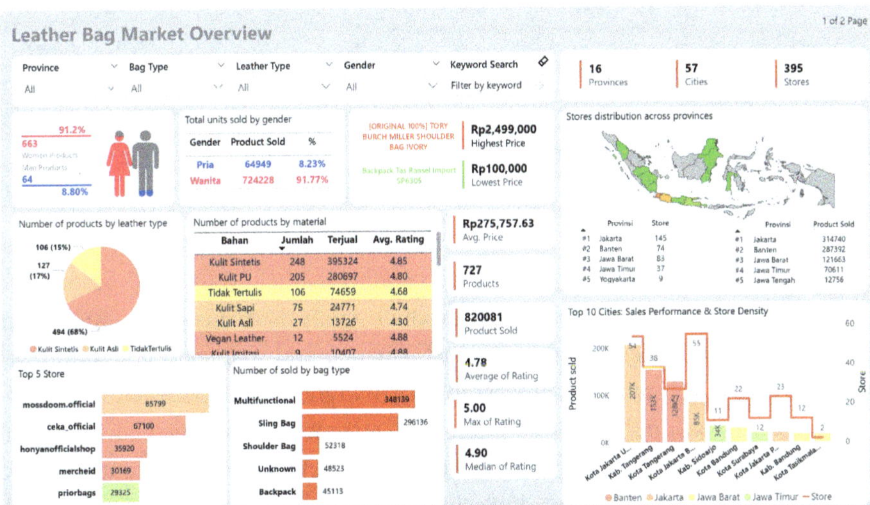

Figure 2. Product Analysis & Insights – The Second Page of the Developed Dashboard

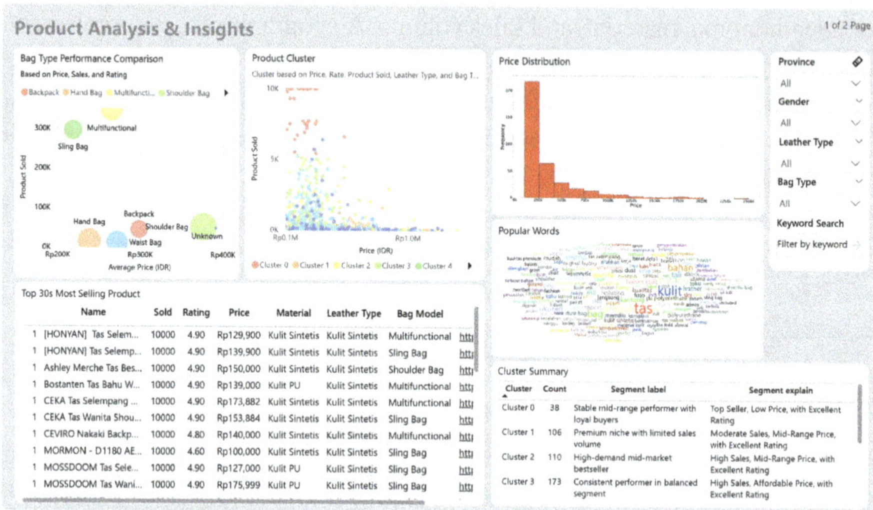

The second page of the dashboard, Product Analysis & Insights, focuses on a more detailed examination of product performance and market segmentation. As shown in Figure 2, this page features a range of analytical visualizations designed to reveal patterns in product behavior and market structure. A bubble chart illustrates the relationship between average price and sales volume across different bag types, while a scatter plot presents product segmentation based on price, rating, sales volume, leather type, and bag type, derived using the K-Means clustering method. This visualization is accompanied by a table that explains the segmentation labels associated with each cluster. Additionally, a histogram depicts the distribution of product prices, providing insight into pricing ranges and market trends. A word cloud highlights the most frequently used terms in product descriptions, offering an overview of the attributes commonly emphasized by sellers. The page also includes a Top 30 Best-Selling Products table, which lists the highest-selling items along with key attributes such as ratings, prices, material types, and bag models.

Together, the two dashboard pages provide the empirical basis for deriving market findings and insights that are required for the subsequent development of the Circular Fashion Business Model.

FINDING AND INSIGHTS

The following findings combine AI-driven market segmentation with BI-based visual analytics to inform the design of the Circular Fashion Business Model. Analysis of the dashboard reveals notable market patterns, particularly with respect to pricing, material composition, and geographic distribution. Based on the dashboard visualizations (Figures 2 and 3), a total of 727 leather bag products were identified from the first 20 pages of Shopee search results for the keyword "tas kulit" as of August 2023. These products recorded 820,081 units sold across 395 stores in 16 provinces. Prices range from IDR 100,000 to IDR 2,500,000, with most products concentrated between IDR 100,000 and 300,000, resulting in an average price of IDR 275,757. This price concentration suggests that competitive positioning in Indonesia's online leather bag market is constrained within narrow affordability thresholds, indicating that circular strategies for Tanggulangin SMEs should prioritize cost efficiency and value enhancement rather than premium price escalation.

Geographically, Jakarta dominates online sales and store density, followed by Banten, West Java, and East Java. The concentration of high-performing cities in these provinces reflects the importance of industrial and logistical hubs within Indonesia's e-commerce ecosystem, where sellers benefit from infrastructure efficiency and proximity to large urban markets.

From a material perspective, synthetic leather accounts for approximately 68% of listed products, while genuine leather represents about 17%. Top-selling products are predominantly synthetic, indicating strong consumer preference for affordable and low-maintenance options. This trend aligns with product-type distribution, where multifunctional and sling bags dominate sales, reflecting demand for lightweight and versatile designs. From a circular business model perspective, this dominance highlights a structural tension between affordability and environmental sustainability, reinforcing the CFBM's emphasis on incremental circular strategies such as durability enhancement, repair services, and selective adoption of recycled or eco-materials.

Overall, Indonesia's online leather bag market is characterized by the dominance of affordable and mid-range products that balance functionality, aesthetic appeal, and customer satisfaction. Products offering good value for money, combining competitive pricing, acceptable quality, and high ratings, tend to achieve the highest sales volumes. Even within similar price ranges, some products significantly outperform others, suggesting that brand recognition and consumer trust play an important role in driving repeat purchases. These market characteristics indicate that demand is concentrated in functional and accessible segments, while premium products occupy a relatively limited niche. Further clustering analysis elaborates these patterns by categorizing products into distinct market segments based on price, sales performance, and consumer ratings.

East Java Market and Product Insight

Given that the Tanggulangin leather bag industry is in East Java, examining the provincial market were also done to assess the characteristics and competitiveness of East Java's leather products, offering comparative insights relevant to strengthening the market position of Tanggulangin-based SMEs. Using the province filter in the BI dashboard, pricing, material composition, and product performance patterns were examined, as illustrated in Figures 3 and 4.

Figure 3. East java leather bag market overview

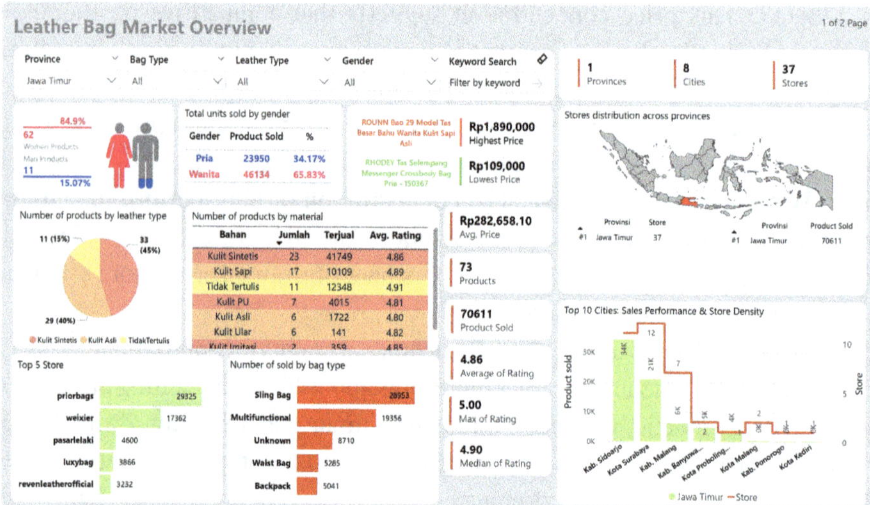

Figure 4. East java product analysis and insight page

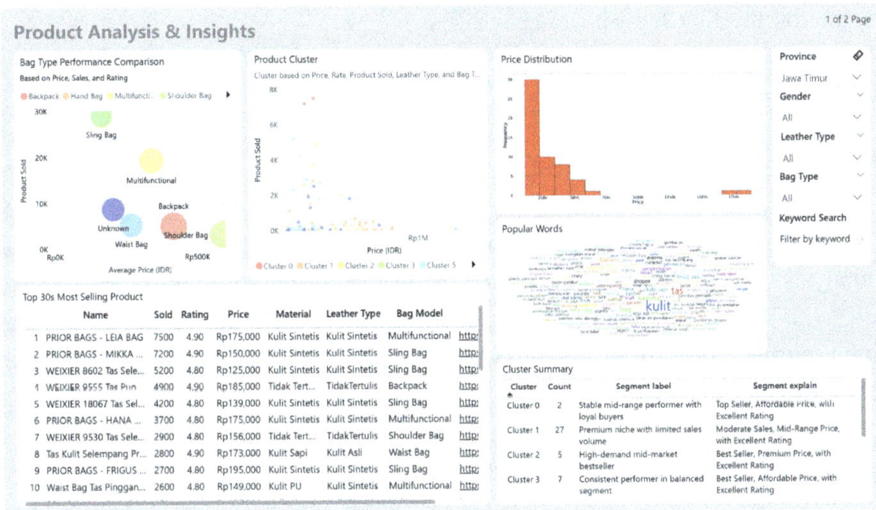

The filtered dataset identified 73 leather bag products from 37 stores across eight cities in East Java, with total sales of 70,611 units. Sidoarjo recorded the highest sales, contributing approximately 34,000 units from 11 stores, followed by Surabaya with around 20,900 units from 12 stores. Consistent with national trends, East Java products are concentrated in the affordable price range of IDR 100,000–250,000, indicating strong positioning in price-sensitive market segments.

Although product listings of genuine and synthetic leather are relatively balanced, sales are dominated by synthetic leather, which accounts for 65.56% of total units sold, compared to 16.95% for genuine leather. This reflects producer and consumer preferences for affordability and ease of maintenance. In terms of product types, sling bags and multifunctional bags dominate market offerings, with sling bags achieving the highest sales volumes, highlighting strong demand for practical and versatile designs.

Customer satisfaction levels are high, with an average rating of 4.78 and a median rating of 4.9, suggesting reliable product quality and service among East Java sellers. Overall, the provincial leather bag market is characterized by high price sensitivity combined with strong quality expectations. Sales are concentrated in affordable and mid-range segments, with limited presence in premium categories, indicating that consumers prioritize functionality, durability, and value for money over luxury positioning.

The similarity between national and East Java market patterns suggests that Tanggulangin SMEs are operating within a demand environment that is already aligned with their regional strengths, indicating that competitiveness can be improved through better market alignment and circular value enhancement rather than fundamental product repositioning.

Product-Level Insights

Product Segmentation and Cluster Result

To better understand Indonesia's online leather bag market, a K-Means clustering analysis was applied to 727 products. Multiple cluster solutions (k = 2–8) were tested, with k = 8 producing the highest silhouette score (0.53), indicating a well-defined segmentation structure with strong internal coherence and clear separation across clusters.

Cluster 1 – Premium Niche Segment

Composed entirely of genuine leather bags, this cluster has high prices (average IDR 390,000, up to IDR 1.47 million) and excellent ratings (4.86) but limited sales (23,000 units), indicating a selective, quality-oriented niche market.

Cluster 2 – High-Demand Mid-Market Bestseller

This cluster combines synthetic and genuine leather backpacks, shoulder bags, and sling bags, with an average price of IDR 302,000. Strong sales (82,000 units) and high ratings (4.84) suggest robust demand for products balancing affordability, durability, and design.

Cluster 3 – Consistent Mass-Market Performer

The largest cluster consists exclusively of synthetic leather multifunctional bags, averaging IDR 206,000. High sales (168,000 units) and ratings (4.87) indicate standardized products that closely match mainstream consumer expectations.

Cluster 4 – Underperforming Mid-to-High Price Segment

Featuring mixed-material bags priced at an average of IDR 559,000, this cluster records very low sales and limited rating data. The results suggest weak value positioning and misalignment between price and perceived benefits.

Cluster 5 – Mass-Market Favorite

This cluster is dominated by synthetic leather sling bags priced at IDR 166,000, achieving strong sales (128,000 units) and high ratings (4.84). It highlights the importance of price-sensitive, functional designs in driving mass-market demand.

Cluster 6 – High-Satisfaction Mid-Range Segment

Primarily composed of shoulder bags, this cluster achieves the highest average rating (4.89) at an average price of IDR 380,000, indicating a favorable balance between perceived quality and affordability.

Cluster 7 – High-Price, Low-Demand Segment

With similar price levels (around IDR 370,000–380,000) and excellent ratings (4.89) as Cluster 6, this cluster represents a niche market with moderate sales (48,000 units), appealing to consumers seeking exclusivity rather than mass appeal.

Overall, the clustering results provide indicative market signals derived from e-commerce data to inform strategic alignment within the proposed Circular Fashion Business Model (CFBM). High-performing clusters emphasize affordability, functionality, and synthetic materials, aligning with the production capabilities of Tanggulangin SMEs. Conversely, higher-priced clusters with lower sales highlight the risks of weak value positioning in digital markets. The analysis therefore serves as a contextual reference rather than a definitive segmentation, supporting BI-informed design and pricing decisions while acknowledging data limitations.

Market Performance Analysis by Bag Type

The previous section classified Indonesian leather bag products into eight market clusters based on pricing, sales performance, customer ratings, leather type, and bag type. This section adopts a product-type perspective by comparing average price, total sales, and customer ratings across different bag categories.

Multifunctional bags show the strongest market performance, leading in product quantity, total sales, and average sales per item while maintaining high customer ratings. This indicates that multifunctional bags effectively combine versatility, affordability, and quality, making them attractive to a broad consumer base. Sling bags rank second, supported by their relatively low average price and strong market traction, with high average sales per product. Shoulder bags place third and achieve the highest customer ratings, suggesting strong user satisfaction despite their smaller market share and positioning toward more style- and comfort-oriented consumers.

Backpacks demonstrate stable performance across all indicators, reflecting consistent demand driven by practicality. Waist bags perform well within a limited niche, appealing to consumers who prioritize portability. Handbags record modest sales and product variety, indicating a smaller, style-focused segment. The unknown category shows the weakest performance, although some sales still occur, suggesting that visual presentation can partially compensate for incomplete product descriptions.

Further analysis highlights the dominance of multifunctional bags, which are designed for flexible use as sling bags, shoulder bags, or handbags. Nearly 90% of multifunctional bags in terms of quantity and total sales can be converted into sling bags through adjustable straps and side hooks. Given that nearly 60% of all products in the dataset are sling bags, this finding suggests that sling bags represent the most preferred and functional bag type, offering comfort, convenience, and versatility for daily use.

Overall, the analysis indicates that Indonesia's online leather bag market is strongly driven by practical and versatile designs, with multifunctional and sling bags consistently outperforming other categories in terms of sales and market reach. Consumer preferences are clearly oriented toward affordable, functional products that offer flexibility for daily use rather than niche or highly stylized designs. These bag-type trends provide a clear empirical basis for subsequent discussions on product strategy and business model development for Tanggulangin leather SMEs.

CIRCULAR FASHION BUSINESS MODEL

After examining the insights generated from the BI dashboard, the next step is to develop a Circular Fashion Business Model (CFBM) for Tanggulangin's leather SMEs to translates digital market analytics into actionable strategies that integrate circular economy principles into the conventional business model structure. The proposed business model will be presented using the Business Model Canvas approach. The proposed CFBM is explained below, and the visual canvas table can be seen in Figure 5.

Figure 5. CFBM Canvas Tables

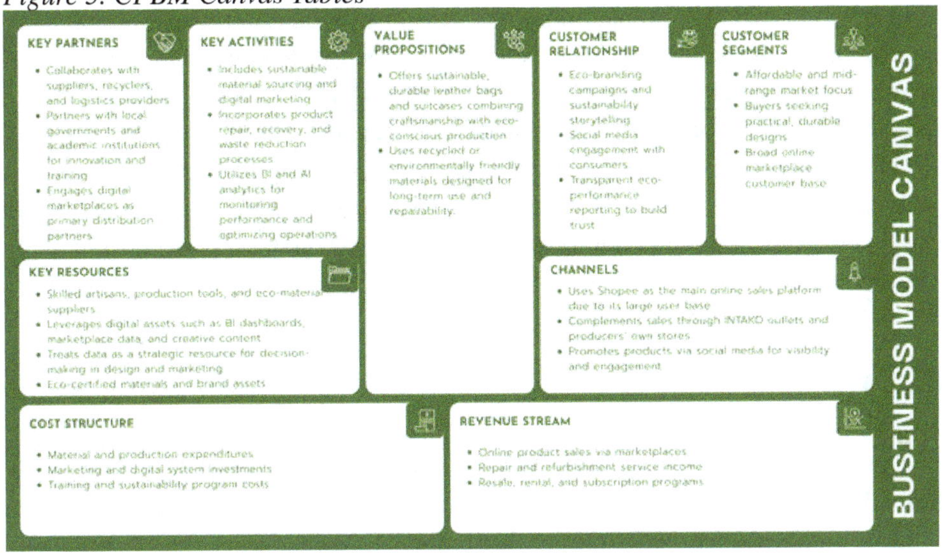

Customer Segments

Tanggulangin leather SMEs have traditionally served domestic buyers, tourists, and custom-order clients. However, declining tourism, economic disruptions, and the rise of online marketplaces have shifted dependence toward custom orders and price-sensitive online consumers. These segments offer limited scope for brand differentiation and constrain movement into higher-value markets.

From a CFBM perspective, targeting broad customer segments that prioritize durability, functionality, and long-term use is more aligned with extending product lifecycles and slowing resource loops. Rather than pursuing premium markets that exceed current branding and cost capabilities, the proposed CFBM focuses on mass and middle-income consumers seeking affordable, practical, and reliable leather products with improved sustainability attributes. BI-derived insights support this direction, showing that affordable to mid-range multifunctional and sling bags dominate national and East Java e-commerce markets, with consistently high sales volumes and customer ratings.

Value Proposition

Historically, Tanggulangin leather products derived value from craftsmanship, durability, and regional reputation. This value has weakened due to increased use of synthetic materials, limited differentiation, and weak branding in online marketplaces, resulting in price-based competition.

The proposed CFBM redefines the value proposition by integrating local craftsmanship with circular design principles, emphasizing durability, versatility, and repairability. Functional and modular designs support longer product lifespans, while gradual adoption of recycled or eco-friendly materials enhances sustainability without imposing significant cost burdens. BI insights indicate that online consumers prioritize functionality, durability, and value for money over luxury branding, suggesting that strengthening longevity and sustainability attributes can improve competitiveness while maintaining affordability.

Key Activities

Current SME activities focus mainly on production and material sourcing, with limited innovation and basic marketing practices. Cost pressures, inefficiencies, and reliance on intermediaries further reduce competitiveness.

Under the proposed CFBM, key activities are expanded to include design for durability, sustainable material sourcing, lean manufacturing, and repair and recovery processes. These activities reduce waste, improve efficiency, and support extended product use, contributing to both narrowing and slowing resource loops.

Key Resources

Tanggulangin SMEs benefit from strong artisanal skills, cooperative support through INTAKO, and established production facilities. However, digital capabilities, branding assets, and structured data remain limited.

In the proposed CFBM, craftsmanship and cooperative coordination remain core resources, complemented by BI-derived market insights to support planning and innovation. Digital content, marketplace data, and access to sustainable material suppliers enhance decision-making while remaining compatible with existing production capabilities.

Key Partnerships

INTAKO currently acts as the primary coordinating partner, while other partnerships remain largely transactional. Engagement with digital innovation and circular practices is limited.

The proposed CFBM expands partnerships to include eco-material suppliers, recycling and repair actors, logistics providers, digital marketplaces, and supporting institutions such as universities and local governments. These collaborations enable material loop closure, capability development, and knowledge transfer, with INTAKO maintaining its central coordinating role.

Customer Relationships

Customer relationships are currently transactional, with limited post-sale engagement and weak brand recognition due to unbranded online sales.

The proposed CFBM shifts relationships toward longer-term engagement through repair and maintenance services, product care guidance, and transparent communication on materials and production processes. BI-derived insights highlight the importance of ratings and reviews, indicating that durability and reliability strongly influence repeat purchases and support the feasibility of relationship-based strategies.

Channels

SMEs currently rely on declining physical stores and intermediary-managed online sales, resulting in weak brand visibility and limited customer interaction.

Within the proposed CFBM, online marketplaces like Shopee could serve as the primary sales channels, complemented by cooperative-managed digital storefronts and social media. This configuration strengthens branding, product storytelling, and direct communication while improving coordination and reducing distribution inefficiencies. BI insights confirm the dominance of e-commerce in Indonesia's leather bag market, validating this channel strategy.

Cost Structure

Costs are dominated by materials, labor, imported inputs, and inefficiencies from fragmented production, limiting pricing flexibility.

The proposed CFBM treats investments in eco-materials, repair systems, and digital capabilities as long-term efficiency improvements. Lean production and coordinated sourcing reduce waste and operational costs, supporting a more stable and resilient cost structure over time.

Revenue Streams

Currently, revenue streams of Tanggulangin leather SMEs are largely concentrated on direct product sales and custom orders, with limited diversification into service-based income. This narrow revenue structure increases vulnerability to demand fluctuations and price competition.

Within the proposed CFBM, revenue streams are expanded to include repair and restoration services, resale of refurbished products, and potential maintenance- or rental-based schemes. These mechanisms enable SMEs to capture additional value beyond the initial sale while supporting product lifecycle extension and closing resource loops. Although product sales remain the main source of income, service-based revenues contribute to greater diversification and business resilience.

BI-derived market insights indicate stable demand for affordable, everyday use leather products and show that consumers often repurchase within similar price ranges. This suggests that value-added services that enhance product longevity can be introduced without relying on premium pricing, making the expanded revenue model both feasible and market aligned.

Based on the nine Business Model Canvas components discussed above, the proposed CFBM offers an integrated and realistic framework for strengthening the competitiveness and sustainability of Tanggulangin leather SMEs. Each component is designed to address existing structural limitations while remaining aligned with local capabilities and BI-derived market insights, ensuring that strategic choices are grounded in observable demand patterns rather than abstract circular ideals. By reconfiguring customer segments, value propositions, channels, relationships, resources, activities, partnerships, revenue streams, and cost structures, the CFBM demonstrates how circular principles can be embedded incrementally into everyday business practices. In this sense, the CFBM functions not only as a conceptual model but also as a practical guide for managerial implementation, indicating how SMEs, cooperatives, and supporting institutions can translate these strategic directions into concrete actions and operational priorities.

IMPLICATION

The proposed Circular Fashion Business Model (CFBM) indicates that implementing circularity in fashion SMEs is primarily a managerial and strategic challenge rather than a purely technological one. As highlighted in the literature, circular fashion faces interconnected cultural, market, technological, and organizational barriers, many of which are evident in the Tanggulangin leather industry. Historical disruptions, cost pressures, limited branding capacity, and low digital maturity have constrained SMEs' ability to respond to changing market conditions and sustainability expectations.

From a managerial perspective, the CFBM emphasizes incremental implementation through existing institutional structures, particularly the INTAKO cooperative.

By acting as a coordinating platform, the cooperative can support collective learning, shared digital channels, coordinated branding, and the use of BI-derived market insights to reduce uncertainty and guide strategic decisions. This collective approach is critical for overcoming fragmentation and minimizing risk for individual SMEs.

Operationally, the model suggests that circular practices, such as repair services, refurbished product resale, and sustainable material sourcing, should be framed as efficiency-enhancing activities rather than additional costs. Lean production, coordinated procurement, and data-informed production planning help reduce waste and improve efficiency, allowing SMEs to address both cost constraints and price-sensitive consumer behavior. BI-based insights further support alignment between product design, pricing, and observable market demand, reducing reliance on intuition and mitigating market resistance.

Finally, the CFBM highlights the importance of expanded partnerships with material suppliers, repair and recycling actors, digital platforms, universities, and local governments. Such collaborations support knowledge transfer, capability development, and access to resources needed to overcome systemic barriers to circularity. Overall, the CFBM demonstrates how BI-supported, cooperative-based decision-making can translate circular economy principles into practical and context-sensitive strategies for traditional leather SMEs such as those in Tanggulangin.

CONCLUSION

This study aimed to develop a Circular Fashion Business Model (CFBM) that embeds circular-economy principles into the business practices of leather-product SMEs by leveraging digital innovation—specifically artificial intelligence (AI) and business intelligence (BI). The objective was to produce a practical, data-driven model that small producers can use to slow, narrow, and close resource loops while remaining market-aligned through the use of AI for market pattern discovery and BI for data organization, visualization, and strategic interpretation.

Empirical results show that AI (via machine-learning clustering) uncovered coherent market segments and dominant patterns, while the BI dashboard consolidated these findings into interpretable indicators for managers. These outputs directly informed the proposed CFBM leading to practical recommendations such as prioritizing multifunctional, durable designs, introducing repair and refurbishment services, strengthening cooperative-led digital channels, and diversifying revenue through service offerings, thereby demonstrating how digital insight can quickly translate into actionable circular strategies.

The proposed CFBM positions data as a strategic asset that bridges environmental objectives with business competitiveness. By embedding circular strategies such as repair, resale, remanufacturing, and recycling within a digital framework, the model empowers local SMEs to extend product lifecycles, reduce waste, and diversify revenue streams. The synergy between craftsmanship and computational intelligence not only revitalizes Tanggulangin's leather industry but also offers a scalable blueprint for other creative clusters in developing economies seeking to balance cultural heritage with sustainable innovation.

Novelty of the Work

The work's novelty lies in combining a decision-support pathway that integrates AI–based methods, such as marketplace data scraping, semantic text embedding, and machine-learning segmentation—with interactive business intelligence visualization to construct a context-specific Circular Fashion Business Model for a traditional cooperative cluster.

Limitations of the Study

This study has several limitations. First, it is based on a single case study of the Tanggulangin leather SME cluster. Therefore, the findings may not be directly generalizable to other regions or industrial sectors. Second, the role of digital technologies was deliberately scoped. AI was employed primarily for market pattern discovery through machine-learning–based analysis only, while BI tools were used to support data organization, visualization, and strategic interpretation. Third, this chapter primarily emphasizes business model development and the analysis of managerial and operational implications for SMEs; consequently, empirical validation or experimental testing of the proposed model was beyond the scope of this study.

Scope for Future Work

For future work, the research can be expanded in several directions. First, artificial intelligence techniques could be expanded beyond basic clustering approaches to provide more predictive and prescriptive capabilities within circular business operations. Second, future research could implement the proposed CFBM within selected SMEs through pilot projects or action-research designs to evaluate its practical impacts on economic performance, operational outcomes, and environmental indicators. Third, comparative studies across different SME clusters, regions, or industries could be conducted to strengthen the generalizability of the CFBM and clarify the contextual factors that influence successful circular business model adoption in developing-economy settings.

REFERENCES

Abdelmeguid, A., Afy-Shararah, M., & Salonitis, K. (2022). Investigating the challenges of applying the principles of the circular economy in the fashion industry: A systematic review. *Sustainable Production and Consumption*, *32*, 505–518. DOI: 10.1016/j.spc.2022.05.009

Abdelmeguid, A., Afy-Shararah, M., & Salonitis, K. (2024). Towards circular fashion: Management strategies promoting circular behaviour along the value chain. *Sustainable Production and Consumption*, *48*, 143–156. DOI: 10.1016/j.spc.2024.05.010

Afifah, N. (2024). Influencer Marketing Strategies And The Use Of Ai Technology In Enhancing Brand Awareness: A Case Study In The Fashion Industry. *Journal of Economic* [COSTING]. *Bussines and Accounting*, *7*(2), 3058–3066. DOI: 10.31539/costing.v7i2.8723

Ahmad, S., Miskon, S., Alabdan, R., & Tlili, I. (2020). Exploration of Influential Determinants for the Adoption of Business Intelligence System in the Textile and Apparel Industry. *Sustainability 2020, Vol. 12, Page 7674*, *12*(18), 7674. DOI: 10.3390/su12187674

Ajax, R., Joseph, O., & Own, J. (2025). *Enhancing Business Intelligence with Data Visualization Tools*.

Akbar, R. Wahyudi, Rahmadoni, J., & Lubis, H. A. (2022). The Implementation of Business Intelligence on Visualisation of Transaction Data Analysis using Dashboard System Case Study: XYZ Convenience Store. *Proceeding - 2022 International Symposium on Information Technology and Digital Innovation: Technology Innovation During Pandemic, ISITDI 2022*, 42–49. DOI: 10.1109/ISITDI55734.2022.9944494

Anjaningrum, W. D., Azizah, N., & Suryadi, N. (2024). Spurring SMEs' performance through business intelligence, organizational and network learning, customer value anticipation, and innovation - Empirical evidence of the creative economy sector in East Java, Indonesia. *Heliyon*, *10*(7), e27998. Advance online publication. DOI: 10.1016/j.heliyon.2024.e27998 PMID: 38689951

APJII. (2022). *Indonesian Internet Profile 2022*.

APJII. (2023). *Survei Penetrasi & Perilaku Internet 2023*.

Arranz, C. F. A., Arroyabe, M. F., & Fernandez de Arroyabe, J. C. (2024). Organisational transformation toward circular economy in SMEs. The effect of internal barriers. *Journal of Cleaner Production*, *456*, 142307. DOI: 10.1016/j.jclepro.2024.142307

Bocken, N. M. P., de Pauw, I., Bakker, C., & van der Grinten, B. (2016). Product design and business model strategies for a circular economy. *Journal of Industrial and Production Engineering*, *33*(5), 308–320. DOI: 10.1080/21681015.2016.1172124

Brismar, A. (2017). *What is Circular Fashion?* https://greenstrategy.se/circular-fashion-definition/

Casciani, D., & D'Itria, E. (2024). Fostering Directions for Digital Technology Adoption in Sustainable and Circular Fashion: Toward the Circular Fashion-Tech Lab. *Systems*, *12*(6), 190. DOI: 10.3390/systems12060190

Colombi, C., & D'Itria, E. (2023). Fashion Digital Transformation: Innovating Business Models toward Circular Economy and Sustainability. *Sustainability (Basel)*, *15*(6), 4942. DOI: 10.3390/su15064942

Ellen MacArthur Foundation. (2016). *Understand circular flows*. https://www.ellenmacarthurfoundation.org/understand-circular-flows

Ellen MacArthur Foundation. (2019). *Fashion and the circular economy*. https://www.ellenmacarthurfoundation.org/fashion-and-the-circular-economy-deep-dive

Ellen MacArthur Foundation. (2021). *Rethinking business models for a thriving fashion industry*. https://www.ellenmacarthurfoundation.org/fashion-business-models/overview

Geissdoerfer, M., Pieroni, M. P. P., Pigosso, D. C. A., & Soufani, K. (2020). Circular business models: A review. *Journal of Cleaner Production*, *277*, 123741. DOI: 10.1016/j.jclepro.2020.123741

Gonçalves, C. T., Gonçalves, M. J. A., & Campante, M. I. (2023). Developing Integrated Performance Dashboards Visualisations Using Power BI as a Platform. *Information 2023, Vol. 14, Page 614, 14*(11), 614. DOI: 10.3390/info14110614

Gong, Y. (2024). The Impact of Big Data on the Fashion Industry. *Advances in Economics. Management and Political Sciences*, *143*(1), 190–196. DOI: 10.54254/2754-1169/2024.GA18973

Hartley, K., Roosendaal, J., & Kirchherr, J. (2021). Barriers to the circular economy: The case of the Dutch technical and interior textiles industries. *Journal of Industrial Ecology*, *26*(2), 477–490. DOI: 10.1111/jiec.13196

IBM. (2021). *What Is Business Intelligence (BI)?* https://www.ibm.com/think/topics/business-intelligence

Kunz, M., Se, Z., Birr, S., Raslan, M., Ma, L., Li, Z., Gouttes, A., Koren, M., Naghibi, T., Stephan, J., Bulycheva, M., Grzeschik, M., Kekić, A., Narodovitch, M., Rasul, K., Stanley, M., Sieber, J., & Januschowski, T. (2023). *Deep Learning based Forecasting: a case study from the online fashion industry*. 279–311. DOI: 10.1007/978-3-031-35879-1_11

Larsson, M. (2018). Circular business models: Developing a sustainable future. *Circular Business Models: Developing a Sustainable Future*, 1–303. https://doi.org/ DOI: 10.1007/978-3-319-71791-3/COVER

Linder, M., & Williander, M. (2017). Circular Business Model Innovation: Inherent Uncertainties. *Business Strategy and the Environment*, *26*(2), 182–196. DOI: 10.1002/bse.1906

Madsen, D. Ø., Silva, E. S., & Hassani, H. (2020). The application of big data in fashion retailing: A narrative review. *International Journal of Management Concepts and Philosophy*, *13*(4), 247. DOI: 10.1504/IJMCP.2020.112160

Maghsoudi, M., & Nezafati, N. (2023). Navigating the acceptance of implementing business intelligence in organizations: A system dynamics approach. *Telematics and Informatics Reports*, *11*, 100070. DOI: 10.1016/j.teler.2023.100070

Muhammad, A., Muhammad, A., & Defit, S. (2022). Analyzing the use of Social Media by Fashion Designers with K-Means and C45. *MATRIK : Jurnal Manajemen. Teknik Informatika Dan Rekayasa Komputer*, *21*(2), 463–476. DOI: 10.30812/matrik.v21i2.1432

Niinimäki, K., Peters, G., Dahlbo, H., Perry, P., Rissanen, T., & Gwilt, A. (2020). The environmental price of fast fashion. *Nature Reviews. Earth & Environment*, *1*(4), 189–200. DOI: 10.1038/s43017-020-0039-9

Pereira, A. M., Moura, J. A. B., Costa, E. D. B., Vieira, T., Landim, A. R. D. B., Bazaki, E., & Wanick, V. (2022). Customer models for artificial intelligence-based decision support in fashion online retail supply chains. *Decision Support Systems*, *158*, 113795. DOI: 10.1016/j.dss.2022.113795

Quan, N. M., & Hien, L. T. (2023). Analyzing the Impact of Big Data Analytics on Supply Chain Efficiency in the Fashion Industry. *Journal of Empirical Social Science Studies*, *7*(4), 64–81. https://publications.dlpress.org/index.php/jesss/article/view/59

Ragazou, K., Passas, I., Garefalakis, A., & Constantin Zopounidis, ·. (2023). Business intelligence model empowering SMEs to make better decisions and enhance their competitive advantage. *Discover Analytics 2022 1:1*, *1*(1), 1–15. DOI: 10.1007/s44257-022-00002-3

Rathinamoorthy, R. (2019). Circular Fashion. In Muthu, S. S. (Ed.), *Circular Economy in Textiles and Apparel Processing, Manufacturing, and Design*. Woodhead Publishing. DOI: 10.1016/B978-0-08-102630-4.00002-9

Saidani, M., Kim, H., & Yannou, B. (2021). Can Machine Learning Tools Support the Identification of Sustainable Design Leads From Product Reviews? Opportunities and Challenges. *Volume 3A: 47th Design Automation Conference (DAC), 3A-2021*. DOI: 10.1115/DETC2021-70613

Silva, E. S., Hassani, H., & Madsen, D. Ø. (2019). Big Data in fashion: Transforming the retail sector. *The Journal of Business Strategy*, *41*(4), 21–27. Advance online publication. DOI: 10.1108/JBS-04-2019-0062

Strengholt, P. (2020). *Data management at scale : best practices for enterprise architecture*. https://books.google.com/books/about/Data_Management_at_Scale.html?id=GunzDwAAQBAJ

Wahyuningsih, D. (2016). PEMBERDAYAAN INDUSTRI TAS DAN KOPER (INTAKO) TANGGULANGIN PASCABENCANA LUMPUR LAPINDO OLEH DISKOPERINDAG KABUPATEN SIDOARJO. *Publika*, *4*(6). Advance online publication. DOI: 10.26740/PUBLIKA.V4N6.P

Xue, Z., Li, Q., & Zeng, X. (2023). Social media user behavior analysis applied to the fashion and apparel industry in the big data era. *Journal of Retailing and Consumer Services*, *72*, 103299. DOI: 10.1016/j.jretconser.2023.103299

Zucchella, A., & Previtali, P. (2019). Circular business models for sustainable development: A "waste is food" restorative ecosystem. *Business Strategy and the Environment*, *28*(2), 274–285. DOI: 10.1002/bse.2216

Zwingmann, T. (2022). *AI-Powered Business Intelligence*. O'Reilly Media, Inc.

KEY TERMS AND DEFINITIONS

Artificial Intelligence (AI): Computational techniques—such as machine learning and deep learning—that enable predictive and prescriptive analytics, automating insight extraction and optimizing decision processes at scale.

Business Intelligence (BI): A set of technologies and practices that transform raw data into meaningful insights through visualization and reporting, supporting strategic and operational decision-making.

Circular Economy: An economic system designed to prolong the resources lifecycle through continuous regeneration and reuse processes, thereby minimizing resource extraction and waste generation.

Circular Fashion Business Model (CFBM): A framework that integrates circular economy principles into fashion businesses to extend product lifecycles, reduce waste, and enhance sustainability through repair, reuse, remanufacturing, and recycling strategies.

Dashboard: A visual interface that presents a collection of key performance indicators (KPIs), metrics, charts, and tables to monitor performance and support data-driven decision-making.

Digital Transformation: The process of integrating digital technologies, such as Business Intelligence (BI), Artificial Intelligence (AI), and data analytics, into business operations to enhance organizational efficiency, innovation, and competitiveness.

Chapter 8
Application of AI in Sustainable Textile Waste Management

Gautam Shivaraj
http://orcid.org/0009-0000-5184-8448
Adarsh Institute of Management and Information Technology, India

M. Gurusamy
http://orcid.org/0000-0002-9425-9368
Adarsh Institute of Management and Information Technology, India

G. Silambarasan
http://orcid.org/0009-0004-6233-4943
Periyar University, Salem, India

Komal Bisht
http://orcid.org/0009-0009-3810-3068
Adarsh Institute of Management and Information Technology, India

ABSTRACT

The textile industry is one of the largest contributors to global environmental pollution, generating vast amounts of waste during production and post-consumer stages. With the increasing demand for sustainable practices, Artificial Intelligence (AI) is emerging as a transformative solution to optimize textile waste management. This chapter explores the various applications of AI in reducing, recycling, and managing textile waste, with a focus on enhancing sustainability. AI technologies such as machine learning, computer vision, and robotics play a crucial role in identifying, sorting, and recycling textile materials more efficiently. Furthermore, AI can facilitate

DOI: 10.4018/979-8-2600-0303-9.ch008

the development of smarter production processes that minimize waste generation from the outset. By analyzing large datasets and improving resource management, AI enables more sustainable decision-making across the textile supply chain.

1. INTRODUCTION

Textile Industry Overview

The World Bank has estimated the global textile market to be valued at over one billion a year and millions of tons worth of textile are produced yearly. Not only does this industry create its share of job markets to masses of people spread all over the world but it also affects significantly through the fashion, home and industrial sectors (Faghih et al., 2025).The textile industry also forms one of the greatest source of environmental abuse in most cases due to the tremendous pressure brought on the resources as well as the high wastes generated. The dynamics of fashion are ever-changing and they are dictated with the wants of the customers, who desire cheap expendable products, thus more waste of the textile and as such, swamping the world with landfills and waste recovery networks to the point of exhaustion.(Peter, n.d.)

Textile Waste

The textile waste will mostly categorize into two including the pre-consumer waste, and the post-consumer waste. Pre-consumer waste is scraps, off-cuts and other materials that are produced during production.(Olawade et al., 2024) This type of wastes has been identified to be disposed off as regular production processes and hence colossal test drop of material. The post-consumer textile waste on the other hand, includes those that have been disposed by the consumers and old cloths, house textiles, and those fabrics that are no longer in use. The monstrosity of the amount of textile wastes is something horrific. According to the Ellen MacArthur Foundation, 90 million tons (driven up or down by 60 percent) of textile waste is generated a year. This colossal garbage has largely been sent to the landfills or has been burnt thereby contaminating the land or the air. Not much of the textile waste is recycled and the rest is normally left to spoil in the landfills or used as energy. (Esposito et al., n.d.)

Modern Issues in managing textile wastes

In as much as there is the heightened awareness with regard to environmental implication of textile waste, there are no powdered solutions to this. The waste management technique, which has been employed in the past and which is environmentally risky in addition to being very ineffective, is landfill and incineration. (Stubbe et al., 2024)There is leakage that is formed in case in textile in landfills meaning that it is highly toxic liquid and may spill into ground water and there is incineration that forms toxic fumes and carbon dioxide, dioxins and other poisonous gasses. The textile recycling systems are ill developed and a material barrier like mix fibres, dyes, finishing in textile fabric does not lend itself conductively to recycling or recycled utilization in the textile industry.(Bhalerao, n.d.)

The Role of AI in Sustainability scenario

Artificial Intelligence (AI) is among the technological revolutions in various industrial sectors and the adoption of the technology in sustainable activities, particularly on the management of waste is gaining prominence more than ever before. Regarding the issue of textile waste management, it is possible that AI can change the way the textile waste is sorted, directed and reshaped. With the help of AI, the waste sorting process can be automated and efficient and thus reduce the cost of labor and increase the effectiveness of the processes. To illustrate an instance, the analysis of the textile can be done on a real-time basis (by the use of machine vision technologies) to know the composition of the material, type of fiber, the color and sort it accordingly. In addition, through the aid of AI, one can also predict the generation of waste through which manufacturers can alter their process of production so as to minimize waste generated. AI can also introduce such new recycling techniques as i.e. introduction of closed-loop systems or once used-up textiles are continuously recycled and converted into the new garments or items. The usage of AI in textile waste management is one of the most exciting things revealing the fact that it can help with the circular economy model. The next method that highlights the importance of reuse, recycling and repurposing of any material, extending the life-cycle of products and reducing wastes is circular economy. The development of the closed loop systems is possible with the help of AI since it assists in raising the material recovery percentage, making the product as close to the maximally recyclable one, and automating the process of using the used textile to produce high-quality fluid.(Bravo & Iturralde, 2024)

Chapter Objectives

The aim of the chapter is that to determine the possibilities of utilizing AI in textile waste management with the intention to promote sustainability. It will be provided with the overview of the textile waste problem, the existing problems related to waste management, and the ways AI could be implemented to address them. By the end of this chapter, the readers will have complete overview of the various AI techniques that could be adopted in waste sorting, recycling and reducing waste in the textile industry. The chapter will also indicate the examples of AI practice in the management of textile waste thus forming a clear picture of the existing situation and of prospects as well. Lastly, the chapter would seek to bring out AI as a factor enhancing sustainability in the textile sector, which can become the solution to curb wastes and pollution, and greener production and consumption of textile in future. (Telfort & Valilai, 2025)

2. TEXTILE WASTE AND ENVIRONMENTAL IMPACT

The extend of Textile wastes

The waste of textile has turned out to be a global challenge and problem that is emitting due to the manufacturing process that takes place in addition to consumer level that indulges into textile wasting rates that occur all over the world. United Nations Economic Commission for Europe (UNECE) discovers that the textile sector is responsible of an approximate proportion of 10 percent in the emission of carbon across the world and approximately 20 percent in the global world of water contamination. It estimates the global textile wastages at a figure of 92 million tons in a year with the larger part of the discards being diverted to the land fills or simply being set ablaze. The industry of fashion mostly fast fashion is a contributor to textile waste given that its growth rate has increased in the recent past because of fast fashion. Environmental De-gradation due to Textile Wastes The outcomes of the pollution of the environment by the textile wastes occurrence are complicated and impact with land and water bodies. The most evident one is the landfill burden that is the first one.(Peter, n.d.)

The pollution of groundwaters and soils can be added to the list of serious problems which can be related to the textile waste in the land fill. Dyes, heavy metal and other toxic chemicals are the hazardous chemicals found in the textile products that may poison the contiguous soil and underground water when the products are in the process of decomposition. These wastes are highly harmful to both the environment and human beings since it can someday flow into the food chain.(Olawade et al., 2024)

They also release textile wastes which pollute the air besides polluting the land. Incineration which is actually one of the most popular ways of removing the textile waste is associated with polluting dioxins and furans, toxic gases, carbon dioxide, and particulate matter. Such pollutants not only initiate the climate change but also causes respiratory diseases amongst the community residing around the incinerators. . Moreover, when the synthetic clothes are put in a washing machine, they prompt the breakdown of millions of miniature fabrics into the environment and they find themselves in the oceans endangering the sea lives and the ecosystems.(Olawade et al., 2024)

Problems of Textile waste management

Another issue that is significant to the proper management of the textile wastes is the absence of an appropriate infrastructure. The systems available in most locations in the world are poor as observed through the process of the collection, sorting of textiles and recycling. By way of example, in the developing nations, majority of the textile waste generated is not recycled and at times is not supported by any type of system. Even in the developed ones, the kind of recycling schemes are there, although not very well formed or productive, i. e. most of the goods still makes its way to the landfills.(Olawade et al., 2024)

3. ARTIFICIAL INTELLIGENCE IN THE MANAGEMENT OF WASTES IN TEXTILE INDUSTRIES

General Insight into the Approaches of AI to Textile Waste Pyramid

One of the largest producers of wastes in the world today is textile industry and thus doing lots of harm to the environment. Sorting and Classification by means of Artificial Intelligence ; In the production of the textiles there are a number of different fibers (both natural and manufactured fibers), dyes and finishes that complicate the recycling process. The AI-based and machine learning (ML) systems have already achieved a fair share of success in automating the process of waste-sorting and making it more efficient as well, especially when it comes to those that use computer vision.(Telfort & Valilai, 2025)

- Artificial intelligence and textile fragment super searching: Computer vision may also automate the process of sorting waste into the form of artificial intelligence that can sort textile material much quicker and efficient. The computer vision unit captures high-resolution images of the textile waste after which the AI algorithms calculate the composition of the material, type of fiber and properties of the dye using the pictures. To illustrate, AI will be capable of assuming that cotton, polyester and wool as well as the combination of fabrics may be sorted out so that these goods could be separated to be recycled or re-used.

- Material Identification and Classification: It will be referenced to machine learning, which will be trained on many thousand images of textiles and will be able to identify a few categories of fabrics, colors and impurities. As soon as the system identifies a material, one may categorize them in one of the modes (e.g. synthetic vs. natural fibers; recyclable vs. non-recyclable). Besides nullifying the sorting accuracy, this automated sorting will take shorter time since the chances of manual intervention would be avoided, and this too would raise the number of sorting mistakes.(Bravo & Iturralde, 2024)
- Smart Sorting Robots: The robotic mechanism that applies computer vision and robotics with the help of AI will physically stack the textile wastes by tracking the found waste material. These robots are also sophisticated in the sense that they assist them to pick and to sort the textile waste in a more effective way such that various materials like cotton, polyester and nylon are separated. This helps to reduce contamination of recyclable products, which is one of the principal concerns in classic sorting system.(Faghih et al., 2025)

Artificial creativity and Textile Recycling and Upcycling

Recycling and upcycling are the most important characteristics of the efforts concerning the minimization of the consumption of textiles and extension of their life cycle.(Karmali & Valilai, 2025) Even though the recycling of textile was subject to such problems as the issues of contamination, decline of quality and lack of technology, the AI technology was applied to increase the recycling process in terms of efficiency and scalability. Artificial intelligence can help to recycle and make it more environmentally friendly and reduce the impacts of the waste of texts. (Bhalerao, n.d.)

- Textile Fiber Recycling: Deprecation of fibers in the process of textile recycling may be seen as one of the most burning problems in the area of recycling textiles. A good example is that polyester fibers might not be stronger because of the multiplicity of the recycling procedures. Machine learning also predicts the durability and recyclability of the different fibers present using the help of AI-driven models to come up with the ways in which the processes that are involved cause the minimum damage to the fibers and ways in which the quality of the fibers is not being compromised.(Karmali & Valilai, 2025)
- Improved Material Recovery: With the help of AI and ML plans, one will be able to use large amounts of data in order to optimize the process of recycling. On the example of this, AI models can be applied to determine the manner in which the most valuable materials can be extracted out of waste

textiles. Analyzing data, AI would be able to recommend which category of belongings would it be possible to recycle most of all, which processes would result in having a fibre, dyes, and other substances extracted. This would help in recycling plants to increase the amount of recyclable materials and to make their total operations fruitful.

- Artificial intelligence in design: The creative process of upcycling is where new applications are discovered in used products so as to come up with more valued items. Upcycling of textiles also can entail the participation of AI in terms of designing new products, which will be made of the waste materials. Generative design algorithm can also assist design to produce sustainable products by highlighting decisions that have a less impact resource-wise on material. The process of upcycling may also be accomplished due to the use of AI, as it would forecast what discarded materials may be re-utilized to process into new materials or products and do not send them to dump sites anymore.
- Circular Economy AI: The model that is created under circular economy is in such a manner that the products and material goes in use as on as many times as possible in order to reduce or avoid the waste materials, therefore sustainable. AI is making the circular economy in the textile possible as this technology makes clothes more recyclable, and designers create clothes with an extended cycle. It is also possible to make the processes more effective because such AI can guarantee that textile goes through sorting, cleaning, and processing in a way that it could be effectively used in regards to closed-loop system where wastes should be minimized, and resources should be recycled. (Karmali & Valilai, 2025)

AI driven Waste Reduction

The most effective way that can be used to resolve the problem of the environment and the textile industry is to ensure that there is no textile waste. AI can possibly come in handy to achieve the space to eradicate waste in production, consumption, and post-consumption setting of products. To give an example, AI may develop the most effective patterns on clothes that should use less fabric and be described as the maintenance of the type of design regarding the beauty value.

Figure 1. Flow diagram of AI waste reduction

• Generation of Wastes: Through the inputting of predictive analytics, artificial intelligence can foresee the waste generation based on the production plans, consumer patterns and history of waste that has been processed before. The prediction of the waste to be generated in the future will assist the manufacturers to synchronize the manufacturing trends thereby consuming minimal amounts of materials. As an example, AI-based models may be applied to calculate the exact amount of fabrics that would be needed in order to manufacture a particular line of clothing and, consequently, prevent the cases of excess manufacturing and wasting. It also helps companies in the optimization of the inventory management system, and an overstock does not become a waste.(Bravo & Iturralde, 2024)

Smart Fabric Waste Management in Manufacturing: through AI, one can intervent in the actual use of fabrics through warning people or machines when they are wasting fabrics unnecessarily. This could also lead to immediate revolution of production techniques in order to curtail wastage. Also, AI has the capability of making acquiring materials simple and therefore raw materials can be effectively laid out and applied in the best possible manner.

Artificial intelligence in Closed loop Textile Systems

- The concept of closed textile loop shall be at the epicenter of coming up with a sustainable textile industry. The closed loop system is more focused on the process of recycling and uses of the textilers without involving the additional materials in the process. AI would be the core of constructing and running closed-loop textile systems since it can contribute to the enhancement of sorting, recycling, and upcycling.

- Textile Collection Systems: AI would enable textile collection activities to be more efficient and textile sorting activities to be optimized in such a way that the left out wastes are well classified and directed to the respective recycling channels. The accuracy of the sorting can become even more accurate with the help of the AI algorithms in the way the used materials are taken through in such a way that it is not flung towards the landfills, but goes into the correct machinery so that it can be refined into fibers that can be used.
- A Continuous Loop: AI can provide an opportunity of networking the players between waste production, recycling, and redesign of products in the textile corporate. Taking an example, AI will allow one to trace the lifecycle of textiles where it will be possible to obtain information on the composition of the material, the way it is used and recycled. Then this can be fed backwards into the design process and manufacturers will be able to make new products using the recycled ones. This way AI introduces the smooth cycle of circular economy in the textile sector where the by-products replenish those of good quality.

4. CIRCULAR ECONOMY OF TEXTILES AI

What is Circular Economy of Textile Industry?

Circular economy concept is characterized by the need to develop systems that will be observed to be aimed at sustainability, reduced level of wastes and recycling of non-renewable resources. On the contrary, a circular economy is expected to cycle around the process by filling a loophole between the so-called take, make, dispose concept which is regarded as the basic structure of the traditional form of eco-economic system. Textile industry: It is another industry that is contributing to enormous wastes compared to any other sector in the world, and it needs to change to circular economy promptly. The given transformation includes the process of the conversion of the traditional linear structure of the textile manufacturing into the one that is in existence under the life cycle of fabrics and garments, waste reduction and recycling of resources.(Candeloro, 2020)

Artificial Intelligence (AI) plays a major role in supporting this change by guaranteeing textile recycling process, sorting garbage and making textile products more recyclable or reuseable. The entire process of the textile industry can be turned eco-friendly, with the assistance of various AI-driven solutions, the textile suppliers and developers, as well as waste disposal agencies can cooperate and organize the decontamination of the textile industry as a whole. The chapter examines what AI is and how it can affect the circular economy of the textile and how it can assist in the efficient management of the textile waste operations.(Cate, 2025; Esposito et al., n.d.)

The Textile Knowledge on Circular Economy

The vision of the circular economy that is being pursued by the textile is that through converting the textiles into a constant process of recycling and reifying, it will have a pre-condition of reducing the raw materials that have to undergo the manufacturing process. The strategy can help in curbing the adverse impact of the textile waste on the environment including carbon, water-use and landfill. The circular economy has the objective of retaining the textiles in the circulation to go to waste but also to propel the sustainability gears along with economic development. (Esposito et al., n.d.)

The principles of Circular economy in Textiles

Design Long Life: The products are designed in such a manner that it may last longer and one is not used to replacing them that much. These involve such aspects as use of sustainable materials, design that is repairable, and use of attire and cloth that is easy to recycle after use. Recycling and Reuse: All products used in textile like the fibers; the dyes and the fabrics are always recycled into other new ones or can be reused. The recycling systems are designed in such a way that there is retrieval of high valued materials in the used textile and therefore they can be recycled to make a new pair of clothes and textiles. Business Model Innovation: Then there is the Business Model Innovation that aims at novel business models, such as product-as-a-service (e.g., leasing textiles, rather than buying them), so that the producers and consumers can get involved in an extended system in which they will not only reuse the products but also recycle them, rotating them and not discarding them into garbage dumps.(Stubbe et al., 2024)

Several Issues on use of Circular Economy in Textiles

One of the challenges that the textile sector must overcome in its climb toward complete acceptance of a circular economy involves that there are no technologies that can enable the efficient recycling of textile materials, that the textile wastes are highly complex (e.g., colourants, finishes, crushed fibers, mixed fibers) and the very low collection and sorting of texts are. Artificial intelligence has been regarded as among the key methods of unlocking this kind of block in increasing recycling performance levels, sorting, and control of the supply chain.(Mauro, 2021b)

Waste-to-Value Model- Artificial Intelligence

Waste value creation is one of the capital ideas of the circular economy. Waste-to-value models in textile: One of the objectives that are to be attained under textile is to resuscitate the valuable fibers, fabrics etc, which are present in the waste textiles and re-manufacture them as new products. AI plays a key role in fully optimizing such operations as it increases the percentage of recovering the materials and the capacity to create new products of considerable value out of textile waste.(Olawade et al., 2024)

- Fiber AI: Conventional recycling will involve textile wastes using huge amounts of fibers during the recovery process. The evidence of the change of the composition of the waste of textile, the evaluation of the fibers quality, and the potential optimal cost-efficient method of fiber recovery can be researched with the help of AI-driven systems. Conducting recycling of materials through machine learning methods can be optimized in a manner that ensures that fibers are not ruined once they are recovered, and can be reused again and that the relative quality loss is still on a relatively low level with the general quality barely being affected.
- Upcycling Textile Waste: AI Upcycling textile waste also involved its help; in this case, it will change the textile wastes to the products of higher value. Using the example of one of them, AI may contribute to creating more environmentally friendly items by considering consumers choices and suggesting to them design variations involving recycled textiles. The generation pattern algorithm can generate optimized pattern to reduce waste, and enhance fabric offcit reuse or waste fiber recycling. Besides, the AI systems can trace waste streams of texts and suggest alternative solutions to the use of certain waste textiles, which this has presented a prospect of upcycling to various fields, including fashion, home furnishing, and industrial textiles.
- New Products with Textile Waste: Another option is finding the opportunity to create totally different types of products with textile waste with the help of AI, which is a possibility of expanding the attitudes of circularity of the textile industry. As an example, AI will have the capability to dissolve waste pipes so that it can make biodegradable or environmentally friend material as a substitution to the popular use of artificial materials. This enables production of nature friendly products thus reduced use of virgin raw materials which is competitive advantage in the market that is keen about the environment.(Bhalerao, n.d.)

AI and Circular Textiles AIs and Circular Textiles

The textile industry should be positioned to obtain a successful circular economy and thereby the concept of transparency should be upheld all through the textile supply chain such as the source of raw materials and the post life cycle disposal. Explaining the textile Industry and making it more sustainable and traceable AI will enable explaining the textile industry and making it more sustainable and trackable: monitoring the supply chain of materials, life cycle of products and reusing textile rather than disposing of it.(Mauro, 2021b)

- Blockchain and AI Combination: The blockchain and AI combination are a prospective instrument in regards to the transparency of the textile waste management. The blockchain will be in a position to record all the transactions or processes involved in the life cycle of a textile product and the block chain data could be then be analyzed and optimized using AI. It can be fully traced and hence it is possible to properly recycle or reuse textile products and the likelihood of losing the products or taking them to the landfills is also minimized upon integration.
- Monitoring in Real-time: With the help of AI, the waste of textiles could be tracked in real-time once combined with sensors and IoT hardware. Information on the type and quantities of textiles entering the waste can be provided in such systems and through this, it is possible to know where the reduction can be increased. Such tracking in real-time will enable the regulation of the handling of the materials effectively and within the range of the circular economy, and manufacturers will be able to change the processes in real-time so that the recycling processes could be as extensive as possible, and wastes can be minimal.
- Supply Chain Optimization: AI holds the key in terms of optimization of textile supply chain towards circularity. AI enables the possibility to identify the inefficiencies of the production, distribution, and handling of waste processes basing on the advanced information analysis. To give an example, the amount of waste in the form of textile produced during a certain time period could be found with the help of historical data and measures aimed at reducing the wasteful behavior could be suggested by AI. (Stubbe et al., 2024)

AI-Textile Design to Sustainability

It is one of the most crucial stages of textile manufacturing during the design under which circularity could be improved. With the AI, the designer can use the garments and fabrics to become more sustainable, recyclable and durable. The design process could be made more optimized through the use of AI and thus AI would allow the creation of designs where more material is not wasted and the design is as easily recycled as possible, through the use of generative design algorithms and predictive analytics.

- Design to Minimize Wastes: Generative design is the application of AI to the field of design, which enables the creator to create the best textile patterns with minimum wastage. It takes into consideration the fabric used, the garment size and the consumer liking and suggests certain patterns that consume less amount of fabric and utilize the available resources at maximum.
- Design in Disassembling: With the help of AI, the designer will be guided to design textile which can be dismantled easily at the time of its end of life services. e.g. AI will suggest certain revisions in the designing to make sure that the components which can constitute clothes can easily be separated at the time of recycling and this separation should not damage the parts. Dis-bly design is also significant to enable the product to stay on the loop in the plan of circular economy since it will be easy to bring them back into the recycling processing with minimal effort.
- Material innovation: AI could help to research a new material, which is more sustainable either it is easier to recycle or it is manufactured using renewable materials. Machine learning will allow such things as the algorithms are capable of analyzing within the large groups of information and discovering which materials will develop into the most sustainable and recyclable as time passes on to enable the development of a greater level of a circular economy made up of textiles such as those existing.

The use of Transparency with AI and Blockchain to Textile Waste

One of the cases when blockchain and AI can be especially useful is the application of these technologies to make the textile waste management responsible and transparent. Blockchain creates a history of all transactions or events throughout the life cycle of any textile product and it is decentralized and cannot be altered and starts at the point of production to the end. The AI will be able to facilitate this aspect of transparency as it will review the data remaining on the blockchain and streamline the flow of materials, identify wastefulness and improve the sustainability outcomes.(Stubbe et al., 2024)

- Recyclability: AI-driven blockchain will have the capability of verifying the recyclability of the textile, the textile is under process of recycling or has gone through the recycling process. It may be of immense assistance in the implementation of the sustainability standards and rules. The solutions that can increase the better accountability and transparency of the textile waste management are AI and blockchain as the supply chain of materials will be traced and recycling could be made traceable.(Stubbe et al., 2024)

Artificial intelligence in Textile Circular Economy-What Is Coming Next?

AI plays a significant role in enabling the sector of textile to adopt the concept of circular economy in future. They will also become more intelligent and complex due to the development of the AI technologies and have the capability of offering an answer to the thorny issues of waste management in the world of textile. Potentials or the AI to play a role in the proverbial paradigm shift in textile recycling, upcycling, and waste minimization are too great to be disregarded, and chances are that the industry is going to witness other breakthroughs whose focus will be on the significance of sustainability. (Olawade et al., 2024)AI-Guided Closed-loop Systems: (The above makes it possible to say that we can be sure that in the future the management of textile wastes is going to be central with regard to the creation of AI-powered closed-loop systems.) All the processes of manufacturing and recycling of the textile products will also be streamlined in the following systems; the selection of the materials, sorting the wastes and the final production of the product such that every step will ensure that very less wastage occurs and that there will always be re-use of the same material.(Esposito et al., n.d.)

5. CASE STUDIES OF AI AND TEXTILE WASTE MANAGEMENT

Background Facts about Textile Waste Management Case Studies of AI Futuristic Project of AI Future Case Studies of AI Textile Waste Management. Textile business is pretty much at the point of being overtaken by the Artificial Intelligence (AI) at least in waste management as Artificial Intelligence has already made serious steps forward. Not only does the use of artificial intelligence assist the work of textile manufacturers, waste management services and designers to make their businesses more efficient and environment-friendly, but is also the transition to new technologies in the field of sorting systems and intelligent recycling systems. In this chapter, some real-life case studies are analyzed when there is a deployment of the AI technologies in the textile wastes management. Such case studies are helpful in giving good ideas on how integration of AI can be practically done in management of textile waste and this has been succeeding, failing and also on how it can be done even better. Through these illustrations, we are also going to realize how the textile industry is becoming efficient, environmentally considerate, and sustainable at other stages of a textile lifecycle, such as production and post-consumer waste. (*HM-Group-Annual-and-Sustainability-Report-2024*, n.d.)

Case Study No. 1 H and M Garment Recycling and Collection Strategy

Swedish based fashion retail chain company namely H M, is one of the largest fashion merchants in the world that has long been concerned with sustainability and circularity in the world of textile. In 2013, the company embarked on its collection initiative on clothing where the clients are asked to drop the old one to H&M stores in order to be recycled. Nevertheless, there is an issue with such an initiative whereby there is problem of sorting and processing the textiles collected that is generally a blended material and therefore it is difficult to recycle.(Candeloro, 2020)

- Impact of AI: H&M has saved so much time and effort as far as sorting of the returned garment is concerned since it has automated the process thereby recycling becomes so much more efficient. The AI system will also increase the grade of the sorted material hence constituting the recycled fiber of better grade. As a result, the firm will be able to recycle even more of its textile waste towards other commodities hence contributing to the goal of circular economy.
- Challenges and Opportunities: This process connected with the AI-powered system can be regarded as more efficient as compared to the past though it should still tackle the problem of the pieces of clothing/fabrics that are highly polluted or made of more than 2 materials. To this effect the company is still spending heavily in research and development in a bid to increase the effectiveness of its recycling processes even more and to recycle the greater percentage of garments.(Candeloro, 2020)

Case study 2: Artificial Intelligence in Part of Textile Fiber Recycling by Renewcell

One of the firms that have invested in innovative way of recycling textile wastes and turning them into new fibers that may be introduced into production of new transactions is a Swedish company known as Renewcell.(We Make Fashion Circular, n.d.) It will do this by converting old textiles made of cotton (old garment pieces and producing waste) into a renewable fiber source that it refers to as Circulose 1, which is a biodegradable source. It can then be reverted into textiles thereby snuffing the pipeline of the textile production process.(Mauro, 2021a)

- AI and fibre identification and sorting: The utilization of AI and fibre identification, as well as sorting, will enable Renewcell to recycle via the deep learning and machine vision, sorting equipment to process the textile waste to identify its fibre type and categorize them accordingly before the opening of the recycling process. These robots will be McLearned to identify different types of fabrics, sort out all the contaminants and ensure that only the right ones will be directed to recycle. This makes the recycling process extremely efficient as the process of sorting would be improved and faster.
- AI in Forecasting Fiber Quality: AI is also being applied by renewcell in predicting the quality of fiber that it produces because it is waste. The machine learning algorithms will examine the data of the previous batches of recycling to determine the nature of the fibers to be supported such as robustness and force that will be yielded. The forecasting functionality will help Renewcell to advance the recycling process to product of higher quality fiber, which could be used to meet a wide range of purposes, such as fashion and home textile.(Mauro, 2021b)
- Challenges and Opportunities: In spite of the success of the AI-powered system of Renewcell, it has some troubles related to the growth of its business activities and access to the supply of enough quantities of textile waste regarding the quality required to recycle it. However, the technological aspect which is innovative by the company has presented an opportunity into what AI can achieve to foster the practice of recycling textile waste on larger scale. (Mauro, 2021a)

Case Study 3: IKEA Madonna samples of Sustainable Waste Management of Textiles

IKEA, a Swedish multi-national furniture company has seen it all the way through in terms of infusion of sustainability with its operations. (Rai, n.d.)As one of its efforts to carry out its mission of small textiles out to waste, IKEA has embarked on various activities towards reuse of materials and recycling of materials where textiles in their home product collections have taken precedence.(IKEA Sustainability Report FY22, n.d.)

- AI in Wastes Sorting: IKEA is even using Artificial intelligence to sort wastes where it has been working with Tomra systems which is expert in automated sorting solutions to implement AI in sorting of wastes at its recycling centers.

It is possible through the AI systems to sort the textile wastes e.g. used carpets and upholstery materials in various categories depending on the nature of material. As AI will aid IKEA to simplify the mechanism of recycling objects, it will also enable it to reduce wastes and parallelly sort the materials in a proper manner to be reused in right manner.

- Predictive Analytics in Waste Reduction in Production: IKEA also has adopted use of AI-based predictive analytics and this assists it to predict the amount of textile waste it has incurred in course of producing its home products as part of its recycling processes. The IKEA can also apply the AI models whereby it looks back into its past records, and decides how much materials consumption was done and how many production cycles are there to end up with minimal materials to be produced and avoid waste at the manufacturing point. The waste reduction strategy is included in the larger goals IKEA is planning to achieve to realize a closed cycle economy and have a less-carbon footprint.
- Impact of AI: The adopted AI in IKEA has not only helped it to improve the efficiency of the sorting process of the textile waste but also helped the firm to reduce the waste generated in its production process. The company has put in place aggressive strategies towards the use of more recycled material in its product and it is at this stage that the AI is central in the realization of its aspirations.
- Challenges and Opportunities: High level of variability of textile waste and difficult aspect of separation of mixed materials are some of the challenges met by the strategy of IKEA on AI in textile waste management. However, the company is currently doing a lot to improve its systems and it invests into AI and other technologies to eliminate these shortcomings and turn a truly circular system into a reality.(Rai, n.d.)

Case Study 4: AI and the fashion Industry

The ways through which AI could assist the fashion industry to curtail its waste issue

The fashion industry forms one of the industries that have led to the issue of textile waste in the world since clothes worth millions of tonne's are disposed of every year. The fast fashion specifically has aggravated the situation even more as it has created the problem of over production that has created waste.(Dawar & Gupta, n.d.) Certain fashion enterprises have commenced to seek AI-founded prospects to minimize the waste disposable and endorse larger recycling.(We Make Fashion Circular, n.d.)

- AI-Powered Design Optimization: Stella McCartney and Adidas are using AI when it comes to designing and manufacturing their clothes and goods so that there was an optimization of building materials used. Generative design Every decision a designer makes is subject to unpredictable variations, but machine learning algorithms can help guide him towards cutting clothing patterns with minimal fabric wastage in the process. Such algorithms can come up with a number of design alternatives basing on the fit, nature of fabric and the preference of the consumer hence ensuring that they do not end up wasting that much material yet they maintain the style and quality of the products.
- Artificial Intelligence in Waste Forecasting and Inventory Management: AI has been used in waste forecasting and inventory management and fashion brands are using it to predict the trends and manage stocks in the most effective manner so that one is left with less material that has gone into production but has ended up in waste products. Analysis of the consumer will help the companies to produce only that many clothes that will have their market and reduce the inventory that will go to waste products by considering the pattern of the consumer, production of clothes according to this pattern and estimation of the amount of clothes which are demanded by the consumer.
- Impacts of AI: AI and textile-based design together with inventory invention have helped the fashion business to significantly reduce clutter of textiles, but be able to address the desires of the customer. Adidas and other brands are also using recycled polyester but through the application of AI in order to close the circle of textile production.(Dawar & Gupta, n.d.)
- Challenges and Opportunities; The opportunities which can be observed regarding using AI to eliminate the negatives that fashion companies impose on the environment are associated with the fact that the major challenge would remain unable to make a proper prediction of demand and prevent the unfortunate cases when the waste that a fashion company is able to produce successfully cannot be recycled.(Dawar & Gupta, n.d.)

6. RESTRICTIONS CONCERNING THE MANAGEMENT OF TEXTILE WASTE WITH THE HELP OF THE AI IMPLEMENTATION

Obstacles in the integration of AI to the textile waste management

Technical, economical, infrastructural, and social challenges that occur in the case of the implementation of AI technologies in the given sphere are grave. With such problems addressed, it will aid in scaling the AI solutions that enable a reduction in the creation of waste and the increase in recycling and the circulatory economy. Then, we propose the opportunities of innovation and improvement and offer the approach of successful integration of AI into the environment of textile waste management.(Faghih et al., 2025)

Technological Resistances to receipt of AI

One of the key issues in the process of integrating the AI in the management of the textile wastes is formed by the technical complexity of the AI technologies themselves. To turn into a productive system of sorting and recycling textile waste, AI has to perform a variety of complex functions, among which there are, first of all, deciding on the type of textile, processing great amounts of information, and operating automated actions. Nonetheless, the use and successful deployment of AI into the industry face a lot of technical barriers.

- Textile materials are intricate: The range of materials out of which textile can be produced is rich: natural products of fibers (e.g. cotton, wool), and also synthetic products of fibers (e.g. polyester, nylon), as well as a combination of them (mixed fiber fabrics). This kind of different materials can be hard to segregate with one another during the process of sorting. AI is used in machine vision and deep learning, and it, in turn, requires adequate and detailed training data to be able to detect such materials. Textile waste is rather complex and dirty and consists of different materials that are not textile-related such as zippers, buttons, and adhesive, which in itself does not permit the system to sort materials efficiently using AI.
- Real-time processing of mass data: Textile waste management is the one that involves massive volumes of material that should be processed throughout time and the AI systems can easily operate under high processing loads. A sorting or recycling based on the AI model must be done by instantaneous analysis of real time (sensors, imaging systems) data. The problem is that

the AI systems must be able to operate with huge chunks of information and deliver high-quality outputs within sufficient time so as not to lead to the backlog in the process of waste management in the future.

- Preservation of Legacy systems and equipment: Many facilities of textile factories and recycling plants might possess legacy systems, and equipment which in general are incompatible with new AI tools. Notably, retrofitting of the existing machinery with the use of the AI-powered solutions can be so difficult, and it is going to require enormous scale of novelties infrastructure, software, and training. Additionally, the compatibility issues may arise in the case of AI integration with the existing waste management system like with automatic sorting or recycling centers.

Information gap and Information quality

- Information plays a significant role in the AI success. Precise and consistent and dependable data is required to train the models of the AI so that the accuracy of the work of the AI can be improved and an assurance that the techniques based on AI will be used in the textile waste management sector.
- Lack of uniform Data Sets: There is lack of uniform sets of data in textile material, recycling and waste management in textile industry. The data must be organized and aligned so that the AI systems could be put into operation. However, it is factual that textile wastes are more or less diversified as per composition, quality and as well as treatment (i.e., dyes or finishes). *Economic Barriers and economic Barriers*

Despite the numerous benefits of the long-term gratifications of application of AI in the management of textile wastes, the cost that a company incurs to start up the project in terms of innovation to enable AI use in the process proves to be a big setback to most companies especially the small firms in the developing nations. Even though AI takes advantage of enhanced productivity and cost reduction in the long term, the upfront costs paid on the way to its implementation can become excessively large.(Cate, 2025)

Regulatory s Compliance

The environment in textile business is highly regulated and the business is governed by a handful of rules and regulations in terms of waste management, recycling standards and impact to the environment. In as much as AI can potentially boost the adherence to such regulations, the same can give rise to new issues as regards whether AI systems should be compliant to these regulations to a certain extent.

- Weak Regulatory Policy of AI: As compared to the traditional mechanisms of waste disposal, even the mechanisms of managing textile waste through AI are too light at the moment and the regulatory policy related to waste disposal through AI is not very clear. The lack of guidelines or the parameter to use the technology in the use of textile recycling can be a challenge to any business organization which might be interested in the application of this technology. Regulatory authorities might need to establish open procedures on the secure and morally acceptable usage of AI in order to inspire consumers to use it in managing textile waste.
- Ethical Implications: Ethical implications also apply in regards to the topic of textile waste management as far as AI is concerned particularly on the data gathering procedure, openness and other key areas of fairness. In an illustration, the AI systems can base their decisions on the data that can end up to forms of discrimination such as avoiding a specific type of textile waste of an end in which the data is not available. In an attempt to curb such challenges, companies ought to ensure that AI-based systems become transparent, accountable and ethically conscious.The remodeling of taking care of these concerns using education, upskilling system, and effective communication of the merits of AI will be essential in offering smooth adoption.(Jayasinghe et al., 2010)

7. AI FUTURE OF THE SUSTAINABLE TEXTILE WASTE MANAGEMENT

Future Studies in AI for Textile Waste Management

1. **Enhanced Recycling Algorithms**: Future AI studies are likely to focus on developing highly efficient algorithms that can identify, sort, and process various types of textile fibers, making recycling a less labor-intensive and more accurate process. Machine learning (ML) can analyze the structure and composition of fibers, enabling automated recycling systems that maximize reuse and minimize waste.
2. **AI-Driven Circular Economy Models**: AI could support models that predict the entire lifecycle of textile products, from manufacturing to disposal, promoting a more circular approach. Using big data, machine learning could predict consumption patterns, reducing overproduction and ensuring that textile waste is minimized at the design stage itself.
3. **Waste Reduction in the Production Process**: Studies are also likely to explore AI's role in minimizing textile waste during the manufacturing phase. AI-powered

tools can optimize cutting patterns for fabrics, ensuring that less material is wasted, and improve production processes to limit offcuts and defects.

4. **AI for Waste-to-Value Solutions**: In the future, AI could assist in transforming textile waste into new products or biofuels. By using deep learning to analyze the chemical composition of waste fibers, AI can help identify potential new uses for discarded textiles, such as creating biodegradable alternatives to plastic or new, sustainable materials for the automotive or fashion industries.

Feature Applications of AI in Textile Waste Management

1. **Smart Sorting of Textile Waste**: AI could power robotic systems equipped with computer vision to sort different textile waste types, such as polyester, cotton, and wool, with high precision. These systems would reduce the labor cost and time typically involved in sorting waste manually, increasing the efficiency and scalability of recycling plants.
2. **AI-Powered Design for Longevity**: AI can play a pivotal role in designing textiles that are not only fashionable but also built for longevity. AI algorithms could predict the most durable materials and fabrics, reducing the need for fast-fashion models that lead to high waste volumes. AI could even provide consumers with recommendations on how to prolong the life of their garments.
3. **Real-Time Waste Tracking**: With AI, textile manufacturers can track their waste in real-time. Sensors and IoT devices, combined with AI algorithms, can monitor production flows, identify waste patterns, and suggest areas for improvement. This could lead to a significant reduction in textile waste in real-time, enabling just-in-time recycling.
4. **AI in Fiber Regeneration**: Advanced machine learning techniques might be used in future AI systems to regenerate and repair textile fibers. This could help in reducing the need for virgin materials, as recycled fibers could be transformed back into high-quality fabrics that can be reused in new clothing or products.
5. **Predictive Analytics for Waste Forecasting**: Machine learning models could predict future textile waste based on trends in production, consumption, and waste disposal rates. This would allow manufacturers to better align production with demand and waste disposal capabilities, ensuring that overproduction and excessive waste generation are minimized

The world is moving towards sustainability, and thus AI has become the powerhouse ensuring that the management of the textile waste becomes transformed. Still, its possibilities are not all used, and even more, impresses what may be further done with the assistance of solutions associated with AI as they can provoke the revolution in the textile industry.(Sivakumar & Mohan, 2020)

- New AI and its possible trend: The future of AI applicability in the textile industry based on waste management is highly dependent on the future evolution of several state-of-art AI technologies that are bound to provide more efficient, scalable, and precise quantification of the issue regarding waste management in the textile industry.
- Deceptive Machine Learning Algorithms: The ML algorithms will keep on advancing as time goes on and more so in the future and will improve different anticipations, classes and optimizations in the textile waste management system. These algorithms will also have opportunities to learn on the basis of large data in real-time and show new structures and reorganize their working processes instantly. As an example, smart sorting algorithms in textile settings and use of AI would allow continuously improving them according to the obtained new information, and new incoming material or waste patterns will not demand much human effort when redesigning and reprogramming.
- Potential Impact: The increase in the performance of the recycle and sorting machine will be reached with the improvement in the development of ML models leading to the drop in the contamination level and the rise in the output of materials obtained. Furthermore, the possible consequence of AI is the molding of the future trends of textile waste rates, which implies that the organizations will be capable of operating with respect to superior production planning and reducing the amount of waste prior to its occurrence.(Karmali & Valilai, 2025)
- Deep Learning: On the Recognition of Composite Materials: Deep learning (DL) as the branch of machine learning will play a significant role to increase the ability of the AI to detect multi-material and complex textiles.
- Potential Impact: This will improve the process of sorting so as to recycle additional textile which is made of complex composite material or mixed fibre. System would also be in position to detect the contaminants in a better way, in that only clean and recyclable processes would be done, thereby increasing the rate of recycling.
- Use of the Artificial Intelligence power smart sorting plants: It is quite likely in future, that the sorting facilities would transform into automated ones powered by the AI power houses, the system of textile wastes sorting is a complex of sorting systems, smart sensors, robotics and alphabet of smart sorting systems. Smart sorting systems will integrate the real-time events of different origins (sensors, computer vision systems, and history data) to provide on-line decisions on how the textiles have to be treated.
- Possible Implication: Introducing such intelligent systems will reduce the labor cost to minimal, increase the precision of sorting and indeed boost the performance of recycling plants. In addition, the facility will operate in a

more sustainability manner with reduced energy consumption and minor waste of materials, which will also add to the overall pattern of the circular economy.(Karmali & Valilai, 2025)

- Waste Reduction predictive Analytics: The other application of artificial intelligence would be waste reduction through predictive analytics, which would be a significant contribution to the reduction of textile wastes generated. An AI is capable of predicting when and where the surplus material will be produced with the help of earlier data collected to evaluate the trends of the production and propose the solution to restrict the number of the instances of waste as these occur even before they might take place.
- The process of production optimization: Predictive analytics will also enable AI models to optimise the entire process of production, such as the materials to be acquired and the way to produce a final garment. To use an example, AI can assist manufacturers by estimating materials with which they can construct a specific design and calculate the quantity of waste that will be manufactured with the intention that they can streamline the process of production. (Karmali & Valilai, 2025)
- Potential effect: With such a projection, there will be a reduction in the amount of raw materials needed to manufacture a particular produce, there will be no over-producing productions and there will be a best way to cut the fabric to avoid loss of the most part of the fabric. The manufacturers will as well be better informed of the quantity they will be producing and as a result so much textile wastage will be eliminated at a production level.(Cate, 2025)

Advances in the Artificial Intelligence-based recycling technologies

Another detail of textile circular economy is recycling. The future of AI in recycle cloths is quite good particularly since a state-of-the-art of AI-driven recycling is on the point of arriving in the phase where it could disintegrate textiles into base cloths and make them completely recyclable in further production of the other cloths.(Telfort & Valilai, 2025)

- Artificial Intelligence in Chemical Recycling: Recycling of fiber as well as textile polymers entails the regeneration of polymer and fiber textiles chemically into their chemical products before using it in the manufacturing of new fibers. Through the AI, one can optimize such processes by studying chemical reactions and establishing the most favorable conditions to recycle different materials.(Karmali & Valilai, 2025)

- Potential Impact: Artificial Intelligence (AI) enabled chemical recycling technology can translate to improved quality of the recycled fibres; and also it opens the possibility of doing closed loop recycling where fabrics can be re-recycled an unlimited number of times without the loss of recycling quality. (Andini et al., 2024)This will prove crucial in reducing on the consumption of virgin materials that eventually will contribute towards the reduction of carbon footprint of producing textile.(Andini et al., 2024)
- Artificial intelligence in Textile fiber regeneration: New technologies of fibre-regeneration those are the technologies, in which the fibres of old textiles are broken by the enzymes or by chemical substitutes and transformed into the new high-grade fibre, which can become the basis of new clothes. Such processes of fiber regeneration can be optimized by the use of AI to ensure that the best enzyme or a chemical solution is present on various materials such that the fibers regenerated can comply with the desired quality criterion. (Andini et al., 2024)
- The Opportunity Scenery: Future application of the AI-based fiber regeneration will present the opportunity of exponentially increasing the volume of textile waste that will be recovered and subsequently used to spin new material of unsurpassed quality thus closing the loop in the process of manufacturing textile and playing in to the environmentally friendly trends.(Stubbe et al., 2024)
- Social and Ecological impact of AI on Textile waste: Base use of AI in the management of waste of textiles will create a great impact sociologically and environmentally, lacking in the integrity of economic effectiveness. Thanks to AI, the textile industry can become more sustainable and circular, consume less and waste less, and the footprint of the textile industry in the environment will be a lot lesser.
- Environmental Advantages: Artificial intelligence can reduce the number of textile wastes, reduce the carbon footprint as well as reduce the application of water use in the making of the textiles. The contribution of AI to the textile industry sustainability will be related to the improvement of the amount of recycling, reduction of material waste, and decreasing of production.(Stubbe et al., 2024)
- Potential Impact: An improved recycling and waste reduction process that is a combination of new AI technology will mean that there are major reductions of the number of waste products that is ending up in the landfill or is being burnt in the incineration center, which will have a very small negative impact compared to the traditional practices of waste management.
- Social amenities: AI facilitated sustainable paradigm in the textile sector will provide better social responsibility to the environment since green jobs will

be generated in the recycling of textile, sorting of waste and technological processes behind the existence of new and sustainable textile. Besides, AI can contribute to a more even distribution of sustainable goods, as it will also be possible to simplify production and distribution chains that are capable of supplying products to the local demand and relieve the environmental inequalities.

- Possible Impacts: AI will also contribute to the generation of jobs in green technologies, and thus, the communities might change into the more sustainable ones due to the implementation of a circular economy. Additionally, AI will assist the consumers and enterprises in choices that are more environmentally-friendly and intelligent.(Olawade et al., 2024)

8. CONCLUSION

Artificial intelligence (AI) is a great chance to alter the process of handling waste in the textile industry. Since the textile industry contributes to some of the largest amounts of waste and deterioration of the environmental situation in the world, the growing number of people tend to make more elements of this industry more environmentally friendly. Most of the issues that arise with the textile waste can be addressed through AI such as textile waste sorting, recycling, lightening waste and creating the circular business models. As we have already talked about in this book however, machine learning, deep learning, computer vision, and predictive analytics AI technologies already began to make a difference, and this trend will become even more dominant in the future as the textile industry tries to make efforts to reduce its footprint on the Earth. With AI technologies in line, new opportunities of sustainable management of textile wastes are on the agenda, and the concept of the more closed waste circle can be introduced, and the resource-efficient building of the textile economy will be given a chance. The extensive use of AI in the next few decades might easily emerge as the solution to the sustainability decisions of the textile industry to reduce its ecological impact and enable building a more sustainable global economy.

Table 1. Summary with key Insights

Aspect	AI Techniques	Benefits	Limitations	Future Directions
Sorting Textile Waste	Computer Vision, Robotic Process Automation (RPA)	High precision in sorting, reduces labor costs, improves efficiency in recycling plants.	Requires high-quality image data; challenges with sorting complex fabrics and mixed waste.	More advanced vision systems for mixed fiber identification and better sorting accuracy.
Recycling Algorithms	Machine Learning (ML), Deep Learning	Improved recycling efficiency by identifying fiber types, enabling higher material recovery.	Needs large datasets for training; may struggle with identifying new or unconventional materials.	Development of self-learning algorithms to improve over time and adapt to new textile innovations.
Circular Economy Models	Predictive Analytics, Big Data	Predicts waste generation, reduces overproduction, and promotes sustainable design practices.	Difficult to integrate real-time data and predict long-term trends accurately.	AI-driven closed-loop systems that track products throughout their lifecycle for ultimate recycling.
Manufacturing Optimization	ML, AI-Driven Process Control	Minimizes waste in production, optimizes cutting patterns to reduce material loss.	Requires real-time data and integration with existing manufacturing systems.	Real-time waste monitoring systems that optimize fabric usage on-the-fly.
Waste-to-Value	Deep Learning, Generative Models	Transforms textile waste into new materials or biofuels, reducing landfill contributions.	Requires advanced material analysis; complexity in ensuring high-quality outputs from waste.	AI models for creating sustainable fibers or alternative materials from textile waste.
Waste Tracking	Internet of Things (IoT), AI Analytics	Provides real-time insights into textile waste, enabling efficient waste management strategies.	Implementation cost of IoT infrastructure and data integration.	Real-time, autonomous waste tracking with AI-driven suggestions for waste minimization.
Fiber Regeneration	Deep Learning, Neural Networks	Potential for regenerating textile fibers, reducing dependency on virgin materials.	Requires high levels of precision in processing; could be costly to scale.	Development of more efficient and scalable fiber regeneration techniques powered by AI.
Sustainable Design	AI-Driven Predictive Modeling	Designs durable textiles, reducing the need for frequent replacements and waste.	Challenges in integrating AI tools with traditional design processes.	AI tools for integrating sustainability into design processes, encouraging eco-friendly material choices.

9. REFERENCES

Andini, E., Bhalode, P., Gantert, E., Sadula, S., & Vlachos, D. G. (2024). Chemical recycling of mixed textile waste.[). *Science Advances*, *10*(27), eado6827. https://www.science.org. DOI: 10.1126/sciadv.ado6827 PMID: 38959304

Bhalerao, K. (n.d.). *Artificial Intelligence Technologies Usage Decides the Success or Failure of Garment Industry Ecosystem*. https://www.researchgate.net/publication/380168904

Bravo, M. V. C., & Iturralde, W. M. P. (2024). Artificial Intelligence in the Management of Textile Companies: A Contextual Analysis. *Open Journal of Business and Management*, *12*(02), 945–960. DOI: 10.4236/ojbm.2024.122050

Candeloro, D. (2020). *Towards Sustainable Fashion: The Role of Artificial Intelligence-H&M, Stella McCartney, Farfetch, Moosejaw: A Multiple Case Study.* DOI: 10.6092/issn.2611-0563/11837

Cate, M. (2025). *Sustainable Supply Chain Strategies in Textile Engineering: A Circular Economy Approach*. https://www.researchgate.net/publication/390489132

. Dawar, R., & Gupta, M. A. (n.d.). *The Rise of AI In the Fashion Industry.*

Esposito, M., Tse, T., & Soufani, K. (n.d.). *The Circular Economy: An Opportunity for Renewal, Growth, and Stability*. https://www.forbes.com/sites/valleyvoices/2015/01/20/the-circular-economy-great-idea-but-can-it-work/

Faghih, E., Saki, Z., & Moore, M. (2025). A Systematic Literature Review—AI-Enabled Textile Waste Sorting. In *Sustainability (Switzerland)* (Vol. 17, Issue 10). Multidisciplinary Digital Publishing Institute (MDPI). DOI: 10.3390/su17104264

. *HM-Group-Annual-and-sustainability-report-2024*. (n.d.).

IKEA Sustainability Report FY22. (n.d.).

Jayasinghe, I., Basnayake, B., Amarathunga, K., & Dissanayake, P. (2010). Environmental Conservation Efforts in Developing Textile Waste Incorporated Cement Blocks. In *Tropical* [). www.wasteonline.org.uk]. *Agricultural Research*, *21*(2), •••.

Karmali, I. M., & Valilai, O. F. (2025). Exploring the Role of Artificial Intelligence for Pattern Recognition of Textile Sorting and Recycling for Circular Economy. *Procedia Computer Science*, *253*, 346–356. DOI: 10.1016/j.procs.2025.01.097

. Mauro, E. (2021a). *Circular fashion.*

. Mauro, E. (2021b). *Circular fashion.*

Olawade, D. B., Fapohunda, O., Wada, O. Z., Usman, S. O., Ige, A. O., Ajisafe, O., & Oladapo, B. I. (2024). Smart waste management: A paradigm shift enabled by artificial intelligence. *Waste Management Bulletin*, *2*(2), 244–263. DOI: 10.1016/j.wmb.2024.05.001

Peter, H. (n.d.). *Innovations in Sustainable Textile Production*. https://www.researchgate.net/publication/389272494

. Rai, K. J. (n.d.). *The IKEA experience in moving towards a Better Cotton supply chain Making sustainability work.*

Sivakumar, V., & Mohan, R. (2020). Sustainable solid waste management in leather and textile industry: Leather & textile waste fibre-polymer composite and nanocomposite–overview and review. *Textile & Leather Review*, *3*(2), 54–63.

Stubbe, B., Van Vrekhem, S., Huysman, S., Tilkin, R. G., De Schrijver, I., & Vanneste, M. (2024). White Paper on Textile Fibre Recycling Technologies. In *Sustainability (Switzerland)* (Vol. 16, Issue 2). Multidisciplinary Digital Publishing Institute (MDPI). DOI: 10.3390/su16020618

Telfort, T. E., & Valilai, O. F. (2025). A Framework for Sustainable Textile Waste Management using Digital Product Passports and Artificial Intelligence. *Procedia CIRP*, *134*, 909–914. DOI: 10.1016/j.procir.2025.02.224

Compilation of References

Aaker, D. A. (2011). *Building strong brands*. Simon & Schuster.

Abdelmeguid, A., Afy-Shararah, M., & Salonitis, K. (2022). Investigating the challenges of applying the principles of the circular economy in the fashion industry: A systematic review. *Sustainable Production and Consumption*, *32*, 505–518. DOI: 10.1016/j.spc.2022.05.009

Abdelmeguid, A., Afy-Shararah, M., & Salonitis, K. (2024). Towards circular fashion: Management strategies promoting circular behaviour along the value chain. *Sustainable Production and Consumption*, *48*, 143–156. DOI: 10.1016/j.spc.2024.05.010

Adulyasak, Y., Cohen, M. C., Khern-Am-Nuai, W., & Krause, M. (2024). Retail Analytics in the New Normal: The Influence of Artificial Intelligence and the Covid-19 Pandemic. *IEEE Engineering Management Review*, *52*(1), 268–280. DOI: 10.1109/EMR.2023.3337415

Afifah, N. (2024). Influencer Marketing Strategies And The Use Of Ai Technology In Enhancing Brand Awareness: A Case Study In The Fashion Industry. *Journal of Economic* [COSTING]. *Bussines and Accounting*, *7*(2), 3058–3066. DOI: 10.31539/costing.v7i2.8723

Ahmad, S., Miskon, S., Alabdan, R., & Tlili, I. (2020). Exploration of Influential Determinants for the Adoption of Business Intelligence System in the Textile and Apparel Industry. *Sustainability 2020, Vol. 12, Page 7674, 12*(18), 7674. DOI: 10.3390/su12187674

Ajax, R., Joseph, O., & Own, J. (2025). *Enhancing Business Intelligence with Data Visualization Tools*.

Akbar, R. Wahyudi, Rahmadoni, J., & Lubis, H. A. (2022). The Implementation of Business Intelligence on Visualisation of Transaction Data Analysis using Dashboard System Case Study: XYZ Convenience Store. *Proceeding - 2022 International Symposium on Information Technology and Digital Innovation: Technology Innovation During Pandemic, ISITDI 2022*, 42–49. DOI: 10.1109/ISITDI55734.2022.9944494

Akram, S. V., Malik, P. K., Singh, R., Gehlot, A., Juyal, A., Ghafoor, K. Z., & Shrestha, S. (2022). Implementation of Digitalized Technologies for Fashion Industry 4.0: Opportunities and Challenges. *Scientific Programming*, *2022*, 1–17. DOI: 10.1155/2022/7523246

Akter, M. M. K., Haq, U. N., Islam, M. M., & Uddin, M. A. (2022). Textile-apparel manufacturing and material waste management in the circular economy: A conceptual model to achieve sustainable development goal (SDG) 12 for Bangladesh. *Cleaner Environmental Systems*, *4*, 100070. DOI: 10.1016/j.cesys.2022.100070

Alanadoly, A. B., Sidhu, S. K., & Richards-Carpenter, N. (2024). AI Landscape in Fashion: Insights on Transforming Design, Supply Chains, Marketing, and Consumer Experiences. In Raj, P., Rocha, A., Dutta, P. K., Fiorini, M., & Prakash, C. (Eds.), *Illustrating Digital Innovations Towards Intelligent Fashion* (Vol. 18, pp. 417–439). Springer Nature Switzerland., DOI: 10.1007/978-3-031-71052-0_16

Alhitmi, H. K., Mardiah, A., Al-Sulaiti, K. I., & Abbas, J. (2024). Data security and privacy concerns of AI-driven marketing in the context of economics and business field: An exploration into possible solutions. *Cogent Business & Management*, *11*(01), 2393743. Advance online publication. DOI: 10.1080/23311975.2024.2393743

Ali, Z. A., Zain, M., Pathan, M. S., & Mooney, P. (2024). Contributions of artificial intelligence for circular economy transition leading toward sustainability: An explorative study in agriculture and food industries of Pakistan. *Environment, Development and Sustainability*, *26*(8), 19131–19175. DOI: 10.1007/s10668-023-03458-9

Allais, F. B., Cappa, C., De Cock, M., Guarcello, L., & Lyon, S. (2021). *Child labour: Global estimates 2020, trends and the road forward*. ILO; UNICEF. Retrieved from https://www.ilo.org/wcmsp5/groups/public/---ed_norm/---ipec/documents/publication/wcms_797515.pdf

Alto, V. (2023). *Modern generative AI with ChatGPT and OpenAI models: Leverage the capabilities of OpenAI's LLM for productivity and innovation with GPT3 and GPT4*. Packt Publishing.

Ameen, N., Cheah, J. H., & Kumar, S. (2022). It's all part of the customer journey: The impact of augmented reality, chatbots, and social media on the body image and self-esteem of Generation Z female consumers. *Psychology and Marketing*, *39*(11), 2110–2129. DOI: 10.1002/mar.21715

Andini, E., Bhalode, P., Gantert, E., Sadula, S., & Vlachos, D. G. (2024). Chemical recycling of mixed textile waste.[). *Science Advances*, *10*(27), eado6827. https://www.science.org. DOI: 10.1126/sciadv.ado6827 PMID: 38959304

Anjaningrum, W. D., Azizah, N., & Suryadi, N. (2024). Spurring SMEs' performance through business intelligence, organizational and network learning, customer value anticipation, and innovation - Empirical evidence of the creative economy sector in East Java, Indonesia. *Heliyon*, *10*(7), e27998. Advance online publication. DOI: 10.1016/j.heliyon.2024.e27998 PMID: 38689951

Anozie, U. C., Onyenahazi, O. B., Ekeocha, P. C., Adekola, A. D., Ukadike, C. A., & Oloko, O. A. (2024). Advancements in artificial intelligence for omnichannel marketing and customer service: Enhancing predictive analytics, automation, and operational efficiency. *International Journal of Science and Research Archive*, *12*(2), 1621–1629. DOI: 10.30574/ijsra.2024.12.2.1436

APJII. (2022). *Indonesian Internet Profile 2022*.

APJII. (2023). *Survei Penetrasi & Perilaku Internet 2023*.

Arranz, C. F. A., Arroyabe, M. F., & Fernandez de Arroyabe, J. C. (2024). Organisational transformation toward circular economy in SMEs. The effect of internal barriers. *Journal of Cleaner Production*, *456*, 142307. DOI: 10.1016/j.jclepro.2024.142307

Aslam, U., & Davis, L. (2024). Analyzing consumer expectations and experiences of Augmented Reality (AR) apps in the fashion retail sector. *Journal of Retailing and Consumer Services*, *76*, 103577. DOI: 10.1016/j.jretconser.2023.103577

Aura Blockchain Consortium. (2025). *Leveraging Blockchain for Supply Chain Transparency in the Luxury Sector*. Retrieved from https://auraconsortium.com/insight/blockchain-for-supply-chain-transparency-luxury-sector

Bag, S., Rahman, M. S., Routray, S., Shrivastav, S. K., & Agrawal, S. (2024). Exploring the potential of blockchain-enabled smart contracts for achieving net-zero emissions: An empirical study. *Business Strategy and the Environment*, *33*(5), 3965–3985. DOI: 10.1002/bse.3691

Baniyani, A., Ahmadi, M. H., Motamedi, M., & Gholami, M. (2021). Providing a model for brand strength in the banking industry using Yazd city banks. *Asia Pacific Management Review*, *26*(2), 78–85. DOI: 10.1016/j.apmrv.2020.08.003

Barman, H. (2013). Web analytics metrics for Internet business models. In *Impact of IT applications in accounting and finance*. Global Publishing House.

Barone, A. M., & Stagno, E. (2023). AI-powered Self-service Technologies. In A. M. Barone & E. Stagno, *Artificial Intelligence along the Customer Journey* (pp. 23–35). Springer Nature Switzerland. DOI: 10.1007/978-3-031-48792-7_2

Barreda, A. A., Bilgihan, A., Nusair, K., & Okumus, F. (2015). Generating brand awareness in online social networks. *Computers in Human Behavior, 50*, 600–609. DOI: 10.1016/j.chb.2015.03.023

Baukh, O. (2024, September 11). How Artificial Intelligence is Revolutionizing the Fashion Industry. Retrieved September 2025, from https://techpacker.com/blog/design/how-artificial-intelligence-is-revolutionizing-the-fashion-industry/

Behare, N., Bhosale, S. P., Sharma, S., Shitole, V. C., & Sane, A. C. (2024, July 23). Quantum ethics: Ensuring integrity and security in supply chain operations. In *Quantum Computing and Supply Chain Management: A New Era of Optimization* (pp. 284–314). IGI Global., DOI: 10.4018/979-8-3693-4107-0.ch019

Bellamy, R. K. E., Dey, K., Hind, M., Hoffman, S. C., Hoey, J., Kanan, C., & Raji, I. D. (2018). AI fairness 360: An extensible toolkit for detecting, understanding, and mitigating unwanted algorithmic bias. *IBM Journal of Research and Development, 63*(4/5), 4–1. DOI: 10.1147/JRD.2019.2942287

Bhalerao, K. (n.d.). *Artificial Intelligence Technologies Usage Decides the Success or Failure of Garment Industry Ecosystem*. https://www.researchgate.net/publication/380168904

bluedesign. (n.d.). Retrieved from bluedesign.com: https://www.bluesign.com/en/ethical-fashion/

Bocken, N. M. P., de Pauw, I., Bakker, C., & van der Grinten, B. (2016). Product design and business model strategies for a circular economy. *Journal of Industrial and Production Engineering, 33*(5), 308–320. DOI: 10.1080/21681015.2016.1172124

Bravo, M. V. C., & Iturralde, W. M. P. (2024). Artificial Intelligence in the Management of Textile Companies: A Contextual Analysis. *Open Journal of Business and Management, 12*(02), 945–960. DOI: 10.4236/ojbm.2024.122050

Briggs, R., & Hollis, N. (1997). Advertising on the web: Is there response before click-through? *Journal of Advertising Research, 37*(2), 33–46. DOI: 10.1080/00218499.1997.12466659

Brismar, A. (2017). *What is Circular Fashion?* https://greenstrategy.se/circular-fashion-definition/

Brynjolfsson, E. a. (2014). *The Second Machine Age: Work, Progress, and Prosperity in a Time of Brilliant Technologies*. W. W. Norton & Company.

Bucea-Manea-Ţoniş, R., Gurgu, E., Martins, O. M. D., & Simion, V. E. (2021). An Overview of How VR/AR Applications Assist Specialists in Developing Better Consumer Behavior and Can Revolutionize Our Life. In Dutta, T., & Mandal, M. K. (Eds.), *Consumer Happiness: Multiple Perspectives* (pp. 231–253). Springer Singapore., DOI: 10.1007/978-981-33-6374-8_12

Burke, H., Zhang, A., & Wang, J. X. (2023). Integrating product design and supply chain management for a circular economy. *Production Planning and Control, 34*(11), 1097–1113. DOI: 10.1080/09537287.2021.1983063

Busalim, A. H., Fox, G., & Lynn, T. (2022). Consumer behavior in sustainable fashion: A systematic literature review and future research agenda. *International Journal of Consumer Studies, 46*(5), 1790–1815. DOI: 10.1111/ijcs.12794

Candeloro, D. (2020). Towards sustainable fashion: The role of artificial intelligence—H&M, Stella McCartney, Farfetch, Moosejaw: A multiple case study. *ZoneModa Journal, 10*(2), 91–105. DOI: 10.6092/issn.2611-0563/11837

Casciani, D., & D'Itria, E. (2024). Fostering Directions for Digital Technology Adoption in Sustainable and Circular Fashion: Toward the Circular Fashion-Tech Lab. *Systems, 12*(6), 190. DOI: 10.3390/systems12060190

Casino, F., Dasaklis, T. K., & Patsakis, C. (2019). A systematic literature review of blockchain-based applications: Current status, classification and open issues. *Telematics and Informatics, 36*, 55–81. DOI: 10.1016/j.tele.2018.11.006

Cate, M. (2025). *Sustainable Supply Chain Strategies in Textile Engineering: A Circular Economy Approach*. https://www.researchgate.net/publication/390489132

Chan, C. K. Y., & Lee, K. K. W. (2023). The AI generation gap: Are Gen Z students more interested in adopting generative AI such as ChatGPT in teaching and learning than their Gen X and millennial generation teachers? *Smart Learning Environments, 10*(1), 60. DOI: 10.1186/s40561-023-00269-3

Chaturvedi, P., Kulshreshtha, K., & Tripathi, V. (2020a). Investigating the determinants of behavioral intentions of generation Z for recycled clothing: An evidence from a developing economy. *Young Consumers, 21*(4), 403–417. DOI: 10.1108/YC-03-2020-1110

Chaudhary, P., Raut, N., Patil, H., & Kate, N. (2024). Up-Skilling in Fashion Retail. In Malik, R., Sharma, A., & Chaudhary, P. (Eds.), *Transforming Education with Virtual Reality* (1st ed., pp. 323–336). Wiley., DOI: 10.1002/9781394200498.ch19

Chee, J. S. (2025, January). The impact of AI chatbot adoption on customer experience in e-retailing. *Issues and Perspectives in Business and Social Sciences*, 27-36. DOI: 10.33093/ipbss.2025.5.1.3

Chen, Y. (2023). How blockchain adoption affects supply chain sustainability in the fashion industry: A systematic review and case studies. *International Transactions in Operational Research*, *0*, 1–29. DOI: 10.1111/itor.13273

Chen, Y., Sherren, K., Smit, M., & Lee, K. Y. (2023). Using social media images as data in social science research. *New Media & Society*, *25*(4), 849–871. DOI: 10.1177/14614448211038761

Choi, D., & Lee, H. (2024, January 20). AI-Designed Clothing and Perceived Values: What can Move Consumers' Minds with the AI-Designed Clothing? *Bridging the Divide*. Bridging the Divide. DOI: 10.31274/itaa.17098

Choi, W., Jang, S., Kim, H. Y., Lee, Y., Lee, S., Lee, H., & Park, S. (2023). Developing an AI-based automated fashion design system: Reflecting the work process of fashion designers. *Fashion and Textiles*, *10*(1), 39. Advance online publication. DOI: 10.1186/s40691-023-00360-w

Christodoulides, G., De Chernatony, L., Furrer, O., Shiu, E., & Abimbola, T. (2006). Conceptualising and measuring the equity of online brands. *Journal of Marketing Management*, *22*(7–8), 799–825. DOI: 10.1362/026725706778612149

Circular economy introduction. (2017). Netherlands. Retrieved Sep 5, 2025, from https://www.ellenmacarthurfoundation.org/topics/circular-economy-introduction/overview

Coleman, N. M. V., & Williams, P. (2015). Looking for My Self: Identity-Driven Attention Allocation. *Journal of Consumer Psychology*, *25*(3), 504–511. DOI: 10.1016/j.jcps.2015.01.001

Colombi, C., & D'Itria, E. (2023). Fashion Digital Transformation: Innovating Business Models toward Circular Economy and Sustainability. *Sustainability (Basel)*, *15*(6), 4942. DOI: 10.3390/su15064942

Cuevas-Molano, E., Matosas-López, L., & Bernal-Bravo, C. (2021). Factors increasing consumer engagement of branded content in Instagram. *IEEE Access : Practical Innovations, Open Solutions*, *9*, 143531–143548. DOI: 10.1109/ACCESS.2021.3121186

Dalal, S., Lilhore, U. K., Simaiya, S., Radulescu, M., & Belascu, L.Surjeet Dalal a. (2024, December 1). Improving efficiency and sustainability via supply chain optimization through CNNs and BiLSTM. *Technological Forecasting and Social Change, 209*, 123841. Advance online publication. DOI: 10.1016/j.techfore.2024.123841

Dasandi, N., Graham, H., Hudson, D., Jankin, S., vanHeerde-Hudson, J., & Watts, N. (2022). Positive, global, and health or environment framing bolsters public support for climate policies. *Communications Earth & Environment, 3*(1), 239. DOI: 10.1038/s43247-022-00571-x

Das, D., & Paul, S. (2024). Promoting consumer engagement in sustainable fashion and circular textile through eco-gamification in Bangladesh. *Proceedings of the International Conference on Industrial Engineering and Operations Management, 37*, 241–252. DOI: 10.46254/BA07.20240037

Davic, N., Vinhas, R., & Hair, F. (2015). Towards a unified theory of brand equity: Conceptualisations, taxonomy and avenues for future research. *Journal of Product and Brand Management, 24*(1), 3–17. DOI: 10.1108/JPBM-06-2014-0639

De Angelis, R., Howard, M., & Miemczyk, J. (2018). Supply chain management and the circular economy: Towards the circular supply chain. *Production Planning and Control, 29*(6), 425–437. DOI: 10.1080/09537287.2018.1449244

De Chernatony, L. (1997). Integrated brand building using brand taxonomies. *Journal of Product and Brand Management, 6*(1), 56–63.

De Oliveira, M. O., Silveira, C. S., & Luce, F. B. (2015). Brand equity estimation model. *Journal of Business Research, 68*(12), 2560–2568. DOI: 10.1016/j.jbusres.2015.06.025

De Paula, E., & Chaves, S. (2017). Identity, positioning, brand image and brand equity comparison: A vision about quality in brand management. *Independent Journal of Management & Production, 8*(4), 1246–1263. DOI: 10.14807/ijmp.v8i4.637

Dear, K. (2019). Artificial Intelligence and Decision-Making. *RUSI Journal, 164*(5–6), 18–25. DOI: 10.1080/03071847.2019.1693801

Deeksha Gupta Ganguly, R. B. (2025). *Sustainable Practices in the Fashion and Retail Industry*. IGI Global., DOI: 10.4018/979-8-3693-9959-0.ch022

Dhatrak, M., Jadhav, S., Harkal, A., Kankrale, A., & Gupta, S. (2024). AI-Powered Virtual Try-On System: Enhancing Fit Prediction and User Comfort Through Deep Learning. *2024 5th International Conference on Communication, Computing & Industry 6.0 (C2I6)*, 1–6. DOI: 10.1109/C2I663243.2024.10895137

Díaz-Soloaga, P., & Pelzer-Peinado, I. (2024). Comunicación de moda e inteligencia artificial:el caso de Neural Fashion AI. *Universitas (Accra), 41*(41), 15–52. DOI: 10.17163/uni.n41.2024.01

Dilmegani, C. (2025, August). *Generative AI in Fashion: Top 10 Use Cases & Examples.* (AI Multiple Research) Retrieved September 2025, from https://research.aimultiple.com/generative-ai-fashion/

Directory, S. (2025, January 29). *How Can AI Improve Supply Chain Transparency in Fashion?* Retrieved September 2025, from https://fashion.sustainability-directory.com/: https://fashion.sustainability-directory.com/question/how-can-ai-improve-supply-chain-transparency-in-fashion/

Dissanayake, D. G. K., & Weerasinghe, D. (2022). Towards circular economy in fashion: Review of strategies, barriers and enablers. *Circular Economy and Sustainability, 2*(1), 25–45. DOI: 10.1007/s43615-021-00090-5

Doshi-Velez, F., & Kim, B. (2017). Towards a rigorous science of interpretable machine learning. *arXiv preprint arXiv:1702.08608.* /arXiv.1702.08608DOI: 10.48550

Drivas, I. C., Sakas, D. P., & Giannakopoulos, G. A. (2021). Display advertising and brand awareness in search engines: Predicting the engagement of branded search traffic visitors. En Business intelligence and modelling (pp. 3–15). DOI: 10.1007/978-3-030-57065-1_1

Dubey, A., Bhardwaj, N., Abhinav, K., Kuriakose, S. M., Jain, S., & Arora, V. (2020). *AI Assisted Apparel Design* (Version 2). arXiv. DOI: 10.48550/ARXIV.2007.04950

Dülek, B., & Saydan, R. (2019). The impact of social media advertisement awareness on brand awareness, brand image, brand attitude, and brand loyalty: A research on university students. *International Journal of Contemporary Economics and Administrative Sciences, 9*(2), 470–494.

Dumitriu, D., Militaru, G., Deselnicu, D. C., Niculescu, A., & Popescu, M. A. M. (2019). A perspective over modern SMEs: Managing brand equity, growth and sustainability through digital marketing tools and techniques. *Sustainability (Basel), 11*(7), 2111. DOI: 10.3390/su11072111

Dwivedi, A., Moktadir, M. A., Chiappetta Jabbour, C. J., & de Carvalho, D. E. (2022). Integrating the circular economy and industry 4.0 for sustainable development: Implications for responsible footwear production in a big data-driven world. *Technological Forecasting and Social Change, 175*, 121335. DOI: 10.1016/j.techfore.2021.121335

Dwivedi, Y. K., Ismagilova, E., Hughes, D. L., Carlson, J., Filieri, R., Jacobson, J., Jain, V., Karjaluoto, H., Kefi, H., Krishen, A. S., Kumar, V., Rahman, M. M., Raman, R., Rauschnabel, P. A., Rowley, J., Salo, J., Tran, G. A., & Wang, Y. (2021). Setting the future of digital and social media marketing research: Perspectives and research propositions. *International Journal of Information Management*, *59*, 102168. DOI: 10.1016/j.ijinfomgt.2020.102168

Elkington, J. (1997). *Cannibals with Forks: The Triple Bottom Line of 21st Century Business*. Capstone.

Ellen MacArthur Foundation. (2016). *Understand circular flows*. https://www.ellenmacarthurfoundation.org/understand-circular-flows

Ellen MacArthur Foundation. (2017). *A new textiles economy: Redesigning fashion's future*. Retrieved from https://www.ellenmacarthurfoundation.org/publications/a-new-textiles-economy-redesigning-fashions-future

Ellen MacArthur Foundation. (2019). *Fashion and the circular economy*. https://www.ellenmacarthurfoundation.org/fashion-and-the-circular-economy-deep-dive

Ellen MacArthur Foundation. (2021). *Rethinking business models for a thriving fashion industry*. https://www.ellenmacarthurfoundation.org/fashion-business-models/overview

Enes, Y. de S. O., Demo, G., Porto, R. B., & Zulato, T. S. (2024). What is next for consumer-based brand equity in digital brands? Research itineraries and new challenges. *Sustainability (Basel)*, *16*(13), 5412. DOI: 10.3390/su16135412

Environmental Sustainability in the Fashion Industry. (2025, May 23). (G. E. Network, Compiler) Geveva. Retrieved 2025, from https://www.genevaenvironmentnetwork.org/resources/updates/sustainable-fashion/

Enyejo, J. O., Obani, O. Q., Afolabi, O., Igba, E., & Ibokette, A. I. (2024). Effect of Augmented Reality (AR) and Virtual Reality (VR) experiences on customer engagement and purchase behavior in retail stores. *Magna Scientia Advanced Research and Reviews*, *11*(2), 132–150. DOI: 10.30574/msarr.2024.11.2.0116

Esposito, M., Tse, T., & Soufani, K. (n.d.). *The Circular Economy: An Opportunity for Renewal, Growth, and Stability*. https://www.forbes.com/sites/valleyvoices/2015/01/20/the-circular-economy-great-idea-but-can-it-work/

Faghih, E., Saki, Z., & Moore, M. (2025). A Systematic Literature Review—AI-Enabled Textile Waste Sorting. In *Sustainability (Switzerland)* (Vol. 17, Issue 10). Multidisciplinary Digital Publishing Institute (MDPI). DOI: 10.3390/su17104264

Faircloth, J., Capella, L., & Alford, B. (2001). The effect of brand attitude and brand image on brand equity. *Journal of Marketing Theory and Practice*, *9*(3), 61–75. DOI: 10.1080/10696679.2001.11501897

Fashion meets AI: The next step in material innovation. (2024, October 25). Premiere Vision The Art & heart of fashion. Retrieved from https://www.premierevision.com/en/articles/6dc27294-75fa-ef11-90cb-00224888722c/fashion-meets-ai-the-next-step-in-material-innovation#:~:text=AI%20adjusts%20these%20processes%20based,reducing%20energy%20and%20material%20waste

Fashion Revolution. (2025). *What fuels fashion?* Retrieved from https://www.fashionrevolution.org/about/transparency/

Fashion, Virtual: Production and Display. (2024). The Frontiers of Society. *Science and Technology*, *6*(7). Advance online publication. DOI: 10.25236/FSST.2024.060720

Forero, M., & Duque, E. (2014). Evolución y caracterización de los modelos de brand equity. *Suma de Negocios*, *5*(12), 158–168. DOI: 10.1016/S2215-910X(14)70038-2

Foroudi, P. (2019). Influence of brand signature, brand awareness, brand attitude, and brand reputation on the hotel industry's brand performance. *International Journal of Hospitality Management*, *76*, 271–285. DOI: 10.1016/j.ijhm.2018.05.016

France, S., Davcik, N. S., & Kazandjian, B. (2025). Digital brand equity: The concept, antecedents, measurement, and future development. *Journal of Business Research*, *181*, 115273. DOI: 10.1016/j.jbusres.2025.115273

Freeman, R. E. (1984). *Strategic Management: A Stakeholder Approach*. Pitman.

Gaitniece, E. (2018). Digital marketing performance evaluation methods. *CBU International Conference Proceedings*, 6, 135–140. DOI: 10.12955/cbup.v6.1145

Gauri, D. K., Jindal, R. P., Ratchford, B., Fox, E., Bhatnagar, A., Pandey, A., Navallo, J. R., Fogarty, J., Carr, S., & Howerton, E. (2021). Evolution of retail formats: Past, present, and future. *Journal of Retailing*, *97*(1), 42–61. DOI: 10.1016/j.jretai.2020.11.002

Gazzola, P., Pavione, E., Pezzetti, R., & Grechi, D. (2020). Trends in the fashion industry. The perception of sustainability and circular economy: A gender/generation quantitative approach. *Sustainability (Basel)*, *12*(14), 5808. DOI: 10.3390/su12072809

Geissdoerfer, M., Pieroni, M. P. P., Pigosso, D. C. A., & Soufani, K. (2020). Circular business models: A review. *Journal of Cleaner Production*, *277*, 123741. DOI: 10.1016/j.jclepro.2020.123741

Gill, S. (2015). A review of research and innovation in garment sizing, prototyping and fitting. *Textile Progress*, *47*(1), 1–85. DOI: 10.1080/00405167.2015.1023512

Gilpin, L. H., Bau, D., Yuan, B. Z., Bajwa, A., Specter, M., & Kagal, L. (2018, October). Explaining explanations: An overview of interpretability of machine learning. In *2018 IEEE 5th International Conference on data science and advanced analytics (DSAA)* (pp. 80–89). IEEE. DOI: 10.48550/arXiv.1806.00069

Godey, B., Manthiou, A., Pederzoli, D., Rokka, J., Aiello, G., Donvito, R., & Singh, R. (2016). Social media marketing efforts of luxury brands: Influence on brand equity and consumer behavior. *Journal of Business Research*, *69*(12), 5833–5841. DOI: 10.1016/j.jbusres.2016.04.181

Goldstein, N. J., Cialdini, R. B., & Griskevicius, V. (2008). A room with a viewpoint: Using social norms to motivate environmental conservation in hotels. *The Journal of Consumer Research*, *35*(3), 472–482. DOI: 10.1086/586910

Gonçalves, C. T., Gonçalves, M. J. A., & Campante, M. I. (2023). Developing Integrated Performance Dashboards Visualisations Using Power BI as a Platform. *Information 2023, Vol. 14, Page 614*, *14*(11), 614. DOI: 10.3390/info14110614

Gong, Y. (2024). The Impact of Big Data on the Fashion Industry. *Advances in Economics. Management and Political Sciences*, *143*(1), 190–196. DOI: 10.54254/2754-1169/2024.GA18973

Good On You. (2023). *How We Rate Fashion and Beauty Brands*. Retrieved from https://goodonyou.eco/how-we-rate

Gorkhe, M., Kudare, R., Behare, N., Kulkarni, M. V., & Waghulkar, S. (July,2024). *Quantum Computing and Supply Chain Management: A New Era of Optimization*. IGI Global. DOI: 10.4018/979-8-3693-4107-0.ch017

Goworek, H. (2011). Social and environmental sustainability in the clothing industry: A case study of a fair trade retailer. *Social Responsibility Journal*, *7*(1), 74–86. DOI: 10.1108/17471111111114558

Guo, Z., Zhu, Z., Li, Y., Cao, S., Chen, H., & Wang, G. (2023). AI Assisted Fashion Design: A review. *IEEE Access : Practical Innovations, Open Solutions*, *11*, 88403–88415. DOI: 10.1109/ACCESS.2023.3306235

Gupta, A. K., & Srivastava, V. (2023). Modelling the impact of social media marketing for apparel brands: Evidence from India. *International Journal of Internet Marketing and Advertising*, *18*(2–3), 242–262. DOI: 10.1504/IJIMA.2023.129665

Gyulai, Z., & Revesz, B. (2023). Nudging in the digital world: An up-to-date systematic literature review. *Proceedings of the European Marketing Academy Conference*, Paper 117268. https://proceedings.emac-online.org/pdfs/R2023-117268.pdf

Hales, R., & Birdthistle, N. (2023). The sustainable development goals–SDG# 12 responsible consumption and production. In *Attaining the 2030 sustainable development goal of responsible consumption and production* (pp. 1–10). Emerald Publishing Limited. DOI: 10.1108/978-1-80455-840-920231001

Hamari, J., Koivisto, J., & Sarsa, H. (2014). Does gamification work?—A literature review of empirical studies on gamification. *2014 47th Hawaii International Conference on System Sciences* (pp. 3025–3034). IEEE. DOI: 10.1109/HICSS.2014.377

Hanan Samir Berry, R. K.-D. (2020, November 27). Measuring Saudi Mothers' Awareness of Sustainable Children's Clothing. *Open Journal of Social Sciences*, *8*, •••. Retrieved August 2025, from https://www.scirp.org/reference/referencespapers?referenceid=2870108

Hariani, M., & Sinambela, E. A. (2020). The effect of price perception, service quality, and product diversity on Superindo customer loyalty in Surabaya. Journal of Science. *Technology in Society*, *1*(1).

Har, L. L., Rashid, U. K., Chuan, L. T., Sen, S. C., & Xia, L. Y. (2022). Revolution of Retail Industry: From Perspective of Retail 1.0 to 4.0. *Procedia Computer Science*, *200*, 1615–1625. DOI: 10.1016/j.procs.2022.01.362

Hartley, K., Roosendaal, J., & Kirchherr, J. (2021). Barriers to the circular economy: The case of the Dutch technical and interior textiles industries. *Journal of Industrial Ecology*, *26*(2), 477–490. DOI: 10.1111/jiec.13196

Has, M. (2024). *Sustainable Products: Life Cycle Assessment, Risk Management, Supply Chains, Ecodesign*. Walter de Gruyter GmbH & Co KG.

Hase, V., Boczek, K., & Scharkow, M. (2023). Adapting to affordances and audiences? A cross-platform, multi-modal analysis of the platformization of news on Facebook, Instagram, TikTok, and Twitter. *Digital Journalism (Abingdon, England)*, *11*(8), 1499–1520. DOI: 10.1080/21670811.2022.2128389

Heidari, S., Zarei, M., Daneshfar, A., & Dokhanian, S. (2023). Increasing sales through social media marketing: The role of customer brand attachment, brand trust, and brand equity. *Marketing and Management of Innovations*, *14*(1), 224–234. DOI: 10.21272/mmi.2023.1-19

Herhausen, D., Miočević, D., Morgan, R. E., & Kleijnen, M. H. P. (2020). The digital marketing capabilities gap. *Industrial Marketing Management, 90*, 276–290. DOI: 10.1016/j.indmarman.2020.07.022

Himmelreich, J., & Köhler, S. (2022). Responsible AI through conceptual engineering. *Philosophy & Technology, 35*(3), 60. DOI: 10.1007/s13347-022-00542-2

Hossain, L., Sarker, S. K., & Khan, M. S. (2018). Evaluation of present and future wastewater impacts of textile dyeing industries in Bangladesh. *Environmental Development, 26*, 23–33. DOI: 10.1016/j.envdev.2018.03.005

Hu, M., Chen, J., Chen, Q., & He, W. (2020). It pays off to be authentic: An examination of direct versus indirect brand mentions on social media. *Journal of Business Research, 117*, 19–28. DOI: 10.1016/j.jbusres.2020.05.032

Husain, R., Ahmad, A., & Khan, B. M. (2022). The role of status consumption and brand equity: A comparative study of the marketing of Indian luxury brands by traditional and social media. *Global Business and Organizational Excellence, 41*(4), 48–67. DOI: 10.1002/joe.22156

Iacovidou, E., Hahladakis, J. N., & Purnell, P. (2021). A systems thinking approach to understanding the challenges of achieving the circular economy. *Environmental Science and Pollution Research International, 28*(19), 24785–24806. DOI: 10.1007/s11356-020-11725-9 PMID: 33289042

IBM. (2021). *What Is Business Intelligence (BI)?* https://www.ibm.com/think/topics/business-intelligence

IEEE Global Initiative on Ethics of Autonomous and Intelligent Systems. (2019). *Ethically Aligned Design: A Vision for Prioritizing Human Well-being with Autonomous and Intelligent Systems (2nd ed.)*. IEEE. Retrieved from https://globalpolicy.ieee.org/wp-content/uploads/2019/06/IEEE19002.pdf

IKEA Sustainability Report FY22. (n.d.).

inGrade. (n.d.). Retrieved from inGrade.io: https://ingrade.io/how-ai-is-revolutionizing-the-fashion-industry/

Ivanov, A., Mou, Y., & Tawira, L. (2023). Avatar personalisation vs. Privacy in a virtual try-on app for apparel shopping. *International Journal of Fashion Design, Technology and Education, 16*(1), 100–109. DOI: 10.1080/17543266.2022.2125589

Jayasinghe, I., Basnayake, B., Amarathunga, K., & Dissanayake, P. (2010). Environmental Conservation Efforts in Developing Textile Waste Incorporated Cement Blocks. In *Tropical* [). www.wasteonline.org.uk]. *Agricultural Research, 21*(2), •••.

Jin, Y., Yoon, J., Self, J., & Lee, K. (2024). Understanding fashion designers' behavior using generative AI for Early-Stage concept ideation and revision. *Archives of Design Research, 37*(3), 25–45. DOI: 10.15187/adr.2024.07.37.3.25

Joy, A., Zhu, Y., Peña, C., & Brouard, M. (2022). Digital future of luxury brands: Metaverse, digital fashion, and non-fungible tokens. *Strategic Change, 31*(3), 337–343. DOI: 10.1002/jsc.2502

Jung, J., Yu, J., Seo, Y., & Ko, E. (2021). Consumer experiences of virtual reality: Insights from VR luxury brand fashion shows. *Journal of Business Research, 130*, 517–524. DOI: 10.1016/j.jbusres.2019.10.038

Kamerer, D. (2020). Reconsidering bounce rate in web analytics. *Journal of Digital & Social Media Marketing, 8*(1), 58–67. DOI: 10.69554/EJGO6858

Kandpal, V., Jaswal, A., Santibanez Gonzalez, E. D., & Agarwal, N. (2024). Circular economy principles: shifting towards sustainable prosperity. In *Sustainable energy transition: Circular economy and sustainable financing for environmental, social and governance (ESG) practices* (pp. 125–165). Springer Nature Switzerland. DOI: 10.1007/978-3-031-52943-6_4

Kapferer, J. N. (2008). *The new strategic brand management: Creating and sustaining brand equity long term* (4th ed.). Kogan Page.

Kar, A. K., Choudhary, S. K., & Singh, V. K. (2022). How can artificial intelligence impact sustainability: A systematic literature review. *Journal of Cleaner Production, 376*, 134120. https://doi.org/doi:10.1016/j.jclepro.2022.134120

Karadayi-Usta, S. (2024). Role of artificial intelligence and augmented reality in fashion industry from consumer perspective: Sustainability through waste and return mitigation. *Engineering Applications of Artificial Intelligence, 133*, 108114. DOI: 10.1016/j.engappai.2024.108114

Karimkhan, F. (2023). Ethics in fashion and Gucci's blackface sweater: Will the fashion industry finally learn from its mistakes? *Journal of Media Ethics, 38*(2), 123–125. Advance online publication. DOI: 10.1080/23736992.2023.2194289

Karimova, G., LeMay, S. A., Müller, A., & Klumpp, M. (2025). From the Shallows to the Shelves and Back: A Review, Synthesis, and Research Agenda for Socially Sustainable, AI -Driven Digital Fashion Supply Chains. *Business Ethics, the Environment & Responsibility*, beer.12839. DOI: 10.1111/beer.12839

Karmali, I. M., & Valilai, O. F. (2025). Exploring the Role of Artificial Intelligence for Pattern Recognition of Textile Sorting and Recycling for Circular Economy. *Procedia Computer Science, 253*, 346–356. DOI: 10.1016/j.procs.2025.01.097

Kasavan, S., Yusoff, S., Guan, N. C., Zaman, N. S. K., & Fakri, M. F. R. (2021). Global trends of textile waste research from 2005 to 2020 using bibliometric analysis. *Environmental Science and Pollution Research International*, *28*(33), 44780–44794. DOI: 10.1007/s11356-021-15303-5 PMID: 34235692

Kaur, M., Palazzo, M., & Foroudi, P. (2024). Circular supply chain management in post-pandemic context. A qualitative study to explore how knowledge, environmental initiatives and economic viability affect sustainability. *Qualitative Market Research*, *27*(4), 572–607. DOI: 10.1108/QMR-10-2023-0140

Kaya, Ö., & Aytaç, S. (2024). *Fashion sector and artificial intelligence applications*. Cankiri Karatekin Universitesi Iktisadi Ve Idari Bilimler Fakultesi Dergisi. DOI: 10.18074/ckuiibfd.1520744

Keller, K. L. (1993). Conceptualizing, measuring, and managing customer-based brand equity. *Journal of Marketing*, *57*(1), 1–22. DOI: 10.1177/002224299305700101

Keller, K. L. (2013). *Strategic brand management: Building, measuring, and managing brand equity* (4th ed.). Pearson.

Khairulanwar, A. B. M., & Jamaluddin, K. A. (2025). Artificial Intelligence in Fashion Design Education: A phenomenological Exploration of Certificate-Level Learning. *International Journal of Academic Research in Business & Social Sciences*, *15*(3). Advance online publication. DOI: 10.6007/IJARBSS/v15-i3/24604

Khan, B. M. (2009). Operationalising Young and Rubicam's BAV™ as a consumer-based brand equity measure. *Journal for International Business and Entrepreneurship Development*, *4*(4), 314–333. DOI: 10.1504/JIBED.2009.033744

Khatib, D. M. E., Al Falasi, F., Anani, H. A., & Shurrab, W. (2023). The Effect of Virtual Reality and Augmented Reality on Managing Projects. *2023 International Conference on Business Analytics for Technology and Security (ICBATS)*, 1–10. DOI: 10.1109/ICBATS57792.2023.10111112

Kholoud, F. A. D. E. L. (2024). *Understanding How Algorithms Shape Consumer Choices: A Retail Consumer Framework*. DOI: 10.5281/ZENODO.11544950

Kiehn, K., & Weller Vojkovic, A. (2018). Millennials motivations for shopping second-hand clothing as part of a sustainable consumption practice.

Kim, J.-H., Kim, M., Park, M., & Yoo, J. (2023). Immersive interactive technologies and virtual shopping experiences: Differences in consumer perceptions between augmented reality (AR) and virtual reality (VR). *Telematics and Informatics*, *77*, 101936. DOI: 10.1016/j.tele.2022.101936

Kincl, T., & Štrach, P. (2012). Measuring website quality: Asymmetric effect of user satisfaction. *Behaviour & Information Technology, 31*(7), 647–657. DOI: 10.1080/0144929X.2010.526150

Koivisto, E., & Mattila, P. (2023). Fashion in the metaverse: Consumer engagement through immersive experiences. *Journal of Business Research, 158*, 113672. DOI: 10.1016/j.jbusres.2023.113672

Konina, N. Yu. (2023). Artificial Intelligence in the Fashion Industry—Reality and Prospects. In Popkova, E. G., & Sergi, B. S. (Eds.), *Anti-Crisis Approach to the Provision of the Environmental Sustainability of Economy* (pp. 273–280). Springer Nature Singapore., DOI: 10.1007/978-981-99-2198-0_29

Konopik, J., Jahn, C., Schuster, T., Hossbach, N., & Pflaum, A. (2022). Mastering the digital transformation through organisational capabilities: A conceptual framework. *Digital Business, 2*(2), 100019. DOI: 10.1016/j.digbus.2021.100019

Kotler, P. (n.d.). *The Marketing Journal*. Retrieved from https://www.marketingjournal.org/: https://www.marketingjournal.org/brand-purpose-to-beneficence-philip-kotler/

Kovács, I., & Keresztes, É. R. (2024). Digital Innovations in E-Commerce: Augmented Reality Applications in Online Fashion Retail—A Qualitative Study among Gen Z Consumers. *Informatics (MDPI), 11*(3), 56. DOI: 10.3390/informatics11030056

Kraus, S., Durst, S., Ferreira, J. J. M., Veiga, P. M., Kailer, N., & Weinmann, A. (2021). Digital transformation in business and management research: An overview of the current status quo. *International Journal of Information Management, 63*, 102466. DOI: 10.1016/j.ijinfomgt.2021.102466

Kreye, M. (2025). Circularity in supply chains versus circular supply chains: Identifying the need for transformation in manufacturing. *Supply Chain Management, 30*(3), 339–352. DOI: 10.1108/SCM-05-2024-0295

Kumar, A., Prakash, G., & Kumar, G. (2021). Does environmentally responsible purchase intention matter for consumers? A predictive sustainable model developed through an empirical study. *Journal of Retailing and Consumer Services, 58*, 102270. DOI: 10.1016/j.jretconser.2020.102270

Kunz, M., Se, Z., Birr, S., Raslan, M., Ma, L., Li, Z., Gouttes, A., Koren, M., Naghibi, T., Stephan, J., Bulycheva, M., Grzeschik, M., Kekić, A., Narodovitch, M., Rasul, K., Stanley, M., Sieber, J., & Januschowski, T. (2023). *Deep Learning based Forecasting: a case study from the online fashion industry*. 279–311. DOI: 10.1007/978-3-031-35879-1_11

Laaber, F., Florack, A., Koch, T., & Hubert, M. (2023). Digital maturity: Development and validation of the Digital Maturity Inventory (DIMI). *Computers in Human Behavior, 143*, 107709. DOI: 10.1016/j.chb.2023.107709

Laitala, K., & Klepp, I. G. (2018). Motivations for and against second-hand clothing acquisition. *Clothing Cultures, 5*(2), 247–262. DOI: 10.1386/cc.5.2.247_1

Larsson, M. (2018). Circular business models: Developing a sustainable future. *Circular Business Models: Developing a Sustainable Future*, 1–303. https://doi.org/ DOI: 10.1007/978-3-319-71791-3/COVER

Lee, G., & Kim, H.-Y. (2024). Human vs. AI: The battle for authenticity in fashion design and consumer response. *Journal of Retailing and Consumer Services, 77*, 103690. DOI: 10.1016/j.jretconser.2023.103690

Lee, J., & Suh, S. (2024). AI Technology Integrated Education Model for empowering fashion Design ideation. *Sustainability (Basel), 16*(17), 7262. DOI: 10.3390/su16177262

Lens, (2025). Scholar search: AI in Fashion https://www.lens.org/lens/search/scholar/list?q=ai%20in%20fashion&n=10

Linder, M., & Williander, M. (2017). Circular Business Model Innovation: Inherent Uncertainties. *Business Strategy and the Environment, 26*(2), 182–196. DOI: 10.1002/bse.1906

Liu, L., Zhang, H., Ji, Y., & Wu, Q. J. (2019). Toward AI fashion design: An Attribute-GAN model for clothing match. *Neurocomputing, 341*, 156–167. DOI: 10.1016/j.neucom.2019.03.011

Llorente-Barroso, C., Kolotouchkina, O., & Ferreira, I. (2023). E-WOM as an asset of branded content strategies: A conceptual approach to the role of consumers in building brand equity. In *Handbook of research on the future of advertising and brands in the new entertainment landscape* (pp. 367–383). IGI Global.

Lorne Michael Cousins, P. P. (n.d.). Fashion Sustainability Directory. Retrieved from https://fashion.sustainability-directory.com/term/social-equity-in-fashion/

Lozano-Oviedo, J., Cortés, C. E., & Rey, P. A. (2024). Sustainable closed-loop supply chains and their optimization models: A review of the literature. *Clean Technologies and Environmental Policy, 26*(4), 999–1023. DOI: 10.1007/s10098-023-02730-w

Madsen, D. Ø., Silva, E. S., & Hassani, H. (2020). The application of big data in fashion retailing: A narrative review. *International Journal of Management Concepts and Philosophy, 13*(4), 247. DOI: 10.1504/IJMCP.2020.112160

Maghsoudi, M., & Nezafati, N. (2023). Navigating the acceptance of implementing business intelligence in organizations: A system dynamics approach. *Telematics and Informatics Reports*, *11*, 100070. DOI: 10.1016/j.teler.2023.100070

Mahajan, A. I., & Taggar, R. (2025). Augmented Reality Adoption: Exploring Security Concerns and Consumer Resourcefulness in the Era of Society 5.0. *International Social Science Journal*, *75*(255), 241–259. DOI: 10.1111/issj.12548

Makrides, A., Vrontis, D., & Christofi, M. (2019). The gold rush of digital marketing: Assessing prospects of building brand awareness overseas. *Business Perspectives and Research*, *8*(1), 4–20. DOI: 10.1177/2278533719860016

Marques, L., & Marques, L. (2020). Waste and Industrial Intoxication. *Capitalism and Environmental Collapse*, 97-129.

Mettler, T., & Pinto, R. (2018). Evolutionary paths and influencing factors towards digital maturity: An analysis of the status quo in Swiss hospitals. *Technological Forecasting and Social Change*, *133*, 104–117. DOI: 10.1016/j.techfore.2018.03.009

Mirbabaie, M., Marx, J., & Germies, J. (2022). Digital nudge stacking and backfiring: Understanding sustainable e-commerce purchase decisions. *Pacific Asia Journal of the Association for Information Systems*, *14*(12), 65–87. DOI: 10.17705/1pais.15303

Mishra, S., Jain, S., & Malhotra, G. (2021). The anatomy of circular economy transition in the fashion industry. *Social Responsibility Journal*, *17*(4), 524–542. DOI: 10.1108/SRJ-06-2019-0216

Mollel, J., & Chen, Y. (2025). Does AR virtual try-on boost online apparel purchase intentions? An integration of TAM, IDT, FIT perception and body esteem. *Young Consumers*, *26*(3), 385–402. DOI: 10.1108/YC-08-2024-2196

Mondalek, A. (2023). Generative AI: Unlocking the future of fashion. *McKinsey & Company*. Retrieved September 2025, from https://www.mckinsey.com/industries/retail/our-insights/generative-ai-unlocking-the-future-of-fashion

Morseletto, P. (2020). Targets for a circular economy. *Resources, Conservation and Recycling*, *153*, 104553. DOI: 10.1016/j.resconrec.2019.104553

Mosarrat, F. (2012). Brand elements lead to brand equity: Differentiate or die. *Information Management and Business Review*, *4*(4), 223–233. DOI: 10.22610/imbr.v4i4.983

Moura, P. D. (2021, January 2). *Live Innovation.* Retrieved September 2025, from https://liveinnovation.org/: https://liveinnovation.org/brand-personality-understanding-aakers-5-dimension-model/

Muhammad, A., Muhammad, A., & Defit, S. (2022). Analyzing the use of Social Media by Fashion Designers with K-Means and C45. *MATRIK : Jurnal Manajemen. Teknik Informatika Dan Rekayasa Komputer, 21*(2), 463–476. DOI: 10.30812/matrik.v21i2.1432

Munten, P., Swaen, V., & Vanhamme, J. (2024). Exploring rebound effects in Access-Based services (ABS). *Journal of Business Research, 182*, 114758. DOI: 10.1016/j.jbusres.2024.114758

Newman, S. (2015). *Building microservices: Designing fine-grained systems*. O'Reilly Media, Inc.

Nguyen, K., Le, M., Martin, B., Cil, I., & Fookes, C. (2022). When AI meets store layout design: A review. *Artificial Intelligence Review, 55*(7), 5707–5729. DOI: 10.1007/s10462-022-10142-3

Nichifor, E., & Brătucu, G. (2021). How the digital maturity level is shaping the connected consumer future? *Journal of Smart Economic Growth, 6*(2), 19–39.

Niinimäki, K. P., Peters, G., Dahlbo, H., Perry, P., Rissanen, T., & Gwilt, A. (2020, April 1). The environmental price of fast fashion. *Nature Reviews. Earth & Environment, 1*(4), 189–200. DOI: 10.1038/s43017-020-0039-9

Nobre, H., & Ferreira, A. (2021). Digital marketing and social media: Why bother? *Business Horizons, 64*(6), 739–749. DOI: 10.1016/j.bushor.2021.09.001

Norman, D. A. (2004). *Emotional design: Why we love (or hate) everyday things*. Basic Books. DOI: 10.1145/985600.966013

OECD. (2019). *Artificial intelligence in society*. OECD Publishing., DOI: 10.1787/eedfee77-

Okeke, N. I., Alabi, O. A., Igwe, A. N., Ofodile, O. C., & Ewim, C. P.-M. (2024). AI in customer feedback integration: A data-driven framework for enhancing business strategy. *World Journal of Advanced Research and Reviews, 24*(1), 2036–2052. DOI: 10.30574/wjarr.2024.24.1.3207

Olawade, D. B., Fapohunda, O., Wada, O. Z., Usman, S. O., Ige, A. O., Ajisafe, O., & Oladapo, B. I. (2024). Smart waste management: A paradigm shift enabled by artificial intelligence. *Waste Management Bulletin, 2*(2), 244–263. DOI: 10.1016/j.wmb.2024.05.001

Olivar Aponte, N. H. (2024, August). ast fashion consumption and its environmental impact: a literature review. *Sustainability: Science. Practice and Policy, 20*(1). Advance online publication. DOI: 10.1080/15487733.2024.2381871

Omkar Singh, N. S. (2024, September). AI, IoT, and Blockchain in Fashion: Confronting Industry. *International Journal of Communication Networks and Information.* Retrieved September 2025, from https://ijcnis.org/

Onwezen, M. C., Bartels, J., & Antonides, G. (2013). The self-regulatory function of anticipated pride and guilt in a sustainable and healthy consumption context. *European Journal of Social Psychology, 43*(7), 671–684. DOI: 10.1002/ejsp.1991

Our vision of a circular economy for fashion. (2023, May 9). *Ellen Macarthur Foundation Periodical.* Retrieved from https://www.ellenmacarthurfoundation.org/our-vision-of-a-circular-economy-for-fashion

Oyebode Kayode, A. L. (2025). Predictive Analytics for Demand Forecasting in Ethical Fashion:. *Research Gate.* Retrieved 2025, from researchgate.net

Pakharuddin, N. D., & Kamarudin, S. (2023). Retail Sector Emerging Technologies: AI and Augmented Reality Present and Future Perspective. *2023 2nd International Engineering Conference on Electrical, Energy, and Artificial Intelligence (EICEEAI)*, 1–7. DOI: 10.1109/EICEEAI60672.2023.10590317

Park, C. I., & Namkung, Y. (2022). The effects of Instagram marketing activities on customer-based brand equity in the coffee industry. *Sustainability (Basel), 14*(3), 1657. DOI: 10.3390/su14031657

Park, H. J., & Lin, L. M. (2020). Exploring attitude–behavior gap in sustainable consumption: Comparison of recycled and upcycled fashion products. *Journal of Business Research, 117*, 623–628. DOI: 10.1016/j.jbusres.2018.08.025

Patel, K. (2024). Revolutionizing Customer Experience: Integrating Blockchain with AR and VR in Retail. In B. Verma, A. Mittal, M. Raman, & B. Sindhav (Eds.), *Augmenting Retail Reality, Part B: Blockchain, AR, VR, and AI* (pp. 1–22). Emerald Publishing Limited. DOI: 10.1108/978-1-83608-708-320241003

Patsy Perry, J. F. (2018). *Luxury fashion supply chain management* (5th ed.). Edinburgh: Kogan Page. Retrieved 2025, from research.manchester.

Paun, D. (2023). Digital presence and competitive advantage in fashion retailing. *Journal of Retailing and Consumer Services, 75*, 103464. DOI: 10.1016/j.jretconser.2023.103464

Pencarelli, T., Ali Taha, V., Škerháková, V., Valentiny, T., & Fedorko, R. (2019). Luxury products and sustainability issues from the perspective of young Italian consumers. *Sustainability (Basel), 12*(1), 245. DOI: 10.3390/su12010245

Pereira, A. M., Moura, J. A. B., Costa, E. D. B., Vieira, T., Landim, A. R. D. B., Bazaki, E., & Wanick, V. (2022). Customer models for artificial intelligence-based decision support in fashion online retail supply chains. *Decision Support Systems, 158*, 113795. DOI: 10.1016/j.dss.2022.113795

Perry, P., Kent, A., & Bonetti, F. (2019). The Use of Mobile Technologies in Physical Stores: The Case of Fashion Retailing. In Piotrowicz, W., & Cuthbertson, R. (Eds.), *Exploring Omnichannel Retailing* (pp. 169–195). Springer International Publishing., DOI: 10.1007/978-3-319-98273-1_8

Peter, H. (n.d.). *Innovations in Sustainable Textile Production.* https://www.researchgate.net/publication/389272494

Peters, J., & Simaens, A. (2020). Integrating sustainability into corporate strategy: A case study of the textile and clothing industry. *Sustainability (Basel), 12*(15), 6125. DOI: 10.3390/su12156125

Pierdicca, R., Frontoni, E., Pollini, R., Trani, M., & Verdini, L. (2017). The Use of Augmented Reality Glasses for the Application in Industry 4.0. In De Paolis, L. T., Bourdot, P., & Mongelli, A. (Eds.), *Augmented Reality, Virtual Reality, and Computer Graphics* (Vol. 10324, pp. 389–401). Springer International Publishing., DOI: 10.1007/978-3-319-60922-5_30

Pimenow, S., Pimenowa, O., Prus, P., & Niklas, A. (2025). The Impact of Artificial Intelligence on the Sustainability of Regional Ecosystems: Current Challenges and Future Prospects. *Sustainability (Basel), 17*(11), 4795. https://www.mdpi.com/2071-1050/17/11/4795. DOI: 10.3390/su17114795

Pina, R., & Dias, Á. (2021). The influence of brand experiences on consumer-based brand equity. *Journal of Brand Management, 28*(2), 99–115. DOI: 10.1057/s41262-020-00215-5

Pubmed, *Search: AI in Fashion* https://pubmed.ncbi.nlm.nih.gov/?term=AI+in+Fashion&sort_order=asc

Qishu, L. (2024). Implementation method of intelligent emotion-aware clothing systembased on nanofibre technology. *Industria Textila (Bucuresti), 75*(01), 3–14. DOI: 10.35530/IT.075.01.202379

Quan, N. M., & Hien, L. T. (2023). Analyzing the Impact of Big Data Analytics on Supply Chain Efficiency in the Fashion Industry. *Journal of Empirical Social Science Studies, 7*(4), 64–81. https://publications.dlpress.org/index.php/jesss/article/view/59

Quattelbaum, B., Breckenfelder, C., Voigt, J., & Maas, L. (2022). Possibilities and limits of virtual and augmented reality in the purchase decision process for clothing. *Communications in Development and Assembling of Textile Products, 3*(1), 42–50. https://doi.org/DOI: 10.25367/cdatp.2022.3.p42-50

Ragazou, K., Passas, I., Garefalakis, A., & Constantin Zopounidis, ·. (2023). Business intelligence model empowering SMEs to make better decisions and enhance their competitive advantage. *Discover Analytics 2022 1:1, 1*(1), 1–15. DOI: 10.1007/s44257-022-00002-3

Raji, M. A., Olodo, H. B., Oke, T. T., Addy, W. A., Ofodile, O. C., & Oyewole, A. T. (2024). E-commerce and consumer behavior: A review of AI-powered personalization and market trends. GSC advanced research and reviews, 18(3), 066-077.

Ramasamy, R., & Subramanian, R. B. (2021). Synthetic textile and microfiber pollution: A review on mitigation strategies. *Environmental Science and Pollution Research International, 28*(31), 41596–41611. DOI: 10.1007/s11356-021-14763-z PMID: 34100210

Ramos, L., Rivas-Echeverría, F., Pérez, A. G., & Casas, E. (2023). Artificial intelligence and sustainability in the fashion industry: A review from 2010 to 2022. *SN Applied Sciences, 5*(12), 387. DOI: 10.1007/s42452-023-05587-2

Rashid, A., Roci, M., & Asif, F. M. (2020). 26. Circular manufacturing systems. *Handbook of the circular economy*, 343.

Rathinamoorthy, R. (2019). Circular fashion. *Circular economy in textiles and apparel: Processing, manufacturing, and design*, 13-48.

Rathinamoorthy, R. (2019). Circular Fashion. In Muthu, S. S. (Ed.), *Circular Economy in Textiles and Apparel Processing, Manufacturing, and Design*. Woodhead Publishing. DOI: 10.1016/B978-0-08-102630-4.00002-9

Ratra, K., & Neelam, N. (2018). Brand awareness quotient: Digital marketing and consumer engagement. En Digital marketing and consumer engagement: Concepts, methodologies, tools, and applications (pp. 460–473). DOI: 10.4018/978-1-5225-5187-4.ch024

Ray, S., & Nayak, L. (2023, April 4). Marketing Sustainable Fashion: Trends and Future Directions. *Sustainability (Basel), 15*(7), 6202. Advance online publication. DOI: 10.3390/su15076202

Redhil, D. (1999). Brand research and the global conundrum. [Former Series]. *Design Management Journal, 10*(1), 75–80. DOI: 10.1111/j.1948-7169.1999.tb00245.x

Robaina, M., Murillo, K., Rocha, E., & Villar, J. (2020). Circular economy in plastic waste-Efficiency analysis of European countries. *The Science of the Total Environment, 730*, 139038. DOI: 10.1016/j.scitotenv.2020.139038 PMID: 32438212

Rodrigues, C., & Rodrigues, P. (2019). Brand love matters to millennials: The relevance of mystery, sensuality and intimacy to neo-luxury brands. *Journal of Product and Brand Management, 28*(7), 830–848. DOI: 10.1108/JPBM-04-2018-1842

Rogers, E. M. (2003). *Diffusion of Innovations* (5th ed.). Free Press.

Romão, M. T., Moro, S., Rita, P., & Ramos, P. (2019). Leveraging a luxury fashion brand through social media. *European Research on Management and Business Economics, 25*(1), 15–22. DOI: 10.1016/j.iedeen.2018.10.002

Rossmann, A. (2018). Digital maturity: Conceptualisation and measurement model. En *Proceedings of the Thirty-Ninth International Conference on Information Systems (ICIS)*, San Francisco, CA.

Ryan, R. M., & Deci, E. L. (2000). Self-determination theory and the facilitation of intrinsic motivation, social development, and well-being. *The American Psychologist, 55*(1), 68–78. DOI: 10.1037/0003-066X.55.1.68 PMID: 11392867

Saidani, M., Kim, H., & Yannou, B. (2021). Can Machine Learning Tools Support the Identification of Sustainable Design Leads From Product Reviews? Opportunities and Challenges. *Volume 3A: 47th Design Automation Conference (DAC), 3A-2021*. DOI: 10.1115/DETC2021-70613

Sanjida Sumaia Mimmo, A. R. (2025). Integrating Artificial Intelligence Across the Fashion. *Applied IT & Engineering*. Eman Publishers. Retrieved from https://publishing.emanresearch.org/CurrentIssuePDF/EmanPublisher_9_5948engineering-3110210.pdf

Sasha, N., & Sarokin, N. M. (2024, March 10). Pursuing profitability in slow fashion: Exploring brands' profit contributors. (Elsevier, Ed.) *Journal of Cleaner Production, 444*. DOI: 10.1016/j.jclepro.2024.141237

Scholz, J., & Smith, A. N. (2016). Augmented reality: Designing immersive experiences that maximize consumer engagement. *Business Horizons, 59*(2), 149–161. DOI: 10.1016/j.bushor.2015.10.003

Schröder, P. (2020). *Promoting a just transition to an inclusive circular economy*. Royal Institute of International Affairs.

Schürmann, C. L., Helinski, C., Koch, J., Westmattelmann, D., & Schewe, G. (2023). Digital Nudging to Promote Sustainable Consumer Behavior? An Experimental Analysis in Online Fashion Retail. https://aisel.aisnet.org/ecis2023_rp/335

Shahbaznezhad, H., Dolan, R., & Rashidirad, M. (2022). The role of social media content format and platform in users' engagement behavior. *Journal of Interactive Marketing*, *53*(1), 47–65. Advance online publication. DOI: 10.1016/j.intmar.2020.05.001

Shahzad, M. F., Xu, S., Rehman, O. U., & Javed, I. (2023). Impact of gamification on green consumption behavior integrating technological awareness, motivation, enjoyment and virtual CSR. *Scientific Reports*, *13*(1), 21751. DOI: 10.1038/s41598-023-48835-6 PMID: 38066018

Shawky, R. (2020). The role of trust in understanding the impact of social media marketing on brand equity and brand loyalty. *Journal of Relationship Marketing*, *19*(4), 287–308. Advance online publication. DOI: 10.1080/15332667.2019.1705742

Shirkhani, S., Mokayed, H., Saini, R., & Chai, H. Y. (2023). Study of AI-Driven Fashion Recommender Systems. *SN Computer Science*, *4*(5), 514. Advance online publication. DOI: 10.1007/s42979-023-01932-9

Shi, W., Cao, J., Zhang, Q., Li, Y., & Xu, L. (2020). Edge computing: Vision and challenges. *IEEE Internet of Things Journal*, *3*(5), 637–646. DOI: 10.1109/JIOT.2016.2579198

Shi, W., Wong, W., & Zou, X. (2025). Generative AI in fashion: Overview. *ACM Transactions on Intelligent Systems and Technology*, 3718098. Advance online publication. DOI: 10.1145/3718098

Silva, E. S., Hassani, H., & Madsen, D. Ø. (2019). Big Data in fashion: Transforming the retail sector. *The Journal of Business Strategy*, *41*(4), 21–27. Advance online publication. DOI: 10.1108/JBS-04-2019-0062

Silvestri, B. (2020). The Future of Fashion: How the Quest for Digitization and the Use of Artificial Intelligence and Extended Reality Will Reshape the Fashion Industry After COVID-19. *ZoneModa Journal, V. 10 N. 2*, 61-73 Paginazione. DOI: 10.6092/ISSN.2611-0563/11803

Singh, H., & Kulkarni, P. (2023). *A review on application of modern AR/VR technologies in brand*. 050010. DOI: 10.1063/5.0175843

Singh, S. (2024). Umetna inteligenca v modni in oblačilni industriji. *Tekstilec*, *67*(3), 225–240. DOI: 10.14502/tekstilec.67.2024001

Sivakumar, V., & Mohan, R. (2020). Sustainable solid waste management in leather and textile industry: Leather & textile waste fibre-polymer composite and nanocomposite–overview and review. *Textile & Leather Review*, *3*(2), 54–63.

Sliyakat, K. (2025). Machine learning-powered IoT (MLIoT) for retail apparel industry. In Tarnanidis, T., Papachristou, E., Karypidis, M., & Manda, V. (Eds.), *Sustainable practices in the fashion and retail industry* (pp. 345–372). IGI Global Scientific Publishing.

Sliyakat, S. (2024). IoT driven by machine learning (MLIoT) for the retail apparel sector. In Tarnanidis, T., Papachristou, E., Karypidis, M., & Ismyrlis, V. (Eds.), *Driving green marketing in fashion and retail* (pp. 63–81). IGI Global., DOI: 10.4018/979-8-3693-3049-4.ch004

Srivastava, M., & Kumar, M. (2020). Impact of Solid Municipal Waste. *Resilience, Response, and Risk in Water Systems: Shifting Management and Natural Forcings Paradigms*, 303.

Srivastava, R., & Shocker, A. D. (1991). Brand equity: A perspective on its meaning and measurement (MSI Report No. 91-124). Cambridge, MA: Marketing Science Institute.

Stern, P. C. (2000). New environmental theories: Toward a coherent theory of environmentally significant behavior. *The Journal of Social Issues*, *56*(3), 407–424. DOI: 10.1111/0022-4537.00175

Strengholt, P. (2020). *Data management at scale : best practices for enterprise architecture*. https://books.google.com/books/about/Data_Management_at_Scale.html?id=GunzDwAAQBAJ

Strubell, E., Ganesh, A., & McCallum, A. (2019). Energy and policy considerations for deep learning in NLP. *Proceedings of the 57th Annual Meeting of the Association for Computational Linguistics*, 3645–3650. DOI: 10.18653/v1/P19-1355

Stubbe, B., Van Vrekhem, S., Huysman, S., Tilkin, R. G., De Schrijver, I., & Vanneste, M. (2024). White Paper on Textile Fibre Recycling Technologies. In *Sustainability (Switzerland)* (Vol. 16, Issue 2). Multidisciplinary Digital Publishing Institute (MDPI). DOI: 10.3390/su16020618

Su, B. (2025). *Ai-Driven Innovations for Sustainable E-Commerce Returns Management. SSRN*. DOI: 10.2139/ssrn.5126388

Sustainability in Fashion and Textiles. (2013). Taylor & Francis., DOI: 10.4324/9781351277600

Swaminathan, K. L. (2019). *Strategic Brand Management Building, Measuring and Managing Brand Equity* (5th ed.). Pearsons., Retrieved 2025, from.

Symeonides, D., Loizia, P., & Zorpas, A. A. (2019). Tire waste management system in Cyprus in the framework of circular economy strategy. *Environmental Science and Pollution Research International*, *26*(35), 35445–35460. DOI: 10.1007/s11356-019-05131-z PMID: 31127515

Takyar, A. (2023, April 19). AI in fashion: Use cases, benefits, implementation and future trends. *LeewayHertz - AI Development Company*. Retrieved from https://www.leewayhertz.com/ai-use-cases-in-fashion/#the-rise-of-ai-in-the-fashion-industry

Tangney, J. P., Stuewig, J., & Mashek, D. J. (2007). Moral emotions and moral behavior. *Annual Review of Psychology*, *58*(1), 345–372. DOI: 10.1146/annurev.psych.56.091103.070145 PMID: 16953797

Telfort, T. E., & Valilai, O. F. (2025). A Framework for Sustainable Textile Waste Management using Digital Product Passports and Artificial Intelligence. *Procedia CIRP*, *134*, 909–914. DOI: 10.1016/j.procir.2025.02.224

Thaler, R. H., & Sunstein, C. R. (2009). *Nudge: Improving decisions about health, wealth, and happiness*. Penguin.

The Business of Fashion and McKinsey & Company. (2021). *The state of fashion 2021*. McKinsey & Company. Retrieved from https://www.mckinsey.com/~/media/mckinsey/industries/retail/our%20insights/state%20of%20fashion/2021/the-state-of-fashion-2021-vf.pdf

Thomassey, S., & Zeng, X. (2018). *Artificial intelligence for fashion industry in the big data era*. Springer Ser Fashion Bus., DOI: 10.1007/978-981-13-0080-6

ThreadUp Inc. (2025). *Resale Report 2024*. Retrieved from https://cf-assets-tup.thredup.com/resale_report/2024/ThredUp_2024_Resale%20Report.pdf

TrendBible. (2023). What is a Micro Trend? *Glossory*. Retrieved from https://www.trendbible.com/trendterms/micro-trend/#:~:text=A%20Micro%20Trend%20is%20a,into%20these%20emerging%20consumer%20mindsets

Udall, A. M., De Groot, J. I., De Jong, S. B., & Shankar, A. (2021). How I see me—A meta-analysis investigating the association between identities and pro-environmental behaviour. *Frontiers in Psychology*, *12*, 582421. DOI: 10.3389/fpsyg.2021.582421 PMID: 33796041

UNFCCC. (2021). *Fashion Industry Charter for Climate Action*. United Nations Framework Convention on Climate Change. Retrieved from https://unfccc.int/climate-action/sectoral-engagement-for-climate-action/fashion-charter

United Nations Environment Programme. (2025). *Fashion and textiles: Environmental impact and solutions*. UNEP Reports. Retrieved from https://www.unep.org/resources/report/fashion-and-textiles-environmental-impact-and-solutions

Upadhyay, Y., Paul, J., & Baber, R. (2022). Effect of online social media marketing efforts on customer response. *Journal of Consumer Behaviour*, *21*(3), 554–571. DOI: 10.1002/cb.2031

Upreti, K., Gangwar, D., Vats, P., Bhardwaj, R., Khatri, V., & Gautam, V. (2024). Artificial Neural Networks for Enhancing E-commerce: A Study on Improving Personalization, Recommendation, and Customer Experience. In Shaw, R. N., Siano, P., Makhilef, S., Ghosh, A., & Shimi, S. L. (Eds.), *Innovations in Electrical and Electronic Engineering* (Vol. 1115, pp. 141–153). Springer Nature Singapore., DOI: 10.1007/978-981-99-8661-3_11

Ushmita Gupta, P. S. (2024). *Revolutionizing Retail IoT Applications for Enhanced Customer Experience*. Taylor & Francis. Retrieved August 2025, from https://www.taylorfrancis.com/chapters/edit/10.1201/9781003458401-5/revolutionizing-retail-ushmita-gupta-pritesh-somani-nitesh-behare-rashmi-mahajan-meenakshi-singh-vishwanathan-iyer

Usui, T. (2024). Uniqlo: A Pathway to Becoming a Multinational Through Global Business Model Development. In Makino, S., Uchida, Y., & Kasahara, T. (Eds.), *Transformation of Japanese Multinational Enterprises and Business* (pp. 161–186). Springer Nature Singapore., DOI: 10.1007/978-981-99-8616-3_5

Verónica Bolón-Canedo, L. M.-F. (2024, September 28). A review of green artificial intelligence: Towards a more sustainable future. *Neurocomputing*, *599*, 128096. Advance online publication. DOI: 10.1016/j.neucom.2024.128096

Vinted. (2023). *Climate Impact Report 2023*. Retrieved from https://www.vinted.com/climate-impact-report

Vishwakarma, A., Mehrotra, D., Agrahari, R., Kharub, M., Gupta, S., & Jagtap, S. (2024). Breaking barriers: Paving the path to sustainable fashion – insights for a greener apparel and textile sector. *Journal of Advances in Management Research*, *21*(3), 376–397. DOI: 10.1108/JAMR-05-2023-0112

Viswanathan, J. (2024). Artificial Intelligence: Transforming the Future of Retail. [IJSR]. *International Journal of Science and Research (Raipur, India)*, *13*(9), 174–178. DOI: 10.21275/SR24901234506

Voigt, P., & von dem Bussche, A. (2017). *The EU general data protection regulation (GDPR): A practical guide*. Springer International Publishing., DOI: 10.1007/978-3-319-57959-7

VOSViewer. (https://www.vosviewer.com/)

Wahyuningsih, D. (2016). PEMBERDAYAAN INDUSTRI TAS DAN KOPER (INTAKO) TANGGULANGIN PASCABENCANA LUMPUR LAPINDO OLEH DISKOPERINDAG KABUPATEN SIDOARJO. *Publika*, *4*(6). Advance online publication. DOI: 10.26740/PUBLIKA.V4N6.P

Warbung, C., Wowor, M., Walean, R., & Mandagi, D. (2023). The impact of social media marketing on beauty clinic brand equity: The case of Zap Manado. *International Journal of Professional Business Review*, *8*(4), 1–26. DOI: 10.26668/businessreview/2023.v8i4.1389

Weinmann, M., Schneider, C., & vom Brocke, J. (2016). Digital nudging. *Business & Information Systems Engineering*, *58*(6), 433–436. DOI: 10.1007/s12599-016-0453-1

Wies, S., Bleier, A., & Edeling, A. (2023). Finding Goldilocks influencers: How follower count drives social media engagement. *Journal of Marketing*, *87*(3), 383–405. DOI: 10.1177/00222429221125131

Wilson, R., & Bowles, O. (2024). Artificial intelligence and trend forecasting in the fashion industry: Ethical and anticipated ethical issues. *Proceedings of the International Conference on AI Research.*, *4*(1), 75–81. DOI: 10.34190/icair.4.1.3186

World Bank. (2019). *How Much Do Our Wardrobes Cost to the Environment*. World Bank Report. Retrieved from https://www.worldbank.org/en/news/feature/2019/09/23/costo-moda-medio-ambiente

Wren, B. (2022). Sustainable supply chain management in the fast fashion industry: A comparative study of current efforts and best practices to address the climate crisis. *Clean Logistics Supply Chain*, *4*, 100032. DOI: 10.1016/j.clscn.2022.100032

Wüst, K., & Gervais, A. (2018). Do you need a blockchain? In *Proceedings of the Crypto Valley Conference on Blockchain Technology (CVCBT '18)* (pp. 45–54). IEEE. DOI: 10.1109/CVCBT.2018.00011

Xie, Z., Yu, Y., Zhang, J., & Chen, M. (2022). The searching artificial intelligence: Consumers show less aversion to algorithm-recommended search product. *Psychology and Marketing, 39*(10), 1902–1919. DOI: 10.1002/mar.21706

Xue, Z., Li, Q., & Zeng, X. (2023). Social media user behavior analysis applied to the fashion and apparel industry in the big data era. *Journal of Retailing and Consumer Services, 72*, 103299. DOI: 10.1016/j.jretconser.2023.103299

Yan, H., Zhang, H., Liu, L., Zhou, D., Xu, X., Zhang, Z., & Yan, S. (2022). Toward intelligent design: An AI-Based fashion designer using generative adversarial networks aided by sketch and rendering generators. *IEEE Transactions on Multimedia, 25*, 2323–2338. DOI: 10.1109/TMM.2022.3146010

Yılmaz, F. (2020). Is there a waste Kuznets curve for OECD? Some evidence from panel analysis. *Environmental Science and Pollution Research International, 27*(32), 40331–40345. DOI: 10.1007/s11356-020-09109-0 PMID: 32666443

Yoo, B., & Donthu, N. (2001). Developing and validating a multidimensional consumer-based brand equity scale. *Journal of Business Research, 52*(1), 1–14. DOI: 10.1016/S0148-2963(99)00098-3

Zeeshan, S., & Hussain, I. (2017). Social Media Marketing and Brand Equity: A Literature Review. *Journal of Marketing Management, 16*(1), 47–64.

Zhang, Y., & Liu, C. (2024). Unlocking the potential of artificial intelligence in fashion design and E-Commerce applications: The case of Midjourney. *Journal of Theoretical and Applied Electronic Commerce Research, 19*(1), 654–670. DOI: 10.3390/jtaer19010035

Zils, M., Howard, M., & Hopkinson, P. (2023). Circular economy implementation in operations & supply chain management: Building a pathway to business transformation. *Production Planning and Control, 36*(4), 501–520. DOI: 10.1080/09537287.2023.2280907

Zorpas, A. A., & Saranti, A. (2016). Multi-criteria analysis of sustainable environmental clean technologies for the treatment of winery's wastewater. *International Journal of Global Environmental Issues, 15*(1/2), 151–168. DOI: 10.1504/IJGENVI.2016.074359

Zucchella, A., & Previtali, P. (2019). Circular business models for sustainable development: A "waste is food" restorative ecosystem. *Business Strategy and the Environment, 28*(2), 274–285. DOI: 10.1002/bse.2216

Zwingmann, T. (2022). *AI-Powered Business Intelligence*. O'Reilly Media, Inc.

About the Contributors

Luzia Arantes (lamorim@ua.pt) as a PhD in Applied Psychology from the University of Minho, Portugal, in addition, she is doing a PhD in Marketing and Strategy at the same institution. She is currently a researcher at Ekonomikas un Kulturas Augstskola (Serbia) and a lecturer at Polytechnic University of Cávado and Ave and at University of Aveiro, Portugal. She has published book chapters in IGI Global on marketing, tourism, consumer behaviour, sustainability and artificial intelligence, as well as the book entitled "Regenerative tourism for social development". She has published in the Journal of International Journal of Marketing, Corporate Social Responsibility and Environmental Management, Journal of Cultural Heritage Management and Sustainable Development, Journal of International Consumer Marketing, Sustainability and the European Journal of Applied Business Management. She has received several awards, including the Best Paper Award in Sustainable Marketing & Digital Perspectives and the Best Paper Award in Consumer Behaviour.

***

Maica Amador-Marrero, dedicated doctoral student at the University of Las Palmas de Gran Canaria, with a background in marketing and international trade. Research interests include applied neuroscience, artificial intelligence, gamification, and user experience, aiming to connect innovation, technology, and business impact.

Komal Bisht is a committed and passionate Assistant Professor in the field of Human Resource Management, bringing over six years of academic experience to her role. She has served at reputed institutions such as Shri Guru Ram Rai University and the Dev Bhoomi Group of Institutions, Dehradun. Currently pursuing her Ph.D. in Human Resource Management, she holds an MBA (HR) and BBA (HR) from Graphic Era Hill University. Her teaching philosophy emphasizes interactive learning, real-world application, and student mentorship. In addition to her academic responsibilities, Komal has hands-on industry experience, particularly in recruitment and selection, having led a team at Placement Dehradun. Her dual experience in academia and industry enables her to bring practical insights into the classroom. She is an active participant in national-level workshops, Faculty Development Programs (FDPs), and academic conferences, and has been recognized for her mentorship and leadership skills. Komal has also contributed significantly to academic research. Her publications include: – 1 authored book – 4 Scopus-indexed research papers – 2 UGC-CARE-listed research papers

Susanta Das is a seasoned educator with a proven record of teaching and mentoring diverse students, working at multiple institutions, and providing service to the various initiatives of organizations. He received his Ph.D. and M.A. degrees from Western Michigan University (WMU), USA, and M.Sc. degree from Banaras Hindu University (BHU), India all in Physics. He continued his research as a Marie-Curie post-doctoral fellow at Stockholm University, Stockholm, Sweden on beam diagnostics for the DESIREE (Double ElectroStatic Ion Ring ExpEriment) in the project DITANET (Diagnostic Techniques for particle Accelerators – a Marie-Curie initial training NETwork), at the Indian Institute of Science Education and Research-Kolkata, India on high-pressure physics as a Project Scientist-B, and at the University of Electro-Communications, Tokyo, Japan on ion-surface interactions as a Post-doctoral fellow. Throughout his career, Dr. Das worked and collaborated with many researchers, Ph.D., master, and visiting students from different countries. He further visited many countries to discuss research and an international conference participant (UK, Italy, Germany, Greece, Belgium, Bulgaria, Romania, Brazil etc.). He worked at several institutions before assuming his current role at Ajeenkya D Y Patil University. He received the Marie-Curie post-doctoral fellowship in Sweden, Science Academies' Summer Research Fellowship in India, Gowen Frostic Doctoral Fellowship, Department Graduate Research and Creative Scholar Award by WMU, and Leo R. Parpart Doctoral Fellowship by Dept. of Physics, WMU, among many others, throughout his academic journey. He co-authored several research articles in WoS/Scopus indexed international journals, conference proceedings, and scholarly book chapters and co-edited several books published by renowned international publishing houses (IGI-Global, Springer Nature, Nova Science Publishers, Wiley, Scrivener-Wiley, Notion Press). At present, Dr. Das continues to delve into cutting-edge fields, with a keen interest in nanotechnology, UN SDGs, and data science. His multifaceted contributions, spanning teaching, research, and administrative leadership, showcase a dedicated professional who is instrumental in advancing the vision and mission of the institutions he serves.

Gonzalo Díaz Meneses (1966) is a devoted and interdisciplinary lecturer of Marketing at Las Palmas of Gran Canaria University (Spain). He earned his PhD degree in Marketing (ULPGC), MSc in Market Research (UNED), MBA (EAE & UB), diploma in Datamining (UNED), degrees in Politics and Sociology (UCM) and History (UCM). His research has focused on marketing, having more than 144 scientific publications in the lines of social marketing, consumer behaviour and tourism. He is a member of several journal scientific boards as The International Journal on Public Policy and Non-Profit Marketing, The Journal of Non-Profit and Public Sector Marketing, The Journal of Social Marketing, the Journal of Fashion Marketing & Management. Finally, he has visited and taught in several European universities such as Lieja, Lathi, Byalistok, Bolonia, Bicocca, Siddansk, Hertfordshire, Sussex, Oxford Brookes, Leeds, Bremen and Berlín, as well as in American universities such as UCA, UAP, Temuco and Lethbridge.

Sreedevi was born and bought up in Payyanur, a small town in northern district of Kannur in Kerala. She did her schooling from PES Vidyalaya and went on to pursue bachelor's in mass communication and journalism from Amrita University, Coimbatore. She did her master's in business administration specializing in lean operations and systems from Christ University, Bangalore and currently working as Business & growth Associate for a Fintech company

Silambarasan G possesses a comprehensive academic foundation, holding a Bachelor of Computer Applications (BCA) and a Master of Computer Applications (MCA), and is currently pursuing a Ph.D. (Full-Time) in the Department of Computer Science at Periyar University, Salem, Tamil Nadu, India. With over 08 years of teaching experience and 02 years of industry exposure, he has consistently demonstrated excellence in both academic and technical domains. His professional journey reflects a strong commitment to research, innovation, and pedagogical advancement in the rapidly evolving field of computer science. Renowned for his expertise in network administration, system architecture, virtualization, and emerging computing technologies, Silambarasan G continues to contribute significantly to the integration of theory and practical application. His academic and research pursuits exemplify a passion for technological innovation and a steadfast dedication to advancing the frontiers of computer science education.

Gayatri Gaware, a second-year B.Tech student specializing in Software Engineering. I'm passionate about using technology to create practical, innovative solutions that make a real impact. My interests span across software development, artificial intelligence, and digital innovation. Currently, I'm actively involved in various technical and leadership initiatives at my college. I've had the opportunity to work on several projects like, Evora a project designed for eco awareness through technology-driven solutions and Viyon —an AI-powered freelancing platform designed to optimize client–freelancer matchmaking and streamline payments through an escrow system. My involvement in the Cyber Alchemist club has allowed me to explore and promote awareness around cybersecurity and emerging digital trends through seminars and collaborative events. I'm always eager to learn, collaborate, and contribute to meaningful work—especially at the intersection of technology, creativity, and real-world problem-solving.

M. Gurusamy, with a comprehensive academic background including an MBA, M.Phil, Ph.D., and a D.Litt. in Marketing, brings an impressive 20 years of teaching experience alongside a brief stint in the industry of 9 months. Currently serving as a Professor and Chairperson for Marketing and Entrepreneurship at the Adarsh Institute of Management and Information Technology in Bangalore, Karnataka, India, he has distinguished himself in the academic and research fields. Dr. Gurusamy has significantly contributed to the intellectual property domain with nine patents in India and 5 in Australia, underscoring his innovative approach to research and development. His scholarly output is remarkable, with 12 articles published in Web of Science journals, 32 in Scopus-indexed journals, and many articles in other national and international journals, totalling 40 books published. As an academic leader, he has evaluated Ph.D. theses and served as an external examiner, showcasing his expertise in guiding research scholars. Dr. Gurusamy's role as a resource person and chairperson in 90 instances, along with his editorial and reviewer memberships in 14 and 16 journals respectively, reflects his esteemed position in the academic community. Additionally, his contributions extend to academic advisory boards and visiting professorships, demonstrating a commitment to enhancing educational standards. His achievements have been recognized with 30 awards, affirming his influence and excellence in marketing and research. Dr. Gurusamy's professional journey is a testament to his dedication to academia, research, and the practical applications of marketing principles in the evolving business landscape.

Samruddhi Kale is a dedicated student at Ajeenkya D. Y. Patil University, Charoli, Lohegaon, Pune. She is known for her strong communication skills and natural leadership qualities. Samruddhi actively engages with others in a confident and positive manner, which helps her work effectively in team environmen. She is highly motivated to improve herself continuously and believes in lifelong learning. With a strong desire to gain new knowledge and skills, she consistently strives to learn more and grow both personally and professionally. Her positive attitude, commitment to self-development, and leadership potential make her a promising individual with a bright future ahea. She has completed her schooling from PM Shri

Kendriya Vidyalay Sangathan No. 1 AFS Pune Lohegaon. Now she is completing her higher education in Ajeenkya D Y Patil university Pune.

Ramakrishnan N is a Professor and Head of Lean Operations and Systems specialization at the School of Business and Management, CHRIST (Deemed to be University), Bangalore. He has 37 years of experience which includes 23 years in senior roles including Global Head responsibilities in leading IT organizations and 14 years in full-time roles in academia. His PhD is in the area of software engineering, and has an M.S. in Software Systems from Birla Institute of Technology & Science, Pilani, after an Engineering degree and a post-graduate diploma in Business Administration. He has certification in 'Global Business Leadership' from U21 Global, Singapore and Harvard Business School Publishing, and is a certified Internal Quality Auditor.

Koteshwar Ramesh Rakesh is a cognitive psychologist, educator, and Senior Researcher at Synapse International. After earning a PhD in Psychology from Jamia Millia Islamia, following an earlier law degree, he has taught at CHRIST University, IIPR, and Jamia Millia Islamia, and mentored numerous student research projects. His clinical research with NIMHANS has focused on schizophrenia and community psychiatry. As an Associate Editor at Shenzhen Seg Scientific Navigations Co., Ltd., he collaborates with international scholars to enhance scientific communication. Dr. Ramesh has published peer-reviewed articles on deception, decision-making, AI in healthcare, and sports psychology, and holds a design patent for an AI-based HR system. He co-authored academic volumes on research methodology and authored popular books namely Stats Without Maths and Once Upon A Mind, and most recently, a self-help manifesto blending internet memes with emotional intelligence.

Jyoti Rani, Assistant professor, school of fashion design and technology. Research and Academic experience. 2 year experience in academics and research. Research area: fashion, textile, natural dyeing, consumer behaviour, AI, merchandising. she has published 28 research paper in refered journal and 5 book chapters.

Saibal Kumar Saha (UGC NET Qualified) holds a Ph.D in Management Studies, a first-class master's degree in MBA and a first-class bachelor's degree in Electronics and Communication Engineering. He has over 15 years of experience and has worked in MNCs like Cognizant Technology Solutions and Tata Aig Life. He has worked for National Institute of Technology - Silchar, Jyotirmoy School of Business – Kolkata, University of Technology and Management - Shillong, Sikkim Manipal Institute of Technology, Christ University and is currently working as Associate Professor at St. Xavier's University, Kolkata. He has published more than 90 research articles in reputed international journals, book chapters and conference proceedings. He has published 4 books and has 5 patents. He has obtained 4 copyrights and has worked in consultancy and government sponsored projects. He is also a reviewer in several international journals and member of editorial advisory boards.

Sunil Sankathala is pursuing B. Tech. in Computer Science and Engineering at Ajeenkya D Y Patil University, with a diverse range of interests that bridge technology, sustainability, and innovation. His academic focus lies in computer science fundamentals like programming, data structures, algorithms, and software development. He actively supplements this with hands-on experience in web development and robotics. Beyond the core curriculum, He has a strong research inclination in emerging and impactful fields. His current research interests include Artificial Intelligence in Healthcare, bioplastics, nano bioplastics, e-waste management, and solid waste management—areas where he believes technology can make a meaningful difference in solving real-world problems. He has been publishing research articles and book chapters in reputed national and international journals and books. He is also part of an ambitious Hyperloop project, which involves interdisciplinary collaboration and cutting-edge engineering aimed at revolutionizing transportation. Working on this project has enhanced his skills in teamwork, innovation, and systems thinking. In the tech domain, he has developed proficiency in web development using technologies such as HTML, CSS, JavaScript, and React. His interests in robotics further reflect building smart, responsive systems that interact with the physical world. Throughout his course, he has helped strengthen problem-solving and collaborative skills. He is proficient in languages such as Python, C, C++, MySQL, Ubuntu, Machine Learning and familiar with frameworks and tools like React, Git. He actively participates in hackathons, coding competitions, and tech events to challenge himself and learn from peers. He is also a quick learner and highly adaptable, with an eagerness to stay updated with the latest trends in the tech world. He aspires to become a skilled software engineer and contribute to building innovative solutions that have a positive impact on society. The long-term goal is to work in a dynamic environment where knowledge, grow professionally, and make meaningful contributions to the field of technology. Driven by a spirit of exploration and sustainability, he aims to contribute to technological solutions that address both human and environmental needs. The long-term goal is to become a versatile engineer and researcher, working at the intersection of computer science, environmental innovation, and human well-being.

Gautam Shivaraj, with a comprehensive academic background including a Bachelor's in Mechanical Engineering, Master of Engineering Management (Australia), MBA, brings an impressive 07 years of teaching experience alongside a brief stint in the industry of 3 years. Currently serving as an Assistant Professor at the Adarsh Institute of Management and Information Technology in Bangalore, Karnataka, India, he has distinguished himself in the academic and research fields. Prof.Gautam Shivaraj professional journey is a testament to his dedication to academia, research, in the evolving world.

Neringa Vilkaite-Vaitone (1984) is a Doctor of Social Sciences (Management). She is a researcher at Vilnius Tech (Lithuania). N. Vilkaite-Vaitone has published research results in more than 40 publications, which address service consumer behavior, marketing communications and green marketing problems. She has presented research results at more than 20 international scientific conferences in Lithuania, Spain, Latvia, Poland and Bulgaria. N. Vilkaite-Vaitone is a postdoctoral fellow in the project "Green Marketing in Lithuania: Critical Evaluation and Development Opportunities", and she participates in the Erasmus + project "Advanced Technology Higher Education Network Alliance – ATHENA". In 2020, she did an internship at the University of Las Palmas de Gran Canaria (Spain). She is a member of the American Marketing Association, the Institute of Marketing Science, the Lithuanian Marketing Association and the editorial boards of scientific journals, and a candidate for the experts at the Foundation for Polish Science.

Index

A

B

C

D

E

F

www.ingramcontent.com/pod-product-compliance
Lightning Source LLC
LaVergne TN
LVHW081525300926
849161LV00006B/1301